Being Spiritual but Not Religious

In its most general sense, the phrase "Spiritual but Not Religious" denotes those who, on one hand, are disillusioned with traditional institutional religion and, on the other hand, feel that those same traditions contain deep wisdom about the human condition. This edited collection speaks to what national surveys agree is a growing social phenomenon referred to as the "Spiritual but Not Religious Movement" (SBNRM).

Each chapter of the volume engages the past, present, and future(s) of the SBNRM. Their collective contribution is analytic, descriptive, and prescriptive, taking stock of not only the various analyses of the SBNRM to date but also the establishment of a new ground on which the continued academic discussion can take place.

This volume is a watershed in the growing academic and public interest in the SBNRM. As such, it will vital reading for any academic involved in Religious Studies, Spirituality, and Sociology.

William B. Parsons is Professor of Religion at Rice University. His publications include *The Enigma of the Oceanic Feeling* (1999); *Religion and Psychology: Mapping the Terrain* (2001); *Teaching Mysticism* (2010); *Mourning Religion* (2008); *Freud and Augustine in Dialogue: Psychoanalysis, Mysticism, and the Culture of Modern Spirituality* (2013); and dozens of articles in multiple journals and edited books. He has served as Chair of the Department of Religion and Director of the Humanities Research Center at Rice University and as Editor (the psychology of religion section) with *Religious Studies Review* and has been a fellow at the Martin Marty Center of the University of Chicago and at the Institute for Advanced Studies at Hebrew University.

Routledge Studies in Religion

Religion, Culture and Spirituality in Africa and the African Diaspora
Edited by William Ackah, Jualynne E. Dodson and R. Drew Smith

Theology and Civil Society
Edited by Charles Pemberton

Neoliberalism and the Biblical Voice
Owning and Consuming
Paul Babie and Michael Trainor

European Muslims Transforming the Public Sphere
Religious Participation in the Arts, Media and Civil Society
Asmaa Soliman

Radical Orthodoxy in a Pluralistic World
Desire, Beauty, and the Divine
Angus M. Slater

Spiritual and Social Transformation in African American Spiritual Churches
More than Conjurers
Margarita Simon Guillory

Liberal Religion
Progressive versions of Judaism, Christianity and Islam
Emanuel de Kadt

Piety and Patienthood in Medieval Islam
Ahmed Ragab

Being Spiritual but Not Religious
Past, Present, Future(s)
Edited by William B. Parsons

For more information about this series, please visit: www.routledge.com/religion/series/SE0669

Being Spiritual but Not Religious

Past, Present, Future(s)

Edited by William B. Parsons

Routledge
Taylor & Francis Group

LONDON AND NEW YORK

First published 2018
by Routledge
2 Park Square, Milton Park, Abingdon, Oxon OX14 4RN

and by Routledge
711 Third Avenue, New York, NY 10017

Routledge is an imprint of the Taylor & Francis Group, an informa business

British Library Cataloguing-in-Publication Data
A catalogue record for this book is available from the British Library

Library of Congress Cataloging-in-Publication Data
A catalog record for this book has been requested

ISBN: 978-1-138-09247-1 (hbk)
ISBN: 978-1-315-10743-1 (ebk)

Typeset in Sabon
by Apex CoVantage, LLC

MIX
Paper from
responsible sources
FSC
www.fsc.org   FSC® C013056

Printed and bound in Great Britain by
TJ International Ltd, Padstow, Cornwall

Contents

Contributors

Joy R. Bostic is Associate Professor in the Department of Religious Studies and the Founding Director for the African and African American Studies Minor at Case Western Reserve University (CWRU) in Cleveland, Ohio. She is also a program faculty member of CWRU's Women's and Gender Studies and Ethnic Studies programs. Her teaching and scholarship focus on such areas as African American religion and culture; religion, healing, and social justice; and womanist/feminist theory. Her publications, which include *African American Female Mysticism, Nineteenth-Century Religious Activism* (Palgrave, 2013), have focused on spirituality and social change in religious traditions of African American women.

Linda C. Ceriello recently received her PhD in religion at Rice University. Her research areas include comparative mysticism, Asian religions in the contemporary West, contemplative studies, and critical theories of popular culture. Publications include 'The Big Bad and the Big "Aha!": Metamodern Monsters as Transformational Figures of Instability' in *Holy Monsters, Sacred Grotesques: Monstrosity and Religion in Europe and the U.S.* (forthcoming, Lexington Books) and "Encoded Ambiguities, Embodied Ontologies: The Transformative Speech of Transgressive Female Figures in Gnosticism and Tantra" in La Rosa di Paracelso (2017). She is co-founder, writer, and editor of the website What Is Metamodern? (*whatismetamodern.com*). She sits on the steering committee for the Religion and Popular Culture group of the American Academy of Religion.

Di Di is a PhD candidate (ABD) in sociology at Rice University. She studies how individuals are both constrained and enabled in social institutions with a specific focus on religion, science, gender, race, and ethnicity. Her work has appeared in *Socius: Sociological Research for a Dynamics World*, *Public Understanding of Science*, the *Journal of Contemporary China*, and *Science and Engineering Ethics*.

Elaine Howard Ecklund is the Herbert S. Autrey Chair in Social Sciences and Professor of Sociology at Rice University, as well as the founding director of the Religion and Public Life Program. Her current research addresses how individuals use race, gender, and religious identities to bring changes to religious and scientific institutions. She is the author of more than sixty peer-reviewed articles and five books. She has received grants from the National Science Foundation, Russell Sage Foundation, John Templeton Foundation, and Society for the Scientific Study of Religion. Her research has been cited more than three thousand times by local, national, and international media. In 2013, she received Rice University's Charles O. Duncan Award for Most Outstanding Academic Achievement and Teaching. She has directed more than seventy undergraduates in conducting research.

Jorge N. Ferrer is Professor of East-West Psychology (EWP) and Integral and Transpersonal Psychology (ITP) at the California Institute of Integral Studies (CIIS), San Francisco. He is the author of *Revisioning Transpersonal Theory: A Participatory Vision of Human Spirituality* (Albany, NY: SUNY Press, 2002) and *Participation and the Mystery: Transpersonal Essays in Psychology, Education, and Religion* (Albany, NY: SUNY Press, 2017), as well as the coeditor (with Jacob H. Sherman) of *The Participatory Turn: Spirituality, Mysticism, Religious Studies* (Albany, NY: SUNY Press, 2008). Ferrer is considered one of the main architects of second-wave transpersonalism, and his participatory approach to religious pluralism is widely discussed in academic journals and conferences. Ferrer received the Fetzer Institute's Presidential Award for his seminal work on consciousness studies and served as advisor to the organization Religions for Peace at the United Nations on a research project aimed at solving global interreligious conflict. He was born in Barcelona, Spain.

Sean Fitzpatrick, PhD, LPC, is Executive Director of The Jung Center of Houston, a nonprofit educational institution that offers more than 200 events each year examining contemporary social and spiritual issues through the lens of depth psychology. He received his master's degree in religious studies from Rice University in 1999; received a second master's degree, in clinical psychology, from the University of Houston–Clear Lake in 2007; and received his professional counseling license in 2012. He completed his PhD in psychology at Saybrook University in 2014, where his research focus was the use of depth psychological models of ethics as tools for theorizing the imagination. He is a psychotherapist in private practice and lectures nationally on topics related to psychology, religion, and spirituality.

Robert C. Fuller is the Caterpillar Professor of Religious Studies at Bradley University. He is the author of thirteen books, including *Spiritual but Not Religious* (Oxford University Press, 2001), *Spirituality in the Flesh* (Oxford University Press, 2008), and *The Body of Faith* (University of Chicago Press, 2013), as well as over forty articles on both the psychology of religion and the history of American metaphysical religion. His current research focuses on the experimental psychology of religion.

Matthew S. Hedstrom is Associate Professor of American Studies and Religious Studies at the University of Virginia (UVA). A historian of religion and culture in the late 19th- and 20th-century United States, his central research questions probe the intersections of American modernity and Protestant and post-Protestant religious modernity in the United States. Hedstrom's first book, *The Rise of Liberal Religion* (Oxford University Press, 2012), awarded the Frank S. and Elizabeth D. Brewer Book Prize of the American Society of Church History, tells the surprising story of religious liberalism's cultural ascendancy in the 20th century. At UVA Hedstrom teaches " 'Spiritual but Not Religious': Spirituality in America" every spring, among other courses in American Studies and American religious history.

Andrea R. Jain is Associate Professor of Religious Studies at Indiana University–Purdue University Indianapolis, editor of *Journal of American Academy of Religion*, and author of *Selling Yoga: From Counterculture to Pop Culture* (Oxford University Press, 2014). Her areas of interest include religion in late capitalistic society; South Asian religions; the history of modern yoga; the intersections of gender, sexuality, and religion; and methods and theories in the study of religion. She is a regular contributor to *Religion Dispatches* and co-chair of the Yoga in Theory and Practice Group of the American Academy of Religion.

Jason James Kelly is Chair of Graduate Studies at the Queen's School of Religion and Head of Education for the Spirituality, Nature, and Culture Lab at Queen's University (Canada). Dr. Kelly teaches courses on Religion and Environment, Indigenous Traditions in North America, Mysticism, and Social Ethics. His research interests include spiritual ecology, the psychology of religion, continental philosophy, and Indigenous philosophy. He has published work on erotic mysticism, spiritual ecology, and process philosophy. His current research project focuses on the history of cosmic consciousness in relation to spiritual ecology and social justice.

Jeffrey J. Kripal holds the J. Newton Rayzor Chair in Philosophy and Religious Thought at Rice University, where he chaired the Department of Religion for eight years and helped create the GEM (Gnosticism, Esotericism, and Mysticism) Program. He is the author of numerous books, including *Esalen: America and the Religion of No Religion* (University of Chicago Press, 2007), *The Serpent's Gift: Gnostic Reflections on the Study of Religion* (University of Chicago Press, 2006), *The Secret Body* (University of Chicago Press, 2017), and *Comparing Religions: Coming to Terms*, with Ata Anzali, Andrea Jain and Erin Prophet (Wiley-Blackwell, 2014). His full body of work can be seen at jeffreykripal.com. Additionally, he is Associate Director of the Center for Theory and Research at the Esalen Institute in Big Sur, California, where he also serves as chair of the board. He is presently working on a three-volume study of paranormal currents in the history of science and American metaphysical literatures.

Linda Mercadante has served as Professor of Theology at the Methodist Theological School in Ohio for more than twenty-five years. She was once a "Spiritual but Not Religious" (SBNR) person. But through an intensive spiritual journey has become a seminary professor, theologian, and ordained minister in the Presbyterian Church (USA). You can read about this in her memoir, *Bloomfield Avenue: A Jewish-Catholic Jersey Girl's Spiritual Journey*. A former journalist, she has won many awards for her research in such areas as the theology of culture, film and theology, addiction recovery spirituality, conversion narratives, and the SBNR movement. She has published five books, more than fifty articles, and speaks internationally on a variety of topics. Her book *Belief without Borders: Inside the Minds of the Spiritual but not Religious* (Oxford University Press, 2014), has become an "academic best seller." Her research was awarded the Henry Luce III Fellowship in Theology and the book was named among "the best spiritual books of the year" by *Spirituality & Practice*. She has been interviewed in many publications, including the *New York Times,* and has been a guest on radio and television, including NBC's *The Today Show.*

William B. Parsons is Professor of Religion at Rice University. His publications include *The Enigma of the Oceanic Feeling* (Oxford University Press, 1999), *Religion and Psychology: Mapping the Terrain* (Routledge, 2001), *Teaching Mysticism* (Oxford University Press, 2010), *Mourning Religion* (University of Virginia Press, 2008), *Freud and Augustine in Dialogue: Psychoanalysis, Mysticism, and the Culture of Modern Spirituality* (University of Virginia Press, 2013), and dozens of articles in multiple journals and edited books. He has served as the chair of the Department of Religion (Rice University), director of the Humanities Research Center (Rice University), editor (the psychology of religion section) with *Religious Studies Review*, and has been a fellow at the Martin Marty Center of the University of Chicago and at the Institute for Advanced Studies at Hebrew University.

Chad J. Pevateaux is Assistant Professor of Religion and Director of Liberal Studies at Texas Wesleyan University in Fort Worth, Texas, where he teaches comparative religions, Christian studies, humanities, philosophy, and ethics. His research focuses on modern appropriations and contemporary implications of Christian mystical and liberation theologies in comparison with other mystical and emancipatory traditions and in conversation with philosophy.

Leigh E. Schmidt is the Edward C. Mallinckrodt Distinguished University Professor in the John C. Danforth Center on Religion and Politics at Washington University in St. Louis. He is the author of *Heaven's Bride: The Unprintable Life of Ida C. Craddock, American Mystic, Scholar, Sexologist, Martyr, and Madwoman* (Basic, 2010); *Restless Souls: The Making of American Spirituality* (Harper, 2005; University of California, 2012); *Hearing Things: Religion, Illusion, and the American Enlightenment* (Harvard University Press, 2000); *Consumer Rites: The Buying and Selling of American Holidays* (Princeton University Press, 1995); and *Holy Fairs: Scottish Communions and American Revivals in the Early Modern Period* (Princeton University Press, 1989). His most recent book, *Village Atheists: How America's Unbelievers Made Their Way in a Godly Nation* (Princeton University Press, 2016), examines how atheists and freethinkers have fared in American public life.

William Z. Vickery is a PhD candidate in East-West Psychology at the California Institute of Integral Studies, San Francisco. He has an MA in social policy and social research from Middlesex University and an MA in Buddhist studies from the University of Hong Kong. His main research interests are in Buddhist Studies and he has been studying and practicing Buddhism for more than sixteen years, lived in Asian Buddhist cultures for nine years, and participated in numerous work studies and retreats in a number of traditions. His other major research interests are in psychedelic studies, entheogenic shamanism, participatory theory, alchemy, comparative mysticism, and transpersonal psychology.

Melissa M. Wilcox is Professor and Holstein Family and Community Chair of Religious Studies at the University of California, Riverside. She is the author or editor of several books and journal issues, and numerous articles, on gender, sexuality, and religion. Her books include *Coming Out in Christianity: Religion, Identity, and Community* (Indiana University Press, 2003); *Sexuality and the World's Religions* (ABC-CLIO, 2003); *Queer Women and Religious Individualism* (Indiana University Press, 2009); and *Religion in Today's World: Global Issues, Sociological Perspectives* (Routledge, 2013). Her newest book, *Serious Parody: Religion, Queer Activism, and the Sisters of Perpetual Indulgence* (2018) is published in the Sexual Cultures Series at New York University Press. She is at work on two textbook projects in the areas of queer studies and sexuality studies in religion.

Introduction

Framing the volume

William B. Parsons

The chapters in this volume speak to what national surveys agree is a growing social phenomenon referred to as being "Spiritual but Not Religious" (SBNR). While the polling data over the years has evinced some variability, the most recent 2017 surveys conclude that *at least* 18% (and some have it closer to 30%) of the current U.S. population confess to being SBNR, a fact which has perked the attention of scholars.[1] But what does being SBNR mean? Is it clear-cut and easy to identify, or is it more like what Gertrude Stein once said about Oakland, California, namely, "There is no there there." It's a good question.

Let's start with the easy. We can say what it is not – it does *not* refer to those who have definitively settled in a particular institutionally based religious tradition, are happy with its ethical and metaphysical postulates, and are consistent in observing its services and rituals. If this is the case, then it would suggest that being SBNR refers to those who are not wedded to a particular tradition – those who are disillusioned with institutional religion yet feel that those same traditions contain deep wisdom about the human condition. To say "I'm Spiritual but Not Religious" would then indicate that a person seeks to integrate religious wisdom without fully committing to what is perceived to be the false trappings and mendacity of religious accouterments of all kinds (i.e., dogma, ideologies, rituals, hierarchies, etc.). At the same time, befitting spiritual shoppers in a consumer age, it also speaks to those who canvass multiple religions, mining their spiritual wisdom and introspective techniques for the juice of peak experience in order to foster a spiritual journey tailored to their individual needs.

This general portrait has been detailed a bit more in contemporary academic literature. To note some pertinent highlights, those who profess to being SBNR contest any claim to absolute authority and point, with regard to traditional institutional forms of religion, to their historical role in perpetuating unfair forms of economic, social, and political power. Those who profess to being SBNR also tend to valorize individualism, free creative choice and expression, egalitarianism, progressivism, a psychological/therapeutic approach to spiritual growth, and a seeker/quester/consumer mentality. They are more apt to see humans as basically good (hence rejecting the stronger claims of "original sin"); are more liable to devalue a traditional community in favor of participating in multiple, diverse, yet entangled institutional forms (think the local Jung Institute, the local Zen center, and, yes, even the Catholic mass); are on the whole pantheistic/monistic in outlook, affirm a liberative ethic, and are more likely to endorse the possibility of reincarnation.[2] A 2015 study by the Pew Research Center concluded that being SBNR maps across multiple segments of the American population, noting that this change is taking place

> across the religious landscape, affecting all regions of the country and many demographic groups. While the drop in Christian affiliation is particularly pronounced among young adults, it is occurring among Americans of all ages. The same trends are seen among whites, blacks and Latinos; among both college graduates and adults with only a high school education; and among women as well as men.[3]

This emerging portrait of being SBNR has also given rise to a variety of depictions of who and what they are in popular media outlets. For example, as Linda Mercadante has noted, one could point to the disillusioned character played by Laura Dern in the HBO series *Enlightened* – a character who spends $50,000 on a Hawaii New Age retreat where she meditates, practices yoga, undergoes therapy, achieves a level of enlightenment, then returns to her corporate job in an effort to change her friends, family, and the world as a popular illustration of what we might mean by being SBNR. Alternately, fans of the television series *Madmen* might recall the final episode where Don Draper, on retreat at that famous "religion of no religion" California center known as Esalen, comes up with a new advertising jingle ("I'd like to buy the world a Coke") – a jingle that, in real life, was recorded by a group known as the New Seekers, the underlying meaning of its lyrics being to bring love and harmony to the inhabitants of earth. Or, to go to the farthest, unflattering extreme, one might view a recent YouTube video (admittedly entertaining) that unabashedly parodies the "church" of the SBNR as narcissistic and vacuous.[4]

That being said, we now have to resort to that time-honored scholarly dance: the qualification. The examples just given link being SBNR to neo-liberal capitalism, pop media, and its consumer culture. But some remind us that being SBNR has taken many forms, ranging back well over a century to the creative self-expression, rugged individualism, and social activism of members of the transcendentalist movement like Emerson, Thoreau, and Margaret Fuller. Again, ethnographic studies reveal that those who profess to being SBNR have a spectrum of allegiance to organized, institutional religion, ranging from those completely divorced from the latter to those who have maintained a certain degree of commitment to them, even to the extent of making a traditional religion their major home but integrating multiple other religious practices and ideation to fit their needs for spiritual individuation. In other words, being SBNR sometimes shades into being spiritual *and* religious.[5] It seems that being SBNR is not a cut-and-dried phenomenon but consists of shades of gray, which suggests that we need more ethnographic studies as well as sustained reflection on what constitutes being SBNR.

Given this variance, it begs the question of whether we are justified in using a phrase like SBNR. As is the case with critiques of a number of terms used in the academic study of religion (including, famously, *religion* itself), some may see it as basically invented by academics and biased census questionnaires and, consequently, fostering an imagined construct on a given segment of the unwitting populace, complete with ideological (not to mention colonialist and orientalist) dimensions. Despite this legitimate reservation it is, in fact, difficult to avoid the term and implausible to say it has been *wholly* invented. Speaking historically, there *is* a there, there. As the initial chapter of the volume (which readers may wish to initially consult) titled "Spiritual but Not Religious: a brief introduction" clearly documents, the phrase is a sociohistorical as well as an academic fact, evinced by the growing literature on the topic and its use in American culture (both academic and public) for almost a century. The contributions to this volume, rather than fueling an imagined dimension of being SBNR, provide a corrective through revising, expanding, and contesting the phrase in an effort to provide avenues for work concerning an academically useful category. In this regard the general circumscription of being SBNR offered thus far is but heuristic and, if left there (it won't), would be subject to the same critique Clifford Geertz once leveled at a cousin term utilized in the academic study of religion, namely, any and all generic definitions of *faith* (such as Paul Tillich's "ultimate concern") – a critique which, by calling attention to its general character, renders such formulations insipid and prescriptively useless (as evinced in the wide variance of "being faithful" found between a ritualized Aztec human sacrifice and a meditator in a Kyoto Zen garden).[6] The collected essays of this volume take this to heart. The reader will find in these pages that there exist historical varieties of being SBNR – a variance that suggests that its meaning is best understood when allowed to accrue specificity through detailed research into particular eras, contexts, and figures. Along these lines it is important to stress that the collected essays of the volume address SBNR in the Western world (primarily the United States). The lone exception ("Global Spirituality among Scientists") is included to introduce issues linked to the need to further contextualize a term like *spirituality*, additionally articulating the hurdles required to begin a dialogue about its comparative utility. Certainly any tentative conclusions about such utility must be subject to monitoring by reflective methodologies and fueled by the desired expectation that any speculation will be bequeathed to an academic social space that, defined as secular, pluralistic, and critical, will subject them to debate and correction.

Framework and content

The original chapters of this volume collectively explore not only the "whence" (the various historical cultural strands that led to its rise) and "what" (its current defining characteristics) of being SBNR but more: a vision for its importance and what it could/should become. Their collective contribution is descriptive, analytic, and prescriptive, taking stock of not only the various analyses of being SBNR to date but also the establishment of parameters on which the continued academic discussion of its "thither" can take place. That being said, and in evoking the image of a Venn diagram, matters concerning past, present, and future are not wholly separable. Each chapter of the volume, then, engages these historical dimensions of being SBNR to a greater or lesser extent. However, insofar as each chapter tends to concentrate on specific aspects of being SBNR, we have adopted a commensurate organizational strategy in grouping the chapters into three linked sections: *Roots*, *Circumscriptions*, and *Future(s)*. This frame also suggests that a multidisciplinary approach incorporating both humanistic and social science methodologies is best suited for studying the varieties of being SBNR. While each of the three major parts of this volume utilize such multiple methodologies Part I, dealing more with the past, leans heavily on historical and cultural methods; Part II, which focuses more on its present characteristics, leans heavily on empirical and social scientific methods; Part III, which looks to the future, evinces a more philosophical flavor.

The chapters in this volume are not designed to present a comprehensive, exhaustive view of the SBNR. We offer a general conceptual frame for its investigation punctuated with individual contributions designed to begin the process of detailing what is a vast historical and cultural landscape. Recognizing that there cannot help but be inescapable gaps and omissions in canvassing such a complex topic we remain content with offering intellectual avenues aimed at advancing the conversation. We expect that the articulation of such parameters will inform and fuel the clear need for additional studies concerning SBNR's past, present, and future.[7]

Roots

Existing studies have pointed to a number of cultural strands and conditions that have colluded to form the contemporary option of being SBNR. Salient points of the latter include the role of neoliberal capitalism, of democracy and pluralism (particularly the role of Eastern religions), the Western religious past (e.g., liberal Protestant thought, Quakerism, New England Transcendentalism, New Thought, Unitarianism, Spiritualism, Theosophy), and the cultural influence of science and psychological modes of introspection. Complicit with these factors is the American stress on individualism and pragmatism, the rise of a secularized consciousness, and the separation of church and state.[8] This incomplete list would have to admit that any attempt at cultural analysis seeking to track any historical manifestation must do away with the concept of cause in favor of a Weberian elective affinity, being further complicated not only because of the degree of difficulty involved in isolating and naming such strands but also because of the degree of impossibility involved in tracking how they morph through their interaction. Nevertheless, taking into account this rabbit hole as a necessary contribution to scholarly humility, one can feel at least relatively confident in beginning to articulate the nature and contribution of such roots and strands in the hopes of better understanding what gave rise to the contemporary option of being SBNR.

Roots seeks to take existing scholarly forays deeper by providing in-depth analyses of factors which have been either wholly unacknowledged or undertheorized. In the initial chapter of *Roots*, titled "Spiritual but Not Religious: a brief introduction," Robert C. Fuller and William B. Parsons offer a map for the section and the volume as a whole by offering a history of the term and its cultural roots. The chapter begins by tracing the genealogy of the "churched" terms *spirituality* and *mysticism* from their historical roots in early Greek and Christian culture to the ministrations of liberal Protestant thought and Transcendentalism in the 18th and 19th centuries to the introduction of the phrase "SBNR" in the early 20th century. It then surveys various cultural movements (i.e., early American strands; the metaphysical "isms"; countercultural currents) that helped to further define the term. Finally, it settles on studies concerning its contemporary demographics.

In "The triumph of the therapeutic and being Spiritual but Not Religious" Sean Fitzpatrick and William B. Parsons, banking off that point in our preferred genealogy (as articulated in the earlier chapter) best spied by Michel de Certeau (who sees the emergence of a "psycho-spiritual" tradition in the early 20th century), link that historical juncture to the claim that the United States has become a therapeutic society. The cultural soup we now inhabit takes for granted a spiritual search guided by psychological terms like *self-actualization*, *individuation*, and *peak-experiences*. Adding socio-scientific sophistication to this line of thought, the chapter shows how this soup was fueled, in part, by the social space of the ritualistic therapy session. The latter, framed as liminal, has served to buttress Paul Ricoeur's notion of psychology as a "hermeneutics of suspicion" insofar as it has helped to deconstruct the reigning religio-cultural super-ego (as with Freud) while authorizing "unchurched" spiritual experiences (as with Jung), together furthering the psychological orientation of being SBNR. The chapter then provides empirical evidence which challenges the claim, most persuasively argued in Carrette and King's *Selling Spirituality*, that such spaces have primarily resulted in a form of spiritual narcissism.

Keeping the focus on the roots of being SBNR, no account of its rise can dispense with the pivotal influence of the 1960s. In "The death-of-God theology and the birth of the SBNR sensibility," Leigh E. Schmidt seizes on a crucial development of that decade by focusing on the death of God theology and its complicity in the cultural rise of SBNR. From the fall of 1965 through the summer of 1966, a small band of self-described radical theologians, led by Thomas J. J. Altizer and William Hamilton, championed a "death of God" theology. The sudden notoriety of these Christian Existentialists revealed a fractured religious terrain. The "Is God Dead?" sensation of 1965–1966 drew on the diffuse seeker sensibilities of the era, further loosened the cultural hold of mainline Protestantism, and blessed a churchless quest for the sacred through and beyond the death of God. As the controversy played itself out, many of the basic lineaments of the SBNR sensibility came into sharpened focus.

Our preferred genealogy also suggests that the cultural fascination with Eastern religious traditions and their introspective techniques have played a distinct role in fueling the orientation of being SBNR. Matthew S. Hedstrom, in his "Buddhist fulfillment of a Protestant dream: mindfulness as scientific spirituality," takes this up by exploring the cultural roots of the contemporary mindfulness craze. Hedstrom documents the liberal Protestant ambition to create a psychological science of religion and how that ambition has been fulfilled in the current fascination with Buddhist-derived but secularly marketed mindfulness. He does so by noting that the 19th-century liberal Protestants in Europe and the United States became greatly excited by the realization that modern science, and especially the emerging science of psychology, seemed to prove the human truth of the teachings of Jesus. Buddhist-derived mindfulness in the 21st century does not merely resemble these earlier intellectual projects but, rather, is a direct genetic descendant. While scholars such as Donald Lopez and David McMahan have chronicled the emergence of so-called Protestant Buddhism, no work yet has connected the Protestant efforts to psychologize Christianity a century ago to today's Buddhist mindfulness mania. Hedstrom's chapter admirably fills this gap.

The influence of marginalized communities in the historical formation of the SBNR is a crucial area of research. Joy R. Bostic's "Plurals, hybrids, and nomads: spirituality and religious practice at the intersections" begins to address this lacuna in SBNR scholarship by focusing on the role of marginalized communities (e.g., those dealing with gender, sexuality, race). She starts by noting that Robert Fuller, in his book *Spiritual, But Not Religious*, outlines three categories of the "unchurched." The subjects of her chapter, self-identified Baptist-Buddhist Janice Dean Willis and activist-artist James Baldwin, grew up in traditional Christian church communities. Later, however, each would reject these communities as their primary spiritual homes. While aspects of Baldwin and Willis's narratives might be aligned with one or more of Fuller's categories of "the unchurched," Baldwin and Willis do not neatly fit into Fuller's description of the SNBR demographic. Bostic notes how an examination of Willis and Baldwin's spiritual quests might help us to think more about how race, gender and sexuality might influence a spiritual seeker's quest in ways that expand our views of SBNR populations.

Circumscriptions

Turning to the present day, a discernable group of studies (historical, psychological, sociological) has, through empirical data, surveys, ethnographic material, and scholarly research, offered some insight into what constitutes the present nature of being SBNR. That being said, the collection of essays in this volume operate on the understanding that those who profess to being SBNR, both historically and currently, constitute a wider spectrum of diversity and depth than has been catalogued to this point in the literature. While all the essays in the volume contribute to this scholarly lacuna, this section, in particular, adds nuance and sophistication to the existing body of literature. As a group these chapters, in acknowledging the need for continued research on being SBNR, offer their conclusions as markers for new discussions.

Robert C. Fuller, in his "Minds of their own: psychological substrates of the Spiritual but Not Religious sensibility," begins the proceedings by offering an overview of contemporary psychological understandings of individual differences in personal religiosity. His chapter summarizes contemporary research on the psychological traits of those who identify as being "Spiritual but Not Religious." Individuals who identify as SBNR are overall higher than others in intelligence, openness to experience, the capacity for both self-forgetfulness and transpersonal identification, and a strong valuation of personal intuitions and subjective experience. Fuller suggests that the psychological traits characteristic of the SBNR sensibility are often elicited by positive emotions, specific neurochemical differences that have at least some genetic basis, and altered states of consciousness.

Linda Mercadante, in "Belief without borders: examining anew the minds of the Spiritual but Not Religious," follows up by drawing on interviews with hundreds of self-identified SBNRs concerning the "big questions" many humans ponder: Are there any transcendent powers greater than myself? What does it mean to be human? Does community help or hinder spiritual growth? Is there an afterlife? These questions also translate into the issues of transcendence/immanence (God), theological anthropology, ecclesiology, and eschatology. The interviewee responses analyzed in this research add surprising features to the information gathered by various social science surveys over the years. Although it is risky to overgeneralize, we might be witnessing a new spiritual consensus on "the big" questions. Once such an analysis is performed, questions abound: Are we seeing the birth of a new American "religion"? If so, is it a religion of immanence? And how might such a religion dialogue with the rich theological and philosophical resources contained in the history of Christianity?

Turning ethnographic, Melissa M. Wilcox, in her "Consuming spirituality: SBNR and neoliberal logic in queer communities," notes that being SBNR as a self-description encompasses many different intersections and engagements with religion, from those who are involved in religious organizations but who see themselves as not tied to or beholden to such organizations to those who seek spiritual wisdom and enrichment entirely outside of the purview of organizational settings. Specifically, her chapter explores SBNR queerness as it is linked to homonormativity and homo-nationalism, examining the exclusions this position consequently enacts and linking it to broader neoliberal patterns of consumption that make religious resources ethically available to anyone with the social and economic capital to access them. It investigates the SBNR's neoliberal complicities in an effort to disentangle why certain neoliberal subjects adopt this identity while others do not and to elucidate the political consequences of making personal fulfillment and sincerity the measures of benefit or harm.

Continuing with the theme of the intersection between neoliberal capitalism and spirituality, now with attention to the influence and contemporary American cultural status of Hinduism, Andrea R. Jain, in her "Yogi superman, master capitalist: Bikram Choudhury and the religion of commercial spirituality," focuses on the dissemination of Bikram Yoga. Playing with critiques of being Spiritual but Not Religious as complicit with contemporary neoliberalism and market capitalism and the reduction of pop spiritualities to mere consumer sellout, Jain suggests such critiques fail to account for the ways being SBNR shares certain qualities with traditional religions, including ritual and mythological components. By analyzing Bikram Choudhury, the multimillionaire who has exploited the cultural cache and economic capital of yoga, she demonstrates how pop-culture yoga can betray ritual, mythological, and other religious qualities, but it is also an industry that operates by the same logic as multinational corporations.

Finally, in "Global spirituality among scientists" Elaine Howard Ecklund and Di Di begin the difficult process of ascertaining to what extent (if at all) being SBNR is a global phenomenon. A close analysis of scientists' narratives confirms that there are indeed scientists who claim to be SBNR across the four national contexts surveyed (Taiwan, France, United States, the United Kingdom) but that culture influences the way in which they construct and hence understand spirituality. In Taiwan, spirituality refers to the continuation of Taiwanese traditions through their occasional practice of folk religions; in French counterparts, the negation of supernatural meaning and the furtherance of humanism; in the United Kingdom and the United States, constructing an alternative value system without affiliating with a specific religious tradition. The chapter highlights the role of history and culture in contextualizing spirituality, calls for more global ethnographic research, and draws attention to the hurdles required to begin a dialogue about comparative utility.

Future(s)

Extant studies have also brought up a number of concerns, issues, and debates concerning the overall nature of being SBNR. Among these include charges concerning spiritual narcissism, the lack of community, an insipid perennialism, a superficial consumerism, an unarticulated ethic and meta-physic, a disjointed connection to the past, a problematic emphasis on direct, unmediated experience, an idiosyncratic eclecticism, and seeming ignorance of the need for social activism. Questions abound concerning its viability, sustainability, and future relation to organized religion. *Future(s)* proceeds on the assumption that being SBNR consists of a wide range of individuals who, while held together by certain general postulates, never-theless defy simple and dismissive labels like "spiritual narcissists." More-over, those that profess the sentiments of being SBNR, if taken as part of a long history reaching back to the 19th and 20th centuries, evince an even greater variety. The chapters in this section, then, contest and critique reg-nant stereotypes that have emerged about being SBNR. By drawing on both past and contemporary resources, and at times putting on the hat of public intellectuals, they propose new ways of thinking about being SBNR and its possible future(s).

Jason James Kelly, in his "Rogue mystics: the ecology of cosmic con-sciousness," begins *Future(s)* in a chapter that speaks to a (if not *the*) pivotal issue of our time: climate change. He starts by unpacking the idea of cosmic consciousness as it developed in the late 19th century in the writings of Walt Whitman, R. M. Bucke, and Edward Carpenter. Drawing on key texts of these intellectuals, he suggests their conception of cosmic consciousness presents an alternative interpretation of spiritual subjectivity that can be characterized as "nondualistic," "embodied" and "socially engaged." Then, drawing on this "cosmic" interpretation of spiritual subjectivity as outlined by these "rogue mystics," he argues for a contemporary and future-oriented SBNR understanding of spiritual ecology and the role it can play in vital-izing political action.

The question of the role of social soil in fermenting the future nature of the SBNR is pivotal, and so Linda C. Ceriello, in her "Toward a meta-modern reading of Spiritual but Not Religious mysticisms," frames being SBNR with respect to what has been described as a *metamodern* epistemic shift – a shift that some are putting forth as a successor to postmodernism. She asks how this new category might help us to account for shifting levels of normativity around mysticism in contemporary culture. Theorizing of a metamodern sensibility is further applied in addressing the significant roles that pop culture and social media have played as the New Age gave way to the SBNR. This move, she suggests, has paved the way for a cultural nar-rative of a different sort – one that may offer not only a new angle on uni-versalist (modern) and constructivist (postmodern) cultural readings, but a kind of reconciliation of the two that is consequently uniquely reflective of, and responsive to, contemporary secular spiritualities. By way of addressing prominent critiques of the SBNR, her analysis culminates in a reconsidera-tion of future manifestations of an SBNR "community" and its attendant social mission.

Jorge N. Ferrer and William Z. Vickery's "Transpersonal psychology and the Spiritual but Not Religious movement: beyond spiritual narcissism in a postsecular age," adds to the discussion by exploring some central lessons being SBNR can learn from the evolution of the field of transpersonal psychology. Ferrer and Vickery focus on the challenge of *spiritual narcissism*, understood as a deep-seated belief in the universal superiority of one's favored spiritual choice, path, or account of ultimate reality. Two major conceptual frameworks fueling spiritual narcissism in the SBNR Movement are identified: experientialism and perennialism. After a brief introduction to transpersonal psychology, the chapter discusses two waves of transpersonalism (perennialist and participatory), arguing that the participatory second wave emerged as a corrective to the religious sectarianism and spiritual narcissism of the first perennialist wave. They suggest that realigning the SBNR Movement with the participatory approach in transpersonal psychology may thus assist the Movement's minimization of sectarianism and support a fuller embodiment of its anti-exclusivist ethos. The chapter concludes with some general reflections on the (im)possibility of fully avoiding sectarian spiritual narcissism in intellectual discourse.

The question of being SBNR in relation to the Other is sorely in need of sustained ethical reflection. Chad J. Pevateaux's "Being spiritual but not hierarchical" begins that process by focusing on the issue of oppressive hierarchies. He argues that a motivating factor for being SBNR lies in part because of their rejection of such churched structures. Indeed, of all systems of human cultures, those we deem religious perhaps fare the worst with respect to hierarchical oppression – of women and people of color, of nonhuman animals, and of the environment. The question at the heart of this chapter, then, is how a move away from oppressive hierarchies of all kinds towards a more just and interconnected egalitarianism can be a central motif of those who proclaim being SBNR. Pevateaux starts this process by taking a detour through the past, from Plato through Derrida, arguing that it is through deconstructing the mistakes of past formulations that a more profitable future can be manifested.

Finally, in his "Comparison gets you nowhere!: the comparative study of religion and the Spiritual but Not Religious," Jeffrey J. Kripal explores how university social spaces function as a cultural feeder for the rise of the SBNR. He does so by centering his analysis on the comparative study of religion and how it helped lay the intellectual and social foundations in the 1960s and 1970s for what would eventually become the SBNR demographic. Kripal then moves on to linked social spaces (like the hospital), offering reflections on what such social spaces, in conjunction with comparativism, might mean for the future of being SBNR.

It is our hope that these chapters, taken together, offer a series of new perspectives on being SBNR that will challenge existing assumptions, call attention to its unarticulated features, and offer prescriptions for its future growth. An anticipated outcome is the formation of new issues, debates, and intellectual trajectories. We offer these chapters, then, as a platform for going forward.

Notes

1 See, for example, two recent 2017 polls, one from the Pew Research Center (www.pewresearch.org/fact-tank/2017/09/06/more-americans-now-say-theyre-spiritual-but-not-religious) and one from the Public Religion Research Institute (www.prri.org/research/religiosity-and-spirituality-in-america). The general conclusion of the polls cited throughout the course of this volume have the percentage of those who profess to being SBNR at no less than 18%. Two caveats: (1) over the years the exact percentage of those who profess to being SBNR has varied from poll to poll; (2) one may question the precision of any quantitative poll, particularly given (as with the SBNR) a moving target. That being said, it is fair to say that we are witnessing a significant cultural phenomenon.
2 See, for example, Brian J. Zinnbauer et al., "Religion and Spirituality: Unfuzzing the Fuzzy," *Journal for the Scientific Study of Religion* 36, no. 4 (1997): 549–64; Courtney Bender, *The New Metaphysicals* (Chicago: The University of Chicago Press, 2010); Linda Mercadante, *Belief Beyond Borders* (New York: Oxford, 2014); *Spirituality in the Modern World*, ed. Paul Heelas (New York and London: Routledge, 2012).
3 Pew Research Center, "America's Changing Religious Landscape," Online report, May 12, 2015, 3.
4 See Linda Mercadante, "The Seeker Next Door," *The Christian Century*, May 30, 2012: 30–33, www.youtube.com/watch?v=Z78_rAg4Ldg.
5 These distinctions are also meted out in the two recent polls by Pew and the Public Religion Research Institute (see note 1 of this chapter).
6 See Clifford Geertz, *Interpretation of Cultures* (New York: Basic Books, 1973).
7 It is challenging to see just how much work needs to be done in this area. Two of our contributors, Matt Hedstrom and Leigh Schmidt, aim to fill many of those gaps and omissions in their new series titled *American Spirituality* (Charlottesville, VA: University of Virginia Press).
8 See Robert C. Fuller, *Spiritual, But Not Religious* (New York: Oxford, 2001); Leigh E. Schmidt, *Restless Souls: The Making of American Spirituality* (San Francisco, CA: Harper, 2005); Jeremy Carrette and Richard King, *Selling Spirituality* (New York and London: Routledge, 2005).

References

Bender, Courtney. *The New Metaphysicals*. Chicago: The University of Chicago Press, 2010.

Carrette, Jeremey and Richard King. *Selling Spirituality*. New York and London: Routledge, 2005.

Fuller, Robert C. *Spiritual, But Not Religious*. New York: Oxford, 2001.

Geertz, Clifford. *Interpretation of Cultures*. New York: Basic Books, 1973.

Heelas, Paul, ed. *Spirituality in the Modern World*. 4 vols. New York and London: Routledge, 2012.

Mercadante, Linda. *Belief Beyond Borders*. New York: Oxford, 2014.

Schmidt, Leigh E. *Restless Souls: The Making of American Spirituality*. San Francisco, CA: Harper, 2005.

Zinnbauer, Brian J., Kenneth I. Pargament, Brenda Cole, Mark S. Rye, Eric M. Butter, Timothy G. Belavich, Kathleen M. Hipp, Allie B. Scott and Jill L. Kadar. "Religion and Spirituality: Unfuzzing the Fuzzy." *Journal for the Scientific Study of Religion* 36, no. 4 (1997): 549–64.

Part I
Roots

1 Spiritual but Not Religious

A brief introduction

Robert C. Fuller and William B. Parsons

Millions of Americans now use the phrase "Spiritual but Not Religious" (SBNR) to identify their complex attitudes toward religion. The phrase probably has as many meanings as there are persons who have used it. Even in the scholarly literature there is some confusion about how the phrase originated, what beliefs or attitudes it is meant to affirm, and what beliefs or attitudes it is meant to exclude.

Existing studies have identified a number of cultural strands that came together to make being SBNR a viable contemporary option. These include democracy, immigration, globalization, pluralism, the high cultural emphasis on individualism and pragmatism, the rise of a secularized consciousness, the impact of visual and social media, and the pervasive networks that constitute neoliberal capitalism.[1] These strands don't constitute direct causal sources of the SBNR movement so much as they represent what historians call a Weberian elective affinity whereby certain cultural forms seem to gravitate toward each other over time. Yet despite being a diffuse cultural expression, SBNR has its own genealogy and its own cluster of traditions that have made it an identifiable mode of personal spirituality over the course of American religious and cultural history. While SBNR stretches back to the nation's origins, it is now one of the fastest-growing segments of the contemporary American religious spectrum and thus appears to be a mode of personal spirituality that is particularly befitting the 21st century. It is important that we become more precise about defining this phrase, tracing its genealogy, explaining its cultural history, and identifying the patterns of belief or practice with which it is most commonly associated.

SBNR: a genealogy

The words *spiritual* and *religious* are themselves difficult to define, let alone distinguish from one another. The two words have, in fact, mostly been synonyms with a slight tendency to use the term *religion* for identifying shared, public, or institutional expressions of belief in the existence of something beyond the physical world while using the term *spiritual* as an adjective describing more personal or subjective efforts to find connection with these more-than-physical aspects of reality. Scholars typically explain that our modern use of the term *spirituality* can be traced to the letters of St. Paul. By the 5th century the words *spiritus* and *spiritualis* (Latin translations of *pneuma* and *pneumatikos*) had come to signify those individuals whose mind, will and heart were ordered and led by the "spirit" over against those egoistically attached to things of the world. Through the centuries the term *spiritualis* carried alternate meanings, at one point being used in a juridical sense to denote ecclesiastical offices and property. By the 17th century it came to be used in the more familiar sense of denoting internal dispositions and states, then finally settling, by the mid-20th century, to denote the aims and goals, practices, and virtues of believers defined relative to the totality of a churched, religious matrix.[2]

The meaning and historical development of this "classic" (i.e., churched) notion of spirituality cannot be untangled from a cousin term: *mysticism*. At first the Greek *mystikos*, derived from the verb *muo* (to close), lacked any direct reference to the transcendent, referring only to the hidden or secret dimensions of ritualistic activities. As Louis Boyer notes, the link between mysticism and the vision of the Divine was introduced by the early church fathers, who used the term as an adjective (mystical theology, mystical contemplation) and defined it with respect to three interrelated contexts (biblical, liturgical, spiritual). Importantly, access to God was always seen within a total religious matrix.[3] Mystical theology and "classic spirituality" were inexorably allied. Bernard McGinn observes that the two terms *mysticism* and *spirituality* are intertwined, and thus

> if we take spirituality as a broad term signifying the whole range of beliefs and practices by which the Christian church strives to live out its commitment to the Spirit present in the Risen Christ (1 Cor. 6:14–20; 2 Cor. 3:17), then we can understand mysticism as the inner and hidden realization of spirituality through a transforming consciousness of God's immediate presence. Mysticism, or more precisely, the mystical element within Christian spirituality, is the goal to which spiritual practices aim.[4]

Importantly, McGinn points out that even though the spiritual quest expresses the desire for personal experience it is "not an individualistic one, because it is rooted in the life of the Christian community and the grace mediated through that community and its sacraments and rituals."[5]

Just as classic spirituality and mystical theology were closely linked through the centuries, modern uses of these terms also overlap. By the 16th and 17th centuries the notion of a mystical theology had migrated to France where it became transformed, being used for the first time as a substantive (*la mystique*). Michel de Certeau reminds us that this shift was linked to the emergence of several innovations: (1) a new understanding of the Divine existing within human beings that was universal and hidden beneath religious traditions and doctrines, (2) the delineation of mysticism as a singular "experience," (3) a new discourse that framed contemplative figures as social types ("the mystics"), and (4) the allowance for such experiences to be investigated scientifically.[6] In the 18th and 19th centuries, liberal Protestantism secured the widespread use of mysticism as a substantive and, as Leigh Schmidt notes, solidified its modern form, now understood as "ahistorical, poetic, essential, intuitive, and universal."[7] With the inauguration of religious studies as a discipline, and the introduction of comparative, philosophical, and social scientific methods into the study of "mysticism," one finds a new invention that signaled, over against the use of the term as found in early Christian discourse, a dramatic reversal. A paradigmatic example is found in the work of William James, who, in his *Varieties of Religious Experience*, treats mysticism as an "experience," which, seen as an innate potentiality of our subconscious mind, was available to all. For James theology, philosophy, liturgy, ritual, and the various aspects of church organizations, all crucial for access to the presence of God for the church fathers, were but secondary phenomena derived from the primary experiential matrix.

Similar historical and cultural forces colluded to produce a modern variant of spirituality. Liberal religious traditions (e.g., Transcendentalists, Unitarians, Quakers, Spiritualists, Vedantists, Theosophists), their values (e.g., individuality, solitude, inner silence and meditation, ethical reforms, creative self-expression, appreciation of religious variety), and their consummate figures (e.g., Emerson, Whitman, Thoreau, James, Howard Thurman, Rufus Jones, Margaret Fuller, Sarah Farmer) produced a specifically American version of spirituality. By the dawn of the 20th century Walt Whitman was able to say, "Only in the perfect uncontamination and solitariness of individuality may the spirituality of religion come forth at all," thereby signaling, as with the term *mysticism*, an unchurched, nontraditional, even antiinstitutional orientation towards the divine.[8]

Historical and cultural forces thus coaxed many Americans into associating spirituality with expressive individualism. These same forces prompted many of the nation's churches to reassert a necessary connection between religion and biblical authority. Modern intellectual thought – as so forcefully encapsulated in the Darwinian challenge to biblical authority – forced religious spokespersons to reassert their commitment to traditional Christian beliefs. Curtis Lee Laws, editor of a Baptist paper, coined the word *fundamentalist* and used it to denote all those who were ready "to do battle royal" for the fundamentals of biblical religion.[9] The so-called mainline Protestant denominations continued their cultural dominance during the middle part of the 20th century. Yet the late 20th century witnessed a dramatic shift toward conservative expressions of Protestantism, Catholicism, and Judaism. Affiliation with religious organizations became increasingly associated with a very deliberate decision to conform to traditional authority. As "being religious" gravitated to unquestioning belief in the Bible, it became inevitable that many Americans would develop a spiritual hunger requiring them to leave established churches and follow Emerson's example of seeking out an "original relation to the universe."[10]

Historical and cultural forces thus fostered unchurched, nontraditional, and noninstitutional forms of modern spirituality. As a consequence, spiritually restless Americans were forced to explain their personal journeys in newly minted terminologies that eventually came to be known as SBNR. One of the earliest references to being SBNR was in 1926 (in a journal called *The American Mercury*) when then president of the Rotary Club described his organization as inclusive, nonsectarian, and, notably, as spiritual but not religious.[11] While sporadic references followed (e.g., in 1934 an article in the *Washington Post* about the great *Lusitania* shipwreck describes the various ways that lives were being memorialized as "spiritual but not religious"), it was Bill Wilson (Bill W., as he is usually referred to) and his twelve-step Alcoholics Anonymous (A.A.) program that most successfully disseminated the phrase into popular parlance. Bill W. had been inspired by the writings of William James to develop a metaphysical rationale for a mode of spirituality that is at once deeply personal, optimistic, and progressivist and is couched in the essentially therapeutic language of self-actualization. Bill W. referred to A.A. as "Not religious, but spiritual" as early as 1940.[12] He later described A.A. as "a spiritual rather than a religious program" – demarcating a path both to personal wholeness and to a felt-connection with a "Higher Power" clearly outside the province of the nation's churches.[13]

The phrase gained cultural cache throughout the 1970s. And thus, when Ellen Burstyn's character in the 1980 movie *Resurrection* undergoes a near-death experience and subsequently gains paranormal powers, the script has her describe this metaphysical event as "spiritual but not religious." In 1985, Norman Lear described himself as a "spiritual but not religious Jew," and in a 1989 *LA Times* personals ad, a woman described herself as a "Lovely Eurasian woman . . . spiritual but not religious. Believes love is the highest representation of the human experience." Two recent 2017 polls have concluded that being SBNR is a movement that commands the allegiance of at least 18% of the general population.[14]

The multiple intellectual sources and social spaces that combined to further develop the "Spiritual but Not Religious" tradition, thus bringing it to contemporary cultural prominence, can't be fully explicated in this brief introductory chapter. However, the basic themes of this historical process and its contributing sociocultural factors can be conveniently sketched out in terms of four interrelated rubrics: (1) early American strands, (2) metaphysical "isms" and new spiritual vocabularies, (3) countercultural streams, and (4) contemporary demographics.

Early American strands

Americans have always felt free to create their own form of personal religiosity outside of formal religious institutions. Fewer than one-third of those living in the American colonies in the late 1600s belonged to a church. This percentage actually declined over the next hundred years. By the time of the Revolutionary War only about 15% belonged to a church. This is not to say that the nation's founders were unreligious. They just weren't joiners and pieced together various supernatural beliefs in ways that fit their own needs and interests. Most early Americans, for example, gave credence to a wide array of magical and occult practices. Astrology, divination, fortune-telling, and witchcraft permeated everyday life in the colonial era. These occult systems filled the same kinds of needs that Christianity did. That is, they provided beliefs concerning superhuman powers as well as techniques for gaining the support, protection, and aid of these powers. Historian Jon Butler has noted that "magic and Christianity in colonial America were not generically different entities but were subsets of the same phenomenon – religion. They posited a resort to superhuman powers and they offered techniques for invoking those powers to control human events."[15]

Interest in the supernatural was as prevalent among the upper classes as it was among the common folk. Inventories of personal libraries from 17th- and 18th-century colonial estates indicate that it was common for the most affluent members of society to own books describing occult practices. Colonial Americans avidly collected works dealing with astrology, alchemy, Hermeticism, Rosicrucianism, and various Neoplatonic mystical philosophies. It is difficult to know just what role these individuals had in laying the foundations for the metaphysical systems that would gain popularity in the 19th century. What is certain is that, from the outset, Americans have had a persistent interest in supernatural or religious ideas that fall well outside the parameters of a Bible-centered theology.

Christian clergy urged colonial Americans to stay clear of unbiblical beliefs about the supernatural. Yet in order to meet the kinds of needs or interests emerging in their daily lives, the laity sometimes turned to Christian ritual and sometimes turned to folk magic. This "spiritual eclecticism" must have exasperated the clergy. Their Puritan theology posited a wide gulf between a majestic deity and His finite creation. It was thought impossible for mortal humans to bridge that gulf and gain access to any "higher" spiritual powers. It followed that apparent supernatural events must either be delusions or the work of the devil. What colonial clergy failed to see was that their insistence on the remoteness of God rendered Christianity largely irrelevant to everyday concerns such as the weather, crops, finances, and the health of family members. Christian theology thus inadvertently helped create a consumer market for unchurched religious practices. Many colonists who turned to magical beliefs and practices had no intention of denying the special divinity of Jesus or the Bible's value as a guide to eternal salvation. They were merely supplementing their biblical beliefs with other ideas seemingly more relevant to their immediate needs. Most of the laity didn't share the clergy's concern for theological consistency and instead readily switched back and forth between magical and Christian beliefs without any sense of guilt or intellectual inconsistency.

Americans have thus always displayed a penchant for what historian Catherine Albanese calls "combinativeness."[16] In every era Americans demonstrate an uncanny ability to synthesize beliefs and practices that tradition-bound theologians deem incompatible. Human beings are acting organisms more so than contemplative organisms. Theoretical consistency means far less to most of us than finding solutions to the problems we face in our daily lives. We therefore become adroit at combining ideas and practices in ways that somehow "work" for us, regardless of whether they originate in theoretically compatible intellectual traditions. While the concept of combinativeness is probably the key to understanding most of American religious life, it is surely the key concept in understanding the origins and current expressions of the SBNR movement.

Metaphysical "isms" and new spiritual vocabularies

In the 1830s and 1840s a group of New England intellectuals formed a loose alliance they called Transcendentalism. Henry David Thoreau, Margaret Fuller, and Ralph Waldo Emerson emerged as their leaders. They believed that there is a higher, transcendental reality beyond what can be detected with the physical senses. They believed that this transcendental reality was pervaded by a divine presence which they envisioned not as the male Supreme Being depicted in the Bible but rather an impersonal, universal spirit. They further believed that under the right conditions our minds can become receptive to the inflow of this universal spirit. As Emerson put it, God "must be found within." Emerson put this poetically when he proclaimed that while walking alone in nature, "all mean egotism vanishes. I become a transparent eyeball; I am nothing; I see all; the currents of Universal Being circulate through me; I am part or parcel of God."[17]

The Transcendentalist movement taught Americans that true spirituality has nothing to do with churches, ancient books, or rituals. Instead, the key to authentic spirituality is learning to become inwardly receptive to the inflow of higher spiritual energies. The poetic stream that started with Whitman and the Transcendentalists were subsequently furthered though a host of like-minded poets and novelists they influenced from H.D. (Hilda Doolittle) and Robert Duncan to the Beat poets to Annie Dillard. So, too, did these early figures advocate a socially activist mentality. Fuller advocated and helped to create an activist, feminist modern spirituality just as, later, Howard Thurman (1900–1981), and his Church for the Fellowship of all Peoples, advocated a spirituality of racial inclusion and a focus on social justice. For perhaps obvious reasons, marginalized communities (LGBT; racial minorities) throughout the 20th century have played no small role in the creation and solidification of the SBNR. Indeed, with respect to the contributions of gay and lesbian figures and communities, one can spy continuities from Whitman and Edward Carpenter's valorization of homoeroticism to Forman Brown's novel *Better Angel* to the later development of institutions such as the Mattachine Society, Chuck Rowland's Church of the One Brotherhood, Prosperos, and the Sisters of Perpetual Indulgence.[18]

The late 1800s and early 1900s also witnessed an explosion of interest in new ways of thinking about how we might think of these higher spiritual energies and techniques and how we might use them to open ourselves to their life-changing powers. Metaphysical systems known as mesmerism, Swedenborgianism, spiritualism, mind cure/New Thought, and Theosophy all attracted widespread interest by expanding on the basic teachings that Transcendentalism had first made popular: there are spiritual dimensions that go well beyond the physical world, the human mind contains untapped potentials for making connection with these metaphysical realms, and thus true spirituality is an individual, inward activity.

These metaphysical systems gave Americans another way of thinking about the human condition and the essence of authentic spirituality. Biblical religion insists that humans are guilty of disobeying God (sin). Churched religion therefore demands that we repent of our sin, become contrite, and restore our covenantal relationship with God by professing obedience and gathering to worship or adore our Heavenly Father. In contrast, metaphysical religion teaches that what separates us from God isn't sin, but ignorance of our mind's inner potentials for connecting with transcendental powers. Authors of metaphysical books explained that we need to study the laws of the mind as a first step to restoring our rightful relationship with the divine. As one of New Thought's best-known authors, Ralph Waldo Trine, put it,

> [i]n just the degree that we come into a conscious realization of our oneness with the Infinite Life, and open ourselves to the Divine inflow, do we actualize in ourselves the qualities and powers of the Infinite Life, do we make ourselves channels through which the Infinite Intelligence and Power can work. In just the degree in which you realize your oneness with the Infinite Spirit, you will exchange dis-ease for ease, inharmony for harmony, suffering and pain for abounding health and strength.[19]

Scholars often refer to this as "harmonial" spirituality – meaning an outlook affirming that spiritual composure, physical health, and even economic well-being are understood to flow from a person's inner rapport with the cosmos.[20] Harmonial piety encourages us to adjust our inner lives in order to better align ourselves with powerful energies operative in the unseen dimensions of the universe. This outlook has not only filtered into a wide array of inspirational literature informing unchurched American spirituality but has shaped the inner meaning of the faith affirmed by many church members as well.

Countercultural streams

After the Second World War a number of interrelated cultural strands further weakened bonds to institutional religion, fostering a migration to unchurched forms of spirituality. The igniting factor may well have been those oft-noted and traumatic national events of the 1960s which impacted the sociopolitical and religious soil. Among those were an unpopular war in Vietnam and the harsh reality of racial segregation, both of which fueled growing distrust of reigning forms of Christianity. In reaction came the rise of the beat and hippie generations, the valorization of nontraditional forms of sexuality, experiments with communal living, and the articulation of alternate political narratives. In the language of Victor Turner, hierarchies and structures were being contested to the point that one can almost speak of a "liminal decade."

Cultural upheaval fueled the creation of new, often revolutionary social spaces. Coffee houses, communes, rock concerts, and protest marches forged bonds between disaffected citizens. These new modes of social interaction helped propagate countercultural attitudes aimed at deconstructing traditional (and often misogynistic and prejudicial) religious narratives. These new social spaces, being entangled with culturally entrenched social spaces and institutions, notably universities and theological seminaries, forced the latter to join the attack on outmoded cultural forms. Feminists issued challenges to a religious bureaucracy created "by men and for men," Existentialist philosophers articulated a "death of God" theology, and social critics of many varieties (Freud, Marx, Nietzsche) encouraged a "hermeneutics of suspicion" which highlighted the inherently oppressive nature of religious institutions.

Throughout the 1960s and 1970s many turned away from scripture, ritual, and participation in traditional communal organizations, instead gravitating towards inwardness, self-discovery, and the fruits of immediate spiritual experiences. A new spiritual pluralism offered multiple resources for such seekers. For example, Americans who had formerly idolized scientific rationality as the one way toward truth now embraced altered states such as those produced by entheogens (e.g., psychedelics, drugs that lead to spiritual insight). Earlier in the century the Harvard philosopher/psychologist William James drew attention to the spiritual value of drug-induced ecstasy when he reported that, under the influence of nitrous oxide, he gained firsthand knowledge of higher spiritual realities, stating that there could be no account of the universe in its totality that neglected to take into account such mystical experiences. But in the 1950s and 1960s such isolated events took on wide cultural import through works like Aldous Huxley's classic *Doors of Perception*, being further fueled through the auspices of a bevy of important figures such as Timothy Leary, Stanislav Grof, Carlos Castaneda, and Jack Kerouac.

The growing popularity of Eastern religions added to the mix. Huston Smith, arguably the most influential scholar of religion during the decade of the sixties, and whose own spiritual enlightenment was triggered in part through the ingestion of entheogens, linked the study of comparative mysticism to the American counterculture's advocacy of a more individualistic, experience-driven, eclectic religiosity. Born of a Methodist missionary to China, Smith immersed himself in Vedanta, Zen, and Sufism, writing his widely read *Religions of Man* and championing the attempt to transcend mere belief through mind-altering meditative techniques. Multiple representatives of Eastern religions were complicit in this new round of missionary activity. As early as 1893, at the World's Parliament in Chicago, adepts like Vivekananda (who traveled to Harvard to meet with James) had found ways to institutionalize meditation and yoga in America. But it was in the 1960s, with the advent of Buddhist and Hindu missionaries like D. T. Suzuki and Maharishi Mahesh Yogi, that such practices found homes in retreat centers like Esalen and were blessed by celebrities and intellectuals alike (e.g., the Beatles, Abraham Maslow, and Alan Watts). The fact that popularized versions of Eastern religions came with no fixed dogmas made it easy for them to be embraced by those who, being disillusioned with the Judeo-Christian tradition and dry, arid dogma, sought relief in immediate mystical experience.

Eastern religions were also introduced to popular audiences through the emergence of a unique American form of introspection: psychospiritualities. Earlier in the 20th century Jung and James had forged connections between psychology and the mystical element in the world's religious traditions. The Canadian psychologist R. M. Bucke, James's friend and correspondent, prophesied that religious institutions would simply disappear as increasing numbers of Westerners experienced the mystical state of "cosmic consciousness." While nothing quite that dramatic occurred, the trend toward identifying spirituality with individual mystical experiences was further disseminated through the therapeutic consulting room, the arts, film and social media. Terms like *individuation, self-realization,* and *peak-experiences,* all of which valorized anti-institutionalism and the primacy of the individual, became the preferred nomenclature for talking about one's spiritual growth.

The "human potential" psychologist Abraham Maslow was a paradigmatic example of how psychospiritualities shaped late 20th-century understandings of personal spirituality. Maslow believed that religion was little more than

> a set of habits, behaviors, dogmas, forms, which at the extreme become entirely legalistic and bureaucratic, conventional, empty, and in the truest meaning of the word, anti-religious . . . Organized Religion, the churches, finally may become the major enemies of the religious experience and the religious experiencer.[21]

Maslow claimed that self-actualizing people move past biblical under-standings of a person-like God or a heaven "up there." Instead, Maslow opined,

> religion's Heaven is actually available in principle all through life. It is available to us now, and is all around us . . . [authentic spirituality ena-bles us to] see the universal in and through the particular and the eternal in and through the temporal and momentary.[22]

Maslow later became the originative figure in the emergence of transpersonal psychology, often characterized as western psychology meeting eastern reli-gion. In Maslow's view, transpersonal psychology was concerned primar-ily with the scientific study of mystical states (defined as being everything from unitive consciousness, peak-experiences, and Being values to feelings of ecstasy, wonder, ultimate meaning, and transcendence of the self). Advo-cates of transpersonal psychology provided a quasi-academic grounding for unchurched spirituality through their empirical testing and neurocogni-tive imaging of meditative states, their experimental interest in entheogens, their study of religion "in the hospital" (e.g., near-death experiences), and curiosity about human paranormal abilities. The popularity and influence of these psychologically phrased forms of unchurched spirituality came to be embodied in the psychiatrist M. Scott Peck's best-selling book *The Road Less Travelled*, which sold more than 3 million copies and was on the *New York Times* nonfiction best-seller list for 288 weeks during the 1980s (a record bested only by *The Joy of Sex*).

Contemporary demographics

Historians have understandably focused on the most articulate and well-published spokespersons for the cultural heritage we now call the SBNR movement. Ralph Waldo Emerson and his fairly affluent Transcendentalist colleagues loom large in most scholarly explanations of this eclectic, ideal-istic, and wholly unchurched approach to American spirituality. It is easy to identify any number of other white, middle- or upper-class individuals who have successfully amplified this Emersonian outlook: Ralph Waldo Trine, William James, Abraham Maslow, Huston Smith, and M. Scott Peck. It should thus not be surprising that when psychologists Brian Zinnbauer and Kenneth Pargament attempted to gather survey-based information about the demographic profiles of SBNR individuals in the mid-1990s, they identi-fied a very white, educated constituency. Zinnbauer and Pargament found that those identifying as SBNR were more likely than other Americans to have a college education, to belong to a white-collar profession, to be lib-eral in their political views, to have parents who attended church less fre-quently, and to be more independent in the sense of having weaker social relationships.[23]

There is no doubt that Zinnbauer and Pargament's findings reflect the most culturally visible segment of those who consciously identify with the "spiritual, but not religious" label. Yet this hardly represents the full sweep of Americans whose religious outlook best falls within this broad category. We might remind ourselves that beginning in the colonial era, Americans have displayed remarkable religious "combinativeness." Divination practices, practical magic, and occult philosophy easily meshed together with Christian belief in early America, and that tradition of religious eclecticism comes right down to the present. Few African Americans ever overtly label themselves as unbelievers or as endorsing clearly heterodox beliefs. The same applies to Hispanic Americans. Yet African Americans and Hispanic Americans are just as likely as any other group to practice the very "combinativeness" that lies at the heart of the SBNR outlook. Consider, for example, the case of a 38-year-old Hispanic woman living in the American Southwest who was interviewed by sociologist Meredith McGuire. This woman was raised Roman Catholic, but though considering herself highly spiritual, she now attends Mass only a few times a year. She set aside at least an hour every day for meditation. She has created a home altar with eighteen candles, an amulet attached to a photo of her grandmother, amethyst crystals used in healing meditations, oriental incense, a Tibetan prayer bell, a representation of the Virgin of Guadalupe, and sundry other Catholic devotional items.[24]

As the above example suggests, it is clearly the case that the SBNR movement stretches into most every segment of the American population. A 2015 study by the Pew Research Center has documented the continued growth of unchurched spirituality and reported that

> these changes are taking place across the religious landscape, affecting all regions of the country and many demographic groups. While the drop in Christian affiliation is particularly pronounced among young adults, it is occurring among Americans of all ages. The same trends are seen among whites, blacks and Latinos; among both college graduates and adults with only a high school education; and among women as well as men.[25]

Arriving at a precise percentage of Americans who might be considered SBNR is nearly impossible. After all, how do you categorize those Americans who maintain at least a nominal affiliation with a religious institution but nonetheless privately subscribe to the very outlook associated with SBNR (as many mainline Protestants, liberal Catholics, and Reform Jews do)? That is to say that they fall under the somewhat vague category of being "spiritual and religious."[26] Or, how do you categorize the highly spiritual individuals who don't belong to a religious institution because they are far more orthodox in their beliefs and don't wish to compromise theologically with members whom they consider in some way lapsed? Sociologist Nancy Ammerman is among those who argue that the very attempt to force

"spirituality" and "religion" into opposing, binary categories is utterly misguided. She notes that

> the "religion" being rejected by self-identified "spiritual" people turns
> out to be quite unlike the religion being practiced and described by
> those affiliated with religious institutions. Likewise, the "spirituality"
> being endorsed as an alternative is at least as widely practiced by those
> same religious people as it is by the people drawing a moral boundary
> against them.[27]

Cautions against facile categorizations of spiritual orientations are well
taken, but there is nonetheless solid, empirical evidence to warrant using
a term such as being "spiritual, but not religious" to spotlight the sizable
segment of the American population that searches for the sacred in a fluid,
eclectic manner outside the Jewish and Christian faith traditions that had
formerly structured Western religiosity. A judicious synthesis of existing
research indicates that somewhere between 18% to 27% of the U.S. population can be considered SBNR as opposed to being either traditionally religious or wholly nonreligious.[28] It is important to note that the percentage of
those who identify as SBNR is increasingly larger among younger generations of Americans. Moreover, as the chapter in this volume titled "Minds of
their own: Psychological substrates of the SBNR sensibility" documents,
it is possible to identify distinct clusters of personality and cognitive traits
that differentiate SNBR individuals from those who are either traditionally
religious or wholly nonreligious.

There is considerable historical, sociological, and psychological evidence,
then, to confirm that the cultural option to be Spiritual but Not Religious is
a distinct, sizable, and growing segment of American culture.

Notes

1 See, for example, Robert C. Fuller, *Spiritual, But Not Religious* (New York:
   Oxford, 2001); Leigh E. Schmidt, *Restless Souls: The Making of American Spirituality* (San Francisco, CA: Harper, 2005); Jeremy Carrette and Richard King,
   Selling Spirituality (New York and London: Routledge, 2005).
2 Walter Principe, "Toward Defining Spirituality," *Studies in Religion* 12, no. 2
   (1983): 127–43; Bernard McGinn, "The Letter and the Spirit: Spirituality as an
   Academic Discipline," in *Minding the Spirit: The Study of Christian Spirituality*,
   ed. Elizabeth A. Dreyer and Mark S. Burrows (Baltimore, MD: John Hopkins,
   2004), 25–41. Readers might wish to consult the Paulist Press's multivolume
   series on the classics of Western spirituality for examples of the many practices
   that have historically been associated with Christian spirituality.
3 Louis Bouyer, "Mysticism: An Essay on the History of the Word," in *Understanding Mysticism*, ed. Richard Woods (Garden City, NJ: Image Books, 1980),
   42–56.
4 Bernard McGinn, "Mystical Consciousness: A Modest Proposal," *Spiritus* 8
   (2008): 44–63.
5 Ibid., 44.

6 Michel de Certeau, "Mysticism," *Diacritics* 22, no. 2 (1992): 11–25.
7 Leigh E. Schmidt, "The Making of Modern Mysticism," *The Journal of the American Academy of Religion* 71 (June 2003): 288.
8 Leigh E. Schmidt, *Restless Souls: The Making of American Spirituality* (San Francisco, CA: Harper, 2005), 4.
9 Curtis Lee Law, "Convention Side Lights," *Watchman-Examiner*, July 1, 1920, 3. A more complete account of the rise of modern fundamentalism can be found in George Marsden, *Fundamentalism and American Culture* (New York: Oxford University Press, 1980).
10 *The Collected Works of Ralph Waldo Emerson*, ed. Robert E. Spiller (Cambridge, MA: Belknap Press, 1971), 1:7.
11 See *The American Mercury*, October 9, 1926: 234. Thanks to Matt Hedstrom for pointing this out.
12 *Spiritual Aspect Most Important* (The Houston Press, 1940).
13 Bill, W., cited in Ernest Kurz, *Not-God: A History of Alcoholics Anonymous* (Center City, MN: Hazelden Press, 1979), 178.
14 See two recent 2017 polls, one from the Pew Research Center (www.pewresearch.org/fact-tank/2017/09/06/more-americans-now-say-theyre-spiritual-but-not-religious) and one from the Public Religion Research Institute (www.prri.org/research/religiosity-and-spirituality-in-america).
15 Jon Butler, "Magic, Astrology, and the Early American Religious Heritage, 1600–1760," *American Historical Review* 84 (1979): 323. See also Jon Butler, *Awash in a Sea of Faith* (Cambridge, MA: Harvard University Press, 1990).
16 Catherine Albanese, *A Republic of Mind and Spirit: A Cultural History of American Metaphysical Religion* (New Haven, CT: Yale University Press, 2007).
17 *The Complete Works of Ralph Waldo Emerson* (New York: AMS Press, 1968), 1:10.
18 We are indebted for this line of thought to Mark Jordan, "Queer Spirits in America: Some Alternative Spiritualities," lecture given at Rice University, February 2016.
19 Ralph Waldo Trine, *In Tune with the Infinite* (New York: Crowell, 1897), 15.
20 Sydney Ahlstrom, *A Religious History of the American People* (New Haven, CT: Yale University Press, 1972), 1019.
21 Abraham Maslow, *Religions, Values, and Peak Experiences* (New York: Viking Press, 1970), viii.
22 Ibid., 112, 115.
23 Brian Zinnbauer et al., "Religion and Spirituality: Unfuzzying the Fuzzy," *Journal for the Scientific Study of Religion* 36 (December 1997): 549–64.
24 Meredith McGuire, "Mapping Contemporary American Spirituality," *Christian Spirituality Bulletin* 5 (Spring 1997): 3–8.
25 Pew Research Center, "America's Changing Religious Landscape," Online report, May 12, 2015, 3.
26 This is not to say that there have not been attempts to differentiate being SBNR from being "spiritual and religious." For the recent data on this see the polls cited in note 14 of this chapter.
27 Nancy Ammerman, "Spiritual But Not Religious? Beyond Binary Choices in the Study of Religion," *Journal for the Scientific Study of Religion* 52 (June 2013): 258–78.
28 In addition to the Pew report and Public Religion data cited in note 14 of this chapter, see, for example, Gerard Saucier and Katarzyna Skrzypinska, "Spiritual But Not Religious? Evidence for Two Independent Dimensions," *Journal of Personality* 74 (2006): 1257–91; Alyana Willard and Ara Norenzayan, "Spiritual But Not Religious: Cognition, Schizotypy, and Conversion in Alternative Beliefs," *Cognition* 165 (2017): 137–46.

References

Ahlstrom, Sidney. *A Religious History of the American People*. New Haven, CT: Yale University Press, 1972.

Albanese, Catherine. *A Republic of Mind and Spirit: A Cultural History of American Metaphysical Religion*. New Haven, CT: Yale University Press, 2007.

Ammerman, Nancy. "Spiritual But Not Religious? Beyond Binary Choices in the Study of Religion." *Journal for the Scientific Study of Religion* 52 (June 2013): 258–78.

Bouyer, L. "Mysticism: An Essay on the History of the Word." In *Understanding Mysticism*, 42–56. Edited by Richard Woods. Garden City, NJ: Image Books, 1980.

Butler, Jon. "Magic, Astrology, and the Early American Religious Heritage, 1600–1760." *American Historical Review* 84 (1979): 317–46.

———. *Awash in a Sea of Faith*. Cambridge, MA: Harvard University Press, 1990.

Carrette, Jeremy and Richard King. *Selling Spirituality*. New York and London: Routledge, 2005.

de Certeau, Michel. "Mysticism." *Diacritics* 22, no. 2 (1992): 11–25.

Emerson, Ralph Waldo. *The Complete Works of Ralph Waldo Emerson*. 12 vols. New York: AMS Press, 1968.

———. *The Collected Works of Ralph Waldo Emerson*. Edited by Robert E. Spiller. Cambridge, MA: Belknap Press, 1971.

Fuller, Robert C. *Spiritual, But Not Religious*. New York: Oxford, 2001.

Jordan, Mark. "Queer Spirits in America: Some Alternative Spiritualities." Lecture given at Rice University, February 2016.

Kurz, Ernest. *Not-God: A History of Alcoholics Anonymous*. Center City, MN: Hazelden Press, 1979.

Law, Curtis Lee. "Convention Side Lights." *Watchman-Examiner*, July 1, 1920, 3.

Marsden, George. *Fundamentalism and American Culture*. New York: Oxford University Press, 1980.

Maslow, Abraham. *Religions, Values, and Peak Experiences*. New York: Viking Press, 1970.

McGinn, Bernard. "The Letter and the Spirit: Spirituality as an Academic Discipline." In *Minding the Spirit: The Study of Christian Spirituality*, 25–41. Edited by Elizabeth A. Dreyer and Mark S. Burrows. Baltimore, MD: John Hopkins, 2004.

———. "Mystical Consciousness: A Modest Proposal." *Spiritus* 8 (2008): 44–63.

McGuire, Meredith. "Mapping Contemporary American Spirituality." *Christian Spirituality Bulletin* 5 (Spring 1997): 3–8.

Pew Research Center. "America's Changing Religious Landscape." Online report, May 12, 2015, 3. www.pewforum.org/2012/10/09/nones-on-the-rise-religion.

Principe, Walter. "Toward Defining Spirituality." *Studies in Religion* 12, no. 2 (1983): 127–43.

Saucier, Gerard and Katarzyna Skrzypinska. "Spiritual But Not Religious? Evidence for Two Independent Dimensions." *Journal of Personality* 74 (2006): 1257–91.

Schmidt, Leigh E. "The Making of Modern Mysticism." *The Journal of the American Academy of Religion* 71 (June 2003): 271–302.

———. *Restless Souls: The Making of American Spirituality*. San Francisco, CA: Harper, 2005.

Spiritual Aspect Most Important. The Houston Press, 1940.

Trine, Ralph. *In Tune with the Infinite*. New York: Crowell, 1897.

Willard, Alyana and Ara Norenzayan. "Spiritual But Not Religious: Cognition, Schizotypy, and Conversion in Alternative Beliefs." *Cognition* 165 (2017): 137–46.

Zinnbauer, Brian J., Kenneth I. Pargament, Brenda Cole, Mark S. Rye, Eric M. Butter, Timothy G. Belavich, Kathleen M. Hipp, Allie B. Scott and Jill L. Kadar. "Religion and Spirituality: Unfuzzying the Fuzzy." *Journal for the Scientific Study of Religion* 36 (December 1997): 549–64.

2 The triumph of the therapeutic and being Spiritual but Not Religious

Sean Fitzpatrick and William B. Parsons

Being Spiritual but Not Religious (SBNR), like any other social phenomenon, did not spontaneously arise but is the product of a long history with multiple contributing cultural strands and roots. In examining this difficult problem we start with the genealogy, offered in the first chapter of this volume ("Spiritual but Not Religious: a brief introduction"), which traces the link between being SBNR and oft-utilized academic terms like *mysticism* and *spirituality*, their rootage in the Western philosophical and religious past and a host of contributing factors (democracy, immigration, globalization, pluralism, liberal Protestant thought, American individualism and pragmatism, Eastern religions, etc.).[1] This chapter seeks to analyze in greater detail the contribution of another such cultural strand that is a distinguishing, if not unique, characteristic of both the SBNR movement and the American ethos, namely, the shift to a therapeutic culture. As Philip Rieff noted some fifty years ago, Western democracies such as the United States have undergone a novel cultural sea change, one that he terms the "triumph of the therapeutic." In her influential book on the SBNR Linda Mercadante concurs, noting that her research concluded that the typical SBNRer surveys the religio-cultural terrain using a psychological lens. The major reason for this, continues Mercadante, is that we live in a cultural soup pervaded by (and here she explicitly cites Rieff) the "triumph of the therapeutic."[2] If Rieff and Mercadante have this right, questions abound as to how to best theorize about its complicity in the past and continued formation of the SBNR movement.

On Rieff's therapeutic

What is Rieff's argument? Central to his thesis is the distinction between "positive communities" (i.e., communal, religious history to the 20th century) and "negative communities" (which is to say, the historically unique rise of psychological culture). In articulating the relation between the two Rieff takes as his example the Weberian notion that what "came before" were the Protestant reformers and "idea men" like Calvin, Protestant culture, the emergence of inner-worldly asceticism, and the "spirit" of capitalism. The

defining characteristic of such positive communities consists in the elabora-
tion of a cultural symbolic in which controls and restraints on behavior
outweigh permissions and an ethic in which the group takes precedence over
the individual. In such communities there exists a "language of faith" that
is deemed authoritative, a cultural superego that is idealized, internalized,
and serves to keep the "lower" socially disruptive instinctual forces (sex
and aggression) in check through repression and guilt. Represented institutionally by the "church" and the "party," positive communities reintegrate
the anomic/neurotic through what Rieff calls "commitment therapies." The
latter are those therapies, typical of all forms of religious healing, which
enable the afflicted to encounter their unconscious in what the self psychologist Heinz Kohut terms an "experience-distant" manner. This is so for
the language of sin and redemption and the multiple symbols, myths, and
narratives that invariably accompany the healing ritual are seen, at least
from a psychodynamic perspective, as cultural containers, being disguised
projections of the unconscious. This religious language, mediated through
rituals and the commanding, idealized figure of a religious functionary, serve
to edify and release aggressive and sexual tensions, further allowing for the
reenactment of the internalization of the cultural superego. In short, "commitment therapies" are "suggestive-supportive" in nature, being in the service of the reigning cultural symbolic.

Negative communities, on the other hand, are of recent historical vintage
and find their origin in a new series of cultural elite championing a psychological and therapeutic mode of self-relating. This new mode of therapy is
not so much "suggestive-supportive" but "analytic" and "uncovering" in
nature. In the case of Freud and his psychoanalytic followers the point is to
engage the unconscious directly ("where id was, there ego shall be"), thus
widening the ego and a sense of one's unique individuality. Indeed, cultural
forms like religion and politics are rendered suspect, being understood as
symbolic manifestations of unconscious contents. An "analytic attitude" of
observation, detachment and tolerance of psychical discontents replaces the
"language of faith" and the command to repress. The result is "deconver-
sion" in the sociological sense, the collapse of the cultural superego, the
replacement of the church and party with the "hospital" and "theater" (as
normative institutions), the valorization of the individual over the group,
and the emergence of a therapeutic character-type: "psychological man."[3]

Rieff's articulation of the rise of "negative communities" gives psychosocial sophistication to the genealogy offered previously, which tracks the
shift from tradition-based mysticism to the historical development of a
"modern," nontraditional, or "unchurched" form of psychologically-based
spirituality. Cited in that genealogy is the research of Michel de Certeau,
who, in tracking the historical emergence of the substantive "mysticism,"
makes note of what he calls a "significant debate," namely, that between
the French professor, social activist, and novelist Romain Rolland and Sigmund Freud, over the nature of the "oceanic feeling" – a debate played

out in the opening chapter of Freud's *Civilization and Its Discontents*. De Certeau thinks it significant for it is here that he finds, in Rolland's efforts to secure a "mystical psychoanalysis," the trend towards a noninstitutional form of mysticism and (psycho)spirituality. This trend eventually led to the fact that for many in contemporary culture psychological formulations have been utilized for the purposes of organizing, monitoring, and expressing the need for wholeness, numinous experiences, and individuation. Such systems (which later included psychospiritualities like those of Jung [archetypal], Maslow [humanistic], and Wilber/Ferrer [transpersonal]), have enabled those who seek a modern, unchurched, nontraditional way of mapping religious proclivities.

Psychological rituals, social spaces

Granting Rieff's general historical move from positive to negative communities, we can add further sophistication and detail to the mechanisms through which "the therapeutic" had an impact on being SBNR. We first focus on the role of religion in the formulations of the originative psychologists, then address the reasons behind their seeming acceptance by an entire culture (as Weber would have it, "whole groups of peoples"). With respect to the former, the methodological "meta" key lies in what Peter Homans dubs a Weberian "double ideal type" – one he refers to as "the tension between a common culture and analytic access."[4] Analytic access, by which is meant the kind of introspective activity found in depth psychology, is in "tension" with what Talcott Parsons refers to as a "common culture" for, sociologically speaking, analytic access always takes place at the margins of culture. The double-ideal type thus presupposes an inclusive concept of "mourning," one that is defined with respect to the psychological concept of disillusionment or de-idealization, involves both the cognitive and affective dimensions of the psyche, and extends what is mourned to social and cultural "objects" like values, ideals, and symbols. In an ideal-typical sense, the process is envisioned as starting when the power of a religious worldview or common culture to command allegiance wanes and symbols "die" (disenchantment, as Weber would have it). What was previously idealized, and hence believed or given allegiance to, becomes de-idealized. This loss leads to mourning, a regressive process that involves, to various degrees depending on the person, an introspective engagement with unconscious contents. This is so for the unconscious, previously worn "on the outside" – that is, projected onto, hence contained and monitored by, religious ideation and hence dealt with in an "experience-distant" manner – no longer finds nourishment on the collective level. Such loss loosens unconscious contents, including in some cases unchurched mystical experiences. The dramatic upsurge of the unconscious may result in breakdown, despair or cynicism. However, it also provides an opportunity for individuation, which is to say the process of growing out of the social womb and the integration of previously unmonitored unconscious contents – a process that can result in a response to the loss of religion in the form of the creation of new ideals and symbols. It is the array of psychologies thus created which have served as the guiding locus, even if in the form of an ascendant and distilled cultural atmosphere, for the self-understanding and introspective probes of those who profess to being SBNR. Among the latter, at least with respect to the originative psychologists, is the formation of psychospirituality. And, as evinced by the latter, such ideas usually display some form of connection with the religious past. While de-idealized and in some sense rejected, religion is never wholly left behind in the creation of such psychologies but rather repudiated and assimilated in varying degrees and proportions. In a very real sense, religion "lives on" in psychological formulations.

The birth of depth psychology, then, is understood as in part dependent on secularization, the de-idealization of religious ideation, and the subsequent theorization of unconscious processes previously expressed through and monitored by public religious narratives. The paradigmatic case here, as Homans notes, is that of Jung.[5] Due to an inability to fully idealize and enter into the world of Protestantism, a fact he attributes to a father who, despite being a pastor, was himself ambivalent about Christian doctrines and communicated as much to his son (Marthe Roberts's "vague father"), significant experiences (catalogued in his *Memories, Dreams, Reflections*) of disillusionment with religion (notably his cathedral fantasy and his reaction to his first communion), and subsequent self-fragmentation and encounter with archetypical material (as catalogued in his famous *Red Book*), Jung literally created, as he himself admits, a "public" psychological theory out of his own "private" experiences. In his view, what had been historically expressed and contained in religious symbols and narratives now became rightly understood as located in the psychological processes of the collective unconscious and its archetypical modes of expression. So it is that, with respect to Jung's works, one can draw a direct correlation between Jung's personal "confrontation with the unconscious" (in chapter 6 of *Memories, Dreams, Reflections* and his *Red Book*) and his theorizing about them (most evident in Part 2 of his *Two Essays on Analytical Psychology*). This theory of mourning, then, provides further psychosocial depth, beyond that of Rieff's notion of negative communities, to the textual and historical analyses found in Schmidt, de Certeau, and others. That is to say, *psychological forms of modern spirituality ("psychospiritualties") are de-idealized and "mourned" cultural products of classical, traditional mysticism ("mystical theologies").*

With respect to how such formulations impacted cultural at large (as the poet W. H. Auden once said of Freud, "to us he is no more a person now but a whole climate of opinion under whom we conduct our different lives"), the matter first turns to the clinical social space, now understood as a form of ritual. For our purposes, a brief, cursory meaning of "social space" can be modeled after the classic example of a house: we perform different tasks in kitchens, bedrooms, living rooms, and bathrooms. Social spaces can and do authorize certain forms of living, thinking, and acting. To spin Mary Douglas a bit, context (which is to say, culture) matters: one's boots are not dirty in the hall foyer but are so if placed on the kitchen table. Similarly, university, religious, and clinical spaces all authorize certain, and often conflicting, forms of thought and action. In each case one can conceptualize such spaces as promoting certain forms of ritualized actions which, in turn, socialize the participants into certain ways of thinking about self, world, Other. For example, in Wahhabi madrassas where scripture, understood as eternal, unchangeable, and revealed, is summoned for memorization, there is little, if any, room for de-idealization or mourning here. On the contrary, what is valorized is the internalization of an ethos and truth that cannot, under any circumstances, be de-idealized (where de-idealization is understood as the psychoanalytic infrastructure of belief: belief necessitates idealization). The Geertzian models "of" and "for" reality are presented as sacred and, internalized as part of the superego, held fast by dynamic psychological forces. To act or even to think otherwise is, in fact, to risk communal ostracization, excommunication or even to incur violence. In such social spaces "mourning" is absent. In stark contrast to this, by participating in a university social space (e.g., "the classroom"), understood (if ideally at least) as being secular, pluralistic, and critical, one is enjoined to analyze, deconstruct, and alter any existing religious text, even to the eventual objection of traditional religious communities. Such spaces promote a kind of mourning, insofar as one gains critical distance and detachment from the object of ultimate concern. Psychological social spaces, like those of the university, are potentially revolutionary. If one thinks of the "double doors" of the psychoanalytic ritualized social space as symbolic of the repression barrier (and hence of the cultural superego that, by definition, is composed of collective representations and categorization schemes) and the actual therapeutic spaces as "liminal" (as Victor Turner would have it), then what is authorized is the de-repression and expression of potentially transgressive desires, thoughts and actions.

This social space is in relation to but ultimately trumps "metapsychology" (i.e., the theory itself). For example, on one hand, the cultural legitimacy of the clinic has promoted a greater tolerance for sexual fantasies as well as sexual aims aside from those of heterosexual monogamy (which Freud critiqued as one facet of the religious cultural superego that fermented *unbehagen* or "uneasiness"). Yet Freud's own views concerning sexuality and gender are problematic. Feminists have long noted the misogynistic elements in his theory (e.g., how he essentialized feminine identity and sexuality). To resolve this tension one can, in separating Freud's creation of a socially legitimated ritual space from his theoretical edifice, view the liminality of the clinic as a progressive social space (among many others) in which women have historically been afforded an opportunity to explore their inner space, theorize about it and, as a result, help change patriarchal social structures. That this is so is evinced by what some call the feminist revolution in psychoanalytic theory (i.e., the ascendancy of object-relations theory). From this perspective, the cultural trend toward gender equality, the legitimation of alternative sexual orientations, and an awareness of the unconscious origins of racial prejudice owe something to the liminal space of the clinic. Along these lines it should be remembered that Freud, as a student at the University of Vienna, aspired at one point to go into politics. It was the arrival of anti-Semitism, in the form of a collusion between Rome and the candidacy of Karl Lueger (who became mayor of Vienna) that dashed his hopes but eventually led to the articulation of what he called a "secular cure of souls" that would be unchurched and could, if slowly, eventuate social change.

The logic of this argument is portable and extends to the multiple other ways in which the social space of the clinic has taken critical aim at cultural forms. To be sure, it has become "entangled" with other social spaces (e.g., social and visual media, the university), institutional structures and, through such entanglements, morphed into new forms of cultural discourse that have invariably altering existing social structures. So envisioned, such change is often subtle, slow, and traceable to multiple, entangled social spaces.

The hermeneutics of suspicion and psychospirituality

The clinical space has impacted religion and the rise of being SBNR in two senses: deconstructive and constructive. The first concerns the well-known psychoanalytical distrust of institutional religion. Freud's view, articulated most succinctly in his *Psychopathology of Everyday Life*, is that the ideation of religion is "nothing but psychology projected into the external world . . . supernatural reality . . . is destined to be changed back once more by science into the psychology of the unconscious."[6] The distrust of modern spirituality vis-à-vis institutional religion owes no small debt to Freud for he was instrumental, as Ricoeur would have it, in developing that "hermeneutic of suspicion" where the narratives of religious traditions are understood as disguised expressions of deeper, latent unconscious proclivities. In the clinical space this has become very evident: religious beliefs, motives, and expressions are traced to their developmental and very human origins – a fact that has led an increasing number of people to think that what is really transpiring in institutional forms of religious narratives reflects less the directive of a holy ontological source than it does that of gendered, class, and cultural interests. In this negative sense, not just Freud but the psychoanalytic tradition has contributed to the rise of modern, unchurched spirituality.

Carl Jung, on the other hand, being illustrative of a case where psychology "becomes" religious, which is to say, of a psychospirituality, insisted that there are germs of wisdom hidden in the deeper, mystical elements of traditional religion – germs that can be siphoned from their rootage in a total religious matrix and translated anew for a disillusioned populace seeking wholeness. Jung is a paradigmatic case of what we referred to above as "de-idealizing" and "mourning" traditional forms of religion. Jung, like James, Maslow, R. M. Bucke, and others, advocated a modern, psychological, non-traditional, or "unchurched" form of mysticism and spirituality. Returning to the genealogical survey offered in this volume, Jung mirrored the spirit, if not the letter, of James in turning to Rudolph Otto, proclaiming that religion "is a careful and scrupulous observation of the 'numinosum' . . . by the term 'religion' I do not mean a creed . . . Creeds are codified and dogmatized forms of original religious experience."[7] Of course, for Jung the experience of the "numinosum" came to mean the emergence of strong archetypical material. And what was true for Jung and his fellow theorists of the psychospiritual was then realized by their analysands and, eventually, culture at large. The clinic has become a praxis which has served to ferment nontraditional forms of mystical experience and spirituality.

The influence of this group of originative psychologists is best seen not as a traceable, one-to-one correspondence so much as a contribution, in con-junction with assorted entangled social spaces, to the more general "cultural soup" that informs the various "spiritual" formulations and nomenclature found in those who profess to be SBNR. Linda Mercadante's theology of culture project in her *Belief beyond Borders*, which has amassed and teased out definite data on the unarticulated ethical and metaphysical horizons of meaning that characterize SBNR views with respect to transcendence ("met-aphysics"), human nature ("anthropology"), community, and the afterlife, offers further evidence that this is, in fact, the case. For example, surveying her respondents' views on human nature, she notes that they look inwards to the self for their source of authority, proclaiming that human nature is good if not divine, utilizing psychological explanations for behavior, and seeing "self-fulfillment" as the path of spirituality.[8] They are conversant with a common nomenclature, namely, terms like *individuation, self-realization*, and *peak experiences*, which are the result of the impact of psychological theories and which are often utilized in the expression of that which constitutes the path of the "spiritual." Again, in her survey of the SBNR take on God and the divine, Mercadante notes how some of her respondents objected to gendered "Father" characterizations of God (Freud), further characterizing "traditional" forms of belief as regressive and childish (Freud), alternately conceiving of the divine as needing humans to evolve, to come to self-awareness (Jung).[9]

To illustrate the influence of these psychologies on contemporary spiritual self-understanding we offer one of our cases, that of David, a 19-year-old undergraduate whose presenting issue was grief following the sudden death of a lifelong friend named Randy. David had moved several hundred miles from his rural home to attend college in Houston, and Randy died in his hometown. In the therapeutic sessions David shared stories about Randy, exploring his feelings of loss and guilt about having left his hometown. The turning point in his work came when he brought a dream to therapy. In it Randy was alive and well, and they were talking and laughing together. As the dream ended, Randy handed David a quarter, which he took, puzzled. On waking, he found that he had a quarter in his hand. David found the appearance of the quarter in his waking life uncanny and troubling. As we worked with the dream, he began to understand it as a communication from his friend. He recalled that it was a common element of their relationship. David was constantly short on funds, and Randy often helped him with the few extra coins he needed to buy a soda or a burger. Randy's generosity was not just a part of his personality; it was a critical part of their relationship. David came to understand the dream as reflecting their enduring connection and as a charge to honor him through his own acts of generosity – to allow Randy to live through him. It was Jung's notion of synchronicity, understood as an inner state connected to an external state in an acausal way and experienced as a "meaningful coincidence" (a concept that can be found by those adopting an SBNR mentality), which gave David a useful frame to understand his experience and assuage his anxiety. David went to some pains to deny that it could have appeared in any conventional way, for example, that change might have fallen out of his pocket on the bed before he fell asleep – a denial that reflected both the uncanny nature of the experience and the ways in which its uncanniness was essential to its meaning. David understood it as a spiritual experience, one that allowed the acute symptoms of his grief to lift and directed him into a gently enhanced ethical relatedness.

"Selling" spirituality?

Mercadante's "theology of culture" approach takes being SBNR seriously and, befitting the dialogical nature of her project, sees both its positive and its problematic elements. Others, notably Carrette and King's *Selling Spirituality*, are less charitable. Carrette and King do leave space for, and clearly valorize, a socially engaged, altruistic form of modern spirituality that is oriented towards social justice (exemplified by, among others, David Loy and his socially engaged Buddhism). Although they evince a nostalgia for the communal solidarity and ethos of service found in past traditional forms of religion, they also acknowledge the value of a Ricoeurian hermeneutics of suspicion vis-a-vis the same. However, their focus is less on articulating a more positive form of modern spirituality than it is on critiquing its complicity in reproducing a steroidal neoliberalism. Their genealogy of being SBNR (which understandably departs from ours mainly in the 20th century in order to help facilitate their argument) siphons through two major historical movements: (1) that which echoes the enlightenment stress on the privatization of religion and focus on the individual and (2) the subsequent

20th-century "corporatization of spirituality" in which neoliberalism has tailored individual desires for self-fulfillment to buttress and continuously reproduce the capitalistic ethos of growth, industrial efficiency, profitability, and success. Their critique, as one might imagine, highlights the economic and cultural problematic offered by Marx and Foucault. But their narrative is hardly devoid of psychological elements. Indeed, they see psychology as a major cultural strand in the formation of both modern spirituality and its problematic focus on the individual. In particular, it is James, who privatized religious experience, and then Maslow and his humanistic psychology – one in which a person's basic needs and the valorization of peak experiences reflects, supports, and reproduces neoliberal capitalism – that evokes their ire.

In unpacking their thesis, Carrette and King evoke Bellah's articulation of *Sheilaism* (a term denoting the myopic individualism of being SBNR) as well as the thesis, promoted by Christopher Lasch in his *The Culture of Narcissism*, that social shifts have led to a culture beset by archaic, pathological narcissism. Here they missed an opportunity, for Lasch's thesis is entirely dependent on Heinz Kohut, who articulated a developmental line of narcissism (a value-neutral clinical term and not a pejorative, evaluative one) that offers resources that, properly applied, balances the one-sided thesis that dominates *Selling Spirituality*. If Carrette and King had fully utilized object-relations theory to make their argument, they could have distinguished between a form of spiritual narcissism driven by archaic narcissistic structures that fits well with neoliberal capitalism and a more mature, socially engaged spirituality indicative of a "transformed" narcissism. In other words, there exists a wide spectrum of psychosocial types linked to being SBNR of which Carrette and King focus on but one pathological strand.

To unpack this a bit, Lasch's diagnosis (through Kohut) is that modern culture is beset by a form of archaic, fragmented narcissism in which narcissistic rage, eruptions of grandiosity, inability to care for the Other, and a lack of empathy reign. His task is to sift through and trace its social, economic, political and familial causes, and to point to the attendant social forms that have issued forth as a result. In the hands of Carrette and King that means calling attention to a modern, private, corporate form of spirituality and how such a system ferments fragmented spiritual narcissism. But neither Lasch nor Carrette and King acknowledge that Kohut's psychology calls for more: a transformed narcissism that eventuates in the capacity for empathy, creativity, humor, object-love, psychologically informed wisdom, and the ability to tolerate transience. Properly disseminated throughout society, Kohut thought such transformed narcissism could produce a new "unchurched" religion. At the root of this was his concept of "cosmic narcissism," a concept that clearly captures the religio-ethical goal of his psychology. Referring to Freud's "oceanic feeling," Kohut notes that cosmic narcissism is statelike, consisting in "a shift of the narcissistic cathexis from the self to a concept of participation in a supraindividual and timeless existence."[10] Cosmic narcissism "transcends the bounds of the individual," and one lives "sub specie aeternitas" without elation or anxiety, bathed in a continual communion with a contentless, supraordinate Self, participating in "supraindividual ideals and the world with which one identifies."[11] It is to this ideal that Kohut links a cultural agenda. In his essay "On Leadership" Kohut elaborates the need for a new, unchurched rational religion, "an as yet uncreated system of mystical rationality which could take the place of the religions of the past."[12] He then points to "instances of heroic men of constructive political action who have achieved a transformation of their narcissism into a contentless, inspiring personal religion," warning that humanity will have to produce such types in greater numbers in order to survive.[13] As to who might paradigmatically embody such an achievement, Kohut points to Dag Hammarskjöld, the former secretary-general of the United Nations, who laid out his mystical vision in his *Markings*:

> Dag Hammarskjöld . . . an example of this type, describes his contentless mysticism in the following words: "Faith is a state of mind and of the soul . . . the language of religion is (only) a set of formulas which register a basic religious experience.[14]

Interestingly enough, an earlier version of Hammarskjöld is found in none other than Romain Rolland, the man responsible for Freud's analysis of the oceanic feeling. Born Catholic, Rolland left the church in adolescence due to schooling (at the prestigious École normale supérieure) and the cultural atmosphere of Paris (which he referred to as "deicidal"). Subject to a series of mystical experiences that were pan-en-henic and unchurched and mourning the loss of his native Catholic faith, Rolland began to construct his own religion. Set down in essay form and dubbed the *Credo Quia Verum* Rolland, prefiguring the eclectic bent of many contemporary SBNRers, produced an essentially mystical and highly individualistic, idiosyncratic document, complete with references to transient "oceanic" mystical experiences, culled from a variety of different philosophical and religious sources. Years later, as a result of the complicity of Catholicism in fermenting the Great War, Rolland, in a state of utter disillusionment, turned eastwards to the figures of Gandhi, Tagore, Ramakrishna, and Vivekananda. There, he said, he found anew the mysticism of his youth and a source for the vital renewal of Western culture. Rolland was convinced that integrating the resources of East and West would take many midwives, and he eagerly accepted the challenge of helping to forge a new cultural whole. Importantly, Rolland reserved a pivotal role for psychology (albeit a mystical one) in this project – one that emphasized the need for a modern spirituality that was psychologically informed and socially concerned. Rolland admired Freud and psychoanalysis, hoping that Freud would see fit to help him create and disseminate what he called a "mystical psychoanalysis." Freud reciprocated, admiring Rolland particularly for his artistry (Rolland won the Nobel Prize for literature in 1915) and social activism (Rolland was dubbed the "conscience of Europe" for his public stance against anti-Semitism and attempts to broker dialogue at the outset of the Great War). What we have with Freud and Rolland, then, is nothing short of the *locus classicus* of the psychoanalytic encounter with modern spirituality.[15] And, in the figure of Rolland, a socially-engaged spirituality at that. This line of thought fits nicely with Leigh Schmidt's emphasis on the shaping of the ethos of an individualistic, socially engaged American form of being SBNR as articulated through, among others, Whitman, Emerson, Sarah Farmer, and Howard Thurman. Significantly, Schmidt uses this more socially engaged, transformational understanding of the roots of being SBNR to explicitly counter what he shows to be Bellah's misappropriation of Sheilaism as well as Carrette and King's one-dimensional valorization of its more corporate dimension.[16]

To add a final piece to our argument, *Selling Spirituality* offers a thesis but no empirical research to back it. Yet such research does exist. In linked essays, Wink et al. and Dillon et al. gathered data on the SBNR movement, focusing specifically on the relation among spirituality, narcissism, and psychotherapy (with a specific emphasis on Maslow and humanistic forms of therapeutic intervention).[17] Citing Rieff's thesis, they note that no empirical studies have yet attempted to empirically adjudicate between two reigning perspectives on the therapeutic, namely, what they refer to as the "cultural criticism" hypothesis (aligned with Bellah and Lasch) and the "self-growth/ self-realization" hypothesis (aligned with humanistic forms of psychotherapy) which states that successful therapeutic intervention leads to a more cohesive self, personal autonomy, and social generativity. In line with our thesis offered earlier, in which distinctions between a spectrum of narcissistic types needs to be introduced into the argument, these studies confirm that some of their findings do support the "cultural criticism" perspective when it is linked to a depleted self and archaic or pathological narcissism. Yet, and on the other hand, their findings "do not support the general claim that an individuated spirituality is antithetical to communal commitment and they challenge any simple model that postulates an inevitable dichotomy between an institutionally autonomous spirituality and concern for others."[18] Indeed, when faced with what they call "autonomous or healthy narcissism," which is the desired outcome of psychotherapeutic intervention, they conclude that the significance of their study lies in showing that such therapeutically transformed spirituality "is associated with a healthy form of narcissism characterized by personal autonomy with concern for the welfare of future generations."[19]

To buttress this empirical data specifically with respect to Jung, the core concept of individuation is similarly confused with a narcissistic, solipsistic self-involvement. But individuation always occurs in complex relationship to collectivity. Indeed, one can never *not* be related. The long line of writers and educators following in the Jungian wake have drawn out the communal and political implications of this core Jungian principle in ways that are increasingly connected to direct social action. For example, the

Jungian analyst Andrew Samuels suggests that "experiences in therapy act to fine down generalized rage into a more specific format, hence rendering emotion more accessible for social action."[20] Again, the post-Jungian scholar and psychotherapist Stephen Aizenstat coined the term *archetypal activism* to express his vision of a social action that emerges from a psychospiritual interiority. He advocated a praxis that emerges from an attention to one's dream life, in which specific actions inspired by the dreams would be "rooted in something deeper than political gain or enhanced self-esteem."[21] As founder of the Pacifica Graduate Institute, which provides accredited graduate academic and clinical training and is one of the leading post-Jungian intellectual hubs, Aizenstat's vision of social action grounded in a nonrational introspection has had broad and increasing influence in Western society.

This characterization extends to the Jungian institutional structure. While the original Jungian institutions were focused on clinical training (and their social engagement typically took the form of low-fee psychotherapeutic clinics that serve the poor), an increasing number of contemporary Jungian organizations serve, and are sometimes led by, the (typically well-educated) public. They are access points to a Jungian psychospirituality, serving as nodes around which new spiritual communities continue to emerge. While precisely how they engage the broader community varies from group to group, a good illustration can be found in The Jung Center of Houston. Founded in 1958 by five Houston women, only one of whom had any formal analytic training, offerings of this center suggest a more complex and socially engaged profile that resist superficial critiques of therapeutic culture and contemporary spiritualities. Since 1997, the center has provided psychoeducational classes for homeless and underserved children in partnership with neighborhood-based nonprofit organizations. The center works to mitigate the effects of vicarious trauma with county forensic investigators, case managers for K–12 students in low-socioeconomic areas of the region, public health workers, frontline social service professionals working with children in both the child welfare and juvenile justice systems, and other similar populations. All these offerings have been provided free of charge to the participants.

Further, Jungian social service has an international reach. A relevant, special case is recent work done in Haiti with the University of Notre Dame of Port-au-Prince and CESSA (the Center for Spirituality and Mental Health in Port-au-Prince). In helping to train paraprofessionals to work with traumatized Haitians, The Jung Center introduced trainees to a psychological understanding of spirituality drawn from William James and post-Jungian thought. Conference organizers suggested that this psychologized spirituality could prove an important tool in opening dialogue between the Christian social service providers and the local community of *vodou* healers, a dialogue intended to advance mental health education nationwide.[22]

The hope of being SBNR

The foregoing has been an attempt to articulate but one cultural strand among many that have contributed to the formation of those who profess to being SBNR. Even so, and harkening back to Weber's elective affinity, any attempt at cultural analysis is bound to be inadequate not only because of the degree of difficulty involved in isolating and naming the various historical strands but also because of the degree of impossibility involved in tracking how they combine, influence each other, and thus morph through their interaction. Nevertheless, our analysis does seem to reveal that the growing hegemony of psychological ways of thinking about self and society is organic to being SBNR.

Looking forward, any questions concerning the future role of psychological cultural strands in the shaping of being SBNR will have to continue engaging issues which have plagued the use of the term as a whole (e.g., questions concerning spiritual narcissism and the problem of articulating an ethic, the nature of an SBNR community, whether one can identity anything like an SBNR metaphysic, and questions concerning its viability, sustainability, and future relation to organized religion). Time will tell whether we are seeing the birth of a new religion of immanence, a passing fad, or something that has yet to fully materialize.

Notes

1 See Robert C. Fuller, *Spiritual, But Not Religious* (New York: Oxford, 2001); Leigh E. Schmidt, *Restless Souls: The Making of American Spirituality* (San Francisco, CA: Harper, 2005); Jeremy Carrette and Richard King, *Selling Spirituality* (New York and London: Routledge, 2005).
2 Linda Mercadante, *Belief Without Borders: Inside the Minds of the Spiritual But Not Religious* (New York: Oxford, 2014), 129.
3 See Philip Rieff, *The Triumph of the Therapeutic* (New York: Harper, 1966). Some of the material presented here can also be found in William B. Parsons, *Freud and Augustine in Dialogue: Psychoanalysis, Mysticism, and the Culture of Modern Spirituality* (Charlottesville, VA and London: University of Virginia Press, 2013).
4 See Peter Homans, *The Ability to Mourn* (Chicago: University of Chicago Press), 122ff. See also William B. Parsons et al., eds., *Mourning Religion* (Charlottesville, VA and London: University of Virginia Press, 2008).
5 See Peter Homans, *Jung in Context* (Chicago: University of Chicago Press, 1975).
6 Sigmund Freud, *The Psychopathology of Everyday Life* (New York: Norton, 1965), 258–9.
7 Carl Jung, *Psychology and Religion* (New Haven, CT: Yale University Press, 1938), 4–6.
8 Mercadante, *Belief Beyond Borders*, chapter 6.
9 Ibid., see chapter 5.
10 Heinz Kohut, "Forms and Transformations of Narcissism," in *The Search for the Self*, ed. Paul Ornstein (New York: International Universities Press, 1978), 456.
11 Ibid., 455–6.

12 Heinz Kohut, "On Leadership," in *Self Psychology and the Humanities*, ed. Charles Strozier (New York: W.W. Norton, 1985), 70.
13 Ibid.
14 Ibid., 71.
15 See William B. Parsons, *The Enigma of the Oceanic Feeling* (New York: Oxford, 1999).
16 See Schmidt, *Restless Souls*, Epilogue; 319–20 ft. 3. It should be noted that *Selling Spirituality*, which has been cited more than eight hundred times (an unusually high number), has for many become the de facto lens through which to view the SBNR. While not dismissing their valuable contribution, this volume aims at expanding and enriching what constitutes being SBNR.
17 P. Wink et al., "Spiritual Seeking, Narcissism, and Psychotherapy: How Are They Related?" *Journal for the Scientific Study of Religion* 44, no. 2 (2005): 143–58; M. Dillon et al., "Is Spirituality Detrimental to Generativity?" *Journal for the Scientific Study of Religion* 42, no. 3 (2003): 427–42.
18 Dillon et al., "Is Spirituality Detrimental to Generativity?" 438.
19 Wink et al., "Spiritual Seeking, Narcissism, and Psychotherapy," 156.
20 Andrew Samuels, *The Political Psyche* (London: Routledge, 1993), 51.
21 Stephen Aizenstat, *Dreamtending: Attending to the Healing Power of Dreams* (New Orleans, LA: Spring Journal Books, 2011), 171.
22 Jean-Charles, W. personal communication.

References

Aizenstat, Stephen. *Dreamtending: Attending to the Healing Power of Dreams*. New Orleans, LA: Spring Journal Books, 2011.

Carrette, Jeremy and Richard King. *Selling Spirituality*. New York and London: Routledge, 2005.

Dillon, M., P. Wink and K. Fay. "Is Spirituality Detrimental to Generativity?" *Journal for the Scientific Study of Religion* 42, no. 3 (2003): 427–42.

Freud, Sigmund. *The Psychopathology of Everyday Life*. New York: Norton, 1965.

Fuller, Robert. *Spiritual, But Not Religious*. New York: Oxford, 2001.

Homans, Peter. *Jung in Context*. Chicago: University of Chicago, 1975.

———. *The Ability to Mourn*. Chicago: University of Chicago Press, 1989.

Jung, Carl. *Psychology and Religion*. New Haven, CT: Yale University Press, 1938.

———. "Adaptation, Individuation, Collectivity." In *The Symbolic Life: Collected Works of C.G. Jung*, vol. 18, 449–54. Princeton, NJ: Princeton University Press, 1950.

Kohut, Heinz. "Forms and Transformations of Narcissism." In *The Search for the Self*, 427–60. Edited by Paul Ornstein. New York: International Universities Press, 1978.

———. "On Leadership." In *Self Psychology and the Humanities*, 51–72. Edited by Charles Strozier. New York: W.W. Norton, 1985.

Mercadante, Linda. *Belief Without Borders: Inside the Minds of the Spiritual But Not Religious*. New York: Oxford, 2014.

Parsons, William B. *The Enigma of the Oceanic Feeling*. New York: Oxford, 1999.

Parsons, William B., Diane Jonte-Pace and Susan Henking, eds. *Mourning Religion*. Charlottesville, VA and London: University of Virginia Press, 2008.

Parsons, William B. *Freud and Augustine in Dialogue: Psychoanalysis, Mysticism, and the Culture of Modern Spirituality*. Charlottesville, VA and London: University of Virginia Press, 2013.

Rieff, Philip. *The Triumph of the Therapeutic*. New York: Harper, 1966.

Samuels, Andrew. *The Political Psyche*. London: Routledge, 1993.

Schmidt, Leigh E. *Restless Souls: The Making of American Spirituality*. San Francisco, CA: Harper, 2005.

Wink, P., M. Dillon and K. Fay. "Spiritual Seeking, Narcissism, and Psychotherapy: How Are They Related?" *Journal for the Scientific Study of Religion* 44, no. 2 (2005): 143–58.

3 The death-of-God theology and the birth of the SBNR sensibility

Leigh E. Schmidt

On Good Friday in April 1966, *Time* magazine published its famously controversial cover story "Is God Dead?" Placing that stark query in large red lettering against an all-black background, the prominent weekly solemnly informed readers that those "three words represent a summons to reflect on the meaning of existence." Written by *Time*'s religion editor, John T. Elson, the article attempted to capture the nation's shifting theological mood from the comfortable faith of the 1950s to the metaphysical confusion of the mid-1960s. The cover itself quickly became an icon of the period's social and religious transformations – apiece with John Lennon's suggestion that the Beatles were more popular than Jesus among contemporary youth or with Timothy Leary's imperative to "tune in, turn on, and drop out."[1]

By Elson's lights, God's death was no longer an old Nietzschean taunt but an imminent cultural threat. The idea had now gained a toehold within American Protestantism itself, thanks to "a small band of radical theologians," self-described Christian atheists, who were quite sure "that God is indeed absolutely dead." As Elson described it, "the new atheism" of the 1960s was a complex blend, including everything from the "scrofulous hobos" of Samuel Beckett – "the anti-heroes of modern art" – to the nation's sundry "practical atheists" who politely disguised their unbelief by still showing up at church on a semi-regular basis. Even as the story raised the cultural profile of the new God-is-dead sloganeers, it dwelled equally on the existential doubt and social disorientation that had come to beset the faithful themselves by the mid-1960s – the youthful alienation from the churches, the believers who have "desperately turned to psychiatry, Zen or drugs" to sooth their search-for-meaning anxieties, and the growing humanistic impulse to submerge religious identity in social-justice activism or the secular city. Notorious for giving cover-story visibility to the Christian atheists, Elson's article actually concluded with inklings of a "new quest for God" – one that "respects no church boundaries" and one that is reverently agnostic about particular Christian truth-claims: "God is not the property of the church," the essay pledged in an ecumenical, almost post-Christian flourish. Perhaps, Elson hinted, this new death-of-God theology did not portend an atheistic secularism so much as an amplified spiritual seeking.[2]

The God-is-dead tempest had been whirling for more than half a year when *Time* emblazoned the controversy on its cover. By the fall of 1965 the news coverage had already become extensive. That October the *New York Times* reported at length on these new "radical Protestant thinkers" who were intent on reimagining Christianity without God and without "traditional church practices." Highlighting a small cadre of death-of-God theologians, the article focused on Thomas J. J. Altizer, a professor of religion at Emory University and a lapsed Episcopalian; William Hamilton, a professor of theology at Colgate Rochester Divinity School and an ordained Baptist; and Paul Van Buren, a professor of religion at Temple University and an Episcopal priest. While Hamilton and Van Buren were presented as maintaining an ethical, if secularized, focus on Jesus, the *Times* singled out Altizer as the "most radical," especially for his "mystical" propensities: "He rejects not only the Christian tradition," the paper reported, "but much of Western culture to explore Eastern and primitive religious phenomena." Having announced his Christian atheism, Altizer was awaiting the dialectical return of the sacred after the death of Christendom's God – an abstruse proposition that the *Times* had trouble mapping onto the familiar liberal Protestant and neoorthodox theological terrain. Less than a week later, *Time* magazine offered its initial wide-eyed foray into "The 'God is Dead' Movement." "God has died in our time, in our history, in our existence" – it would be one thing if that claim was being made by some "moody French Existentialist," the weekly observed, but coming from a religion professor at a Methodist school in Atlanta, that was head-shaking news. Again, it was Altizer's "eclectic theology" – the merger of his Christian atheism with "a strong streak of mysticism" – that proved especially hard for the journal to pin down in familiar Protestant or secular terms.[3]

After the extensive news coverage in the fall of 1965 the death-of-God brouhaha reached a peak that winter with two feature stories on the CBS Evening News with Walter Cronkite on back-to-back nights in February 1966. Altizer was again the center of attention, pronouncing God's death with a wild-eyed, prophetic confidence. The CBS coverage managed to add a new theatrical wrinkle, shocking many viewers by showing "a funeral service for God," a requiem written by an assistant professor at North Carolina Wesleyan College. Focusing especially on the face of an innocent-looking undergraduate as she chanted the "God is dead" mantra, CBS lingered over the bleak liturgy that Altizer and his colleagues had inspired: "He was our guide and our stay / He walked with us beside still waters / He was our help in ages past . . . He is gone, He is stolen by darkness . . . Heaven is empty." Two months later the death-of-God commotion culminated in *Time* magazine's cover story; by then, *Newsweek* and *U.S. News and World Report* had also given concerted attention to the controversy. The excitement finally played itself out over the summer, slowly dwindling away after Altizer's especially dismal reception on the *Merv Griffin Show* that August. Hissed and booed, he found the clock running out on his fifteen minutes of pop-culture celebrity. Within a year or two, his radical theology looked like it had been nothing so much as a passing fad. "Pop Theology via TV," the *Christian Century* dubbed one of Altizer's performances; he had offered little more than "adolescent daydreaming," the sober mainline Protestant weekly suggested, on par with the espionage show *The Man from U.N.C.L.E.* For its part, *Christianity Today* assured its evangelical readership in May 1967 that "the death-of-God stir has passed like an overnight storm" and that Altizer's "bizarre and aberrational" claims would "soon be forgotten" in the face of the enduring proclamation of the gospel.[4]

A half century on, the whole death-of-God hubbub warrants reexamination. The advent of the Christian atheists revealed a fissured religious terrain: evangelicals seething over the death-of-God heresy and the liberal betrayals of the Supreme Court; secularists, atheists, and humanists wishing these radical theologians could get over their lingering Christian hang-ups; mainline Protestants, by turns, proud and wary of the existential dissent their theological liberalism had generated; and sundry seekers inviting the death-of-God fraternity to join them in a spiritual counterculture of heady, wide-ranging exploration. Altizer himself hardly needed that last invitation. Once on course to have become an Episcopal priest – he failed the church's required psychiatric evaluation – Altizer had channeled his energies instead into PhD work in theology and the history of religions at the University of Chicago, ultimately coming under the sway of Mircea Eliade's comparative, esoteric vision of the field. Altizer's first book, published in 1961, was on *Oriental Mysticism and Biblical Eschatology*; his second book, which appeared two years later, was entirely devoted to an exposition of Eliade's work, including the "archaic ontology" of shamanism, with sections on alchemy and yoga to boot. Shaped by his own early visionary experiences – one of being in Satan's presence was especially formative – Altizer called himself a "disciple" of Eliade's and meant it. He even reported undergoing, some years later, a "contemporary shamanic initiation" at the Chicago professor's own hands during a ghostly gathering in Hyde Park. The "Is God Dead?" sensation of 1965–1966 had many sources and upshots. Prominent among them were the ways it drew on the diffuse seeker sensibilities of the era and blessed a churchless quest for the sacred through and beyond the death of God.[5]

The death-of-God provocateurs generated plenty of outrage, particularly from Bible-believing Protestants, including a good number of southern Methodists who could not fathom that the theology's most visible spokesman was employed by one of their church-related colleges. Altizer's archived correspondence files are filled with letters from aggrieved evangelicals, several of whom included soul-saving tracts, handwritten biblical extracts in red lettering, or even condolence cards for the professor's loss of his Father (God). One writer, C. A. Kelly, from South Carolina struck a relatively loving tone in a letter he wrote to Altizer after seeing him on Walter Cronkite's news program:

> Mr. Altizer you should not say God is dead. . . . We Christians who have had an experience of Salvation through the atoning blood of Jesus Christ know different. A dead God could not have saved my soul when all hope was gone. It was a living Christ that came into my heart April 16, 1950 and delivered me from alcohol, tobacco, a cursing tongue and all the other filthy habits of the flesh and the devil. . . . You may not believe it, you may not accept it but in spite of [your] belief or I should say unbelief[,] God still loves you.

Many of Altizer's correspondents simply wanted to witness to him, to tell him about their own experiences of a living God, and to let him know that salvation could yet be his as well. "I would like to ask you to turn away from your Phd degree, or BD degree," one North Carolinian exhorted, "and for a moment consider the B. A. Degree given to those who are *Born Again* by the Holy Ghost."[6]

Other evangelicals were far less prayerful in approach, hoping rather that God would swiftly punish Altizer – along with various other enemies of the faith and the nation. "You and Martin Luther King Jr. have several things in common," a preacher from Brownsville, Texas, informed Altizer.

> The first one being your unsaved states. In the second place you are "wolves in sheep's clothing" . . . Your four hands will be bloodied by the lives of those you two have deceived and encouraged to go to Hell with you all. One day, my God will triumph!

A correspondent from Kansas City added to the chorus of hostility: "We have too many of your kind in our schools and colleges today. This country was built by Christians who had faith and believed in God. . . . Maybe Russia would be your choice!" For many white evangelicals, the God-is-dead furor played on a crescendo of fears – of godless communism, civil-rights activism, and liberal secularism made tangible by atheist college professors and by the Supreme Court in its recent decisions against prayer and Bible reading in the public schools. Altizer became the perfect bête noir – a treasonous blasphemer of the nation's most elemental pieties, more threatening in some ways than the atheist activist Madalyn Murray O'Hair because his subversive rhetoric arose from within the Protestant fold. "I became one of the most hated men in America," Altizer reflected four decades later in his theological memoir. Judging from the conservative Christian hate mail he received, he was not inflating his infamy by much. "You are one of Satan's people – you are Anti-Christ," a woman from Wisconsin raged against Altizer. "True Christians want to kick you right out of the U.S." With deep southern roots, Altizer knew the world of tent revivals well, but he found himself utterly at odds with America's assertive evangelical subculture.[7]

At the other end of the religious spectrum were Unitarians, humanists, secularists, and outright atheists who were delighted to have God's demise getting so much attention, even if the funeral retained a distinctly Protestant tenor. "It's high time," the leader of a Unitarian fellowship in Savannah wrote to Altizer, "we replaced the sentimental ideas about God and started practicing a universal religion based on respect for all mankind and an Ultimate Concern for all Life." A Christianity shorn of God but not of its prophetic social imperative resonated with many American secularists and humanists – not exactly a large contingent, of course, but organized enough to sustain small federations such as the American Ethical Union and to issue the occasional manifesto of progressivist striving. Others were less impressed, though, with the way the Christian atheists held onto Jesus as an ethical paragon for radical theology. "Congratulations in having given the heave-ho to that worst of Theological frauds – God," a former colleague at Wabash College wrote Altizer before advising him to take a harder look at "Christ's ethical system." It "seems rather second rate to me," his old associate wrote. "So why the 'Christian' atheism?" Other letter writers wanted to push Altizer and company into more obviously secular political postures: "Do you think it's right for the government to keep putting 'In God We Trust' on our money, when it spends 50 billion dollars a year for man made military protection?" a Georgia nonbeliever asked.

> I think it is a bad thing that the American feeling is that everybody should belong to some religious group, and that agnostics are looked down on as second class citizens. I think the constitution of the U.S. should read *freedom from religion.*

To have this new brand of atheism featured in *Time* or on the CBS Evening News gave heart to a freethinking minority long habituated in the Cold War to the routine association of their secularist dissent with godless communism and moral degradation.[8]

G. Vincent Runyon, one of the humanists and rationalists who wrote Altizer, wanted to nudge the death-of-God theologians in the direction of a more thoroughgoing atheism. A graduate of Drew Theological Seminary in 1925, Runyon had been a Methodist preacher of the modernist variety for twelve years in New York before being won over by the "constructive" humanism he encountered initially among Unitarians. He left the Methodist pulpit and found fellowship instead with the Los Angeles Society of Humanists. "There are many roads to atheism but I came in through the door of Humanism," Runyon observed in his short memoir, *Why I Left the Ministry and Became an Atheist*, published in 1959, six years before he reached out to Altizer. As a materialist, Runyon did not understand the mystical yearning that persisted among the Christian atheists for the return of God or why they continued to patronize Protestant journals like the *Christian Century* rather than the *American Rationalist*. Mostly, though, Runyon wanted to express his sincere appreciation to Altizer and his companions for prompting such wide-ranging inquiry into the death of God in a country that seemed otherwise reflexively God-affirming. For Runyon, all the media attention given to Christian atheism pointed to a religious journey rarely afforded that kind of cultural recognition – the passage out of Protestantism into open nonbelief. Runyon, in short, spoke for the avowedly irreligious segment of the population long before sociologists had drawn attention to the "Nones."[9]

For their part, mainline Protestants – at least, at leadership levels – were caught in the middle, disinclined to offer an evangelical altar call or a ringing post-Christian endorsement. Largely at home with the liberal modernist values of academic freedom, intellectual innovation, and avant-garde artistic expression, ecumenical Protestants defended Altizer from those who thought he had no business teaching at a church-related college. He was not going to get fired from Emory on their watch, even if his presence jeopardized the school's recently announced capital campaign. Like the young Thomas Ogletree (eventual dean of Yale Divinity School) who wrote a whole primer on the controversy for puzzled churchgoers, ecumenical Protestants mostly responded with curiosity and engagement, even as they regretted the journalistic sensationalism that Altizer especially invited. The tagline of the National Council of Churches television advertisement, which ran in response to the whole melee, was purposefully irenic, almost anemically so: "Keep in circulation the rumor that God is alive." For ecumenical Protestants, already attuned to Paul Tillich and Rudolf Bultmann, the radicals rarely seemed as wildly radical as they announced themselves to be. The Methodist youth magazine *motive* embraced the new theology with puckish glee, running its own mock obituary under the headline: "God Is Dead in Georgia: Eminent Deity Succumbs during Surgery – Succession in Doubt as All Creation Groans." The questioning and questing sensibility that Altizer and Hamilton represented already had deep roots within ecumenical Protestantism. A syllabus featuring Blake, Melville, Nietzsche, Camus, and Ingmar Bergman was not going to scare off too many in this constituency.[10]

In 1975, when Altizer's lieutenant William Hamilton looked back at "The Death of God after Ten Years" for the *Christian Century*, he positioned the radical theology's significance not in terms of its impact on a new atheism or a transformed Protestantism. Instead, he highlighted the ways in which it had been "profoundly connected to the outburst of American religiosity, Oriental and otherwise, in the late 1960s." The death-of-God controversy, Hamilton suggested, had helped fuel the post-Christian, pluralistic, and eroticized spiritual strivings on the countercultural left. (The erotic piece was important to Hamilton; he liked to talk up his time spent on the "sex circuit" promoting the "unrepressed life" on college campuses, including a gig with Hugh Hefner at Johns Hopkins University.) "To affirm the death of God," Hamilton wrote, was "to remove the Mosaic-Calvinist censor from the door of the Holy of Holies" and to break open the white, masculine,

Protestant world of divinity. Without that old custodian of the sacred in place, Hamilton surmised, American religiosity had been able to take wing away from the churches and alight on all kinds of "new polytheisms and syncretisms."[11]

It goes without saying that the death-of-God theology was more a symptom than a cause of this wider spiritual and metaphysical ferment. Years earlier, in a more sober moment, Hamilton had acknowledged that the radical theologians were little more than "a loose coalition of drinking companions," a small bunch of academic Existentialists and "profane mystics" connected mostly through conference sessions and hotel bars, but he was nonetheless right – ten years later – to highlight the cultural portentousness of the requiem that he and his colleagues had performed. Their insistent emphasis on the death of God – the irretrievable loss of the divine in the common experience of many American Christians (who were usually universalized as "modern man") – was paired with a hopeful posture of revolutionary possibility, that substantive change was imminent in the religious as much as the political and social realms. God would return, in other words, just not as the guardian of mainline Protestantism's cultural authority. The accustomed homeland of American Christian faith, in Altizer's view, had been lost, but the archaic force of the sacred, its numinous reality, beckoned the grieving inquirer away from modern nihilism into explorations of Buddhism, mysticism, shamanism, and "various forms of Indian Yoga." For Altizer, Eliade's initiate, America's desacralized Christianity was to be reborn through its encounter with "the universal sacred," and modern theological inquiry was to be revivified through the primordial ontology revealed in the history of religions.[12]

Altizer had many correspondents who agreed with him that the time had come for "a radical quest for a new mode of religious understanding." Often, though, they thought he had fallen short of exploring territory that needed to be explored. Alvin Miller wrote from nearby Decatur to tell Altizer of how he had long stared into the Existentialist void and eventually found rescue through a multilayered "quest for the Spiritual." He wondered why Altizer had not done more to engage Zen Buddhism and the search for "Totality by not-searching." "In the beginning mountains are mountains and rivers are rivers," Miller wrote, echoing a passage from Alan Watts's *The Way of Zen* (1957). "Then a point comes when the mountains are not mountains and the rivers are not rivers. But with time the mountains are once again mountains and the rivers are again rivers." The Zennists, as Miller called them, very much needed to be part of radical theology's expanded spiritual horizon.[13]

Other correspondents, of course, had different recommendations for Altizer's announced quest. Had he read Swedenborg, Aldous Huxley, and the British theosophist Paul Brunton? How about Swami Vivekananda, Thomas Merton, and Huston Smith? The litany of book recommendations that Altizer received underlines the importance of a middlebrow book culture in spreading the seeker sensibility – a point that Matthew Hedstrom has amply documented in *The Rise of Liberal Religion*. One college student from Wittenberg University in Ohio, Ted Nelson Tatman, wrote Altizer to describe how he had encountered the works of the new radical theologians against a backdrop of ever-shifting reading. His copy of *Radical Theology and the Death of God* had fast become "dog-eared and over-underlined," and Tatman and his friends had discussed the volume's "revolutionary" claims "in the student union, at work in the dishroom, over beer." The work was disorienting to Tatman's Lutheran faith, and he wondered now how he could "put up with the liturgy of my sect," its "so-called sacraments, the dogmas, the credos." Yet, Tatman placed Altizer's challenge within a very bookish series of inquiries about the faith:

> Here some of us have run through all sorts of exploratory cycles. Kierkegaard and the modern pessimists, Nietzsche, Schleiermacher, and other more hopeful people . . . Then someone discovered J. D. Salinger. The next month Kahlil Gibran was the rage. And then Tillich.

It was all such an intoxicating mix, especially, as Tatman related, for someone who had "grown up half way in the 1950's." Altizer's work had "shocked" him, so much so that law school suddenly "looked better" than seminary. A whirl of reading had cracked open Tatman's "semi-pietistic, semi-fundamental, dogma-bound" Protestant world.[14]

Altizer received not only recommendations for additional books to read, but also suggestions for new practices to try and experiments to conduct. One of his former undergraduates, who had gone on to get his PhD in psychology from Berkeley, wrote to thank his professor for sparking his initial spiritual curiosities – a trek that had led him from Zen to LSD to an Indonesian movement, known as Subud, which offered its own program of meditation and spiritual training. Likewise, another former student, who had also migrated to California for graduate work, fondly recalled the course on world religions that he had taken with Altizer and then remarked,

> I thought I'd drop you a note about something of mutual interest – mysticism – or to spell it another way – *LSD*. Yes, the LSD experience and the mystical experience are much the same thing. It's completely preposterous getting religion out of a pill, I know, but nevertheless.

New realms of consciousness were opening up, and his former student felt sure that Altizer very much deserved to be among "the enlightened." For these admirers, Altizer had become a celebrated spokesman for spiritual seeking beyond familiar religious institutions and moribund theologies. One correspondent summed up the entire drift of these letters in his sign-off to Altizer: "Yours for more honest searching and less ecclesiastical Bull shit[t]ing."[15]

No one more richly embodied the interconnections between the God-is-dead moment and post-Christian spiritual striving than the beatnik-hippie poet George Dowden, another of Altizer's correspondents. An American expatriate living in England, Dowden was especially devoted to Walt Whitman and Allen Ginsberg – an artistic lineage absolutely critical for birthing the SBNR sensibility. Like Whitman and Ginsberg, Dowden was adept at playing the role of the poet-prophet, the bearer of a literary and religious counterculture that courted the obscene and the blasphemous. Dowden sent Altizer a mimeographed copy of his underground poem *Renew Jerusalem*, only published in book form three years later in 1969. A section titled the "Novum Theologicum" saluted the "latest theological avant-garde" – including Altizer, Hamilton, and Paul van Buren by name – and proclaimed the death of both the "Executive God" and "the white man's religion." Dowden lingered for contrast over the youthful seekers of his own generation who had rediscovered the divine in the ecstasy of the "bodysoul mystery" and in the Whitmanian embrace of the artist as revelator.[16]

The renewed Jerusalem that Dowden imagined would be orgiastic and psychedelic – and spiritually diverse. Near the poem's opening he is in a monastery, collecting bugs as they come in an unscreened abbey window: "Pure task as I meditate on the matter – Benedictine Pent[e]costal Christian Hebrew Buddhist Hindu Moslem Taoist Zoroastrian Christian Voodoo Jain Native Church of American Indian League for Spiritual Discovery yoga." Running all the religious possibilities together – with no commas to separate them – the poet then sees himself reflected naked in the abbey window, his body adorned only "with colored glass beads – spiritual jewels." A few years later Dowden would find himself far removed from an English abbey, a "Sixties Man" at an ashram in India, reinventing himself once again through a yearlong spiritual journey with the acclaimed guru Swami Muktananda, savvy popularizer of Siddha Yoga as a meditative path of self-realization. (Here, of course, was another critical strand in the development of the SBNR posture, the convergence of Indian swamis and American seekers that stretched from Vivekananda in 1890s' Chicago through Prabhavananda in 1930s' Hollywood through Muktananda in 1970s' Aspen.) Given Dowden's sweeping eclecticism and his highly eroticized spirituality, he quickly concluded that Altizer's theological musings were, on the whole, all too timid. "I of course do not find you radical enough," the poet informed the professor, but he did find him sufficiently provocative to discern a fellow traveler in a heterogeneous, post-Christian landscape.[17]

"Is God Dead?" – the *Time* cover augured less a new atheism than a transformed American religious terrain. The bells were tolling not for Christendom's God but for the ecumenical Protestant establishment. Embodying a moment of theological and cultural crisis, Altizer's promulgation of Christian atheism proved a last hurrah for the public voice of mainline Protestantism. Lacking the establishment clout of Reinhold Niebuhr, Paul Tillich, or G. Bromley Oxnam – all *Time* cover honorees in the years following

World War II – Altizer became a Warhol-like figure in his brief fling of cultural notoriety. Ecumenical Protestant intellectuals became much easier to ignore after the very public requiem that Altizer and his companions staged in 1965 and 1966. Over the next decade and a half, it would be resurgent evangelicals who became media darlings; the Year of the Evangelical arrived in 1976. Ronald Reagan, who was elected governor of California in November 1966 a half year after *Time*'s cover story, sealed the ascent of the Religious Right with his presidential victory in 1980.

Conservative evangelicals, however, were not the only ones to benefit from the religious and cultural space opened up by the dwindling authority of liberal Protestants. The ascendancy of those who identify as Spiritual but Not Religious, as unaligned seekers, points to an equally momentous development of the last fifty years, and, in that context, Altizer and his companions look less like fleeting celebrities than clear-eyed seers. The spirituality-without-religion phenomenon has deep cultural roots, of course, and innumerable sources – from Emersonian transcendentalism to twelve-step recovery regimens, from Blavatsky's theosophy to Huxley's perennial philosophy. But, the death-of-God controversy provided an important impetus at a critical moment in the diffusion of that religious outlook. Altizer, in all his theological notoriety, embodied many of the different strands that went into the making of the SBNR phenomenon: most conspicuously, the Existentialist, countercultural alienation from conventional Protestant Christianity and the mystical esotericism woven into much of the scholarship on comparative religions. "An angry young (sha)man" Altizer's friend William Hamilton had called him affectionately, and Emory's heretical professor was certainly as much Eliade's disciple as Nietzsche's madman.[18] Likewise, the *Time* cover story of a half century ago – with its bold query, "Is God Dead?" – was not so much a prognostication of the latest New Atheists; instead, it foreshadowed the nation's proliferating questors for the sacred apart from the church and its departed deity.

Notes

1 [John T. Elson], "Toward a Hidden God," *Time*, April 8, 1966, 60. On Elson, see William Grimes, "John T. Elson, Editor Who Asked 'Is God Dead?' at *Time*, Dies at 78," *New York Times*, September 17, 2009. A shorter version of this chapter appeared in April 2016 in the online journal *Religion & Politics*, a venture of the John C. Danforth Center on Religion and Politics, under the title "Is God Dead? A *Time* Cover Turns 50."
2 "Toward a Hidden God," 60–5.
3 " 'New' Theologians See Christianity Without God," *New York Times*, October 17, 1965; "Christian Atheism: The 'God Is Dead' Movement," *Time*, October 22, 1965, 61–2. On how this controversy played out in Methodist circles especially, see Christopher Demuth Rodkey, "Methodist Heretic: Thomas Altizer and the Death of God at Emory University," *Methodist History* 49 (2010): 37–50. For an excellent overview of Altizer's work, including the formative episode in the mid-1960s, see Lissa McCollough and Brian Schroeder, eds., *Thinking Through the Death of God: A Critical Companion to Thomas J. J.*

Altizer (Albany, NY: State University of New York Press, 2004), particularly McCollough's "Historical Introduction."

4 "Pop Theology via TV," *Christian Century*, February 23, 1966, 229; "The Waning Death-of-God Tumult," *Christianity Today*, May 26, 1967, 856, 859. Audio tapes of the Walter Cronkite programs as well as a printed copy of the *Requiem for God* are in the Thomas J. [J.] Altizer Papers, Special Collections Research Center, Syracuse University Libraries, Syracuse, NY. A video portion of these two programs, preserved as part of a CBS News Special in December 1966 recapping the biggest stories of the year, is available from the CBS News Archive, New York, New York. For accounts of the *Merv Griffin Show* debacle, see Thomas J. J. Altizer, *Living the Death of God: A Theological Memoir* (Albany, NY: State University of New York Press, 2006), 17, and Ruth H. Baum to Altizer, August 16, 1966. All cited letters are from Altizer's correspondence files at the Special Collections Research Center, Syracuse University, Syracuse, New York. They are quoted with permission.

5 Altizer, *Living the Death of God*, 3–11, 47–8; Thomas J. J. Altizer, *Mircea Eliade and the Dialectic of the Sacred* (Philadelphia, PA: Westminster, 1963), 41.

6 C. A. Kelly to Altizer, February 8, 1966; unsigned letter from North Carolina, June 8, 1966.

7 Malcolm H. Brown to Altizer, February 9, 1966; M. E. Higginbotham to Altizer, April 21, 1966; Altizer, *Living the Death of God*, 16; Ruth Brissette to Altizer, December 20, 1965.

8 Milton H. Rahn to Altizer, January 13, 1966; John Moore to Altizer, November 29, 1965; Sam Holton to Altizer, October 31, 1965.

9 G. Vincent Runyon to Altizer, November 6, 1965; G. Vincent Runyon, *Why I Left the Ministry and Became an Atheist* (San Diego, CA: Superior Books, 1959), 6–20.

10 Anthony Towne, "God Is Dead in Georgia," *motive* 26 (1966): 74. For Ogletree's measured engagement, see Thomas W. Ogletree, *The Death of God Controversy* (Nashville, TN: Abingdon, 1966). The advertising response of the National Council of Churches is mentioned in various places, including in "Pop Theology via TV" and Sherman D. Wakefield to Altizer, January 27, 1966.

11 William Hamilton, "*In Piam Memoriam* – the Death of God after Ten Years," *Christian Century*, October 8, 1975, 872–3; William Hamilton to Altizer, May 16, [1965].

12 William Hamilton to Altizer, undated "Monday"; Altizer, *Mircea Eliade*, 16, 19. For the importance of an anti modern esotericism in shaping the history of religions as both academic inquiry and religious quest, see particularly Steven M. Wasserstrom, *Religion after Religion: Gershom Scholem, Mircea Eliade, and Henry Corbin at Eranos* (Princeton, NJ: Princeton University Press, 1999). Also crucial is the work of Jeffrey J. Kripal's *Esalen: America and the Religion of No Religion* (Chicago: University of Chicago Press, 2007), esp. 6–8, 47–68.

13 Altizer, *Mircea Eliade*, 13; Alvin W. Miller to Altizer, May 16, 1966.

14 Ted Nelson Tatman to Altizer, May 2, 1966. For a sampling of the reading recommendations that Altizer received, see Mary Watson to Altizer, November 29, 1965; Barbara A. Ashbaugh to Altizer, October 29, 1965; Stephen Drane to Altizer, October 18, 1966. For Hedstrom's work, see Matthew S. Hedstrom, *The Rise of Liberal Religion: Book Culture and American Spirituality in the Twentieth Century* (New York: Oxford University Press, 2013). The specific book that Tatman had mulled over so intently was Thomas J. J. Altizer and William Hamilton, *Radical Theology and the Death of God* (Indianapolis, IN: Bobbs-Merrill, 1966).

15 Jim Sorrells to Altizer, December 2, 1966; David Whitman to Altizer, May 2, 1966; Lee Perkins to Altizer, May 10, 1966.

16 George Dowden to Altizer, November 19, 1966; George Dowden, *Renew Jerusalem* (New York: Smyrna Press, 1969), unpaginated. On Whitman's legacy for religious seekers, see especially Michael Robertson, *Worshipping Walt: The Whitman Disciples* (Princeton, NJ: Princeton University Press, 2008).
17 Dowden, *Renew Jerusalem,* unpaginated; George Dowden, *The Moving I: Episodes in the Life of an American Expatriate 'Sixties Man' in England & India & Around* (Oakland, CA: Inkblot, 1987); Dowden to Altizer, November 19, 1966. On Muktananda's place amid the wider American embrace of yoga and gurus, see Andrea R. Jain, *Selling Yoga: From Counterculture to Pop Culture* (New York: Oxford University Press, 2014), 50–5 (and see her chapter in this volume).
18 William Hamilton to Altizer, July 30, [1965].

References

Altizer, Thomas J.J. *Mircea Eliade and the Dialectic of the Sacred*. Philadelphia: Westminster, 1963.

———. *Living the Death of God: A Theological Memoir*. Albany: State University of New York Press, 2006.

Altizer, Thomas J.J. and William Hamilton. *Radical Theology and the Death of God*. Indianapolis, IN: Bobbs-Merrill, 1966.

[Elson, John T.] "Toward a Hidden God." *Time*, April 8, 1966, 60–5.

Hedstrom, Matthew S. *The Rise of Liberal Religion: Book Culture and American Spirituality in the Twentieth Century*. New York: Oxford University Press, 2013.

Jain, Andrea R. *Selling Yoga: From Counterculture to Pop Culture*. New York: Oxford University Press, 2014.

Kripal, Jeffrey J. *Esalen: America and the Religion of No Religion*. Chicago: University of Chicago Press, 2007.

McCollough, Lissa and Brian Schroeder, eds. *Thinking Through the Death of God: A Critical Companion to Thomas J.J. Altizer*. Albany: State University of New York Press, 2004.

Ogletree, Thomas W. *The Death of God Controversy*. Nashville, TN: Abingdon, 1966.

Robertson, Michael. *Worshipping Walt: The Whitman Disciples*. Princeton, NJ: Princeton University Press, 2008.

Rodkey, Christopher Demuth. "Methodist Heretic: Thomas Altizer and the Death of God at Emory University." *Methodist History* 49 (2010): 37–50.

Wasserstrom, Steven M. *Religion After Religion: Gershom Scholem, Mircea Eliade, and Henry Corbin at Eranos*. Princeton, NJ: Princeton University Press, 1999.

4 Buddhist fulfillment of a Protestant dream

Mindfulness as scientific spirituality[1]

Matthew S. Hedstrom

Mindful Eating. Mindful Knitting. The Mindful Child. The Mindful Way through Anxiety. The Mindful Path through Shyness. Mindful Recovery. A Mindful Nation. The Joy of Mindful Sex. These recent book titles reflect both the current vogue and the utopian promise of contemporary mindfulness. It's the cure for what ails you, no matter what that might be, from addiction and shyness to a dull love life and even, according to Congressman Tim Ryan, the social and political problems of the nation itself. His 2012 book, *A Mindful Nation*, according to the subtitle, describes "How a Simple Practice Can Help Us Reduce Stress, Improve Performance, and Recapture the American Spirit."[2] Mindfulness retreats and seminars are now commonplace in the most powerful institutions of American life, from major corporations and the military to health care and public schools. The Compassionate Schools Project, for example, a partnership of the Contemplative Sciences Center at the University of Virginia and the Louisville, Kentucky public schools, represents only the most prominent and ambitious of efforts to bring mindfulness to schoolchildren. This program "integrates mindfulness for stress management and self-control; contemplative movements, postures and breathing for physical awareness and agility; nutritional knowledge for healthy eating; and social and emotional skills for effective interpersonal relationships." Through this curriculum, the program website continues, "[e]lementary school students will learn to cultivate focus, resilience, empathy, connection, and wellbeing as the basis for academic and personal success."[3] Few of these endeavors ask about the structural economic or political sources of our stress, or what ends our improved performance, productivity, or success are supposed to serve. There are problems, problems in us, and mindfulness can fix them.

As the Compassionate Schools Project indicates, universities stand at the forefront of the modern mindfulness movement, through partnerships such as these but also in their own curricula. The University of Virginia (UVA), University of California, Los Angeles; Emory; the University of Wisconsin; Brown; and many other prominent universities have large-scale mindfulness programs and research centers. At UVA, where I work, the ambitious and well-funded Contemplative Sciences Center is meant to integrate student affairs and academic life, serving as the one site at the sprawling modern university to educate, and care for, the whole person, in mind, body, and spirit. Contemplative Sciences aims to create space and provide tools for the college community to think about the learning that comes from the disciplines in the context of the larger questions of life, questions about meaning, values, identity, and right living. The humanistic psychologist Abraham Maslow described peak-experiences a generation ago as those moments of clarity that allow one to see the universal in and through the particular and the eternal in and through the ephemeral.[4] College, according to proponents of mindfulness on campus, is very much about the particular, about assignments and requirements, majors and minors, with little space for reflection about what it all adds up to and few resources to stay sane and focused, and perhaps even happy, through it all. Mindfulness practices, in contrast, endeavor to help students and educators to think about, and experience, their lives and their educations holistically.

The capacity of Buddhist-derived mindfulness to carry on these functions relies on a particular popular narrative about Buddhism that has existed for almost a century: that Buddhism is wholly compatible with modern science. In my class on "Spirituality in America," for example, I regularly invite representatives from the Contemplative Sciences Center to speak, and in the course of their presentations they invariable describe their enterprise as empirical, rooted in carefully controlled studies. After a long presentation of this kind recently, I asked the speaker about the bell he had rung to initiate the mindfulness exercise at the start of class. "Was that bell ringing Buddhist?" I asked. "No," he replied. "I bought it at a local shopping center." The incongruity of the response reflected the speaker's uncomfortableness with the question after thirty minutes presenting scientific findings. This kind of Buddhism – represented by what the scholar Donald Lopez has called "The Scientific Buddha" – is a reenvisioned Buddhism that was brought to life in the late nineteenth century, a philosophical and psychological Buddhism stripped of the rituals and beliefs that characterized the religion in Asia for centuries.[5] The Scientific Buddha's most lasting, and most easily recognizable, contribution has been the psychologized mindfulness practices that are so in vogue today.

The creation story of the Scientific Buddha is complex, entailing the intertwined histories of colonialism, science, orientalism, and capitalism. But today's Scientific Buddha is also, quite clearly, a reincarnation of the Scientific Christ. Protestant Christianity in the 19th century underwent a process very similar to what Buddhism underwent in the 20th century, a renovation in the light of psychology, with the aim of making the religion more relevant to modern life. This Protestant history from a century ago directly influenced the creation of scientific, therapeutic Buddhism, often called Protestant or Protestantized Buddhism for just this reason. But its importance is more than historical. The Protestant prehistory of Buddhist mindfulness matters today for two interrelated reasons. First and more broadly, the reasons these psychologizing campaigns moved from liberal Christianity to a Westernizing Buddhism helps us understand the prospects and potential pitfalls for mindfulness in our times. Second and more narrowly, the Protestant story helps us understand why mindfulness has gained a particular foothold in colleges and universities. Mindfulness research at modern American universities stands at the convergence of humanistic and scientific disciplines, and in many respects represents the leading edge of research in religious studies, psychology, and neuroscience. But modern mindfulness, as a descendant of these 19th-century Protestant reform efforts, also represents the culmination of more than a century of thought and practice about the very purpose of higher education in America. While "of the moment" in the 21st century, today's mindfulness in this way harkens back to intellectual and pedagogical trends that are older, in fact, than modern universities themselves. This chapter seeks to untangle this history of Protestantism and Buddhism, science and spirituality, as it developed on American college campuses.

Mindfulness as we currently recognize it arrived in the United States in a significant way only in the 1970s, when it hit the best-seller lists with pioneering books by the American medical school professor and Zen practitioner Jon Kabat-Zinn and the Vietnamese Zen monk Thich Nhat Hanh, among others.[6] Not coincidentally, this modern emergence of mindfulness took place just as American Christians began leaving their churches in significant numbers, first a slow but steady stream flowing out of mainline congregations, then a rising tide, and before long a tsunami that swept evangelicals and Catholics along as well. This flood, by the 21st century, had washed away nearly a quarter of American Christianity. The numbers are indeed stark. The percentage of Americans who identify as Christian dropped from 95% in 1960 to 82% in 1999 to 72% in 2008.[7] On the other hand, as the percentage of Christians has plummeted, the percentage who claim no religious affiliation has skyrocketed. About 7% in 1970, the religiously unaffiliated remained below 10% through the early 1990s, at which point their number began to rise steadily.[8] The best accounting in recent years shows that roughly 25% of the population is now unaffiliated, including at least one in three of those under the age of thirty.

The turn away from institutionalized Protestant Christianity and toward more capacious forms of spirituality – forms, like mindfulness, that appear scientific – is marked by a great irony. It was Protestantism itself, after all, that first presented to American young people a form of religion that purported to be scientific and universal. How Protestant Christianity lost its place to Buddhism as the preeminent American "religion of science" is one of the great stories in the history of American spirituality – a story that goes back to the college curricula of the 19th century. Protestant moral philosophy and psychology courses stood in the vanguard of efforts to cast Christianity in a scientific light, and thereby prefigured – and even influenced – today's interest in Buddhist-derived contemplative and mindfulness practices. Mindfulness, especially on college campuses, functions in fact as a form of moral philosophy for the 21st century. The ambitions of 19th-century moral philosophy – especially those capstone courses, typically taught by preacher-presidents, that aimed to apply learning to the development of character and virtue and citizenship – and even more the intellectual frameworks that informed these courses – were the same ones that generated the Scientific Buddha in the late 19th and early 20th centuries. Moral philosophy faded with the rise of the specialized research university, yet the Scientific Buddha, in the form of psychologized mindfulness especially, lives on.

Courses in moral philosophy became a regular feature of American colleges early in the 19th century, as historian George Marsden has written in his very useful *The Soul of the American University*. Critically, these courses aimed to bolster traditional Christianity rather than replace it and to do so by providing a firm basis in reason for Christian morals and character. In this way, these courses sought to serve not only their students but also the needs of the new nation, to bridge sectarianism and inculcate virtue, a key, it was thought, to proper republican citizenship. As Marsden notes,

> by the end of the [18th] century American colleges were instituting courses in moral philosophy, taught by the clergymen-president, as the capstone and integrating feature of their curricula. Rigorous theology might still be preached in required Sunday services . . . but moral philosophy provided a common ground for building a republic of virtue.[9]

By the middle of the 19th century, these courses were firmly established as standard fare in American colleges. Noah Porter, for example, president of Yale in the 1870s and 1880s and one of the last of the great preacher-presidents of a major American research university, regularly taught the college's courses in moral philosophy and insisted on retaining these courses even as Yale professionalized and specialized.

These courses in many ways were in the vanguard of liberal Protestant theology. Since their ambition was to be nonsectarian, public-minded, and up-to-date, they continuously adapted across the 19th century, most especially to the historical critical study of the Bible and advancing scientific knowledge but really to the whole range of advances that were occurring across the emerging disciplines. And this was the point: to show that Christian morals were universal morals, reasonable and American morals, and to reapply them to the needs of the students, the society, and the nation for each new generation.

Critically for the subsequent history of American spirituality, and for the later history of Buddhist mindfulness in particular, it was in the context of these collegiate moral philosophy courses that psychology first emerged as a distinct intellectual endeavor in the United States. This history charts the increasingly imperial reach of psychology and its related transformation from a philosophical enterprise to a laboratory science. A good place to begin is with a book called *Psychology: A View of the Human Soul*, published in 1840 by the Rev. Frederick A. Rauch (1806–1841), which was the first book published in the United States with the word *psychology* in its title. Rauch, the founding president of Marshall College in Pennsylvania and a German-born Protestant Reformed theologian, argued in this work for the common purpose of psychology and theology in crafting a rational basis for religion. Theology, Rauch contended, is the science of religion, by which he meant the exploration of religion through applied reason. Psychology, though not yet an experimental science, Rauch nevertheless still grouped alongside medicine and anthropology as what we might call a human science, meaning an instrument to illuminate human nature. Psychology and theology in this way were twinned enterprises for Rauch. "Man as the subject of psychology," Rauch proclaimed,

> is created for religion and cannot do without it. Religion is not a mere quality, but the substance of man . . . He ceases to be man in the full sense of the term when he has no religion; – he is then only an animal.[10]

Rauch wrote *Psychology* to be the first volume of an intended trilogy, to be followed by works on Moral Philosophy and Aesthetics, though he was not able to complete the other volumes before his early death, at age 34, in 1841. He concluded the work with a section on religion – including an early effort at comparative religion – that proclaimed, in good evangelical fashion, true religion to be the work of God on the human heart. Though Rauch faced accusations of pantheism for his rather impersonal understanding of God, in this manner his *Psychology* nevertheless served the same ultimate purpose as Jonathan Edwards's *Religious Affections* had a century earlier, probing the inner workings of mind and soul in order to better understand and facilitate human receptivity to divine grace.

Rev. Oliver S. Munsell (1825–1905), like Rauch, was a clergyman and a college president, leading Illinois Wesleyan College at the time he authored *Psychology; Or, The Science of Mind* in 1871. Munsell in this work followed the typical approach of the faculty psychologists and phrenologists in developing a complex taxonomy of the mind, applied here as in Rauch's case to the moral instruction of college men. Munsell's work, written thirty years after Rauch's, reveals a greater self-consciousness about psychology as a science, especially as a science rooted in structures of mind and body. "Psychology," Munsell wrote, "is the science of embodied mind, and not of pure spirit. . . . It must not, therefore, be confounded with pure metaphysics," though, he noted, "the two have their necessary and legitimate points of contact."[11] Most of the book, therefore, consisted of rather straightforward efforts to explain the faculties of intellection and reason, the senses, and the will. Munsell recognized, however, that human beings, as "half dust" and "half deity," in his phrasing, have spiritual capacities, meaning that "our perception of the spiritual world, through intuition, is just as direct, just as comprehensible, and just as valid, as our cognition of the material world through sensation."[12]

Though an orthodox Methodist minister, Munsell was pressed by application of the scientific method to expand his spiritual horizons. "It is neither wise nor safe for Christian psychologists," he wrote, to neglect the "strange border-land of dreams, somnambulism, visions, and clairvoyance." These phenomena, he declared, "are an open door through which we may look in upon the human soul and its mysteries, under conditions which, properly investigated and comprehended, cannot fail to add to our intelligent comprehension of its real nature and capacities."[13] Munsell's book, like Rauch's before it, served as a standard college textbook in psychology for decades and likewise aimed to harmonize natural philosophy and moral philosophy. But while Rauch had seen his work on psychology as a prologue *to* moral philosophy, Munsell's text served as a standard text *in* moral philosophy. Just as moral philosophy had displaced theology earlier in the century, now psychology, with all it strange parapsychological attendants, was likewise storming the castle.

The influence of psychology on the moral philosophy courses of the late nineteenth century was such that by the 1880s and 1890s many colleges had ceased to call these courses moral philosophy at all, and began instead to use the label "Logic, Ethics, and Psychology" (LEP). The new LEP title matched the moment, as it indicted quite clearly the belief that reason applied to human nature (logic and psychology) would result in a workable and universal moral framework (ethics). This change in the teaching of moral philosophy occurred in conjunction with the single greatest transformation in the history of psychology, the establishment in research universities in Europe and the United States of first psychology departments in the 1880s. Here, for the first time, psychology seemed to have made a decisive break with moral philosophy. The first laboratories in experimental psychology were founded in Germany, by Wilhelm Wundt (1832–1920) at Leipzig in 1879, and soon thereafter in the United States, by William James (1842–1910) at Harvard and by James's and Wundt's student G. Stanley Hall (1846–1924) at Johns Hopkins; Hall had earned the first American doctorate in psychology at Harvard in 1878, soon after James began teaching the nation's first courses in the field.

Though less well known today than his teacher and mentor William James, Hall is a critical figure in the story of religion, science, and spirituality at American colleges, not only as one of the founders of laboratory psychology in the United States but also as a teacher early in his career of the capstone "Logic, Ethics, and Psychology" course at Johns Hopkins. He soon moved from Johns Hopkins to the presidency of Clark University, which only had graduate students, yet never lost his sense that psychology as a field should remain a vital bridge between science and religion. "The new psychology, which brings simply a new method and a new standpoint to philosophy, is I believe Christian to its root and center," he had proclaimed in his inaugural lecture in psychology at Hopkins in 1884.[14] William James, in fact, criticized Hall for the "religious cant" that remained in his approach to the field, but it is true broadly that the new psychology of the 1880s and 1890s, while now a laboratory science, nevertheless continued to engage religious concerns. This is not surprising. Many of the discipline's American founders – men such as not only Hall but also George Coe, James Leuba, Edwin Starbuck, and James Mark Baldwin – had evangelical childhoods and yet were unable, as adults, to experience conversion or sustain conventional religious faith.[15] William James's unorthodox youth stands as a notable exception, yet he, too, wrote wistfully of religious experiences, noting in his 1902 masterpiece, *The Varieties of Religious Experience*, "[M]y own constitution shuts me out from their enjoyment almost entirely, and I can speak of them only at second hand."[16] Not surprisingly, adolescence and conversion were prominent early topics in the psychology of religion.

Out of this background – his own evangelical youth; his experience teaching the capstone Logic, Ethics, and Psychology course at Hopkins; and his foundational work in laboratory psychology at Hopkins and then Clark – Hall produced his profoundly important and now sadly little-studied magnum opus, the massive two-volume *Jesus, the Christ, in the Light of Psychology*, published in 1917. This work better than any other captures the liberal religious effort to renovate Christianity in the light of psychology – and it thereby serves as the best point of reference for thinking about the similar cultural and intellectual and religious work performed by mindfulness on college campuses today.

In this work Hall told a distinctively progressive story, arguing that religion had moved from its earliest stages, characterized as he put it by "faith and mystic intuition," into the pivotal historical-critical phase of the 19th century, which did the great and noble work of pruning away the dead wood of superstition, myth, magic, and lore, thereby allowing the great energy, the life force of religion, to be channeled into new growth – which, for Hall, meant a newly scientific Christianity, a psychologically reimagined Christianity. "The psychological Christ," Hall wrote, "is the true and living Christ of the present and the future." "I believe in the historical Jesus," he continued, "but I have tried to show how even the Church can get on, if it should ever have to do so, without him, and that this might possibly ultimately make for greater spirituality."[17] To transcend history was to transcend the limits of particularity – of religion, language, culture; to embrace psychology was to embrace the scientific, and therefore the universal, especially the great universal of human nature itself.

Hall was keenly aware that he was writing amid the great conflagration in Europe – remember this is 1917 – a war that for many revealed in stark relief the power of history and the empty promises of theological and political liberalism, especially of liberal optimism about human nature. Yet he was not to be dissuaded. "Two millennia under the Prince of Peace," he wrote,

> have not prevented this colossal and atrocious war, and the Church of Christ cannot now fail to suffer a great increase of neglect and reproach unless it can have a radical reincarnation. Would that psychology, by re-revealing Jesus in a new light, and re-laying the very foundations of belief in him, might contribute to bring in a real third dispensation, so long predicted yet so long delayed.[18]

Psychological science, in other words, especially a psychological reinterpretation of religion, would be the agent of this new millennium. "We must go back to the first principles and elemental forces of human nature," Hall proclaimed, and "realize in a deeper sense that Bibles and religions arose out of it, and thus we must build the latter up again from the very foundations – but," he went on, "these foundations will be and must be the true psychological Jesus Christ, gross, material misinterpretations of whom have made the Church today almost a body without a soul."[19] After all this labor, labor that was for Hall deeply personal as well as of social and even global significance, Hall declared at the end of the work's introduction,

> As a result of all this, I believe I can now repeat almost every clause of the Apostles Creed with a fervent sentiment of conviction. . . . To me not a clause of it is true in the crass, literal, material sense, but all of it is true in a sense far higher.[20]

Hall's *Jesus, the Christ, in the Light of Psychology* is a fascinating book in its own right, but for our purposes we must consider it in the light of the history of the use of psychology as a tool of religious revitalization through liberalization and the implications this has had for American religion and spirituality ever since. Perhaps most representative of the evangelistic embrace of psychology at a more popular level was the psychologist Henry C. Link's best-selling *The Return to Religion* (1936), in which he declared "the findings of psychology in respect to personality and happiness" to be "largely a rediscovery of old religious truths." "The greatest and most authentic textbook on personality," he concluded, "is still the Bible."[21] A more scientific Christianity, proponents argued, would unite religious factions rent by schism and would make religious teaching relevant again to modern life. Many religious critics, from evangelical and Roman Catholic circles especially, but also from within liberal Protestantism, decried the incorporation of psychology into religion as a "sterile union," in the words of theologian H. Richard Niebuhr (1894–1962) from a 1927 essay in *The Christian Century*, the leading journal of liberal Protestantism.[22] The Presbyterian fundamentalist J. Gresham Machen (1881–1937) was characteristically more blunt as he decried "the dangerous pseudo-scientific fads of experimental psychology" in *Christianity and Liberalism* (1923), his celebrated assault on Protestant modernism.[23] Later in the century, secular critics likewise lamented the psychologization of religion, fearing it made Americans more consumerist, more narcissistic, and less able to offer prophetic critiques of the liberal, capitalist political order.[24] Liberal Protestants, nevertheless, kept producing scholarly works that updated or reaffirmed Christianity in the light of psychology, such as famed theologian, physician, and humanitarian Albert Schweitzer's (1875–1965) *The Psychiatric Study of Jesus*, which was first published in German in 1913 but appeared in multiple American editions in the 1940s and 1950s.

Other Americans embraced the union of religion and psychology, however, not to affirm Christianity, however reformulated it might be, but precisely because of the space and legitimacy it afforded religious minorities, dissenters, and heterodox believers. Historian Andrew Heinze, for example, has written of the significant role played by American and European Jews in both academic and popular psychology in the 20th century, noting that psychology afforded a vocabulary and, often, an institutional location that allowed non-Christians to address moral, spiritual, and mental life authoritatively. The Viennese founder of psychoanalysis stands as the most prominent example, certainly, but Harvard's Hugo Münsterberg, and later in the century, popular writers such as Rabbi Joshua Loth Liebman and Dr. Joyce Brothers, also brought distinctively Jewish perspectives to psychology and through psychology to religious and moral concerns. Not coincidentally, Americans of Jewish background, such as Jon Kabat-Zinn as well as Jack Kornfield, Joseph Goldstein, Sharon Salzberg, and Jacqueline Schwartz, have played an outsized role in the history of American mindfulness, finding in the Scientific Buddha a moral vocabulary rooted in psychology that afforded even more space to speak with authority on matters of spiritual significance.[25]

Moral philosophy courses began, as noted, in an effort to cast a wider net, to craft a capacious, integrative intellectual space that would bridge sectarian divides and even help unite the nation into a republic of virtue. Psychology was drafted as a critical ally in this enterprise, and yet by the early 20th-century psychology had become a tool that undermined Protestant hegemony, both in the hands of post-Protestant like Hall and in the hands of religious minorities, dissenters, and skeptics. Over the course of the 20th century, many of the academic disciplines sought to satisfy the old role of moral philosophy, to integrate learning with life. Psychology, sociology, history, and literature curricula all served in some capacities, with literature and psychology, especially mid-century humanistic psychology, probably the most successful.

Modern mindfulness, vaguely spiritual but cast in the authoritative vernacular of science – especially psychology and neuroscience – now serves this function on many campuses and for many young adults. Even in the golden age of the Scientific Christ a century ago, various scholars and practitioners, both Asian and Euro-American, argued that Buddhism functioned better than Christianity as a modern religion of science. Rather than determine who was right, the Christians or the Buddhists – a question of concern, certainly, to religious partisans on each side – it is more historically revealing to see each as part of the same transatlantic and transpacific enterprise to craft a modern, scientific, spiritual vernacular. Hall's *Jesus, the Christ, in the Light of Psychology* stands in this regard in the same lineage as the writings of Paul Carus, D. T. Suzuki, Thich Nhat Hanh, and Jon Kabat-Zinn, the principal architects of the Scientific Buddha. Donald Lopez charts the birth of the Scientific Buddha in the 19th century, in the same milieu and for the same reasons that liberal Protestants were crafting their scientific, psychologized Christianity. The German American editor and philosopher Paul Carus, for example, in an essay on "Buddhism and the Religion of Science" in 1896 wrote of the Buddha as "the first positivist, the first humanitarian, the first radical freethinker, the first iconoclast, and the first prophet of the religion of science."[26] Buddhists, Lopez argues, "wrested the weapon of science from the hands of the Christians and turned it against them" by affirming the liberal Protestant ambition to craft a modernized, rationalized, psychologized faith. As scholars of modern Buddhism Erik Braun and David L. McMahan have observed, attacks on the purportedly primitive or superstitious nature of Buddhism were standard fare among colonial authorities, yet enterprising nationalists in Burma, Ceylon, and elsewhere turned these critiques back at the colonizers. "Arguments against Buddhism's rationality and compatibility with science were a preeminent means of attack," Braun and McMahan write. Yet Buddhist modernizers such as Anagarika Dharmapala and Ledi Sayadaw appropriated the discourse of science for their own ends. "It would not go too far to say that Christianity," write Braun and McMahan, "often riding on the back of colonialism, was the means through which Buddhists first grappled with science."[27] These Buddhist nationalists and modernists engaged the Christians on their own terms, in other words, the terms of the religion of science, and merely argued that Buddhism provided better materials to work with and that the Scientific Buddha was simply more plausible and sustainable in the modern world than the Scientific Christ. Many modern college students and administrators seem to agree.

That Buddhism is understood to offer greater promise as a religion of science than Christianity would have mystified earlier generations of American educators, but the key to making sense of this, I think, comes again from Donald Lopez, who notes that the crafting of the Scientific Buddha required the absence of actual Buddhists with their messy rituals and beliefs and yet, at the same time, the development of sufficient philological skill to read Buddhist texts. In this way one could have a philosophical and psychological Buddhism rather than an actually religious or, as the colonizers might have said, superstitious Buddhism. Some theorists in religious studies claim that all religion is a creature of the scholars' study, and in this case at least they have a point.

A recent look at the work of the Contemplative Sciences Center at the UVA shows how the Scientific Buddha lives today as a reincarnation of Stanley Hall's Scientific Christ. Dr. Daniel Goldman, journalist and psychologist, for example, delivered a lecture at UVA titled "A Force for Good: The Dalai Lama's Vision for Our World," a talk that focused "on the central concepts of the Dalai Lama," according to the published description, "empirical evidence that supports them, and true stories of people who are putting his ideas into action." Through the work of contemplative sciences one can "wake up to wisdom and wellbeing," study "conscious social change," "invest in a sustainable future," or attend monthly lunches "for teachers to deepen their personal mindfulness practice as well as learn ways to weave mindful practices into the classroom."

Once we see the shared intellectual lineage of the Scientific Buddha and the Scientific Christ – a common trajectory that stretches from the mindfulness programs on college campuses today back to those moral philosophy courses taught by 19th-century preacher-presidents – a number of otherwise obscure dimensions of contemporary American spirituality come to light. The first is that moral philosophy and psychology a century ago and mindfulness today each represent a form of liberal religious apologetics rooted in a pragmatic epistemology. The American psychologist and pragmatic philosopher William James expressed this orientation to religious truth most influentially in *The Varieties of Religious Experience* (1902). *Varieties* is rightly understood as an effort to salvage the conditions for religious belief in the modern world, a post-Protestant reclamation endeavor after the acids of modernity had scoured away appeals to older forms of religious authority. James sought to rebuild a foundation for faith on what he called a science of religions, a science rooted in the foundational pragmatic appeal to the effect of religious ideas for the living of life. Religion is true to the extent that it works, in the main and on the whole, over time, as an aid to well-being in this world. James's pragmatism undergirded much of 20th-century self-help, especially Alcoholics Anonymous and other recovery programs. But James also inspired the work of D. T. Suzuki, the great modernizer and popularizer of Japanese Zen across the first half of the 20th century who was married to Beatrice Erskine Lane, an American student of James at Harvard.

In addition to a shared Jamesian pragmatism, mindfulness also shares with earlier liberal Protestant projects an origin in 19th-century nationalism. Recall that one of the aims of moral philosophy courses in the 19th century was to unite Americans across sectarian lines for political as well as religious purposes. As Erik Braun has written in *The Birth of Insight*, meditation also arose in the context of 19th-century nationalism, as an effort at cultural revitalization and integration in the face of colonial occupation. Though of great importance in the history of Buddhism across cultures and traditions, meditation was exclusively a monastic practice until anti-colonial activists in Burma crafted revised forms of mediation for the masses as an act of revival and resistance to British rule. The purported universalism of mindfulness meditation, like that of moral philosophy, stems in other words from a nationalist program of religious revitalization. Yet when deracinated from this Buddhist, anti-colonial context and placed in the hands of Google, for example, which teaches mindfulness to its employees, or the U.S. military or UVA, the universalizing pretentions of mindfulness take on a different cast, more hegemonic than resistive.

Finally, understanding the Christian as well and Buddhist heritage of mindfulness helps us see more clearly the significance of the "Why Buddhism?" question – the question of why it is that Buddhism has come to be seen, in the modern West, as the most promising basis for a religion of science, a role that Christianity seemed destined to fill a century ago. Donald Lopez has observed that "Buddhism has often served as a kind of safe surrogate for Christianity, avoiding all the problems of religion and science by being a religion that is also a science" but I don't think that's quite right.[28] After all, it is only after a century and a half, at least, of often fierce cultural contestation about religion and science that we now look back and see "all the problems of science and religion" that Christianity poses. Frederick Rauch and Oliver Munsell and Stanley Hall saw no such problems; they saw a story of seamless unity, of science as a tool of religious renewal and revitalization. They saw liberal Christianity precisely as so many Americans now see in Buddhism, or, more to the point, many Americans now see Buddhism through the religion of science lens first crafted by these Protestant educators more than a century ago. Many of their fellow Americans, however, fellow Christians like H. Richard Niebuhr and Gresham Machen, saw psychologized Christianity not as progress but as a threat and had the cultural and political capacity to resist the reformulation of their religion into mere science. The Scientific Christ, the psychological Christ, lives on, to be sure, in liberal Christianity as well as in post-Christian forms of self-help and spirituality. Yet on today's college campuses, and among today's Spiritual but Not Religious youth, it is the Scientific Buddha who now speaks with a louder voice. Mindfulness represents a fulfillment of 19th-century liberal Protestantism, a scientific spirituality for the modern age, now better than Protestantism itself, because its message offers a cleaner, purer form of therapeutic pragmatism.

In our times, certainly, both Buddhists and non-Buddhists have leveled sharp criticisms of the psychological reformulation of Buddhism as mere mindfulness, as a therapeutic tool for distracted and stressed moderns, and yet it remains an open question whether they have the cultural resources and political standing to resist the juggernaut of mindfulness. Such reformulations, these critics contend, wrest Buddhism out of traditional contexts – something akin to 19th-century archaeologists plundering the treasures of Asia for western museums – and thereby transform it utterly. On one hand, such moves have the potential to wrest control of the dominant face of Buddhism away from its traditional practitioners, though this remains debatable, as Asian Buddhists have been as involved in these transformations as

Western appropriators. More worryingly, however, these transformations have the great potential to defang Buddhism, making it familiar rather than other, safe rather than dangerous, easy rather than hard, comfortable for comfortable Westerners rather than a powerfully foreign alternative or even rival to the neoliberal, consumerist, and therapeutic order. Now more than ever, amid a society rent by inequality on a planet facing climactic calamity, Americans need rival visions, alternative modes of being, bracingly other ways to imagine human life and human flourishing. To lose such alternatives is to lose our very humanity.

Notes

1 A condensed version of this chapter appeared as "Scientific Spirituality: How Mindfulness Became the Buddhist Fulfillment of a Protestant Dream," *Tricycle* (Spring 2017): 56, 58–9, 102.

2 Tim Ryan, *A Mindful Nation: How a Simple Practice Can Help Us Reduce Stress, Improve Performance, and Recapture the American Spirit* (Carlsbad, CA: Hay House, 2012).

3 "Educating the Whole Child," www.compassionschools.org/program/

4 Abraham H. Maslow, *Religion, Values, and Peak Experiences* (Columbus: The Ohio State University Press, 1964).

5 Donald S. Lopez, Jr., *The Scientific Buddha: His Short and Happy Life* (New Haven, CT: Yale University Press, 2012). See also David L. McMahan, *The Making of Buddhist Modernism* (New York: Oxford University Press, 2008) and Erik Braun and David L. McMahan, eds., *Meditation, Buddhism, and Science* (New York: Oxford University Press, 2017).

6 See Erik Braun, "Mindful But Not Religious: Meditation and Enchantment in the Work of Jon Kabat-Zinn," in Braun and McMahan, eds., *Mediation, Buddhism, and Science.* See also Jeff Wilson, *Mindful America: The Mutual Transformation of Buddhist Meditation and American Culture* (New York: Oxford University Press, 2014) and Erik Braun, *The Birth of Insight: Meditation, Modern Buddhism, and the Burmese Monk Ledi Sayadaw* (Chicago: University of Chicago Press, 2013).

7 The Pew Forum, "U.S. Religious Landscape Survey," February 22, 2008, 10; Bass, "The Obama Doctrine: American Civic Spirituality."

8 *Nones on the Rise*, Pew Forum on Religion and Public Life, October 9, 2012.

9 George M. Marsden, *The Soul of the American University: From Protestant Establishment to Established Nonbelief* (New York: Oxford University Press, 1994), 51.

10 Frederick A. Rauch, *Psychology: Or, a View of the Human Soul, Including Anthropology, Adapted for the Use of Colleges* (New York: M.W. Dodd, 1853), iv.

11 Oliver S. Munsell, *Psychology: Or, the Science of Mind* (New York: D. Appleton and Co., 1871), 4.

12 Ibid., 115.

13 Ibid., 191.

14 Quoted in Marsden, *The Soul of the American University*, 162.

15 On the relationship of religious biography to the disciplinary history of psychology, see Christopher White, *Unsettled Minds: Psychology and the American Search for Spiritual Assurance, 1830–1940* (Berkeley: University of California Press, 2009). See also the autobiographical essays by Coe, Leuba, and Starbuck

collected in Vergilius Ferm, ed., *Religion in Transition* (New York: Macmillan, 1937), and the series, which began publication in 1930, *A History of Psychology in Autobiography* (Washington, DC: American Psychological Association, 1930–2007), now in nine volumes. See also Peter Homans, "A Personal Struggle with Religion: Significant Fact in the Lives and Work of the First Psychologists," *Journal of Religion* 62, no. 2 (1982): 128–44.

16 William James, *The Varieties of Religious Experience* (New York: Random House, 1999 [1902]), 413.

17 G. Stanley Hall, *Jesus, the Christ, in the Light of Psychology* (New York: Doubleday, Page, and Co., 1917), vii, viii.

18 Ibid., xvii.

19 Ibid.

20 Ibid., xviii–xix.

21 Henry C. Link, *The Return to Religion* (New York: Macmillan, 1936), 7, 103.

22 H. Richard Niebuhr, "Theology and Psychology: A Sterile Union," *Christian Century*, January 13, 1927, 47.

23 J. Gresham Machen, *Christianity and Liberalism* (Grand Rapids, MI: Eerdmans, 1923), 18.

24 See especially T. J. Jackson Lears, "From Salvation to Self-Realization: Advertising and the Therapeutic Roots of the Consumer Culture, 1880–1930," in *The Culture of Consumption: Critical Essays in American History, 1880–1980*, ed. Richard Wightman Fox and T. J. Jackson Lears (New York: Pantheon Books, 1983), 1–38; and Philip Rieff, *The Triumph of the Therapeutic: Uses of Faith After Freud* (Chicago: University of Chicago Press, 1966).

25 See most famously in this regard Rodger Kamenetz, *The Jew in the Lotus: A Poet's Rediscovery of Jewish Identity in Buddhist India* (San Francisco, CA: HarperSanFrancisco, 1994).

26 Paul Carus, "Buddhism and the Religion of Science," quoted in Lopez, *The Scientific Buddha*, 7.

27 Braun and McMahan, "From Colonialism to Brainscans: Modern Transformations of Buddhist Meditation," in Braun and McMahan, eds., *Mediation, Buddhism, and Science*, 8.

28 Lopez, *The Scientific Buddha*, 112.

References

Bass, Diana B. "The Obama Doctrine: American Civic Spirituality." www.onfaith. co/onfaith/2014/01/24/the-obama-doctrine-american-civil-spirituality/30562

Braun, Erik. *The Birth of Insight: Meditation, Modern Buddhism, and the Burmese Monk Ledi Sayadaw*. Chicago: University of Chicago Press, 2013.

Braun, Erik and David L. McMahan, eds. *Meditation, Buddhism, and Science*. New York: Oxford University Press, 2017.

"Educating the Whole Child." www.compassionschools.org/program/

Hall, Stanley G. *Jesus, the Christ, in the Light of Psychology*. New York: Doubleday, Page, and Co., 1917.

Hedstrom, Matthew S. "Scientific Spirituality: How Mindfulness Became the Buddhist Fulfillment of a Protestant Dream." *Tricycle*, Spring 2017.

Homans, Peter. "A Personal Struggle with Religion: Significant Fact in the Lives and Work of the First Psychologists." *Journal of Religion* 62, no. 2 (1982): 128–44.

James, William. *The Varieties of Religious Experience*. New York: Random House, 1999 [1902].

Kamenetz, Rodger. *The Jew in the Lotus: A Poet's Rediscovery of Jewish Identity in Buddhist India*. San Francisco, CA: HarperSanFrancisco, 1994.

Lears, T.J. Jackson. "From Salvation to Self-Realization: Advertising and the Therapeutic Roots of the Consumer Culture, 1880–1930." In *The Culture of Consumption: Critical Essays in American History, 1880–1980*, 1–38. Edited by Richard Wightman Fox and T.J. Jackson Lears. New York: Pantheon Books, 1983.

Link, Henry C. *The Return to Religion*. New York: Macmillan, 1936.

Lopez, Donald S. *The Scientific Buddha: His Short and Happy Life*. New Haven, CT: Yale University Press, 2012.

Machen, J. Gresham. *Christianity and Liberalism*. Grand Rapids, MI: Eerdmans, 1923.

Marsden, George M. *The Soul of the American University: From Protestant Establishment to Established Nonbelief*. New York: Oxford University Press, 1994.

Maslow, Abraham H. *Religion, Values, and Peak Experiences*. Columbus, OH: The Ohio State University Press, 1964.

McMahan, David L. *The Making of Buddhist Modernism*. New York: Oxford University Press, 2008.

Munsell, Oliver S. *Psychology: Or, the Science of Mind*. New York: D. Appleton and Co., 1871.

Niebuhr, Richard H. "Theology and Psychology: A Sterile Union." *Christian Century*, January 13, 1927.

Pew Forum. "U.S. Religious Landscape Survey." February 22, 2008.

Pew Forum on Religion and Public Life. *Nones on the Rise*, October 9, 2012.

Rauch, Frederick A. *Psychology: Or, a View of the Human Soul, Including Anthropology, Adapted for the Use of Colleges*. New York: M.W. Dodd, 1853.

Rieff, Philip. *The Triumph of the Therapeutic: Uses of Faith After Freud*. Chicago: University of Chicago Press, 1966.

Ryan, Tim. *A Mindful Nation: How a Simple Practice Can Help Us Reduce Stress, Improve Performance, and Recapture the American Spirit*. Carlsbad, CA: Hay House, 2012.

White, Christopher. *Unsettled Minds: Psychology and the American Search for Spiritual Assurance, 1830–1940*. Berkeley, CA: University of California Press, 2009.

Wilson, Jeff. *Mindful America: The Mutual Transformation of Buddhist Meditation and American Culture*. New York: Oxford University Press, 2014.

5 Plurals, hybrids, and nomads
Spirituality and religious practice at the intersections

Joy R. Bostic

In his book *Spiritual, But Not Religious*, Robert C. Fuller outlines three categories for what he refers to as "unchurched Americans." These categories are (1) those whom Fuller refers to as "secular humanists" or those who do not define themselves as religious and "who deny the supernatural and base their views of the world on reason," (2) those who maintain "ambiguous" connections with religious institutions but "still believe in [the] basic teachings" of their "native" religious tradition, and (3) those who, while not a member of an organized body, still think seriously about spiritual concerns and view themselves as "highly active seekers" working to obtain spiritual growth. Those who fit within category three are what Fuller refers to most explicitly as the "spiritual but not religious," or SNBR. Conflict with religious authority is often a characteristic of those who fit categories two and three. The members of group three also hold more negative views about clergy. Those who fit into this third category also tend to be more comfortable with religious "experimentation" and highly value direct spiritual or mystical encounters.[1]

The subjects of this chapter, avowed Baptist-Buddhist Janice Dean Willis and Pentecostal preacher turned prophetic-activist-artist James Baldwin, each began their religious lives in traditional black church communities. Each would later, however, come into conflict with their traditions and reject Christianity as a centering or exclusive belief system. While aspects of Baldwin's and Willis's narratives might be aligned with one or more of Fuller's categories of "the unchurched" (including category 3, or the SNBR category), these two personalities represent those seekers who do not neatly fit into the SNBR demographic. Yet, these figures and an examination of their spiritual journeys can help us to think more deeply about how race, gender, and sexuality might influence a spiritual seeker's quest in ways that expand our views of SBNR populations. The conflicts that Baldwin and Willis experience within each of their church traditions are related to their multiply-marginalized statuses, not only within the dominant culture but also with in their respective African American communities. As a poor, black gay male coming of age and struggling to exercise freedom in the 1940s and 1950s, Baldwin is marginalized because of sexuality, race, and class. For

Willis, coming into her own voice as a poor, black female confronting racial violence and segregation in the U.S. South in the 1960s and 1970s, gender, race, and class constitute the basis for her marginalized status.

Baldwin and Willis would later reject, at least in part, the Christian communities of their youth as being too restrictive to fully empower them to express themselves fully and to actualize their activist passions. Of course, neither would be the first to do so. In *Restless Souls*, Leigh Schmidt argues that the nature of spiritual journeys or quests of religious seekers who engage in experimentation and eclectic spirituality are a part of an "American" intellectual history and relates to the "pioneering spirit" that is a part of an American mythos that is grounded in the "Protestant right to private judgment."[2] I would also argue that the right to voluntary association that lies at the heart of the First Amendment also creates a climate for religious experimentation and creative identity constructions, especially as a response to conflicts with traditional church settings.[3] While, according to Fuller's categorical definitions for the SBNR, Baldwin and Willis may be considered "unchurched," Fuller's categories do not go far enough for us to fully understand or explicate the quests of seekers, such as Baldwin and Willis, who exist at the margins in society. As persons who are multiply marginalized, subjects such as Willis and Baldwin embark on spiritual quests that invariably involve a search for a particular place to dwell – a place in which she or he can work through and live out an identity that is emancipatory and multifaceted.[4]

Baldwin, complex subjectivity, and Afro-Protestant blues

In his book *What Is African American Religion?* Anthony Pinn describes the religious quest of marginalized African Americans as a quest for "complex subjectivity."[5] In effect, Pinn suggests that this desire for complex subjectivity is the central organizing impulse within black religion. In other words, it is a core concept in African American religiosity.

The difficulty of pursuing the African American quest for complex subjectivity lies in the fact that as seekers, African Americans must often confront oppressive structures in society and the controlling images that operate to maintain these structures. It is these structures that, according to Patricia Hill Collins, make up the matrix of domination.[6] Controlling images serve to construct and constrain human identity by targeting persons as the "Other." Hierarchies of being are established within the matrix that turns on axes such as race, religion, gender, class, sexuality, and gender identification. Controlling images reduce the complexity of being for subordinates within the matrix in ways that reflect these multiple axes. This "Othering" reduces a person's humanity as he or she is boxed in by what Emilie Townes calls the "fantastic hegemonic imagination."[7] The fantastic hegemonic imagination operates to deny a person's complexity of being, mask the troubling features of dominant identities, and justify acts and structures that perpetuate violence against, and the exploitation and exclusion of, people with marginalized identities.

In using the term *quest*, Pinn points both to existential and imaginative terrains in which persons transition from being defined as the Other, that is, "corporeal object[s] controlled by essentializing forces" to multifaceted and multi-situated subjects or "complex conveyor[s] of meaning" who possess "creative identit[ies] expressed in the world of thought and activity."[8] As "complex conveyor[s] of meaning," marginalized black folks seek to move beyond the controlling images society and institutional structures often impose upon them. For these seekers, this subjectivity

> is understood as complex in that it seeks to hold in tension many ways of existing in spaces of identification – having numerous ways of understanding and expressing oneself in relationship to oneself, others, and the world – as opposed to reified notions of identity that mark dehumanization.[9]

The spatial aspects of this quest include internal and external inquiry and movement. Thus, these quests take on a layered, nomadic quality that is evident in both Baldwin's and Willis's life narratives and their respective searches for flexible spaces and expansive sources that can serve as containers for these complex identities.

Born in 1924, James Baldwin grows up poor in New York City during the height of segregation. Living in New York City and specifically Harlem, Baldwin witnesses a diverse set of lifestyles. Within his segregated neighborhood where poverty is pervasive, he sees hardworking men and women struggling to make ends meet. He is also exposed to sex workers and hustlers, those who traffic in or are trafficked by way of the shadow economies of the urban landscape. Baldwin is also exposed to art and culture – movie houses, theaters, libraries, jazz clubs, and museums. His stepfather, David Baldwin, is a Baptist "itinerant preacher" from the South. Although he grows up within a Christian-centered household, it is not until his teenage years when Baldwin is introduced to the holiness tradition that he becomes deeply immersed within the life of the church.[10] In *The Fire Next Time*, Baldwin describes how at the age of 14 he undergoes "a prolonged religious crisis." By "religious" Baldwin means that he

> discovered God, His saints and angels, and His blazing Hell. And since I had been born in a Christian nation, I accepted this Deity as the only one. I supposed him to exist only with the walls of a church – in fact, *our* church – and I also supposed that God and safety were synonymous . . . I became . . . for the first time in my life, afraid – afraid of the evil within me and the evil without.[11]

Initially, Baldwin follows a Pentecostal preacher named Rosa Artimas Horn or "Mother" Horn. Mother Horn preaches a theology that is marked by a rejection of culture and the ways of the world. Therefore, going to the movies, dancing, and listening to jazz music were all viewed as sinful and as being "of the devil." Mother Horn's church taught that followers should separate themselves from "the world" to avoid being tempted or tainted by the wiles of the devil. In this way, Baldwin is exposed to a dualistic world-view in which clear lines are drawn between good and evil, the church and the world. His fears are compounded. Baldwin joins Mother Horn and others in the holiness church to belong and find refuge from evil. He believes that the church can protect him and insulate him from the fate of those living within the urban shadow economies. During these teenage years Baldwin serves as a preacher, and he views the church as a communal space in which he can tap into the "fire" of God's spirit so that he can maintain a communion with the divine and remain protected from life's temptations.

Eventually, Baldwin becomes disillusioned with the ministry and church. He is critical of the clergy and the power they can wield over the lives of their congregants. Baldwin also believes that too often there exists a vast difference between the ministry of Jesus and the tone and tenor of white Western Christianity. He makes a distinction between white Christianity and what he refers to as "Afro-Protestantism."[12] Baldwin is particularly critical of white Christianity as an institution that has too often supported the structures of white supremacy. Baldwin describes "Afro-Protestantism" as arising out the experience of "black suffering."[13] He sees Afro-Protestantism as a fusion of African "pagan" and white American Christian ideas and ritual and, therefore, a departure from white Western Christianity. Nevertheless, Baldwin sees both black and white Christianity as life-denying because of the oppressive ways in which churches suppress the sensual embodiment of its people and the sensual aspects of human identity.

Following his rejection of Christianity, Baldwin is freed to more deeply immerse himself in places where art, literature, and theater are produced. Baldwin embraces these locales as life-affirming spaces in which the embodied passions of the human encounter with the world can be confronted, expressed and engaged. He believes that communion can be achieved in the experience of theater as much if not more than in the breaking of bread in the church. For Baldwin, American Christians are often disconnected from the graces of atonement and the salvation that it offers because of America's inability to tell the truth about its history of racial oppression and objectification of "the Other." While Baldwin rejects institutional churches (both black and white) as life-denying structures, he does not reject the "Outsider" Jesus or the meaning of the Gospel as one that offers salvation to the lost.

As he embraced these aesthetic forms as the ground of his identity, Baldwin embarks on a quest that leads him out of Harlem to New York City's Greenwich Village. On his journey, he first meets the painter Beauford Delaney, who reintroduces him to the black classical artists and their music – Ma Rainey, Louis Armstrong, Bessie Smith, and Duke Ellington. Under Delaney's tutelage, Baldwin "began to hear what he had never dared hear," within the dualistic structures of the institutional churches to which he had belonged. These sources of black musical structures were no longer bearers of sin and evil, but life-giving sources of creativity and empowerment. Baldwin began to understand this music and these artists as a "part of [his]inheritance."[14] He is deeply affirmed in a blackness and a cultural heritage that had long been denigrated by aspects of the dominant culture and conservative quarters of African American religious institutions.[15] Rather than see black religion and black "secular" musical forms as opposed to one another, Baldwin understands them to be rooted in the same soil of black suffering, and he elevated them as arising out of the beauty and genius of black people. Later, Baldwin would come to describe the power of black music in the same way that he describes the power of Afro-Protestantism. Baldwin writes that "the blues are a historical creation produced by the confrontation precisely between . . . the black pagan from Africa and the alabaster cross."[16] Conversing with artists and participating in the performance of art, music, and theater become part of Baldwin's set of spiritual practices that began to reshape and reform his own identity.

It is Delaney who enables Baldwin to imagine that a black man can be a painter, an artist. Having encountered an internal shift beyond the constraints of the segregated city, Baldwin can now imagine himself as an artist. But the political and social landscape of a country still gripped by the power of white supremacy and homophobia still meant that Baldwin had to struggle with finding a space to freely dwell as a black gay artist within the United States. Baldwin becomes disillusioned by the constraints of what it means to live as a gay black man in a country where racial segregation is maintained in law and custom. He moves to France and lives in Paris and Saint Paul de-Vence. Later, he also travels back to the United States and contributes to black freedom struggles. Both within the United States and abroad, artists and activists, such as Nina Simone, Harry Belafonte, and Lorraine Hansberry, become Baldwin's community. They help shape and provide hallowed space for constructing an identity as an activist artist. Although Baldwin's community is rooted in what Fuller refers to as secular humanism, Baldwin does not entirely abandon religious ideas and values that he formed within the context of the black church. During his quest, Baldwin locates the true power of communion in human invention and the genius of black creativity. Rather than fully discounting or "disengaging" himself from the influence of the black church, Baldwin mines the theological and ethical resources within Afro-Protestantism to ground his humanism in the power of religion as black cultural production created in response to black suffering. Baldwin describes the power of the black church as it relates to his own sense of identity:

> There is still, for me, no pathos quite like the pathos of those multi-colored, worn, somehow triumphant and transfigured faces, speaking from the depths of a visible, tangible, continuing despair of the goodness of the Lord. I have never seen anything to equal the fire and excitement

that sometimes without warning, fill a church, causing the church, as Leadbelly and so many others have testified, to "rock." Nothing that has happened to me since equals the power and the glory that I sometimes felt when . . . the church and I were one. Their pain and their joy were mine, and mine were theirs. . . . [17]

Janice Dean Willis, black liberation, and Afro-Buddhism

Janice Dean Willis also grew up poor, but unlike Baldwin, Willis grew up in the South. She was born in Docena, Alabama, during the later years of Jane and Jim Crow. Her parents were active in one of the town's only two black churches – St. Matthew's Baptist Church. In Docena, Klan beatings occurred on a regular basis. In her autobiography, *Dreaming Me: Black, Baptist, and Buddhist*, Willis describes the fear that penetrates the black community because of Klan violence and ongoing acts of racial terror. She writes,

> The messages were crystal clear: Don't get out of line! Don't begin to feel safe! This unimaginable psychic terror would prove effective in helping to cripple my self-esteem and the self-esteem of many black people. I am a witness to their scars.

Willis speaks often about the anger that raged within her, as a child, when she would witness these demonstrations of white supremacist power or find herself battling with internalized fear.

Willis's experiences at St. Matthews illuminate internal conflicts and cultural tensions that Willis has with the Afro-Protestant tradition. As a child, she witnesses scenes that are similar to what Baldwin describes as the ecstatic "power and glory" of black church communal encounters with the Spirit. She also questions the formality and rigidity of church structures of authority. Although Willis expresses fear of these spiritual goings on and tensions with institutional forms of authority, one day when she hears the choir singing, "Don't you want to go?" something inside her shouts. "Yes! I've got my traveling shoes on." She consents to being baptized. Willis describes her baptism, saying that

> something wonderful happened. I couldn't see anything very clearly, but from all around the sides of the tank, arms and hands were extended down, reaching out to me, for me. Hands welcoming me into the community of the faithful. Into the community. Reaching out for me. Joyously welcoming me. I had a new home now. A much bigger family.[18]

By way of baptism, Willis is initiated into the black church community. She experiences black church space as a safe space – a collective communion and a haven from the violence of white supremacy and racial segregation. Conflict is awaiting her, however, when "the next day things would return to normal and" she finds herself once "again in a divided camp, with whites on one side and blacks on the other. This spiritual connection with all things did not erase the racism of the everyday world [she] inhabited."[19]

As a child, Willis is also exposed to dualistic thinking related to good and evil. For Willis, exposure, however, takes on a different kind of gendered dynamic. Prior to Willis's baptism, her mother worries constantly about the fate of her daughter's soul. Willis's mother constantly chastises her and warns her about the dangers of evil. But Willis also learns that as a female child being "smart" and speaking one's mind are dangers in and of themselves. Willis recounts an exchange with her mother when Willis is only 5. Her mother would often tell her daughter that she was "strange" and "smart." But on this occasion, her mother associated this intelligence and this strangeness with evil. Willis's mother becomes exasperated with her daughter. She shouts at her, calling her a "little devil" and telling her to "shut [her] mouth."[20] Through this exchange, Willis learns that as a female exercising the power to use her voice and to question the world around her, she would be demonized by authority figures who want her to be quiet and not use her intellect to challenge them. Willis determines then and there that she is going to immerse herself in learning and if that means "making a pact with the devil then [she] would do it."[21] Confronted by the power of white supremacy within the dominant culture and gendered forms of silencing and dismissal within African American institutions, Willis shifts between moments of rage and low self-esteem as she grows into young womanhood.

Willis's anger and disillusionment resurface when she leaves home to attend Cornell University. On the long bus ride from Docena, Alabama, to Ithaca, New York, Willis feels a profound sense of loneliness. This loneliness is compounded by the anxiety and fear she faces as she travels through segregated public spaces. As a black female, Willis cannot eat at lunch counters during stops, and she is vulnerable to racial and sexual harassment and violence throughout the trip. But during her journey she encounters a "traveling companion that no one else could see."[22] Willis, like her mother, "had been born with cauls over [her] eyes. This meant that [they] saw things that other human beings did not." During this harrowing bus trip, Willis has a vision of Jesus lying down on his side with "His head supported by His right hand." Willis remembers:

> [L]ater, I would see this exact position on depictions of the Buddha's passing away, His so-called Complete Nirvana posture. But then, I knew nothing about Buddhism. I only know that Jesus rode with me on that first bus ride to Cornell and that His gently smiling eyes comforted me throughout the journey.[23]

She goes on to describe how she prayed throughout the journey

> for safety, for food, for a welcoming place. And my prayers were answered: I was not traveling alone. Jesus floated there, with me. And whenever I doubted or felt particularly afraid, I had only to glance to the window to see that He was still there, riding wind currents, a holographic epiphany, life-size, reclining, gently smiling Jesus.[24]

Willis's description includes an eclectic array of religious symbols, imagery, beliefs, and practices that combine African American mystical cultures, traditional Christianity, and Buddhism. For Willis these traditions converge to form a container or welcoming space of safety and accompaniment that support her on what for her as a black female made for a treacherous journey.

As a student at Cornell University, Willis is active in black liberation protests and she participates in civil rights marches. She is constructing her identity as a social justice activist committed to black freedom struggles. As a junior, Willis travels to India. It is during her time there that she meets Tibetan monks who are living in exile in Nepal. She also meets Lobsang Chonjor. After Willis returns to Cornell, she corresponds with Chonjor and turns to Buddhism as way of confronting the destructive aspects of her anger as she continues to grapple with the deleterious effects of racism and sexism in her life. Although she had participated in civil rights marches and learned nonviolent tactics, she could never expel the anger she felt inside. Violence and strategies of self-defense became viable options.

Upon graduation, Willis is faced with a difficult choice: to join the Black Panther Party or return to the Tibetan monastery in Nepal to study Buddhism. Willis initially decides to travel back to Nepal, but the death of Fred Hampton, in 1969, affects her deeply. She states that "after returning to Cornell, I was convinced that as a thinking Black person in this country I was left no choice" but to pick up a gun and join the movement.[25] She resolves to join the Black Panther Party and "lay her life on the line for [her] beliefs and for [her] people's freedom."[26] At the last minute, however, Willis changes her mind. Although she at first feels "tossed and pushed along, it seemed inevitably, toward guns and violence," she discerns that traveling to Nepal "offered the best opportunity for clarity" and "at least the possibility of peaceful transformation."[27] So she embarks on a journey of discovery and healing as a resident of the Bodhanath monastery and becomes a student of Lama Yeshe. During her initiation as a lay follower in the Tibetan Buddhist community, Willis sees a parallel between her baptism and initiation into the Christian church and her Buddhist naming ceremony in which she is given the Tibetan name for "Joy of the Dharma." Willis writes that in both contexts she is resistant to "following the rules," yet she feels completely welcomed into both communities.[28]

Later, Willis comes to not only recognize parallels between her Baptist upbringing and her Buddhist experiences but she also begins to apply language and terminology in ways that create hybrid relationships between the two. Mikhail Bakhtin defines *hybridization* as "a mixture of two social languages within the limits of a single utterance, an encounter, within the arena of utterance, between two different linguistic consciousnesses, separated from one another by an epoch, by social differentiation or by some other factor."[29] Willis combines language from two different religious traditions that arise out of different geographical and cultural contexts to identify her own hybrid dwelling place. She declares herself a Baptist-Buddhist as she recognizes her need for both the black church and the Buddhist sangha. The need for this hybrid relationship becomes evident when she visits her father's church, Sixth Avenue Baptist Church in Middletown, Connecticut. Willis identifies a familiar chant "Lord have mercy" as a "new mantra" in her spiritual practice.[30] Willis is also reminded of the ways in which what Baldwin refers to as "Afro-Protestantism" is rooted in the blues tradition and, thus, can serve as a space of healing and collective transformation as the experience of black suffering is acknowledged and recognized as divine struggle. Willis writes,

> [B]y now my own floodgates had completely opened up. Here, in this sanctuary, you could let your tears stream forward. Everyone had seen tears before. Here you were a part of a community of worshippers a community of people who knew about hardship and at the same time, knew that it did not last forever. . . . This group knew that misery and joy can stand side by side. Indeed, it is this very knowledge that black people call "the blues."[31]

Red pills, blue pills: constructing religious identities within the matrix

For some operating within the matrix, the experiential dimensions of life take place not on a single axis of being within the matrix but at intersecting axes that speak to multiple forms of oppression. This makes finding a place to dwell and be at home in complex being even more difficult. African Americans have sought solace in black institutions that in many ways provide a haven for black bodies assaulted by the systemic power unleashed within the matrix. Even within these institutions, however, hierarchies of being may persist on other axes beyond race. For women or LGBTQ persons, the very institutions that provide relief from the structures of racism and white privilege may hedge on or altogether decry the full-fledged freedoms of women and queer members within their midst. Thus, finding spaces in which dark-skinned, female, and sexually queer communities can be at home can be a difficult task, and the quest for home can take on a nomadic quality as marginalized seekers search for a place to dwell.

Because the very same institutional structures that served as partial havens in which marginalized persons construct and develop identity as related to one axis may end up functioning as structures that help perpetuate controlling images and suppress complex subjectivity with regard to other axes, African American seekers may find it difficult to make a commitment to a specific religious community or may altogether reject these "home" institutions as inadequate to meet their needs. This may be due to tensions and conflicts around issues of identity, sexuality, or social location and the feelings of marginalization within a single institution; the inability of an individual religious tradition or community to speak to the needs and concerns related to complex identities and multiple modes of being or the limitations of particular belief systems to encompass the shifting or expanding worldviews of practitioners.

While in their respective quests, neither Baldwin nor Willis rejects black church communities in absolute terms, each of them embarks on a nomadic journey to identify sources of spiritual sustenance and construct sustaining spaces in which to dwell. James Baldwin becomes a humanist. Therefore, there are aspects of his narrative that might fit into Fuller's first category. Baldwin's humanist vision is one that is very much in concert with his view of social justice in the world. While he rejects the institutional church, Baldwin still incorporates religious ideas such as communion and salvation into his social commentary. Willis may fit more specifically into category three, but she still views community and at least the sangha or the Buddhist community as a home. The Buddhist sangha does not serve as Willis's only spiritual home, however; the black church and activist communities are also homes for Willis's spiritual and social engagement.

Baldwin maintains that Christianity's focus on moral taboos and the prohibitions against engaging in sensual pursuits is life-denying to human beings, particularly those whose bodies are the targets of violence and oppression. Thus, he makes a distinction between white and black Christianities. While Baldwin identifies with Jesus as a darker-skinned outcast who was killed for confronting the power structures of his time, Baldwin rejects the imperial Christianity that arose during the time of Constantine as an oppressive institution. Baldwin views "Afro-Protestantism," however, as a departure from imperial and later white supremacist Christianities. He describes Afro-Protestantism as a black creation that is a blend of African "pagan" and "White Christian" ideas and rituals. Here Baldwin recognizes black, African structures, language, and forms that influence Afro-Protestantism. Baldwin likens the cultural forms present in Afro-Protestantism to those that structure the blues. Willis makes a similar connection between black church religious practices and the blues. Although Willis does not reject the black church with the same conviction as Baldwin, she resists the rules and regulations of the institutional church. At the same time, she identifies with black churches such as St. Matthews as places of welcoming community that serve as a balm and salve that heal the wounds ripped open by the segregation, racism, and sexism she faces as a black woman in the United States.

What Willis and Baldwin both appreciate about the black church is its expression of black/African ritual structures – the same ritual structures that are the basis of other African American cultural productions such as the blues. Both Baldwin and Willis use the concept of the blues as a way of describing religious spaces that can hold the complexities and contradictions of black life. As James Cone insists,

> the blues express a black perspective on the incongruity of life and the attempt to achieve meaning in a situation fraught with contradictions . . . the blues are true because they combine art and life, poetry and experience, the symbolic and the real. They are an artistic response to the chaos of life.[32]

Cone's assertion is echoed in the work of Charles Long, who recognizes that African American cultural productions such as religion, music (the blues and jazz), dance, literature, and so on are oriented by, and arise in direct response to, black involuntary presence in the Americas and the absurd contradiction that enslavement, dehumanization and the change in status from human to chattel creates. These productions carry memory, image, and history of African origins and notions of a God or divinity that are active in history and committed to justice.[33]

African American cultural practices and forms oriented by these three perspectives provide literal and imaginative spaces in which Willis and Baldwin can construct and perform subjectivities that affirm their blackness and African ancestry. These spaces enable seekers such as these to better complexify spiritual practices and religio-cultural community in ways that affirm black identity. While neither Willis nor Baldwin adhere to theistic notions of a personal deity, each of them certainly acknowledges and challenges the "worldly" structural evils that are manufactured by human hands. By embracing and engaging in practices that affirm African diasporic ritual forms, Baldwin and Willis embrace the sanctification aspects of Afro-Protestantism in which black church and blues communities alike maintain relationships with ancestors who engage these aesthetic technologies in response to the difficulties of black life. While Baldwin and Willis embrace and celebrate the flexibility and freedom attached to African American cultural forms that are found in black religious expressions such as Afro-Protestantism, both reject the restrictive views, exclusivism, and authoritarian aspects of institutional Christianity.

Baldwin engages life, art, and activism as a nomad. Willis engages in a hybridization of communal spaces and concepts as a way of maintaining dwelling places that are all necessary for her spiritual quest and activist life.

Each of their quests involves not only internal movements that enable them to exorcise internalized oppression and embrace self-love but also external movements that enable them to identify and construct expanded notions of community.

Baldwin and Willis both searched for religio-cultural communities that made room for them each to exercise complex subjectivity. Their religious quests are not wholly unique, however. Again, as Schmidt suggests in *Restless Souls*, the religious quest for eclectic or at least more flexible spiritual practices and communities are a part of U.S. intellectual and social history, although the religious quests of those who are marginalized by race, gender, and sexuality have been dismissed more readily as outside the "normative" boundaries of "real religion."[34] Spiritual seekers and activists have sought ways to build communal structures that allow for more humane places to dwell. Howard Thurman, for example, rejected racial segregation and religious exclusiveness and society and co-founded the Church for the Fellowship of All Peoples, the first interracial, interfaith congregation. Thurman was a part of a movement to employ the arts as a means of connecting religious seekers across difference.[35] Baldwin and Willis, as did Thurman, seek to construct communal spaces that support their respective activist visions for social justice. These spaces allow for expansive, critical, and flexible thinking and emancipatory practices to facilitate complex subjectivity and transformative visions. These spaces also allow both Willis and Baldwin to engage in practices of multiply belonging as a way of constructing and being in community. Love and hope for communal/national/global salvation are at the core of these activists' social visions.

As we further explore identity and belonging in SBNR cultures, it will be important to examine the ways in which some religious seekers are in search of places in which they can wholly dwell and work through and live out complex subjectivity. Religious denominations and institutions may incorporate belief systems, doctrinal assertions and leadership models that inhibit complex subjectivity of followers, especially those who are marginalized because of gender, race, sexuality, ability, or socioeconomic status and who may be multiply situated. Thus, authoritarian and exclusivist structures can serve as barriers to seekers who are trying to make sense out of this multiplicity and lead such persons to disengage from traditional religious institutions and set out on a path in search of extra-institutional ways to engage the divine and to find a place to dwell in that multiplicity. This manner of seeking is rooted in a desire for expansive or even hybrid systems rather than traditional structures that suppress complex subjectivity.

Notes

1 Robert C. Fuller, *Spiritual, But Not Religious* (New York: Oxford University Press, 2001), 4.
2 Leigh Schmidt. *Restless Souls* (Berkeley and Los Angeles, CA: University of California Press, 2012), 2.

3 Joy R. Bostic, *African American Female Mysticism: Nineteenth Century Religious Activism* (New York: Palgrave, 2013). I argue that practices of voluntary association were a part of the religious and cultural milieu that influenced African American women's spiritual quests in the 19th century.
4 I also argue this with respect to 19th-century black women's spirituality in *African American Female Mysticism*. In this book, I contend that marginalized black women are seeking a place which they can call "home."
5 Anthony B. Pinn, *What Is African American Religion?* (Minneapolis, MN: Fortress Press, 2011), 62.
6 See Patricia Hill Collins, *Black Feminist Thought* (New York: Routledge, 2008).
7 Emilie M. Townes, *Womanist Ethics and the Cultural Production of Evil* (New York: Palgrave, 2006).
8 Pinn, *What Is African American Religion?*, 3.
9 Ibid.
10 Clarence E. Hardy III, *James Baldwin's God: Sex, Hope, and Crisis in Black Holiness Culture* (Knoxville, TN: The University of Tennessee Press, 2003).
11 James Baldwin, *The Fire Next Time* (New York: Vintage, 1992).
12 Ibid.
13 Hardy, *James Baldwin's God: Sex, Hope, and Crisis in Black Holiness Culture*, 9.
14 James Baldwin, *The Price of the Ticket* (New York: St. Martins/Marek, 1985).
15 See Renee K. Harrison. *Enslaved Women and the Art of Resistance in Antebellum America*, (New York: Palgrave, 2009) for a discussion of denigration and black cultures.
16 Hardy, *James Baldwin's God: Sex, Hope, and Crisis in Black Holiness Culture*, 18.
17 Ibid.
18 Janice Dean Willis, *Dreaming Me: Black, Baptist, and Buddhist One Woman's Spiritual Journey* (Boston, MA: Wisdom Publications, 2008), 57.
19 Ibid., 57.
20 Ibid., 28.
21 Ibid.
22 Ibid., 83.
23 Ibid., 84.
24 Ibid., 83.
25 Ibid., 139.
26 Ibid.
27 Ibid., 144.
28 Ibid., 187.
29 Bakhtin, *The Dialogic Imagination*, Edited by Michael Holquist, translated by Carl Emerson and Michael Holquist (Austin, TX: University of Texas Press, 1981) 359.
30 Willis, *Dreaming Me: Black, Baptist, and Buddhist One Woman's Spiritual Journey*, 299.
31 Ibid.
32 James Cone, *The Spirituals and the Blues* (Maryknoll, NY: Orbis Books, 1992), 103.
33 Charles Long, *Significations: Signs, Symbols, and Images in the Interpretation of Religion* (New York: The Davies Group Publishers, 1992), 187–9.
34 Leigh E. Schmidt mentions David Brooks's and Martin Marty's respective critiques of Melissa Etheridge's and Oprah Winfrey's efforts to construct alternative spaces for that are welcoming of LGBQ and women of color. See his *Resltess Souls* (Berkeley: University of California Press, 2012), 283–4.
35 Howard Thurman, *Footprints of a Dream: The Story of the Church for the Fellowship of All Peoples* (Eugene, OR: Wipf and Stock Publishers, 2009).

References

Bakhtin, Mikhail. *The Dialogic Imagination: Four Essays*. Edited by Michael Holquist, translated by Carl Emerson and Michael Holquist. Austin, TX: University of Texas Press, 1981.

Baldwin, James. *The Price of the Ticket*. New York: St. Martins/Marek, 1985.

———. *The Fire Next Time*. New York: Vintage, 1992.

Baldwin, James and Randall Kenan. *The Cross of Redemption: Uncollected Writings*. 1st ed. New York: Pantheon Books, 2010.

Bostic, Joy. *African American Female Mysticism: Nineteenth-Century Activism*. New York: Palgrave, 2013.

Collins, Patricia Hill. *Black Feminist Thought*. New York: Routledge, 2008.

Cone, James H. *The Spirituals and the Blues*. Maryknoll, NY: Orbis Books, 1992.

Fuller, Robert C. *Spiritual, But Not Religious*. New York: Oxford University Press, 2001.

Hardy, Clarence E. III. *James Baldwin's God: Sex, Hope, and Crisis in Black Holiness Culture*. Knoxville, TN: The University of Tennessee Press, 2003.

Hayes, Diana L. *Forged in the Fiery Furnace: African American Spirituality*. Maryknoll, NY: Orbis Books, 2012.

Long, Charles H. *Significations: Signs, Symbols, and Images in the Interpretation of Religion*. Aurora, CO: The Davies Group Publishers, 1992.

Mercadante, Linda A. *Belief Without Borders: Inside the Minds of the Spiritual But Not Religious*. New York: Oxford University Press, 2014.

Pinn, Anthony B. *What Is African American Religion?* Minneapolis, MN: Fortress Press, 2011.

Schmidt, Leigh. *Restless Souls*. Berkeley and Los Angeles, CA: University of California Press, 2012.

Thurman, Howard. *With Head and Heart: The Autobiography of Howard Thurman*. Harvest Book. San Diego, CA: Harcourt Brace and Company, 1979.

———. *Footprints of a Dream: The Story of the Church for the Fellowship of All Peoples*. Eugene, OR: Wipf and Stock Publishers, 2009.

Townes, Emilie M. *Womanist Ethics and the Cultural Production of Evil*. New York: Palgrave, 2006.

Willis, Janice Dean. *Dreaming Me: Black, Baptist, and Buddhist One Woman's Spiritual Journey*. Boston, MA: Wisdom Publications, 2008.

———. "Buddhism and Peace." www.buddhachannel.tv/portail/?article4291.

Part II
Circumscriptions

6 Minds of their own

Psychological substrates of the Spiritual but Not Religious sensibility

Robert C. Fuller

America's religious landscape is almost unrecognizable to scholars monitoring institutional membership. Each new survey chronicles the continued decline of mainline Protestant organizations, weakening commitments among nonimmigrant Roman Catholics, and the resilience of both evangelical Protestant groups as well as nondenominational megachurches. What generates the most headlines, however, is the growing number of U.S. adults who don't identify with any religious organization. Surveys report that

> these changes are taking place across the religious landscape, affecting all regions of the country and many demographic groups. While the drop in Christian affiliation is particularly pronounced among young adults, it is occurring among Americans of all ages. The same trends are seen among whites, blacks and Latinos; among both college graduates and adults with only a high school education; and among women as well as men.[1]

Yet the majority of America's unaffiliated or "unchurched" population still believes in some kind of God or higher spiritual power. Most still ponder life's big questions: Where did the universe come from? Why is there life rather than an endless void? What should I do with my life? What happens when I die? Some of America's religiously unaffiliated have only mild interest in such metaphysical speculation and relegate religion to the periphery of their lives. Yet others are continuously reading, attending lectures, or even engaging in practices that might cultivate a felt connection to higher realities. Thus, at least some of America's unchurched population still find themselves trying to come to terms with the existential and ethical issues traditionally associated with religion.

Coming up with labels to designate these religiously unaffiliated, yet religiously searching individuals is not easy. Three such labels have been particularly helpful. Robert Wuthnow's concept of "seeker spirituality" identifies a mode of spirituality that conceptualizes spirituality more as a journey than a destination, rendering individuals tentative in their spiritual commitments and continually motivating them to seek out new sources of spiritual edification. Daniel Batson's notion of "quest spirituality" similarly identifies a form of personal religiosity recognizing that humans will probably never know the final truth about religious matters and that all beliefs should therefore be continually revised in light of life's challenges and tragedies. The most common label for unchurched spirituality, however, has been the designation of being "Spiritual but Not Religious."[2] The words *spiritual* and *religious* have historically been synonyms. Recent efforts to make a distinction between being religious (religiosity generally following the doctrinal and ritual patterns of an established religious tradition) and being spiritual (spirituality that is self-consciously eclectic and tentative) are themselves symptoms of biblical religion's decreasing viability among citizens of Western cultures. We might note sociologist Nancy Ammerman's caution that scholarly attempts to force "spirituality" and "religion" into opposing, binary categories are misguided. Ammerman notes that many religiously affiliated individuals actually endorse many of the same attitudes as those who are unaffiliated.[3] Ammerman's cautions against facile categorizations of people's spirituality are well taken, but there is nonetheless solid, empirical evidence to warrant using a phrase such as "being Spiritual but Not Religious" to spotlight the sizable segment (now estimated at between 18% to 27%) of the American population that searches for the sacred in a fluid, eclectic manner outside the Jewish and Christian faith traditions that had formerly structured Western religiosity.

We know a few things about those who identify as SBNR. They are, for example, more likely than conventionally religious individuals to hold paranormal beliefs (e.g., mental abilities for telepathy or other forms of extrasensory perception, humans' capacity for out-of-body experiences). They are also more likely to report more encounters with the mystical realm and experience connectedness with everything around them. We also know that SBNRers are more likely than other Americans to have a college education, to belong to a white-collar profession, to be liberal in their political views, to have parents who attended church less frequently, and to be more independent in the sense of heaving weaker social relationships. Yet several questions remain: Why haven't these individuals abandoned religion altogether? That is, if reason led them to reject the "truth claims" behind existing religious traditions, why haven't they followed this line of analytic reasoning to a wholly secular conclusion? Why are so many attracted to ideas that are overtly metaphysical (i.e., testifying to a more-than-physical or more-than-sensory aspect of existence)? Why are so many attracted to practices that privilege nonrational or nonanalytical modes of experience?

Those who consider themselves "Spiritual but Not Religious" clearly have minds of their own. They have not embraced established religious institutions as have their traditionally religious contemporaries. They assert their right to decide for themselves what is true and what meaningfully connects with their lives. Yet they have not followed reason, doubts, and independent thought to wholly nonreligious conclusions as have their secular contemporaries. They retain a lively curiosity about the possibility that our highest good lies in adapting ourselves to some higher or metaphysical reality. Psychology – particularly modern cognitive science – provides some important clues to just how the SBNR segment of the American population came to have such minds of their own.

Homo religiosus: a psychological profile

Academic psychology strives to explain human thought, feeling, and behavior. This includes explaining why humans think religiously, feel religiously, and behave religiously. Important breakthroughs have been made in the psychological study of religion in recent decades as researchers situate humanity's religious propensities within our species' long evolutionary history. The human brain is the product of a millennia-long process driven by genetic mutations and natural selection. What we commonly call "the mind" is a complex organization of neural networks shaped by natural selection to ensure the species' biological survival. As psychologist Stephen Pinker puts it, "[t]he mind is what the brain does . . . the mind is organized into modules . . . their operation was shaped by natural selection to solve the problems of the hunting and gathering lives led by our ancestors."[4] Foremost among the problems that our ancestors needed to solve in order to survive (as measured by the ability to reproduce viable offspring) were (1) identifying causal agents in their immediate surroundings, (2) forging tightly knit coalitions characterized by large-scale cooperation among strangers, and (3) attaching themselves to protective figures.

Understanding *homo religiosus* in a fully naturalist perspective requires insight into religion's connection with the neural networks (modules) shaped by natural selection to solve these and other adaptive problems.[5] It is important to understand that most cognitive activity is unconscious in the sense that it is performed without an individual's awareness. We breathe, digest food, fight off infections, and execute habitual behaviors with no deliberate mental effort. Indeed, most of the thoughts, feelings, and behaviors that guide our adaption to the surrounding world are coordinated by our most evolutionary ancient and "hardwired" neural networks. At the risk of oversimplification, it is helpful to think of the brain as a complex compilation of two very different kinds of cognition. Type 1 cognition is immediate, automatic, universal, and executed by genetically evolved neural networks that are mostly impervious to cultural conditioning. Type 1 cognitive activities are spontaneous and appear natural or intuitive to the acting person. Type 2 cognition is deliberative, requires sustained attention, and largely dependent on learned or acquired abilities.

We should be cautious about taking this distinction between Type 1 and Type 2 cognition too literally since it obscures the brain's organic unity. It might also suggest overly simplistic understandings of concepts such as "reason" or "logic." But the distinction does draw attention to the different kinds of cognitive operations that comprise the human brain. It also high-lights the psychological foundations for Robert McCauley's observation that modern cognitive science shows that "religion is natural, science is not."[6] Religious thought, feeling, and behavior arise naturally from many of the neural networks that compose Type 1 cognition. As such, they are not themselves the product of sensory information or evidence-based rational-ity. Type 2 reasoning, on the other hand, is more likely to be associated with the kinds of evidence-based analyses that are metaphysically agnostic. Type 2 reasoning tends to support intellectual independence and to under-mine the credibility of supernatural concepts. In sum, the kinds of cognition associated with intuitive forms of cognition lean toward religious thought, feeling, and behavior while the kinds of cognition associated with rational deliberation lean toward nonreligious thought, feeling, and behavior.

Modern cognitive science is thus in full agreement with the author of Hebrews 11:1 who writes that "faith is the substance of things hoped for, the evidence of things not seen." Conventional religiosity is not generated by sense experience or reasoned reflection. Instead, religious faith is generated by cognitive processes that aren't dependent on sensory input. Faith is gen-erated by feelings and sensibilities hardwired in the brain rather than being generated by realities external to the brain. Faith is intuitive. It emerges naturally from the human brain's adaptive networks. Foremost among these networks is the capacity for agency detection. Natural selection favored brains containing intricate mechanisms for detecting causal forces or agents in our surroundings since these agents might pose a danger or provide an opportunity. Natural selection also favored brains that automatically imbue these agents with sentience and intentions (i.e., we intuitively think of them as having thoughts, feelings, and motives similar to our own – something that psychologists refer to as "theory of mind"). Experimental studies support the view that our brain's tendency to detect agency underlies the nearly universal human belief in supernatural beings. We are hardwired to anticipate intention in the unseen causes of uncertain or ambiguous events. Our brains spontaneously construct hypothetical, imaginative candidates (particularly if our culture provides us with preformed candidates for such causal influence in our lives). The existence of neural networks for agency detection (that intuitively imbue causal agents with sentience, intention, and basic humanlike thought patterns) thus form the basic psychological sub-strate of the near-universal belief in gods or supernatural beings. In sum, evolution has equipped humans with cognitive tendencies to view the mind as separate from the body (mind/body dualism), to discern the presence of unseen ghosts or gods, and to think that there is meaning or purpose in otherwise ambiguous events. All of these underlie the formation of religious or spiritual beliefs and are perhaps more operative in SBNR individuals given that their spirituality is somewhat less shaped by established cultural institutions.

Human survival is also dependent on our capacity to form tightly knit, cohesive social units. Humans need to form cooperative groups in order to survive. Evolution shaped human brains to make such cooperation not only possible but also deeply woven into human thought, feeling, and behavior. Humans have inborn, innate moral intuitions. We experience powerful emotions such as fear, guilt, and shame that motivate them to abandon self-centered strategies and instead align themselves with the interests of the group. We readily pledge allegiance to tribal units that help us distinguish between tribal insiders to whom we owe loyalty and moral conduct from tribal outsiders to whom we owe neither and toward whom we can justify even the cruelest forms of violence.

Humans are thus innately prone toward "authoritarianism," a cluster of personality traits that incline individuals toward social systems characterized by submission to group authority. Every human has some genetic disposition toward authoritarianism that is displayed through conventionalism, conformity to social standards, submission to authority figures, legitimation of aggression to outsiders, and some forms of prejudice. It should thus not be surprising that authoritarianism and the most pronounced form of conservative religion, fundamentalism, are highly correlated with each other. Nor should it be surprising that authoritarianism is inversely related to the quest, seeker, or SBNR spiritual sensibility.[7]

Another adaptive need served by the brain's genetically evolved neural networks is that of attaching ourselves to protective figures. Just as ethological studies of young members of species ranging from ducklings to baby rhesus monkeys have shown the powerful role of "imprinting" to secure protective attachment, evolution endowed the human brain with intricate attachment systems ensuring that young children stay in close physical proximity with their caregivers. The attachment system works by creating feelings of anxiety or insecurity whenever we are separated from the safety and security associated with the attachment figure. These uncomfortable visceral feelings motivate us to reestablish a connection to our accustomed attachment figure or see out a new attachment figure. It seems that some of our most powerful emotions (e.g., fear, guilt, shame) similarly mobilize these attachment behaviors. As we grow older, God increasingly serves as a substitute attachment figure. People seek proximity to God through prayer, reading scripture, and worship. This is especially true in times of crisis and distress.

These last two psychological substrates of *homo religious*, authoritarianism and attachment systems, draw attention to the fact that religion traditionally thrives in environmental conditions characterized by uncertainty and stress. The genetically evolved neural mechanisms that typically motivate conventional religiosity are most strongly evoked in conditions marked by uncertainty or threat. To this extent we might think of religious thoughts, feelings, and behaviors as cultural elaborations (extended phenotypes) of neural mechanisms needed to soothe stressed brains.[8]

In sum, humanity's most "hardwired" neural networks render us prone to religious thought, feeling, and behavior. These genetically evolved mechanisms are particularly likely to be evoked in environmental conditions characterized by uncertainty and stress. Throughout history and in almost every cultural setting humans intuitively and automatically generate conceptions of spirit beings – at least some of whom monitor our behavior, readily believe in supernatural causal influence, yearn to form secure relationships with supernatural beings, and engage in public displays of allegiance to tribal symbols. Religious proclivities are as universal as the psychological substrates that engender them.

Spiritual sensibilities and the psychology of individual differences

Humans vary in almost every complex cognitive or affective trait – including religiosity. A principal goal of academic psychology is thus identifying variables that reliably explain and measure individual differences. Among the most widely known of these variables are the Big Five personality traits that collectively account for a great deal of the differences in how people think, feel, and behave. The five clusters of personality traits that best capture individual differences are conscientiousness (tendency to be organized, disciplined, dutiful, careful), agreeableness (tendency to be trusting, helpful, cooperative), neuroticism/emotional stability (tendency to be insecure, anxious), openness to experience (tendency to be imaginative, curious, independent, interested in novelty), and extraversion (tendency to be sociable, assertive, initiate social interaction). All the "Big Five" traits are heritable to at least some degree, with openness, neuroticism, and extraversion being more heritable than agreeableness or conscientiousness. We might also note that women typically score higher on measures of agreeableness, conscientiousness, and neuroticism than men, while men typically score higher on measures of openness to experience.

Research indicates that conventional religiosity is most highly associated with the traits of agreeableness and conscientiousness. SBNR individuals are instead associated with higher levels of openness to experience and are lower in both agreeableness and conscientiousness than their more conventionally religious counterparts. One study that located personalities along a scale ranging from "communal" to "individual agency" found that "communal" personality orientations correlated with conventional religiosity while "agentics" tended to be religious contrarians of differing kinds. We know, too, that conventionally religious people measure higher than SBNRs on "collectivism" and "traditionalism," while lower on "individualism" – or putting it differently, SBNRs score higher on measures of individualism and lower on measures of collectivism and traditionalism.[9]

These correlations between personality traits and differing religious sensibilities are especially interesting given that early researchers of the SBNR movement noted a disproportionately high number of males and noted that SBNR individuals were relatively independent in the sense of having weaker social relationships. These early observations of the SBNR movement are consistent with what modern psychology would predict about individuals with higher levels of openness and lower levels of "communal" traits such as agreeableness and conscientiousness. It is also at least possible that SBNR individuals, much like what Abraham Maslow discerned about what he deemed to be "self-actualizing individuals," have a secure sense of self-esteem and are thus less motivated to have their self-worth affirmed by peer groups.

Many cultural commentators have insinuated that SBNR individuals are more narcissistic than their conventionally religious counterparts since they engage in self-focused practices rather than join congregations or engage in shared, public ritual.[10] Empirical research using the Narcissism Personality Inventory (NPI) shows, however, that SBNR and conventionally religious individuals have almost identical NPI measures – with both groups having higher measures than wholly nonreligious individuals.[11] Importantly, the higher NPI scores in both SBNR and conventionally religious individuals were because of slightly higher scores in the so-called healthy or adaptive dimensions of the NPI (i.e., self-absorption and self-admiration) while both SBNR and conventionally religious individuals measured low in the so-called pathological or maladaptive dimensions of the NPI (i.e., entitlement and exploitativeness).

The connection between "openness to experience" and the SBNR sensibility invites further exploration. We know that openness is a personality trait associated with intelligence, creativity, liberal social views, fantasy, and a need to enlarge and examine experiences – all traits that we would expect to be associated with decreasing conventionality and a willingness to challenge traditional ideas. This would account for the negative relationship often found between openness and affiliation with a religious organization. Yet because openness is associated with intelligence, creativity, fantasy, and a need to examine experience, openness also favors increased interest in metaphysical and spiritual ideas as is common among SBNR individuals.

We are thus faced with an apparent contradiction. On one hand, higher levels of openness and higher capacities for analytic reasoning may lead to questioning of traditional beliefs, eventually resulting in a wholly nonreligious worldview. Yet openness may also lead to increased interest in metaphysical ideas – though usually with deistic or pantheistic conceptions of God rather than traditional theism.

This seeming contradiction concerning the effect of openness and cognitive style on personal religiosity lessens when we distinguish between two different cognitive styles that individuals high in openness might bring to reflection on religion. It is helpful here to note that overall there is a negative relationship between intelligence and religion. Yet it is not intelligence per se that negatively affects conventional religiosity as much as it is cognitive style – specifically an individual's propensity to think critically or analytically.[12] This brings us back to our earlier distinction between Type 1 (intuitive, automatic, and spontaneous understanding of the world as mediated through "hardwired" cognitive mechanisms) and Type 2 (deliberative, discursive, more evidence-based, analytic) forms of cognition. Type 2 cognition invariably leads to scrutiny, detecting logical inconsistencies, often culminating in "unbelieving" conventional religious beliefs. Awareness of how Type 2 cognition leads away from conventional religiosity prompts many cognitive psychologists to

> hypothesize that more religious people, compared to less religious people, may be both less skilled at logical inference (cognitive ability) as well as *more prone to be misled by immediate intuitions (cognitive style) that essentially foreclose on the logical processes that might draw inferences that would weaken them.*[13]

There is at least some empirical evidence that SBNR individuals are characterized by stronger-than-average capacities for analytic reason.[14] Yet despite their analytic reasoning capabilities, their overall openness, their intelligence, and their education, SBNR individuals are more likely than either their nonreligious or conventionally religious counterparts to be guided by their immediate cognitive intuitions (Type 1 cognition) – albeit in ways that are more flexible and less characterized by authoritarian sentiments. SBNR individuals are also characterized by such cognitive/affective traits as having feelings of connectedness to the universe or higher powers, having mystical experiences, and believing in paranormal phenomena. SBNR individuals are, more-over, more prone than nonreligious or conventionally religious individuals to immediate intuitions such as viewing the mind being separate from the body, attributing humanlike intentionality to nonhuman objects, or readily attributing mental states to others SBNR individuals are, finally, also more likely than either their nonreligious or conventionally religious counterparts to be characterized by cognitive tendencies toward transpersonal identification, self-forgetfulness, fantasy-proneness, belief in magical powers, and reliance on both personal intuitions and subjective experience.[15]

Understanding how the "minds" of SBNR individuals differ from their nonreligious or traditionally religious counterparts requires that we further explore why those drawn to being "Spiritual but Not Religious" are, in fact, "more prone to be misled by immediate intuitions (cognitive style) that essentially foreclose on the logical processes that might draw inferences that would weaken them." Why, we might ask, do individuals high in openness (and seemingly high in the potential for analytic reasoning) nonetheless display great interest in spiritual and metaphysical ideas? Why are SBNR individuals more likely than their nonreligious counterparts to view the mind as separate from the physical body, and more likely to think that both animate and even inanimate objects possess mental states? In short, why does the

SBNR sensibility place such emphasis on internal and subjective sources of knowledge as opposed to valuing only the external and objective sources of knowledge usually associated with analytic thinking?

Understanding the SBNR sensibility, then, requires sensitivity to the psychological variables that might cause individuals otherwise high in intelligence, education, and openness to be "prone" to internal and subjective valuations. Family background and other factors related to socialization undoubtedly help explain a great deal about why some individuals continue to explore spiritual ideas or practices even though they have intellectually disengaged from conventional religiosity. There are, however, at least three other variables that might render otherwise intellectually adventuresome individuals "more prone" to internal, subjective cognitive processes: positive emotions, genetic predispositions to spiritual feelings, and experiences with altered states of consciousness.

Positive emotions and spiritual sensibilities

Recent advances in the study of emotions have made it possible to explain many observed differences in individuals' religious lives. Emotions are basic features of the genetically evolved mechanisms that guide our immediate, automatic, and largely unconscious interactions with the surrounding world (what we earlier conveniently labeled "Type 1" cognition). Our neural systems are programmed to respond to specific kinds of sensory cues by triggering emotional programs whose purpose is to mobilize the organism for an appropriate response. Emotions mobilize such biologically important activities as goal setting, information gathering, selective attention, retrieving goal-specific memory, regulating physiological processes, communicating, intent, and shifting energy levels. Emotions thus exert significant influence on perception and cognition.

It is important that we do not think of emotion as a single category that might, for example, be contrasted with logical rationality (e.g., claiming that someone is "too emotional" and not thinking clearly). Emotions vary greatly from one another. Many (e.g., fear, guilt, anger, disgust) are universal and sufficiently hardwired in the brain's adaptive mechanisms as to be all but impervious to cultural learning. Others, however, seem more connected with deliberative thought and manifest quite differently depending on cultural context.

Researchers have also found it useful to distinguish between *positive* and *negative* emotions. Negative emotions (e.g., fear or anger) are those emotional programs triggered when new experiences fall short of expectations, thereby frustrating or threatening the organism's overall well-being. In general, negative emotions rapidly mobilize fight/flight defensive responses, narrow attention to the presumed source of threat (tunnel vision), communicate alarm, and prioritize tribal solidarity and related boundary-setting or boundary-defending behaviors.

In contrast, positive emotions (e.g., joy, interest, or wonder) are those emotional programs triggered when new experiences exceed expectations. Positive emotions elevate an individual's level of pleasure or enthusiasm thereby motivating sustained interest in the surrounding world. Psychologist Barbara Fredrickson notes that

> positive emotions broaden (rather than narrow) an individual's thought-action repertoire . . . this broaden-and-build model of positive emotions explains why the propensity to experience positive emotions has evolved to be a ubiquitous feature of human nature and how, in contemporary society, positive emotions might be taped to promote individual and collective well-being and health.[16]

The positive emotion that would appear to be most clearly associated with the SBNR sensibility is wonder, though joy also factors prominently in this distinctive mode of spirituality. Wonder is elicited by novel or unexpected stimuli that defy assimilation to our current understandings of the world. It is frequently triggered by things that strike us as intensely powerful, intensely real, or intensely beautiful – motivating contemplation of the putative source of such more-than-ordinary causal power. Wonder is thus often stimulated by sights of natural beauty or by the sudden recognition that life is a 'gift." Wonder widens the field of perception and attention. It heightens our interest in the object that defied immediate understanding, thereby motivating sustained engagement with our surroundings. In this way, wonder "broadens and builds" both our conceptual repertoire and our sense of connection with the world. It tends to imbue the world with an alluring quality, fostering increased openness and receptivity rather than immediate utilitarian action.

Wonder differs from other emotions in at least three important ways. First, wonder is an emotion linked with approach and affiliation rather than avoidance. Wonder is thus rare among the emotions in its functional capacity to motivate persons to venture outward for increased rapport with the environment. Second, and perhaps most importantly for this study, wonder differs from many other emotions in that it awakens our mental capacity for abstract, higher-order thought. That is, positive emotions motivate contemplation of what possibly lies at a higher or molar level of causal agency rather than motivating cognition seeking to discern causality in proximate mechanisms. Whereas most emotions narrow or focus attention to specific aspects of the environment that portend promise or threat, wonder prompts us to contemplate hypothetical or possible causal powers that are somehow behind, above, or beyond observed phenomena. Although such abstract, hypothetical contemplation rarely contributes to our immediate physical survival, it is indispensable to humanity's existence as cultural beings. SBNRs, though relatively well educated and thus capable of analytic thought, are characteristically inclined toward fantasy, magical ideation, and imaginative thought. They entertain notions of possible causal agency rather analyze events in terms of proximate, material causality. Third, wonder temporarily suspends utilitarian striving. Wonder renders us relatively passive and receptive, frequently giving rise to the sensation that we participate in a more general order of life. The experience of wonder thus often leads to forms of empathy and selfless concern quite different than would arise in a life shaped solely by the active will. Ethical theorist Martha Nussbaum pondered this fact and concluded that wonder is the emotion that most clearly enables humans to move beyond self-interest to recognize and respond to others in their own right. Wonder, she writes, is the emotion that responds

> to the pull of the object, and one might say that in it the subject is maximally aware of the value of the object, and only minimally aware, if at all, of its relationship to her own plans. That is why it is likely to issue in contemplation, rather than in any other sort of action toward the object.

Insofar as persons remain bound by ego-centered perspectives of the world, their ethical orientation is largely eudaemonistic (i.e., geared toward personal well-being as regulated by rational calculations of self-interest). Yet, "wonder, as non-eudaemonisitc as an emotion can be, helps move distant objects within the circle of a person's scheme of ends . . . seeing others as part of one's own circle of concern."[17] Nussbaum thus contends that no emotion matches wonder in its capacity to evoke true empathy or compassion. Wonder redraws our world of concern, establishing true mutuality with a wider sphere of life.

In sum, we don't fully know whether specific psychological traits predispose individuals to experiencing positive emotions or whether positive emotions create specific psychological traits. We do know, however, that the historical record clearly indicates an intimate connection between positive emotions and the SBNR sensibility.[18] This relatively higher incidence of positive emotions helps explain why individuals who might otherwise follow logical rationality to a wholly nonreligious perspective nonetheless remain "prone" to internal, subjective cognitive processes. SBNR individuals naturally and spontaneously value nonsensory intuitions about life. And, for the most part, these subjective and intuitive valuations "work" for them – getting them in touch with the unitary and relational aspects of reality that give rise to visions of peace and wholeness.

Genetics and the neurochemistry of spiritual sensibilities

Geneticist Dean Hamer proposes a very different way of understanding individual differences in spirituality. His argument is straightforward: (1) a person's sense of self is central to her or his spirituality, (2) this sense of self and its relationship to the world arises from distinctive brain processes, and

(3) variables that affect these brain processes can therefore also affect our spirituality.

Hamer successfully identified one such variable: monoamines (i.e., serotonin, dopamine, noradrenaline). Monoamines play a central role in consciousness by lending value to perceptions. Monoamines are what make us feel good, bad, or somewhere in between about other people, places, and experiences. They also control the degree to which we feel either intimately connected with our surroundings or feel distinctly separate from our surroundings. Hamer identified a very specific gene, the VMAT2 gene, that codes for the ebb and flow of monoamines and thus crucially affects how we perceive ourselves and our relationship to the surrounding world. Most important, Hamer found that individuals with one particular version of the VMAT2 gene score significantly higher on a questionnaire-based measure of self-transcendence than did individuals with a different version of that gene. Assuming that proclivity for self-transcendence is a reasonable way of conceptualizing spirituality, Hamer feels we can confidently proclaim that spirituality is hardwired in our genes.

Hamer asks us to visualize two people attempting to meditate. Both focus all their mental energy on the association area of the brain. This results in a partial shutdown of the orientation area that is mediated by the thalamus, which in turn sends signals resulting in varying degrees of mental excitement depending on the individual.

> In one individual, with one particular version of the VMAT2 gene, these signals result in only a modest alteration of monoamine signaling. The call is received, but it's not urgent. It doesn't feel important. . . . In another individual, with a different VMAT2 gene, the same signals have a more dramatic effect because they are received by a different monoamine transporter. Serotonin, dopamine, and noradrenaline rush in and out of this individual's vesicles, setting off a reverberating circuit that is accelerated by ever stronger signals from the cortex and ever weaker input to the parietal lobes. The result is a radical shift in the communication between the front and back of the brain – a shift that, in this individual, brings a profound sense of joy, fulfillment, and peace.[19]

The major point here is that spirituality is more about feelings than it is about Type 2 intellect. It is our genetic makeup that determines how spiritual we are. No book or sermon can teach us to feel more joyful or feel more intimately connected with the wider universe. We do not know God; we feel God. Our genes – and the monoamine flow they control – determine the extent.

Hamer's research is provocative. New studies will undoubtedly refine or redirect this line of inquiry. But his major point holds. Spirituality is affected by a person's sense of self (and the self's relationship to the world). This sense of self arises from very specific neurochemical and neurophysiological processes. There is genetic variance in these neurochemical and neurophysiological processes and this variance must therefore account for at least some of our individual differences when it comes to spirituality. More specifically, higher levels of neurochemicals such as dopamine and/or serotonin would help explain why individuals who might otherwise follow logical rationality to nonreligious conclusions nonetheless remain "prone" to valuing more emotional, intuitive sources of cognition.

While Hamer focused on the causal role of specific neurotransmitters in the genesis of spiritual feelings, other researchers have examined the neuro-physiological correlates of spirituality. We know, for example, that spiritual beliefs and experiences are correlated with changes in parietal lobe activity. A recent review and extension of these studies conclude

> that neural activity in the inferior parietal lobe regions is a central neu-rophysiological substrate of implicit religiousness or spirituality . . . the data suggest that fast alteration in parietal lobe functions may lead indi-viduals to experience an extended self-awareness in which the self is projected into dimensions that transcend sensorimotor contingencies of the body and more easily connect with things beyond the self.[20]

Those individuals who find themselves spiritually engaged despite not capable of affirming conventional spirituality may well be genetically pre-disposed to the kinds of neurophysiological activity that yield spiritual sen-sations. It is also likely the case that they engage in activities that alter either their neurochemistry or their neurophysiology in ways that make them "prone" to valuing subjective and intuitive cognitive processes. Among these activities might be various forms of meditation or the use of mood-altering substances.

Altered states, openness, and spiritual sensibilities

It is also clear that experiencing certain kinds of altered states of con-sciousness (e.g., meditation practices, drug-induced mystical states) is con-nected with the SBNR sensibility. SBNR individuals consume alcohol and use drugs more than their conventionally religious counterparts. We must again acknowledge some uncertainty whether specific spiritual sensibilities cause people to seek out altered states or whether the altered states engen-der SBNR sensibilities – though there is at least some evidence to prove that the latter is the more likely and typical scenario. Individuals who use psychedelics such as psilocybin, as well as lesser inebriants such as alcohol and marijuana, demonstrate sustained higher levels of spirituality.[21] That altered states have a causal effect in eliciting spirituality would seemingly be indicated by the significant neurochemical and neurophysiological changes they create which we know to constitute the psychological substrates of the SBNR sensibility. Most inebriants, from alcohol to psilocybin, accel-erate production of serotonin and/or dopamine and thus predispose indi-viduals to experiences of self-transcendence. The same is also true of many meditation practices. The very act of inducing alterations in consciousness is frequently associated with cultural settings that further render individuals "prone" to valuing cognitive styles that are simultaneously intellectually open or eclectic (thereby avoiding conventional religiosity) and placing a high value on subjective and intuitive cognitive processes (thereby avoiding wholly secular perspectives). In other words, altered states are directly connected to the cognitive processes peculiar to the SBNR sensibility.

The best-known study of altered state-born spirituality was conducted by Walter Pahnke and extended years later by Rick Doblin.[22] In the spring of 1962, Pahnke enlisted the help of twenty theology students who gathered on Good Friday at Boston University's Marsh Chapel. He provided his subjects with identical-looking capsules ninety minutes before the Good Friday service began. Half the capsules contained 30 milligrams of psilocybin. The other half contained 200 milligrams of a vitamin that cause feelings of warmth and tingling but has no effect on the mind. The subjects then attended a two-and-a-half-hour religious service consisting of organ music, prayers, and personal meditation. The subjects later filled out a 147-item questionnaire designed to measure hypothesized features of mystical experience. Nine of the ten subjects who ingested the psilocybin reported having religious experiences. Only one of the subjects who had been given a placebo reported such sensations. One of Pahnke's group leaders, psychologist Walter Clark, surmised that the miracle of Marsh Chapel was the most cogent single piece of evidence that psychedelic chemicals do, under certain circumstances, release profound religious experience. In more recent years Roland Griffiths, William Richards, and others at Johns Hopkins University have extended Pahnke's line of research by conducting several methodologically rigorous studies of psilocybin and similar substances. These studies provide empirical evidence that, at least with some individuals in some controlled conditions, substances like psilocybin can reliably trigger mystical experiences and lead to long-lasting psychological benefits. It is important to note that Griffiths and others have also shown that altered states have a causal role in producing sustained increases in the personality trait of "openness to experience" that is instrumental to the distinctive attributes of the SBNR sensibility.[23]

A surprisingly large number of the leading proponents of the SBNR sensibility have pointed to the pivotal role of chemically induced altered states in the formation of their distinctive views. William James, Huston Smith, Timothy Leary, Abraham Maslow, Ram Das, Carlos Castaneda, Aldous Huxley, and Alan Watts are but a few of the "high priests" of the unchurched American religious tradition. It is also noteworthy that a poll of more than 1,300 Americans engaged in Buddhist practice showed that 83% had taken psychedelics.

This connection between experiencing altered states and the SBNR sensibility is easy to understand. Even a substance as seemingly innocuous as caffeine has historically triggered exhilaration, joy, and a "proneness" to subjective and intuitive cognitive processes. Caffeine is really an indirect stimulant. It binds to cells in the brain in such a way as to block the effect of adenosine, a chemical that ordinarily has a quieting effect on the brain. By blocking the quieting effect of adenosine, caffeine impairs the brain's ability to keep its own excitatory neurotransmitters in check. Caffeine consequently clears the way for the brain's own stimulants – neurotransmitters such as glutamate, dopamine, and the endorphins – to do their job without interference. Coffee drinkers thus "get wired" only to the extent that their own natural excitatory neurotransmitters produce exhilarating signals. Humans vary in this regard. For those susceptible to such excitation, coffee becomes an elixir quite capable of producing sensations ripe with spiritual salience. By altering the subject–object structure of ordinary experience, caffeinated beverages usher us temporarily into a world of richer connections.

From the coffeehouses that surfaced during the 1950s in New York's Greenwich Village to those that emerged during the 1960s in San Francisco's North Beach or Haight-Ashbury districts, American coffeehouses have been at the vanguard of the nation's drift toward seeker-style spirituality. It is not coincidental that a good many of the nation's coffeehouses have included bookshelves filled with texts celebrating Eastern religions, occult practices, and ecologically sensitive worldviews. Even chain bookstores such as Barnes and Noble provide locations where people browse the large New Age book collections while drinking strong coffee beverages. Such locations provide settings where individuals can gather and, even if they never directly engage others, realize that they belong to a much larger community of like-minded seekers.

Marijuana has proved an even more direct conduit to experimental spirituality. Although marijuana lacks the hallucinatory or vision-giving powers of the major hallucinogens, it can be used more casually and more frequently. Smoking marijuana creates unique social settings that allow young cultural rebel to bond with a countercultural community centered around the spiritual goal of personal growth or individuation (even at the expense of traditional cultural values). A great deal of this experience has to do with socialization. Even the "marijuana high" is to some extent a learned feeling state. Peers typically direct newcomers' attention to specific kinds of sensations, feelings, and attitudes. Experienced users often report an almost childlike openness to inner sensations. The marijuana high is thus thought to be helping them cut through social conditioning and get in touch with themselves and with the deeper currents of nature. In this way marijuana use deepens a person's appreciation of interiority and helps establish the ideal of religion as an inner-directed mystical pursuit.

The principal lesson most marijuana users attribute to their altered state is the perception that reality can be viewed from more than one perspective. While under the influence of marijuana attention fluctuates rapidly. Users often report that they find themselves connecting the same sensory data to two or more different sets of concepts. This gives them the sensation that there is not just one reality but several realities, depending on one's current frame of mind. These multiple associations give the experience a highly symbolic character. Many users also conclude that life contains multiple dimensions that are ordinarily obscured from human awareness. While the waking state of consciousness attends to the physical dimension, there are nonetheless other levels of reality that are best discerned in altered states of consciousness, and these levels yield valuable insights into life's intrinsic beauty and spiritual purpose.

Marijuana thus predisposes users to the alternative conceptions we associate with seeker or quest spirituality. Users learn through firsthand experience that religious and cultural authorities have extremely limited perspectives on life. The dire warnings about the moral evil of marijuana use proved wrong. Nor can users any longer proclaim one single truth. Their interest in alternative perspectives often takes them to mystical philosophies advocated by counterculture heroes such as Alan Watts, Aldous Huxley, William James, Carl Jung, Carlos Castaneda, Zen Buddhism, or Vedanta Hinduism. These and other exotic philosophies comport well with the physiological contours of marijuana smoking. All provide a verbal framework for concluding that authentic religion has nothing to do with church attendance or adherence to ancient scriptures but instead comes down to creating one's own original relationship to the universe.

Altered states can be acquired in other ways, too – especially through various meditation practices. From yoga to mindfulness, seeker spirituality is rife with practices that relax muscles, release serenity-producing neurotransmitters, or produce subtle changes in brain functioning. Many of these practices produce novel sensations – mobilizing curiosity and potentially evoking the perceptual and cognitive changes motivated by the emotions of joy and wonder. They also alter activity in brain regions such as the temporoparietal junction or the inferior parietal cortex that alters a person's sense of self. As a consequence, meditation practices afford an experience that could foster intuitive feelings of an extended self, including feelings of a connection with nature and other individuals at large or a sense of relationship with a transcendent power.

Minds of their own

There are, then, distinct psychological substrates of the SBNR sensibility. The SBNR orientation to life is characterized by relatively high levels of openness to experience, lower levels of agreeableness and conscientiousness (either the cause or the consequence of the fact that they are somewhat independent and less motivated to conform to the group), no indications of maladaptive narcissism, less authoritarian, and yet "prone" to intuitive and subjective valuations. These intuitive and subjective valuations include viewing the mind being separate from the body, attributing humanlike intentionality to nonhuman objects, or readily attributing mental states to others SBNR individuals are, finally, also more likely than either their nonreligious or conventionally religious counterparts to be characterized by cognitive tendencies toward transpersonal identification, self-forgetfulness, fantasy-proneness, belief in magical powers, and reliance on both personal intuitions and subjective experience. Prone to cognitive outlooks structured by positive emotions, identifiable neurochemistry, and altered states of consciousness, SBNR individuals possess psychological traits that empirically distinguish them from those who identify as nonreligious or conventionally religious.

Notes

1 Pew Research Center, "America's Changing Religious Landscape," Online report, May 12, 2015, 3.
2 See Daniel Batson, *Religion and the Individual* (New York: Oxford University Press, 1982) and Robert Wuthnow, *After Heaven: Spirituality in America Since the 1950s* (Berkeley: University of California Press, 1998). Conceptual and historical overviews of the "Spiritual But Not Religious" outlook can be found in Brian Zinnbauer et al., "Religion and Spirituality: Unfuzzying the Fuzzy," *Journal for the Scientific Study of Religion* 36 (1997): 549–64 and Robert C. Fuller, *Spiritual, But Not Religious: Understanding Unchurched America* (New York: Oxford University Press, 2001). The best research demonstrating that SBNR represents a distinct and empirically defined cluster of personality/cognitive traits is Gerard Saucier and Kararzyna Skrzypinska, "Spiritual But Not Religious? Evidence for Two Independent Dimensions," *Journal of Personality* 74 (2006): 1257–91.
3 Nancy Ammerman, "Spiritual But Not Religious? Beyond Binary Choices in the Study of Religion," *Journal for the Scientific Study of Religion* 52(2013): 275.
4 Stephen Pinker, *How the Mind Works* (New York: W. W. Norton, 1997), 21.
5 An overview of the biological substrates of religion can be found in Robert C. Fuller, *Spirituality in the Flesh: Biological Sources of Religious Experience* (New York: Oxford University Press, 2008). The best explanations of the cognitive substrates of religion are Pascal Boyer, *Religion Explained: The Evolutionary Origins of Religious Thought* (New York: Basic Books, 2001); Justin Barrett, *Why Would Anyone Believe in God? Cognitive Science of Religion* (Walnut Creek, CA: Alta Mira Press, 2004); and Paul Bloom, "Religion Is Natural," *Developmental Science* 10 (2007): 147–51. A comprehensive overview of religion's connection with humanity's genetically evolved mechanisms guiding prosocial behavior is Ara Norenzayan et al., "The Cultural Evolution of Prosocial Religions," *Behavioral and Brain Sciences*, Online (December 2015). The best explanation of the role of attachment systems in human religiosity is Lee Kirkpatrick, *Attachment, Evolution, and the Psychology of Religion* (New York: Guilford, 2005).
6 Robert N. McCauley, *Why Religion Is Natural, and Science Is Not* (New York: Oxford University Press, 2011).
7 Bob Altemeyer and Bruce Hunsberer, "Authoritarianism, Religious Fundamentalism, Quest, and Prejudice," *International Journal for the Psychology of Religion* 2 (1992): 113–33; Bruce Hunsberger, "Religion and Prejudice: The Role of Religious Fundamentalism, Quest, and Right Wing Authoritarianism," *Journal of Social Issues* 51 (1995): 113–29; and K. Mayor et al., "Religion, Prejudice, and Authoritarianism: Is RWA a Boon or Bane to the Psychology of Religion?," *Journal for the Scientific Study of Religion* 50 (2011): 22–43.

8 For the analyses of the relationship between religion and environmental stress see John Jost et al., "Political Conservatism as Motivated Social Cognition," *Psychological Bulletin* 129 (2003): 108–25. See also Gregory Paul, "The Chronic Dependence of Popular Religiosity Upon Dysfunctional Psychosociological Conditions," *Evolutionary Psychology* 7 (2009): 398–441. A succinct argument that religion's principal function is "brain soothing" can be found in Michael McGuire and Lionel Tiger, "The Brain and Religious Adaptations," in *The Biology of Religious Behavior*, ed. Jay Feierman (Santa Clara, CA: Praeger, 2009), 125–37.

9 See Saucier and Skrzypinska, "Spiritual But Not Religious?" See also the analysis of links between religion and Big Five traits in David Schmitt and Robert C. Fuller, "On the Varieties of Sexual Experience: A Cross-Cultural Exploration of the Links Between Religiosity and Human Mating Strategies," *Psychology of Religion and Spirituality* (December 2015) and Jochen E. Gebauer et al., "Big Two Personality and Religiosity Across Cultures: Communals as Religious Conformists and Agentics as Religious Contrarians," *Social Psychological and Personality Science* 4 (2013): 21–30.

10 Among the most widely cited works linking SBNR individuals to a cultural drift toward narcissism were Paul Pruyser, "Narcissism in Contemporary Religion," *Journal of Pastoral Care* 32 (1978): 219–31; Christopher Lasch, *The Culture of Narcissism: American Life in an Age of Diminishing Expectations* (New York: Norton, 1979); Robert Bellah et al., *Habits of the Heart: Individualism and Commitment in American Life* (Berkeley: University of California Press, 1984).

11 Anthony Hermann and Robert Fuller, "Trait Narcissism and Contemporary Religious Trends," *Archive for the Psychology of Religion* (2017): 99–117. We might note that Hermann and Fuller found that individuals inclined to mystical forms of spirituality were slightly higher in the NPI subscale of vanity.

12 Studies that examine the relationship between religion and intelligence include S. Bertsch and B. Pesta, "The Wonderlic Personnel Test and Elementary Cognitive Tasks as Predictors of Religious Sectarianism, Scriptural Acceptance, and Religious Questioning," *Intelligence* 37 (2009): 231–7; C. Reeve, "Expanding the G-Nexus Further Regarding the Relations Among National IQ, Religiosity, and National Health Outcomes," *Intelligence* 37 (2009): 495–505; G. Lewis, S. Ritchie and T. Bates, "The Relationship Between Intelligence and Multiple Domains of Religious Belief," *Intelligence* 39 (2011): 468–72. Studies examining the inverse relationship between analytic cognitive style and religiosity include Gordon Pennycook et al., "Analytic Cognitive Style Predicts Religious and Paranormal Belief," *Cognition* 123 (2012): 335–46; M. Zuckerman et al., "The Relation Between Intelligence and Religiosity: A Meta-Analysis and Some Proposed Explanations," *Personality and Social Psychology Review* 17 (2013): 325–54; W. Gervais and A. Norenzayan, "Analytic Thinking Promotes Religious Disbelief," *Science Magazine* 336 (2012): 493–6.

13 Pennycook, "Analytic Cognitive Style Predicts Religious and Paranormal Belief," 336.

14 See Hasan Bahcekapili and Onurcan Yilmax, "The Relation Between Different Types of Religiosity and Analytic Cognitive Style," *Personality and Individual Differences* 117 (2017): 267–72.

15 See Saucier and Skrzypinska, "Spiritual But Not Religious?" Also see A. Willard and A. Norenzayan, "Spiritual But Not Religious: Cognition, Schizotypy, and Conversion in Alternative Beliefs," *Cognition* 165 (2017): 137–46.

16 Barbara Frederickson, "What Good Are Positive Emotions?" *Review of General Psychology* 2 (1996): 311. The best overall analyses of the link between religion and emotion are Robert C. Fuller, *The Body of Faith* (Chicago: University of

Chicago Press, 2013), 38–43, 84–98 and *Religion and Emotion*, ed. John Corrigan (New York: Oxford University Press, 2004).

17 Martha Nussbaum, *Upheavals of Thought: The Intelligence of Emotions* (Cambridge: Cambridge University Press, 2001), 54, 57. A comprehensive look at the role of wonder in human spirituality can be found in Robert C. Fuller, *Wonder: From Emotion to Spirituality* (Chapel Hill: University of North Carolina Press, 2006).

18 The link between positive emotions and openness is examined in Paul Silvia et al., "Openness to Experience and Awe in Response to Nature and Music: Personality and Profound Aesthetic Experiences," *Psychology of Aesthetics, Creativity, and the Arts* 9, no. 4 (2015): 376–84. For the link between positive emotions and spirituality see Bruce Smith et al., "Spirituality, Resilience, and Positive Emotions," *The Oxford Handbook of Psychology and Spirituality*, ed. Lisa Miller (New York: Oxford University Press, 2012), 437–54.

19 Dean Hamer, *The God Gene: How Faith Is Hardwired in Our Genes* (New York: Doubleday, 2004).

20 See Andrew Newberg et al., "The Neural Basis of the Complex Mental Task of Meditation: Neurotransmitter and Neurochemical Considerations," *Medical Hypotheses* 61 (2003): 282–91. Also see B. Tomasino et al., "Meditation-Related Activations Are Modulated by the Practices Needed to Obtain It and by the Expertise: An ALE Meta-Analysis Study," *Frontiers in Human Neuroscience* 6 (2013): 346, and C. Crescentini et al., "Neurophysiological and Personological Aspects of Spirituality," in *Being Called: Scientific Secular, and Sacred Perspectives*, ed. David Yaden, Theo McCall and J. Harold Ellens (Santa Barbara, CA: Praeger, 2015), 47–65.

21 The higher incidence of alcohol and drug use among SBNR individuals is documented in Saucier and Skrzypinska. Also, for studies of the relationship between spirituality and altered states, see R. Doblin, "Pahnke's "Good Friday Experiment": A Long-Term Follow-Up and Methodological Critique," *Journal of Transpersonal Psychology* 23 (1991): 1–28; Katherine A. MacLean et al., "Mystical Experiences Occasioned by the Hallucinogen Psilocybin Lead to Increases in the Personality Domain of Openness," *Journal of Psychopharmacology* 25 (2011): 1453–61.

22 See Walter Pahnke, "Drugs and Mysticism," *International Journal of Parapsychology* 8 (1966): 295–314.

23 See MacLean et al., "Mystical-Type Experiences Occasioned by Psilocybin Mediate the Attribution of Personal Meaning and Spiritual Significance 14 Months Later," *Journal of Psychopharmacology* 22 (2008): 621–32; and R. Griffiths et al., "Psilocybin Can Occasion Mystical Experiences Having Substantial and Sustained Personal Meaning and Spiritual Significance," *Psychopharmacology* 187 (2006): 268–322.

References

Ammerman, Nancy. "Spiritual But Not Religious? Beyond Binary Choices in the Study of Religion." *Journal for the Scientific Study of Religion* 52, no. 2 (2013): 258–78.

Bahcekapili, Hasan and Onurcan Yilmax. "The Relation Between Different Types of Religiosity and Analytic Cognitive Style." *Personality and Individual Differences* 117 (2017): 267–72.

Batson, Daniel. *Religion and the Individual*. New York: Oxford University Press, 1982.

Frederickson, Barbara. "What Good Are Positive Emotions?" *Review of General Psychology* 2 (1996): 300–19.

Fuller, Robert C. *Stairways to Heaven: Drugs in American Religious History*. Boulder, CO: Westview Press, 2000.

———. *Spiritual, But Not Religious: Understanding Unchurched America*. New York: Oxford University Press, 2001.

———. *Wonder: From Emotion to Spirituality*. Chapel Hill, NC: University of North Carolina Press, 2006.

———. *Spirituality in the Flesh*. New York: Oxford University Press, 2008.

Hamer, Dean. *The God Gene: How Faith Is Hardwired in Our Genes*. New York: Doubleday, 2004.

Hermann, Anthony and Robert C. Fuller. "Trait Narcissism and Contemporary Religious Trends." *Archive for the Psychology of Religion* (2017): 99–117.

Jost, John, Jack Glaser, Arie W. Kruglanski and Frank J. Sulloway. "Political Conservatism as Motivated Social Cognition." *Psychological Bulletin* 129 (2003): 108–25.

MacLean, Katherine A., Matthew W. Johnson and Roland R. Griffiths. "Mystical Experiences Occasioned by the Hallucinogen Psilocybin Lead to Increases in the Personality Domain of Openness." *Journal of Psychopharmacology* 25(2011): 1453–61.

McCauley, Robert N. *Why Religion Is Natural, and Science Is Not*. New York: Oxford University Press, 2011.

Newberg, Andrew and J. Iverson. "The Neural Basis of the Complex Mental Task of Meditation: Neurotransmitter and Neurochemical Considerations." *Medical Hypotheses* 61 (2003): 282–91.

Nussbaum, Martha. *Upheavals of Thought: The Intelligence of Emotions*. Cambridge: Cambridge University Press, 2001.

Panke, Walter. "Drugs and Mysticism." *International Journal of Parapsychology* 8 (1966): 295–314.

Pennycook, Gordon, J.A. Cheyne, P. Seli, D.J. Koehler and J.A. Fugelsang. "Analytic Cognitive Style Predicts Religious and Paranormal Belief." *Cognition* 123 (2012): 335–46.

Pinker, Stephen. *How the Mind Works*. New York: W. W. Norton, 1997.

Saucier, Gerard and Katarzyna Skrzypinska. "Spiritual But Not Religious? Evidence for Two Independent Dimensions." *Journal of Personality* 74 (2006): 1257–91.

Schmidt, Eric. *Restless Souls: The Making of American Spirituality*. San Francisco, CA: Harper, 2005.

Silvia, Paul, K. Fayn, E.C. Nusbaum and R.E. Beaty. "Openness to Experience and Awe in Response to Nature and Music: Personality and Profound Aesthetic Experiences." *Psychology of Aesthetics, Creativity, and the Arts* 9, no. 4 (2015): 376–84.

Smith, Bruce, J.A. Ortiz, K.T. Wiggins, J.F. Bernard and J. Dalen. "Spirituality, Resilience, and Positive Emotions." In *The Oxford Handbook of Psychology and Spirituality*, 437–54. Edited by Lisa Miller. New York: Oxford University Press, 2012.

Willard, Alyana and Ara Norenzayan. "Spiritual But Not Religious: Cognition, Schizotypy, and Conversion in Alternative Beliefs." *Cognition* 165 (2017): 137–46.

Wuthnow, Robert. *After Heaven: Spirituality in America Since the 1950s*. Berkeley, CA: University of California Press, 1998.

Zinnbauer, Brian and Kenneth Pargament. "Religiousness and Spirituality." In *Handbook of the Psychology of Religion and Spirituality*, 21–42. Edited by Raymond Paloutzian and Crystal L. Park. New York: Guilford Press, 2005.

Zinnbauer, Brian and Kenneth Pargament, Brenda Cole, Mark S. Rye, Eric M. Butter, Timothy G. Belavich, Kathleen M. Hipp, Allie B. Scott and Jill L. Kadar. "Religion and Spirituality: Unfuzzying the Fuzzy." *Journal for the Scientific Study of Religion* 36 (1997): 549–64.

7 Belief without borders

Inside the minds of the Spiritual but Not Religious

Linda Mercadante

Salad-bar spiritualists. Narcissistic commitment-phobes. Anti-dogma experience seekers. Victims of religious abuse. Rich white women in expensive yoga outfits. These are some of the stereotypes I've heard about those nonreligious "nones" who self-identify as "Spiritual but Not Religious" (SBNR). Having been an SBNR myself, and knowing many SBNRs for years, I have long felt these hyperbolic labels do an injustice to the thoughtful, determined spiritual questers that SBNRs often can be. To dispel the stereotypes, SBNRs need to speak in their own voices and be heard. They deserve our attention because they are rapidly contributing to a profound change in the spiritual narrative of the United States.

Today nones make up nearly a quarter of the U.S. population, and the numbers continue to rise dramatically.[1] While there have always been non-religious people in the United States, their numbers were estimated at only about 3% to 5% until a discernable increase in nones was recognized as a result of what Robert Putnam in *American Grace* calls "the Long Sixties."[2] The current growth spurt began during the late 1980s, becoming more evident by the 1990s. Each year during the 1990s, 1.3 million U.S. adults became nones. Between 1990 and 2001, this group more than doubled, going from 14.3 million to 29.4 million. Between 2008 and 2012, the percentage jumped another 3.2%.[3]

At first there was only a little scientific research on this trend.[4] But attention to the reality of documentable decline in religious affiliation began to grow by the 2000s as sociologists, religious leaders, and journalists realized this phenomenon was not going away. Quantitative research and statistical analysis have been the major tools used to chart this,[5] but until recently very little qualitative work had been done.[6] Surveys are not limited to specialists. More popular media outlets such as *Newsweek* and *Parade* have also jumped in.[7] Whether simply charting, celebrating, or worrying about these numbers, the various voices have agreed on some core insights about nones. These include an anti-institutional bent, changes in commitment styles, increasing individualism, secularization, and other features which reflect a globalized, post-modern world.[8]

It is noteworthy that during this same period the number of Christian evangelicals rose as well. Putnam explains that the "Long Sixties" was followed by an "aftershock" that resulted in the rise of conservative Christianity, which was a reaction to the loosened mores of the 1960s.[9] Charles Taylor in *A Secular Age* attributes this seeming resurgence of religion as an aspiration to return America to its theistic roots and being "one nation under God."[10] In fact, it was tempting at first to not take the rise in nones seriously, thinking instead that the rise in evangelicalism heralded a religious revival. But this was no simple increase in religious devotion. For, under the surface, conservative Christians began distancing themselves from their apolitical heritage as they were increasingly being courted by and drawn into right-wing politics.[11]

Both sides of the response to the Long Sixties continues still. There are now more nones in the United States than mainline Protestants. In addition, the 9/11 attacks and increasing fears of global terrorism have caused many people not only to reject religion but also to identify it with extremism. This negative impression has been buttressed by the results of the 2016 presidential election when 81% of white Evangelical Christians voted for a reactionary regime determined to roll back progressive political gains. Thus, many now not only reject religion but also identify American Christianity with an exclusivist hyper-nationalism that puts "America first," rather than the inclusive, justice-, and mercy-inspired faith that large numbers of contemporary Christian practitioners still affirm. As a result, it seems likely that the numbers of nones will continue to rapidly increase rather than subsiding or stabilizing.

Spirituality versus religion?

It is hard to gauge accurately just what percentage of nones falls into the SBNR category, but it appears to be nearly 40%. This percentage only includes those who self-identify as SBNRS. The percentage rises dramatically when those are included who believe in a higher power, feel a deep connection with nature and the earth, and pray.[12] While stereotypes often abound on the more popular level,[13] scholars, too, have identified SBNRs' spiritual seeking as often fickle, staying on the surface, intent on "detraditioning," showing a "wannabe" attitude toward non-Western or folk cultures, and displaying a dramatic amount of religious illiteracy.[14] Dismissive or ironic comments mix with catastrophic predictions about the potential societal effects of the surge in nones and SBNRs. Sometimes there is instead a celebratory insistence that this trend signals the end of organized religion.

But few commentators consider theology as an important aspect of this phenomenon. Even when the topic of belief does come up occasionally, there is often an assumption that SBNR beliefs are disorganized and eclectic, with very little agreement across the group. Others speculate that the SBNR ethos shows that religious "dogmatism" (a negative code word for belief) has come to an end.[15] On the surface, the explanation for divorcing spirituality from religion is fairly standard among SBNRs. Spirituality is said to be individual, personal, holistic, and malleable while religion is considered institutional, dogmatic, moralistic, and nonessential to spiritual growth.

These surface distinctions are inadequate, however, for there is much functional overlap between spirituality and religion. Each consists of four basic components: (1) belief in some kind of larger reality or transcendent force, (2) desire to connect with this force, (3) rituals and practices that aid in this connection, and (4) behaviors that foster or demonstrate that connection. But even when this overlap is recognized, few if any commentators give a crucial place to belief. Some, such as Nancy Tatom Ammerman, suggest instead that the SBNR separation of spirituality from religion is largely a "boundary-maintaining discourse" rather than an actual rejection of the behaviors often considered "religious." Even in this cogent analysis, however, belief does not play a central role except to be identified with religion and rejected by SBNRs as "implausible."[16] Others, such as Meredith B. McGuire, insist that everyday behavior is being re-sacralized as religion bleeds out of its artificial confines within organizations.[17]

I agree that the SBNR discourse is a boundary-setting activity, a rejection of the sacred/secular dichotomy, a recognition that spirituality infuses everyday life, and clearly a weakening of the bonds of religion. But there is more than that in the SBNR ethos. My research reveals that belief – rather than being ancillary or unimportant – is a critical aspect of the SBNR ethos and cannot be taken out of the equation. This boundary-setting rhetoric has a purpose beyond the re-sacralization of everyday life. Instead, it is one that specifically allows its participants to carve out new theological territory. Charting this new territory is critical because it will inevitably affect all of us, just as the dominant Protestant ethos has done for centuries in the United States.

Although there is never a one-to-one correspondence between belief and behavior, the two are invariably and synergistically linked. Therefore, before speculating what effects the SBNR rhetoric might have on society, we need to first understand the new theological territory being carved out. For me the critical question is, What does a contemporary spiritual thought-world or even a "belief system" look like as a dominant theology recedes? As a former journalist, and now a scholar specializing in theology, culture, and spiritual narrative, I felt the need to contribute to the discourse around the burgeoning of nones. The SBNR segment of nones is particularly important because these people are the ones intentionally creating new theological territory.

Method

To study this, I constructed a qualitative research project, consisting of an open-ended semistructured interview format. To find volunteers, I used a convenience and a snowball sampling method. Thanks to being selected as Henry Luce III Fellow in Theology, as well as other grant support, I was able to conduct research all over North America, including both the United States and Canada. I also did some forays into Mexico and the United Kingdom. The result is a book, *Belief without Borders: Inside the Minds of the Spiritual but not Religious.*[18]

Interviewees were discovered in a variety of ways. I visited many types of retreat centers, yoga classes, bookstores, coffeehouses, sweat lodges, Reiki and energy-work centers, meditation classes, public presentations by prominent gurus, and any other logical venues. I posted flyers, hosted a blog, used social media, and was invited to advertise on selected email lists. It was not difficult to find volunteers. When visiting relevant venues, I would announce I was looking for SBNRs to interview and invariably several people would raise both hands in a kind of victory salute and say excitedly "That's me!"

I interviewed volunteers from four main age groups: the silent generation, baby boomers, gen Xers, and millennials. I found both men and women, LGBTQ participants, some racial and ethnic diversity, and people from both coasts as well as the Midwest and Canada. In this pool I had theists, nontheists, agnostics, and even some atheists. The main criteria to participate in the study were, first, that a potential interviewee should resonate with and/or self-identify as SBNR and, second, that they should be willing to discuss their spiritual journey, views, and beliefs. As word spread in the venues and locations I visited, I was inundated with requests to participate. As a result, I had hundreds of informal conversations and conducted one hundred structured interviews.

I explained to each volunteer that we would cover four major themes in the interview: transcendence, human nature, community, and afterlife. I chose these areas because they seemed topics on which most people might speculate, at least those in a Western culture. That is, (1) Is there a power greater than myself? (2) What does it mean to be human? (3) Do we need community to flourish spiritually or is this essentially an individual effort? and, finally, (4) What if anything will happen to humans after death? Of course, as a Protestant theologian, these themes come naturally to me and can be cross-referenced with the "theological loci" of (1) God, (2) theological anthropology, (3) ecclesiology, and (4) eschatology. But I felt no need to apologize for using these "big questions" as a framework since we live in a Western society where the echoes of these theological themes still reverberate.

From the outset, I was clear in identifying myself as not only a researcher but also a professor of theology in a United Methodist seminary and an ordained Presbyterian minister. I was also clear that I was not there to teach, preach, or counsel but instead was deeply interested in them, especially their spiritual journeys and beliefs. I found no hostility to my close connection with religion and very little evidence that SBNRs care a great deal about spiritual "practice" and very little about belief. In fact, no one balked at being asked about their beliefs. Nor did anyone claim that their beliefs were uninvolved in their spiritual journeys. No one argued that in turning away from "dogma" they refrained from thinking about these things. Nor did anyone claim that having beliefs would impede their spiritual practice. Indeed, few volunteers seemed unclear about what these themes meant, and no one objected to this organizing schema. Instead, people were deeply interested in these topics and grateful to be asked their thoughts on them. Many claimed that this was the first opportunity anyone had given them to talk freely on these topics.

An exploration of prior religious background, or lack of it, was part of the interview. The older interviewees often had some or even extensive exposure to religion, but this exposure became less common among the younger interviewees. A significant percentage of interviewees of all ages had either sporadic or very little experience of organized religion. When I asked "How was spirituality expressed in the environment you grew up in?" many answered simply "It wasn't." Nevertheless, interviewees seemed hungry to talk about their spiritual journeys and ideas. The interview lasted up to two hours, and usually it could have gone on much longer. Although I assured them that their identities would be kept anonymous, many were disappointed by this legal requirement. Most interviewees were not ashamed but proud of their new spiritual paths and very much wanted their stories to be made public.

The interviews were recorded, transcribed, and then inputted into a software program specifically for qualitative research (NVivo). The open-ended yet structured interview format enabled me to compare the interviewees' reflections within discreet areas. I systematically analyzed and organized them, looking for main themes, subthemes, and linked categories. I did not set out to prove a correlation between religious background and current beliefs; neither did I set out to simply generate "thick descriptions" of interviewee stories. Instead, I wanted to discover if there are some recurrent belief patterns that would be recognized by other SBNRs, both affiliated and non-affiliated.

All the interviewees seemed eager to give their reasons for avoiding or withdrawing from organized religion. It is highly significant that "religious distress" did not emerge as a main motivator. I identify "religious distress" as being seriously hurt by organized religion in some tangible way, whether physically, emotionally, or relationally. This paucity of evidence held even for those who had been involved in organized religion as children and young adults. This finding challenges the reason many religious leaders give for the increase in nones. Because I had heard this reasoning so frequently in gatherings of liberal clergy, I was ready to hear tales of abuse, rejection, hurt feelings or even violence. Although I did not solicit horror stories, for that would be leading rather than listening, I nevertheless was prepared for it. But there was little of it. In fact, many interviewees remembered their religious exposure fondly. Even so, many felt compelled to leave or avoid organized religion. Some of their reasons were social and political. Given the changing political climate, they now identified organized religion with repression, conservativism, and backwardness. Not surprisingly, virtually all of them were progressive and liberal in their social and political views.

But the most important reason for leaving or avoiding organized religion had not to do with abuse or politics but with belief. Many said that they could not support some of the beliefs they identified with organized religion, in particular Christianity. For those previously involved in organized religion, theology was so important to them that when they realized they did not agree with one or more official teachings, they felt "honor-bound" to leave. Whether or not they had been previously involved in religion, practically all my conversation partners felt they had "outgrown" the need for religion. They routinely considered religion nonessential, unimportant, or a practice that would thwart their spiritual growth.

But there was often more to it than that. Many felt it was more mature to give up former religious beliefs – such as belief in a personal God or in heaven – even if they still felt emotionally attached to them. Some felt guilty or even weak for not being able to successfully clear these beliefs from their minds. Others felt liberated from old ideas and free to pursue their spiritual explorations anywhere they chose. Rather than rejecting belief, interviewees saw the constructing of new theological territory as a crucial part of their spiritual journey.

Types of interviewees

When I speak with religious adherents about the rise in nones, it is sometimes suggested that such people are self-indulgent, lazy, or self-absorbed. Common comments are "They just don't want to give up their Sunday mornings," or "They don't want to commit," or "They just want it to be all about themselves." While there is always some of this in any human behavior, I did not find that to be especially the case with the interviewees. None of them seemed particularly amoral, hedonistic, or any more narcissistic or self-absorbed than the average American. In fact, many of them were quite self-disciplined especially in the areas of diet, exercise, and spiritual practice. They were often spending much time and money on their spiritual explorations, sometimes even building their lives around it. Also, against the hopes of religious leaders who often assume all SBNRs are "seekers," I found few of them actually looking to settle down in a long-lasting spiritual home. In fact, not everyone was equally committed to the process of honing an SBNR identity. Instead, the ways they identified with and practiced being SBNR could be arranged along a continuum.

I distinguished five types of SBNRs: "Dissenters" had a bone to pick with religion, finding certain beliefs or practices not to their liking anymore. Others simply had drifted away. This group represented a small percentage of my pool, and they were often the older cohorts. The next group, and by far the largest, I called the "casuals." They took spirituality on an "as-needed" basis, adopting and discarding practices as they served or stopped serving their personal needs. The third group I labeled "spiritual explorers." These were the spiritual tourists of the pool, trying new practices, enjoying them, and then moving on to the next thing. They had no intention of settling down anywhere. They represented the second-largest percentage of the pool. The fourth group I labeled "seekers." These SBNRs were actually looking for a spiritual home and were willing to commit if the right one came along. They were a small percentage, about equivalent to the "dissenters." Finally, I discovered a few I called "immigrants." These were SBNRs who had chosen a new tradition very different from their native one, if they had one. This was the smallest group and – like actual geographic immigrants – most I met were working hard to adjust to their new spiritual home but not always successfully.

Beliefs rejected

As stated earlier, many had broken with or avoided organized religion because they disagreed with official teachings. Most felt that if they disagreed with one important tenet they should leave to preserve their integrity. Yet this form of integrity did not hold for their spirituality. Instead, many were proud to call themselves hybrid or syncretistic in beliefs, on the order of the Alcoholics Anonymous motto "Take what you like and leave the rest." One woman said, "I'm a Druid-Celtic-Native American-Judeo-Christian." What was more striking, from a theological perspective, was the significant convergence of the theological positions they chose to reject and those they chose to accept.

Interviewees were nearly unilateral in rejecting certain positions they identified with organized religion, particularly Christianity. For example, all of them rejected "exclusivism," that is, the "my way or the highway" theology that declares that some people are "in," (in God's good graces, saved, favored, destined for heaven, etc.) and others out (i.e., condemned by or out of relationship with God, rejected, damned, destined for hell, etc.). Few seemed aware that this is hardly a unilateral position within contemporary Christianity. They were unacquainted with the fact that there exist many different theological streams within this religion, many of which stress individual choice (a more "Pelagian," "Arminian," or free-choice model) or a combination of divine and human intentionality. Instead, the majority of interviewees believed that all Christianity promoted "double predestination," meaning some are destined for heaven and others for hell. Not only was this belief seen as unfair; it was also seen as unrealistic given the strong cultural belief in "second chances." They felt Christianity presented a capricious, arbitrary, or inscrutable God, and they thoroughly rejected this God.

But interviewees went further with this rejection. They did not simply posit a loving, accepting or fair God, or perhaps a more "feminine," "soft," or motherly God (even though using gendered terms for God is simply metaphorical, not literal). Only a few were aware that for decades within progressive elements of Christianity there has been a movement to present a more "feminine" divine image that might empower women and lessen sexism. Although some interviewees did use "feminine" metaphors for the sacred, it is doubtful that their knowing about this usage within religious circles would encourage them to reconsider organized religion. They were not simply looking for a gentler, kinder, more "feminine," and less overbearing God. Simply putting God in a dress just wasn't going to do it.

Instead, God was thrown totally out of the picture. In fact, nearly all the interviewees hesitated or completely avoided using the word *God*. In addition, almost all of them rejected any kind of transcendent deity, even if conceived in nonpatriarchal terms. Transcendence of a "vertical" sort was almost entirely closed off for them. Thus, the vast majority pulled away from any kind of sacred force which was intentional, self-conscious, personal, involved, and/or capable of intervening from beyond the immanent frame. Many felt this kind of a belief was immature and superstitious. Most felt it was more adult to give up the hope of a personal, caring God, seeing it as a vestige of humanity's childhood. As one interviewee put it, "I don't have to believe in some clown in the sky to make my life complete or to give me help."

On another note, all rejected the idea of "sin." The word itself particularly rankled them. They especially hated the idea of original sin, misinterpreting it as God creating humans bad and then punishing them for it. Corollary to that, most rejected traditional views on the afterlife, in particular traditional notions of heaven and hell. Hell was easy to give up because they saw it as an entirely unfair arrangement since everyone should be given another chance. As for heaven, they saw it as some kind of boring holding pattern, with angels sitting on clouds bound to do nothing but meet the demands of a narcissistic God who just wanted to be praised all the time.

Even though they weren't always pleased with giving up the idea of a happy place after death, most felt this was the mature position to take, even if it came at some psychological cost. And, of course, all of them rejected the need for organized religion. Most felt it would stifle spiritual growth. A few admitted that these institutions did often help promote morality in society and/or help the poor and marginalized. But nearly all felt they themselves did not need the sanctions or rewards offered by religion to keep believers "in line," and they felt they could do good without belonging to an organization.

Although there was some fine-tuning of these rejections among various interviewees, these were key areas where interviewees agreed to disagree with Western religion. In fact, I could have taken an unemployed factory worker interviewee from rural Ohio and sat him down with a white middle-class yoga teacher interviewee from Boulder, Colorado, and – although they would be quite different socioeconomically and educationally – they would find an amazing number of themes to agree on, especially those they were rejecting. These findings confirm Charles Taylor's contention that many today live within the "immanent frame."[19] They clearly have ruled certain things out of their believability framework.

Beliefs proposed

Transcendence

Rejection of certain beliefs was not the whole story, however. The interviewees also had beliefs that they affirmed and that cohered across the group in some important ways. It is no surprise that they rejected the traditional stereotype of a bossy old white man in the sky and were determined to live within the "immanent frame." Yet almost all insisted that they nevertheless "believed in something." For them, transcendence – the idea that there is a sacred dimension that is larger than your self – was "horizontal." Many affirmed that divinity resided solely within. Some went so far as to confidently state, "I am God."

However, this "immanence" of the sacred was not always and entirely focused on the self. Some went beyond that, seeing the "power greater than oneself" as the linking with others, the human race, the earth, or the universe. I call this a "horizontal transcendence" because, in theological terms, it shows two things. First, it does demonstrate the triumph of immanence, that is, the idea that the sacred or spiritual dimension is entirely present and active within the universe, not outside of it. Yet it also shows a longing for or intimation of something larger and beyond our "immanent frame." Some hints of transcendence were revealed when interviewees spoke of "the Universe." Although that word sometimes was used similar to the word *God*, the majority speculated that the "Universe" was entirely unconcerned with them. Instead, it was a benign force that was constantly available to everyone. The benefit of this "Universal Energy Source" was that they could tap into at will, recharge their batteries, and then go on until they were drained.

Even for all this, however, there were some interviewees who found it hard to give up the comforting images of a God who guided and cared personally for them. Some handled this by almost personifying the "Universe," making it sound somewhat interactive and benevolent for everyone – but also specific to their own needs and desires. They expected guidance as needed but no unwanted attention and certainly no demands. Interestingly, a few felt that this force was unconscious at present but was coming to consciousness through these interviewees' own self-development. In a strange twist on evolution, it was not humans who were evolving but some kind of immanent deity in the making.

Many interviewees had views close to monism, believing that all reality is one, such that distinctions are not real but only apparent. Their frequent use of the idea that everything is ultimately just "energy" also indicated this. When many said they felt the divine was within or that they were God – one of the only ways most would use this word – the monistic view peeked out. Surprisingly few could be categorized as pantheists, that is, believing that the sacred resides solely in the earth. Although nature was definitely a source of inspiration and spirituality for virtually all interviewees, it was seen as empowered by a larger force rather than being worshipped in itself.

Human nature

The very first thing each interviewee said when I asked them, "What does it mean to be human?" was "Everyone is born good." Again, this is likely a widespread cultural repudiation of the stereotype of original sin. As one interviewee succinctly put it,

> I don't want someone to tell me I'm born fallen and God is punishing me for it. I believe everyone is born good and has the right to seek their own self-fulfillment. No one has the right to tell me how to live or express myself.

The interviewees were willing to speculate about the extent and causes of human problems, how free or determined we are, and the inherent state of humankind. Many wanted to bracket the words *good* and *bad* to describe human behavior. Most took a therapeutic, psychological, and even deterministic approach to human dysfunction and pathology. If someone misbehaved, many suggested, it was likely the result of environmental causes, distorted family dynamics, or unhealthy brain chemistry.

Yet they often also counterbalanced this determinism by claiming that all behavior is freely chosen. Many resorted to the idea of an impersonal and unbendable "karmic process" to ensure that wrong actions matter greatly and have consequences. Not only did this dignify individual choice, but it also helped them understand all human problems as a learning experience on the spiritual path. Some posited that past lives produced karma in this life. A few claimed to remember those past lives, but even for those who did not, many seemed to accept the justice of the process. Others, however, felt this was unfair and insisted that karma was restricted to this life alone. In the end, the traditional view of a God who judges and rewards or punishes has been replaced by an anonymous process that ensures beneficial consequences for those who "wake up" and pay attention – and dire consequences for those who don't.

Almost all of them agreed that well-being, comfort, human flourishing, or happiness were the standards by which to measure a successful human life. True to the shift in the "locus of authority" from external to internal, almost all of them felt it was their own ethical determinations that made the final evaluation. Some interviewees went beyond claiming the inherent goodness of human beings and claimed humans are perfect and even divine, thus carrying over some monistic understandings of divinity. Yet given this clear emphasis on the "sacralization of the self,"[20] it was striking to find some who saw the self as the problem, not the solution. Some saw human rationality – or too much thinking – as the core problem while others blamed the ego. This was in tension with the "divine within" and "everyone is born good" themes.

Community

Interviewees' views on community were fairly straightforward. Many had participated from time to time in various alternative spiritual communities, classes, and some occasionally followed various spiritual masters. Some were introduced to spirituality through twelve-step addiction recovery groups. They also got reading suggestions from friends or the media and followed trends that they could discuss with others. Although they credited teachers, groups, and readings with helping them along the spiritual path, in the end, few made long-lasting commitments to any of this.

As for religious communities, most of the interviewees held to a type of perennialism, believing either that all religions, at their core, ultimately taught the same basic principles or that all religions get things partly right and partly wrong. Thus, it was unnecessary or even harmful to commit to any one religion. Instead, they credited themselves with the ability to see the universal truths or teachings common to all religions and to practice them on their own. They believed they could more safely avoid the unhelpful aspects by keeping their independence.

In spite of their self-referential stance and minimal long-term commitment to spiritual groups, these were not anarchists, nihilists or loners. All went to work, paid taxes, and took care of friends and family. Most wished the world blessings and peace and took an interest in world problems. Many felt that moral values were obvious and even universal but saw the religions they were rejecting as actually immoral for their social positions, such as opposing gay rights and objecting to abortion. Few interviewees were aware that many progressive religious groups would hold social and political positions similar to theirs. Some SBNRs I met had chosen to contribute to the world's well-being – as well as their own – by dedicating their lives to service as yoga teachers, Wicca leaders, or therapists. Many focused their efforts on lifestyle choices such as recycling, diet, meditation, or gardening. But there was a decidedly anti-organizational bent that seemed to get in the way of them uniting around the topics they cared about. I met few who had made ongoing commitments to activist groups or issues that required long-term organization in order to create change.

When I asked in the interview what a really functional and healthy spiritual community would look like, the majority said it would be one that supported them and their growth, one where everyone was free to believe and practice as they wished, and one that didn't make too many demands. When I asked how they would recognize such a community if they went looking for one, many said, "[E]veryone would believe as I do." In general, however, when I asked my interviewees who supports them spiritually, many answered, "I do."

Afterlife

Finally, we discussed afterlife. A few believed that mature people should recognize that after death they would simply return to the earth or become "energy." The majority did not leave it at that, however, but believed strongly in reincarnation. The idea of choice was very instrumental here, with many believing they would choose – perhaps with the help of spiritual guides in an afterlife sort of counseling session – their next iteration. But unlike traditional Eastern notions of reincarnation, which posit the possibility that we might regress rather than progress, for the interviewees it was a very American version of endless second chances to "get it right." Some suggested they would go on to new galaxies rather than returning to this earth. But whether they believed karma only applied to this life or visited on them consequences because of past lives, reincarnation was a chance to rectify past mistakes. Heaven and hell seemed too static to them and unfair in limiting the timeframe allowed for this progress. Unlike more traditional views of reincarnation, the majority of interviewees did not believe there was a set teleological goal for this process, no end point or nirvana or heaven or final resting place. Most believed we could endlessly progress and enjoy happier and more successful lives going forward.

Conclusion

What does this movement suggest about the continuities and discontinuities from traditional Western religion, especially Christianity? It certainly shows the triumph of immanence, a theme that has only grown since the Enlightenment.[21] Yet this movement is not simply a large step on the road toward secularism – even though it continues to distance increasing numbers away from organized religion. Instead, the interviewees in this study demonstrate an implicit protest against what they see as an arid secularizing trend in society. They want to know there is "something more" than the consumerism, status seeking, and focus on body image promoted by our society. They also implicitly protest against our society's overreliance on science, both its methods and its seemingly tightly drawn parameters. This is shown in part through their interest in "natural" health treatments, food, and lifestyle. It is not that science is totally distrusted, but "scientism" – or science as the total explanation for everything – certainly is. At other times, science is used to buttress their emerging theology, especially with reference to "quantum physics," "energy," "chaos theory," and the like.

But there are "intimations of transcendence" in the current culture, especially in the SBNR ethos. We are witnessing, as Charles Taylor says, "the story of closed immanence . . . beginning to come apart." Our whole culture is experiencing "cross pressures, between the draw of the narratives of closed immanence on one side, and the sense of their inadequacy on the other." This is a profound theological reorientation that will have important effects on our culture. This reorientation could go in several different directions. On one hand, it could be a draining out of the dregs of traditional religion. Even if everyday life takes on increasing spiritual significance, this may not coalesce into a new religiosity, a culture-wide acceptance of one dominant spirituality, or a renewed formal affiliation.

After all, the Pew Forum recently noted that the longer nones stay away from organized religious practices, the less spiritual they become.[22] And Ammerman notes that the ones who are the most "spiritual" turn out to be religious practitioners: "The people with the most robust sense of sacred presence in everyday life are those who participate in religious activities that allow for conversation and relationship."[23] Thus, even when simply looking for a sense of the sacred in everyday life, a full-orbed spirituality needs to be embedded in some sort of organized religious community. However, I don't expect that current forms of religion can be reenergized by the SBNR movement unless there are significant and dramatic changes.

I can't speak for all religions in the United States, but it makes sense that change is always possible. History shows that religions adapt to cultural changes through contact with other groups and through global interactions. In fact, change is already happening within Christianity through such movements such as the Emergent Church,[24] the New Monastics,[25] Church-Next,[26] and other experiments. There is a growing desire in many churches to appeal to and learn from SBNRs, even if this impulse sometimes begins as a need to fill pews again.

Because of my book, I've spoken to a wide spectrum of interested parties: secular hospitals, progressive political groups, college chaplains, social workers, hospice directors, and others. I've also been invited by Christian denominations across the whole range, from Unitarian Universalists all the way to evangelicals. Each group is challenged by the burgeoning of nones, and each is confident it has something to offer SBNRs that SBNRs want and need. Religious leaders say to me, "Please tell us how to reach SBNRs because, deep down, they really should be our people." Nearly everyone who invites me wants a piece of the SBNR pie. I have to let each of them know that this SBNR pie doesn't really want to be eaten . . . at least not by any kind of organized group.

But that might not be the whole story. For the SBNR movement could be the harbinger of something spiritually new, whether that's the coming of a New Age or, as some theologians suggest,[27] a cleansing and revitalization of religion. I doubt it will look much like anything we have now, however. In order for a new movement or a spiritual revitalization to take place in Western culture, there would need to be some structure, some recognized common vision, and some core concepts. At this point, the anti-institutional bent present in the SBNR ethos will make such organization difficult. In fact, most SBNRs I've met are quite positive that their spiritual journeys, reasons for avoiding organization, and beliefs are self-created and unique. They seem unaware that many others reject the same doctrines and promote similar theological themes. In fact, some are even disappointed when I tell them how similar they are to so many others.

Whatever may emerge from this important trend, there is no doubt this is a spiritual revolution. It is like a train that can't be stopped and is sweeping people up as it rolls along. While our culture prizes individualism, we are often unaware how influenced we are by the others around us. I found this to be particularly true in my work with SBNRs. While they might not yet recognize or embrace the commonalities I've laid out, at some point a common vision might become necessary and organization desperately needed. In fact, the current political climate may push SBNRs to move beyond limiting their efforts for change to the personal or lifestyle level. In any case, there is reason to find hope in the SBNR movement. Through it there may be emerging a new way to experience, find, and theologically explain the deep feeling that what you see is not all that you get.

Notes

1 "America's Changing Religious Landscape," Pew Research Center, May 12, 2015. In the period between 2007 and 2014, the numbers of unaffiliated rose by nearly 7%. The number of professed Christians dropped by nearly 8% in the same period, going from 78.4% to 70.6%. The number of those who identify with non-Christian religions has "inched up" by 1.2% in the same period, from 4.7% to 5.9%. www.pewforum.org/2015/05/12/americas-changing-religious-landscape. As for those who profess being SBNR, the most recent polls conclude that at least 18% self-describe as such. See, for example, one from the Pew Research Center (www.pewresearch.org/fact-tank/2017/09/06/more-americans-now-say-theyre-spiritual-but-not-religious) and one from the Public Religion Research Institute (www.prri.org/research/religiosity-and-spirituality-in-america).

2 Robert Putnam, *American Grace: How Religion Divides and Unites Us* (New York: Simon & Schuster, 2012), passim.

3 Many sources document this. See, for example, "The Global Religious Landscape," Pew Forum on Religion & Public Life, December 18, 2012 and also its October 2012 report "Nones on the Rise," Pew Research Center. See also Barry Kosmin and Ariela Keyser, *Religion in a Free Market: Religious and Non-Religious Americans, Who, What, Why Where* (Ithaca, NY: Paramount Books, 2006).

4 Some earlier polls, such as the 1948 Gallup Poll, began tracking this, and a few scholars took notice, as reported in John G. Condran and Joseph B. Tamney who chart this in "Religious 'Nones': 1957 to 1982," *Sociological Analysis* 46, no. 4 (1985): 415–23. But one of the only earlier religious scholars who took this rise seriously was Russell Hale, *The Unchurched: Who They Are and Why They Stay Away* (San Francisco, CA: Harper & Row, 1980).

5 Many began to document this. See, for example, Michael Hout et al., "More Americans Have No Religious Preference: Key Findings from the 2012 General Social Survey," Institute for the Study of Societal Issues, University of California,

Berkeley, March 2013. See also the American Religious Identification Survey (ARIS 2008), Barry A. Kosmin and Ariela Keyser, Trinity College; the Pew Forum on Religion & Public Life, *Faith in Flux: Changes in Religious Affiliation in the U.S.*, 2009 and *Religion Among the Millennials*, February 2010; Knights of Columbus, Marist Poll, *American Millennials: Generations Apart*, February 2010, and others.

 6 Oliver Robinson, senior lecturer at the University of Greenwich, says that my *Belief Without Borders: Inside the Minds of the Spiritual But Not Religious* is "one of only a few major empirical studies on the SBNR revolution." "Seeking the Essence of 'Spiritual But Not Religious,'" *Network Review: Journal of the Scientific and Medical Network*, no. 122 (2016): 3.

 7 *Parade*, "Has America Become More Spiritual?" October 4, 2009; *Newsweek*, "Spirituality in America," August 29–September 5, 2005.

 8 For more details and data, please see chapter 1, "Introduction," and especially chapter 2 "Waking from the Dream," in Linda Mercadante, *Belief Without Borders: Inside the Minds of the Spiritual But Not Religious* (New York: Oxford University Press, 2014).

 9 Robert Putnam, *American Grace: How Religion Divides and Unites Us* (New York: Simon & Schuster, 2012), passim.

10 Charles Taylor, *A Secular Age* (Cambridge, MA: Belknap Press, Harvard University, 2007), passim.

11 There are many sources documenting this, but for an engaging personal narrative perspective, see Frank Schaeffer, *Crazy for God: How I Grew Up as One of the Elect, Helped Found the Religious Right, and Lived to Take All (or Almost All) of It Back* (New York: Caroll & Graf, 2007). Also see Randy Balmer, *Thy Kingdom Come: How the Religious Right Distorts the Faith and Threatens America: An Evangelical's Lament* (New York: Basic Books, 2006) and David Kuo, *Tempting Faith: An Inside Story of Political Seduction* (New York: Free Press, 2006).

12 Pew Research Forum, "'Nones' on the Rise," March 9, 2012. This report states that "a new survey by the Pew Research Center's Forum on Religion & Public Life, conducted jointly with the PBS television program Religion & Ethics NewsWeekly, finds that many of the country's 46 million unaffiliated adults are religious or spiritual in some way. Two-thirds of them say they believe in God (68%). More than half say they often feel a deep connection with nature and the earth (58%), while more than a third classify themselves as 'spiritual' but not 'religious' (37%), and one-in-five (21%) say they pray every day. In addition, most religiously unaffiliated Americans think that churches and other religious institutions benefit society by strengthening community bonds and aiding the poor."

13 Although many religious leaders issue such critiques online, the words of minister Lillian Daniels have gotten much attention, see "Spiritual But Not Religious"? Please Stop Boring Me," www.huffingtonpost.com/lillian-daniel/spiritual-but-not-religio_b_959216.html; and *When "Spiritual But Not Religious" Is Not Enough: Seeing God in Surprising Places, Even the Church* (New York: Jericho Books, 2013).

14 For a range of views on spiritual seeking, see, for example, Matthew C. Graham et al., "A Phenomenological Analysis of Spiritual Seeking: Listening to Quester Voices," *International Journal for the Psychology of Religion* 18 (2008): 146–63; Rodney Stark et al., "Exploring Spirituality and Unchurched Religions in America, Sweden, and Japan," *Journal of Contemporary Religion* 20, no. 1 (2005); Dick Houtman and Stef Aupers, "The Spiritual Turn and the Decline of Tradition: The Spread of Post-Christian Spirituality in 14 Western Countries,

1981–2000," *Journal for the Scientific Study of Religion* 46, no. 3 (2007); Paul Heelas, *Spiritualities of Life: New Age Romanticism and Consumptive Capitalism* (London: Blackwell, 2008). On rampant religious illiteracy, see Stephen Prothero, *Religious Literacy: What Every American Needs to Know – and Doesn't* (San Francisco, CA: HarperOne, 2007).

15 Among the few who takes New Age or SBNR theology seriously is Wouter J. Hanegraaff, *New Age Religion and Western Culture: Esotericism in the Mirror of Secular Thought* (Albany: State University of New York Press, 1998). A more popular writer who also tackles this is Dan Kimball, *They Like Jesus But Not the Church: Insights from Emerging Generations* (Grand Rapids, MI: Zondervan, 2007). A scholar who traces out the themes from the past that often show up in SBNR thinking is Catherine Albanese, *A Republic of Mind & Spirit: A Cultural History of American Metaphysical Religion* (New Haven, CT: Yale, 2007). The history of these themes with roots in liberal Protestantism is charted by Leigh Schmidt in *Restless Souls: The Making of American Spirituality* (New York: Harper Collins, 2005). A brief job is done by Robert Fuller in *Spiritual, But Not Religious: Understanding Unchurched America* (New York: Oxford, 2001).

16 Nancy Tatom Ammerman, *Sacred Stories, Spiritual Tribes: Finding Religion in Everyday Life* (New York: Oxford, 2015), 47–52.

17 Meredith B. McGuire, *Lived Religion: Faith and Practice in Everyday Life* (New York: Oxford, 2008).

18 Linda Mercadante, *Belief Without Borders: Inside the Minds of the Spiritual But Not Religious* (New York: Oxford University Press, 2014).

19 Taylor, *A Secular Age*, passim.

20 Paul Heelas says the crux of the new thought-world is a "self-spirituality." See *Spiritualities of Life*, passim. See also Heelas, *The New Age Movement: Religion, Culture and Society in the Age of Postmodernity* (Cambridge, MA: Blackwell, 1996).

21 See Stanley J. Grenz and Roger E. Olson, *20th Century Theology: God & the World in a Transitional Age* (Downer's Grove, IL: InterVarsity Press, 1992).

22 "Religious 'Nones' Are Not Only Growing, They're Becoming More Secular," Pew Research Forum, November 11, 2015, www.pewresearch.org/fact-tank/2015/11/11/religious-nones-are-not-only-growing-theyre-becoming-more-secular/

23 Ammerman, *Sacred Stories, Spiritual Tribes*, 302.

24 The Emerging or Emergent Church is nondenominational and seeks to make Christianity more contemporary, https://en.wikipedia.org/wiki/Emerging_church

25 The New Monasticism is an attempt to revitalize the church via contemplative traditions, www.scribd.com/doc/101981052/New-Monasticism-An-Interspiritual-Manifesto-for-Contemplative-Life-in-the-21st-Century

26 NextChurch is a Presbyterian group that seeks to reinvent church, http://next church.net/

27 Diana Butler Bass, Phyllis Tickle, and Harvey Cox, to name just a few.

References

Albanese, Catherine. *A Republic of Mind & Spirit: A Cultural History of American Metaphysical Religion*. New Haven: Yale, 2007.

Ammerman, Nancy Tatom. *Sacred Stories, Spiritual Tribes: Finding Religion in Everyday Life*. New York: Oxford, 2015.

Balmer, Randy. *Thy Kingdom Come: How the Religious Right Distorts the Faith and Threatens America: An Evangelical's Lament*. New York: Basic Books, 2006.

Condran, John G. and Joseph B. Tamney. "Religious 'Nones': 1957 to 1982." *Sociological Analysis* 46, no. 4 (1985): 415–23.

Daniels, Lillian. *When "Spiritual But Not Religious" Is Not Enough: Seeing God in Surprising Places, Even the Church*. New York: Jericho Books, 2013.

———. " 'Spiritual But Not Religious'? Please Stop Boring Me." www.huffingtonpost.com/lillian-daniel/spiritual-but-not-religio_b_959216.html.

Fuller, Robert C. *Spiritual, But Not Religious: Understanding Unchurched America*. New York: Oxford, 2001.

Graham, Matthew C., Marvin J. McDonald and Derrick W. Klassen. "A Phenomenological Analysis of Spiritual Seeking: Listening to Quester Voices." *International Journal for the Psychology of Religion* 18 (2008): 146–63.

Grenz, Stanley J. and Roger E. Olson. *20th Century Theology: God & the World in a Transitional Age*. Downer's Grove, IL: InterVarsity Press, 1992.

Hale, Russell. *The Unchurched: Who They Are and Why They Stay Away*. San Francisco, CA: Harper & Row, 1980.

Hanegraaff, Wouter J. *New Age Religion and Western Culture: Esotericism in the Mirror of Secular Thought*. Albany, NY: State University of New York Press, 1998.

Heelas, Paul. *The New Age Movement: Religion, Culture and Society in the Age of Postmodernity*. Cambridge, MA: Blackwell, 1996.

———. *Spiritualities of Life: New Age Romanticism and Consumptive Capitalism*. London: Blackwell, 2008.

Hout, Michael, Claude S. Fisher and Mark A. Chaves. "More Americans Have No Religious Preference: Key Findings from the 2012 General Social Survey." Institute for the Study of Societal Issues, University of California, Berkeley, March 2013.

Houtman, Dick and Stef Aupers. "The Spiritual Turn and the Decline of Tradition: The Spread of Post-Christian Spirituality in 14 Western Countries, 1981–2000." *Journal for the Scientific Study of Religion* 46, no. 3 (2007): 305–20.

Kimball, Dan. *They Like Jesus But Not the Church: Insights from Emerging Generations*. Grand Rapids, MI: Zondervan, 2007.

Knights of Columbus, Marist Poll. *American Millennials: Generations Apart*. February 2010.

Kosmin, Barry and Ariela Keyser. *Religion in a Free Market: Religious and Non-Religious Americans, Who, What, Why Where*. Ithaca, NY: Paramount Books, 2006.

———. *American Religious Identification Survey* (ARIS 2008), Trinity College.

Kuo, David. *Tempting Faith: An Inside Story of Political Seduction*. New York: Free Press, 2006.

McGuire, Meredith B. *Lived Religion: Faith and Practice in Everyday Life*. New York: Oxford, 2008.

Mercadante, Linda. *Belief Without Borders: Inside the Minds of the Spiritual But Not Religious*. New York: Oxford University Press, 2014.

Newsweek. "Spirituality in America." August 29–September 5, 2005.

Parade. "Has America Become More Spiritual?" October 4, 2009.

Pew Forum on Religion & Public Life. *Faith in Flux: Changes in Religious Affiliation in the U.S.* 2009.

———. *Religion Among the Millennials*. February 2010.

———. "The Global Religious Landscape." December 18, 2012.

Pew Research Center. "America's Changing Religious Landscape." May 12, 2015. www.pewforum.org/2015/05/12/americas-changing-religious-landscape/

Pew Research Forum. "Religious 'Nones' Are Not Only Growing, They're Becoming More Secular." November 11, 2015. www.pewresearch.org/fact-tank/2015/11/11/religious-nones-are-not-only-growing-theyre-becoming-more-secular/
———. "Nones on the Rise." October 2012.

Prothero, Stephen. *Religious Literacy: What Every American Needs to Know – and Doesn't*. San Francisco, CA: HarperOne, 2007.

Putnam, Robert. *American Grace: How Religion Divides and Unites Us*. New York: Simon & Schuster, 2012.

Robinson, Oliver. "Seeking the Essence of 'Spiritual But Not Religious.' " *Network Review: Journal of the Scientific and Medical Network*, no. 122 (2016/3).

Schaeffer, Frank. *Crazy for God: How I Grew Up as One of the Elect, Helped Found the Religious Right, and Lived to Take All (or Almost All) of It Back*. New York: Caroll & Graf, 2007.

Schmidt, Leigh. *Restless Souls: The Making of American Spirituality*. New York: Harper Collins, 2005.

Stark, Rodney, Eva Hamburg and Alan S. Miller. "Exploring Spirituality and Unchurched Religions in America, Sweden, and Japan." *Journal of Contemporary Religion* 20, no. 1 (2005): 3–23.

Taylor, Charles. *A Secular Age*. Cambridge, MA: Belknap Press, Harvard University, 2007.

8 Consuming spirituality

SBNR and neoliberal logic in queer communities

Melissa M. Wilcox

This chapter is framed by a tale of two Sisters. Both belong to the same order of nuns, and both identify as queer or gay men. I interviewed one at the outset of my research on their order; the other was among my final interviewees, so their stories frame not only my argument in this chapter but also my research process itself.[1] This tale of two Sisters – or perhaps more accurately, these two Sisters' tales – echo many others I have encountered over the course of nearly two decades of research on religion in queer communities, and in their complexity they serve to highlight the tangled nature of power, complicity, and resistance in SBNR under conditions of colonialism and global neoliberal capitalism.

Story 1: Sister Baba Ganesh[2]

Sister Baba Ganesh has been a fully professed member of the San Francisco house of the Sisters of Perpetual Indulgence since the late 2000s. This international order of self-described "queer nuns" founded in 1979 is neither residential nor religiously affiliated; *house* is a term of art. Yet, while the order is not in any official way a religion and some members are ardent atheists, neither of these facts stops many members from understanding their work as Sisters of Perpetual Indulgence to be an expression of, or even central to, their spirituality.

Sister Baba Ganesh speaks of her "calling" to the Sisters as "deeply rooted in spirituality" and of the order as "presenting new ways of believing, presenting new ways of being. . . . I think," she told me, "it's some kind of spiritual blueprint." Much of that spirituality is deeply communal, based in and expressed through the network of Sisters on four continents that guarantees members an instant family and a warm welcome anywhere they might travel. Sister Baba also sees something more intrinsic, more internal, in the calling to be a Sister. "The nature, I think, of the Sister heart," she explained, "is the ability to pull disparate, seemingly unrelated things together toward a kind of queer, spiritual, and socially beneficial purpose." Elaborating on this observation, she added,

There's so much connected to the divine. It's in that place of unknowing, it's in that place of tricking oneself out of knowledge and into intuition, that connection can happen, miracles can be performed, the unimaginable is manifest. So I think it's in those liminal spaces that I see a Sister embodied, down to the outsiderness of it. And the outsiderness of it has to do with the fact that I think in general the kind of classic Sister persona is that one of a prophet, and prophets don't fuckin' choose, man. . . . They're made *crazy* by their lack of choice. You know what I mean? And there are Sisters who are prophets *and* saints, who are conscious of their calling.

Sister Baba must count herself among the latter, because when I asked whether she considered herself religious, spiritual, both, neither, or something else entirely she answered, "I'm a prophet. I didn't get to choose."

Born in the Philippines to a family of Filipino and Chinese political activists who drew on Roman Catholicism to resist the Marcos regime, Sister Baba is herself an activist who works for greater support and inclusion of queer people of color both broadly in the community and more specifically within her largely white order and who sees her spirituality as central to her activism. Although the Sisters are a volunteer order who spend the majority of their time as what they term their "secular selves" and generally only manifest their "Sister selves" on evenings or weekends in order to carry out the community service and activism for which they are known, Sister Baba echoes many other experienced members of the order in understanding these two selves to be interwoven. "I'm Sister Baba right now," she told me, as we sat in her beautifully appointed office at a prominent art center with no habit or veil in sight.

Sister Baba's spirituality, and that of Joël, her secular self, combines influences from across her life and across a variety of cultural and religious traditions. Her novice project (a required undertaking for any Sister wishing to reach the rank of fully professed) blended a guided walking meditation through San Francisco's Castro District with recorded segments from oral history interviews of early members of the order, timed so that participants listening to the guided meditation as they walked would hear an interviewee recount an event as they passed by the location in which that event took place. Although the meditation can be undertaken alone by anyone who knows the walking route, it is typically performed as a procession of over a hundred members and friends of the order during the Sisters' anniversary on Easter Saturday. Everyone dresses in white, and Sister Baba refers to the procession as a "new queer hajj." At least in the year when I participated in this procession, Sister Baba led it wearing the traditional red-and-white habit of Filipina Roman Catholic nuns, and during my interview with her she also described the procession as "darshan," a "queer ritual," and a "queer prayer."

Sister Baba's name, too, points to the range of religious influences in her life and work. As a child in the Philippines, Joël was fascinated by the elephants at the zoo. "I grew up with a mother who allowed me *not* to go to church on Sundays," Sister Baba explained,

> but instead thought it better for me to stand in front of the elephant pit for hours. Because, you know, I told her, "I'm talking to them," and she's like, "Cool! There's church." . . . And there's my connection to Ganesh. And it's true. I *can still* connect with elephants.

In addition, however, Sister Baba sees the Hindu god Ganesh as her "queer god of choice," understanding Ganesh's role as the remover of obstacles to parallel the Sisters' official mission of "the promulgation of universal joy and the expiation of stigmatic guilt." Even more interesting in this regard is the way in which Sister Baba's name was given to her by a more senior Sister:

> During my initiation, I went through easily a year and a half . . . of coming into work . . . wearing non-Western clothes. I was wearing skirts and *kurtas*, my hair was down to here, I had bone hair picks. I could do that in San Francisco in an art center and be part of the Sisters. And so I would dress like that, and then [Sister] Mary Juanita just [at] one point [said], "Well, look at Baba, look at Barbra Ganesh over there." And it just stuck.

Blending what was perhaps a sly reference to gay icon Barbra Streisand with a Hindu deity beloved by the San Francisco house of the Sisters and currently very much in fashion in the United States as an icon of so-called Asian spirituality, along with an exotic food reference, the name was too good to pass up. Sister Baba's name, along with the other aspects of her life and her ministry, points toward the complexity of the "Spiritual but Not Religious" that becomes increasingly perceptible when one brings an intersectional lens to bear.

Story 2: Sister Krissy Fiction[3]

Raised by a lesbian mother who came out to him when he was 14, Kurt – who later became Sister Krissy Fiction – discovered early in his college career that he, too, was same-sex attracted. Around the same time, although he'd been raised nonreligious, Kurt began attending a congregation of the Lutheran Church-Missouri Synod with a friend whose father was a pastor there. His new co-religionists did not take well at all to Kurt's same-sex attraction and, as Sister Krissy tells it: "I went back in the closet and decided homosexuality was a sin." He joined Exodus and remained a member for a decade. Called to youth ministry, Kurt attended a denominational school and eventually was hired by a church in San Antonio. Soon thereafter, his superiors nominated him for a position as a missionary in Brazil. There was just one catch: the church refused to send unmarried ministers to this position. If he wanted the new job Kurt would have to marry a woman whom he'd been dating "halfheartedly" and for only a short time. "I thought, this is what God wants me to do," Sister Krissy recalled when I interviewed her. "You know, he's put this woman in my life, he's opened all of these doors. I still thought of God as a he at that time. And, so you know, if I could just, quote-unquote, 'straighten myself out.'" Like many ex-gays Kurt was still sexually attracted to men, but he had been refusing to act on that attraction. The marriage and the move to Brazil, though, brought things to a breaking point, and when he and his wife returned stateside for a medical procedure that she needed, Kurt was placed under investigation by his denomination, whose leaders eventually told him to "find another career." Instead, Kurt decided to accept his attraction to men and to find another outlet for his call to ministry. He moved to Portland on the word of an online acquaintance and started over.

Kurt's first religious move after coming to Portland was into the United Church of Christ, an enormous leap theologically for someone coming from the Missouri Synod Lutherans. He resumed his youth ministry there, but in the highly unchurched, Spiritual but Not Religious environment of the Pacific Northwest he soon began to explore further afield, into Gnosticism, Wicca, and neopagan revivals of ancient Mediterranean practices. When I interviewed her, Sister Krissy gifted me with what is still one of the most quotable statements I have heard from a Sister of Perpetual Indulgence about religion. "I joke and say I'm a spiritual slut," she told me. Elaborating on this remark took Sister Krissy, who was at that time also pursuing a master's degree in theology, quite some time. But in trying to frame her perspectives, she offered a metaphor. Religion, she suggested to me, is

> like language. . . . [I]t gives us a vocabulary to speak about something which we ultimately can't describe. And so I say I'm fluent in Christianity and fluent in neopaganism, I can kind of ask where the bathroom is in Buddhism, you know. Sometimes I feel like I'm an atheist almost, and on the other end of the spectrum I believe in everything. But I'm kind of a monotheist, too. I'm a nondualist. So it's really complicated for me sometimes.

In the years since that 2009 interview, Sister Krissy has moved away from both Christianity and British Traditional Wicca, becoming increasingly focused on a small movement that has revived the worship of Antinous, the deified lover of the Roman emperor Hadrian. In late 2015, she – not Kurt – became one of three new magistrates of the Ekklesia Antinoou. Kurt is also currently involved in a shamanic movement called (somewhat ironically) the Unnamed Path.

Sister Krissy grew up in the San Francisco Bay Area and identifies as white and cisgender. She is an outspoken antiracist advocate in a very white city. She has committed herself to work for women's rights, and although the Portland house as a whole was on a bit of a steep learning curve regarding transgender issues during the course of my research, Sister Krissy was one of the members who dedicated herself to learning more rather than leaving out of frustration at the tensions that resulted from misconceptions and outright transphobia. While she shares with Sister Baba a deep commitment to spirituality and to the very spiritual social justice work and ministry for which both find an outlet in the Sisters, Sister Krissy has also had very different experiences with both religion and race from those of her fellow Sister in San Francisco. Both the differences and the similarities in their stories are helpful in thinking through the broader patterns and questions regarding SBNR within queer communities.

Queer and spiritual, but not religious

As self-declared "prophet" and "spiritual slut," Sister Baba and Sister Krissy fit easily within the rather amorphous category of "Spiritual but Not Religious" even through Sister Krissy, with her background in religious studies, is happy to claim both spirituality and religiosity. Their approach to spirituality places them within a larger pattern in queer communities, more pronounced for cisgender women and trans people of all genders than it is for cisgender men and possibly (though the data are thinner here) for whites than for people of color, at least in the United States.[4] Thus, one pattern that this tale of two Sisters brings into relief is the particular prevalence of SBNR in queer communities and its ongoing inflection by race and gender. Equally clearly indicated by these two stories is the style of *bricolage* that animates these Sisters' spiritual lives and decision making: Sister Baba's reinterpretation of Ganesh as a queer god and her conceptualization of the procession as simultaneously hajj, darshan, queer prayer, and queer ritual, and Sister Krissy's "fluency" in Christianity and neopaganism, her basic functionality in Buddhism, her explorations of shamanism, and her reclaiming of Antinous.[5]

Although bricolage represents a certain found-object approach to religion, it is also perhaps the logical end point of the neoliberal "spiritual marketplace," in which one can not only shop for religion but buy into it à la carte in a build-your-own approach that offers each religious consumer a perfectly personalized product and the freedom to consume without considering the global context of production.[6] Resistant queer activists though they are, these two Sisters also take part in a neoliberal religious economy, drawing their very ability to navigate religion in a homophobic world from the fragmentation and decontextualization that allows all religion to be for sale in a guilt-free market. And yet, their engagement and their social location within these dynamics raise questions that further complicate what could be an all-too-easy analysis of Western queer plundering of global religious resources. The following exploration of these complexities of neo-liberal religious consumption in queer communities consists of four moves. First, I briefly discuss some of the existing literature addressing changes in religious practice and state management that have resulted from neoliber-alism. Second, I draw on queer settler colonial studies and queer work on homonormativity and homonationalism in order to demonstrate a circula-tion between non-Native queer settler colonialism, homonationalism, neo-liberalism, and religion in North America, a circulation that has resonances with franchise colonial histories such as those in Europe although those resonances fall outside of the scope of this chapter. Third, I show how this circulation creates queer religious consumers for whom religious appropria-tion can be justified through an appeal to the fulfillment of the consuming individual. Fourth, I attempt to complicate this reading by returning to Sis-ter Baba and Sister Krissy in order to examine the challenges of navigating the neoliberal management and marketing of religion from within a system to which there is, in a Foucauldian sense, no outside on which to stand. In exploring this complexity, I end not with a definitive claim but with further questions that arise from these case studies.

Religion and neoliberalism

Jeremy Carrette and Richard King's 2005 book, *Selling Spirituality*, may be the best-known analysis of neoliberalism and religion to date. A polemical work that at times evinces some of the same sense of crisis and gendered scorn that was earlier evoked by much sociological commentary on reli-gious individualism and the pseudonymous Sheila Larson,[7] the book focuses on a supply-side analysis of what its authors term the "corporate takeover of religion" through the individualizing language of spirituality, the mon-etization of the term *spirituality*, the use of orientalist exotification to sell a fragmented and decontextualized mélange of Asian traditions as "Asian spirituality," and the corporate turn to spirituality as a way to improve profit margins. While their critique of the appropriation of Asian religions tends at times to betray an underlying sense of the ancient and static purity of tradition that is itself problematic, and their framing of an earlier time before the neoliberal "hostile takeover of religion" smacks suspiciously of nostalgia, nevertheless, Carrette and King's concern over spirituality as a corporate player in a globalizing neoliberal marketplace in which culture itself has become a commodity is indeed well placed. At the same time, their supply-side focus on religious production leaves mostly unexamined the role of the consumer of such religious goods.

While much other writing on neoliberalism and religion concerns shifting state regulations and changing social norms, with little of the Foucauldian approach to power and regulation that is so useful in Carrette and King's work, Foucauldian analyses appear several times in a more recent collec-tion of articles on the topic from 2013.[8] In the introduction to the volume,

François Gauthier, Tuomas Martikainen, and Linda Woodhead argue that because neoliberalism is an all-encompassing economic system that turns even culture into a commodity, those who study religion must turn our attention to the ways in which neoliberal principles and modes of regulation have come to impact religion in the broadest sense. They add in a footnote the following astute observation about sociological analyses of contemporary religion in North America and Europe:

> Analytics such as Rational Choice Theory, salvation goods and the spiritual marketplace therefore start from a neoliberal epistemology, the ideology of which is thus naturalized, and legitimized. The value of such analytics is very poor as a consequence, as they merely mime what they set out to understand, smuggling as they do so a particularly impervious brand of ethnocentrism in which the historic and social context of the emergence of such realities are thwarted.[9]

Contributors to this volume such as Breda Gray, David Ashley and Ryan Sandefer, Tuomas Martikainen, and Lori Beaman examine specific cases of the intersection of neoliberalism and religion through the Foucauldian lens that the introduction suggests, including state management of religion, privatization of state functions and their outsourcing to religious organizations, and the relationship of neoliberalism to "the political, the social, and the subject."[10]

The subject, though, or more precisely subjectification, is the missing piece so far.[11] Studies of religion and neoliberalism rooted in a Foucauldian analysis of power have examined the monetization and "corporate takeover" of religion, state regulation of religious organizations, the outsourcing of state functions to religious organizations, and the consequent shifts in power, in multiple and complex directions, between religion and the state. The role of the subject is likely to be equally complex.

Queer studies, the neoliberal subject, and colonialism

Some of Foucault's lectures at the Collège de France take up neoliberalism, particularly in his development of the concept of governmentality. As Foucault notes in the lectures published as *The Birth of Biopolitics*, "[t]he problem of neoliberalism is . . . how the overall exercise of political power can be modeled on the principles of a market economy."[12] This is a question, he argues, "of taking the formal principles of a market economy and referring and relating them to, of projecting them on to a general art of government." Importantly, he goes on to add that "[n]eoliberalism should not therefore be identified with laissez-faire, but rather with permanent vigilance, activity, and intervention."[13] Arguing that "the stake in all neoliberal analyses is the replacement every time of *homo oeconomicus* as a partner of exchange with *homo oeconomicus* as entrepreneur of himself,"[14] Foucault concludes that "the individual's life itself – with his [*sic*] relationships to his private property, for example, with his family, household, insurance, and retirement – must make him into a sort of permanent and multiple enterprise."[15] Particularly in the case of the United States, Foucault sees already in 1979 that neoliberalism suffuses all of society and all of social control with economic models.[16] "[*H*]*omo oeconomicus*," he adds, "is someone who is eminently governable": the perfect subject, or, in Foucault's words, "correlate," of governmentality.[17]

What is the role of religion in this neoliberal system of biopolitical management of society and the subject? Foucault and Foucauldian or even post-structuralist scholars more broadly outside of the field of religious studies pay little heed to contemporary religion despite the centrality of Roman Catholic confession to Foucault's understanding of the development of biopower.[18] Foucault's last lecture of the spring of 1979 may offer a clue when the philosopher argues that

> [c]ivil society is like madness and sexuality, what I call transactional realities. That is to say, those transactional and transitional figures that we call civil society, madness, and so on, which, although they have not always existed are nonetheless real, are born precisely from the interplay of relations of power and everything which constantly eludes them, at the interface, so to speak, of governors and governed.[19]

Given the many years now of historical critiques of religious studies and more precisely of its foundational concept of religion,[20] given Carrette and King's persuasive history of the development of the contemporary concept of "spirituality,"[21] it seems reasonable to suggest that religion and spirituality are also among these transactional realities arising from this "interplay of relations of power and everything which constantly eludes them."

Just as neoliberalism creates the subject as enterprise, regulated but perhaps also resisting in part through the concepts and practices of religion and spirituality, so, too, does it create the sexual subject. This creation is, of course, the focus of the first and best-known volume of Foucault's *The History of Sexuality*,[22] but because Foucault's attention did not turn to neoliberalism until several years after he wrote that book it is queer studies scholars who have traced the specific linkages between neoliberalism and the queer sexual subject. Particularly important in this regard is Lisa Duggan's work on homonormativity, in which Duggan argues that what she calls "the new neoliberal sexual politics" that arose in the 1990s "does not contest dominant heteronormative assumptions and institutions but upholds and sustains them while promising the possibility of a demobilized gay constituency and a privatized, depoliticized gay culture anchored in domesticity and consumption."[23] A few years after Duggan's article was published, and in the aftermath of the September 11th attacks, Jasbir Puar added patriotism more explicitly to the concept of homonormativity, arguing that what she terms "homonationalism" provides a route by which white gays and lesbians and highly homonormative gays and lesbians of color can be, as she terms it, biopolitically "folded into life" through patriotism and the privatization of sexuality.[24] In queer communities, then, the particular biopolitics of neoliberalism creates not only the consuming and self-enterprising *homo oeconomicus* but also the perfectly privatized subject. This linkage has important implications for the privatization of religion, a phenomenon already clearly connected to neoliberalism by Carrette and King but also one that becomes more complex when we examine it through the privatization of sex noted by queer studies scholars. In queer communities, as I have argued elsewhere, the privatization of sex and the privatization of religion come together in particularly insidious ways to create obediently consuming, homonational religious – or in their own terms, spiritual – subjects who keep both their sexual and their religious dissidence safely behind closed doors.[25] In the context of the present analysis, one might add that religious privatization indicates not only keeping dissident religious perspectives in the private realm but also deciding the ethics of religious consumption on the private basis of personal spiritual enrichment – with the economic reference most definitely intended.

In addition to religion, neoliberalism, and homonationalism, colonialism makes up the fourth aspect of this circulation of power. Since much of the research on religion in queer communities remains focused on the United States, and since there are closely linked but significantly different circulations among religion, sex, and power in the contexts of franchise and settler colonialism, I focus in this argument on the latter, relying in particular on Scott Morgensen's study of white supremacist settler colonialism within non-Native queer activism. Central to Morgensen's argument is his claim that "[w]hite settler heteropatriarchy creates queers who resolve their [sexual] exile through land-based relationships to disappeared Native people."[26] That is, just as settler colonial societies, in general, stabilize their ongoing claims to Native land through the literal and discursive erasure of living Native people, this erasure takes a specific form in the context of non-Native queer people who "return to the land" – a land to which they often have never been, to which they have no ancestral claim, and therefore to which the claim to "return" is a politically significant misnomer – and who claim Native histories of sexual and gender diversity for themselves with no recognition of their implication within settler colonialism and no support of the efforts of living Native Two-Spirit and queer people to assert their sovereignty and to battle the homophobia and transphobia often instilled in their communities through the colonial process. Morgensen links this non-Native queer settler colonialism to Puar's discussion of homonationalism, through non-Native queer claims to sexual citizenship and through the argument that settler colonialism engages in both civilizationalism – claiming sole possession of the quality of being civilized, and of the ability to be such – and primitivism – objectifying Native cultures as "primitive" and then claiming to celebrate them through appropriation. "In this context," Morgensen argues, "homonationalism will define modern queers within quests to achieve settler citizenship; and civilizationalist and primitivist practices will derive from and express homonationalism."[27]

For Morgensen, the prime example of this settler colonial claim to sexual citizenship can be found in the so-called berdache, a figure more of Western homophobic and eventually queer-positive fantasies than of actual Native histories or presents. Finding few same-sex-attracted or gender-variant fore-bears in Europe who had not ended their lives in cinders, non-Native queers appropriated through the figure of the berdache a sexual and gender history that had been invented through settler colonialism, and in so doing enacted a double erasure of Native histories and living Native people. While he indicts this move in which non-Native queer liberation is bought with settler colonial currency, Morgensen also nuances his analysis with the following comment:

> I do not mean to imply that all activists agreed with the hegemony of white settler colonialism. Some vociferously opposed all structural oppressions, as was the case for [gay activist and Radical Faerie co-founder] Harry Hay's Marxist-inspired critiques of white racism and capitalism as sources of antihomosexual prejudice. Nevertheless, adapting berdache to justify sexual rights for U.S. citizens reflects the desire of white sexual minorities to absorb Native American roots as their own in order to claim – even critically – the rights of settler citizenship.[28]

I see a similar complexity and complicity in queer communities' reliance on spirituality and neoliberal, settler colonial, spiritual appropriation and consumption in their efforts to fight against internalized religious homo-phobia and transphobia, to battle racism, and to establish a certain – even if radically antinormative – queer citizenship in the settler colonial state and within a larger, globalized, neoliberal political and religious economy.

Colonialism and neoliberal religious consumption

In the Western contexts in which most such research has taken place, there are two key ways in which religion in queer communities is caught up in neo-liberalism and in the contemporary forms of colonialism that exist in a sym-biotic relationship with neoliberalism: through religious individualism and through bricolage. For the purposes of this discussion, I use a fairly narrow definition of religious individualism as a derivative of the classically Protes-tant "priesthood of all believers" – that is, a perception that it is laudable and even valuable for religious believers to mediate their own relationship to God – but with an awareness that this phenomenon also includes prac-tice. Thus, religious individualism can be glossed as "individual negotiations of religious practice and belief." This definition includes strategies whereby people within a single and specific religious tradition create space for their own experiences, identities, and perspectives and engage selectively in the religious practices from their tradition which they find most rewarding or meaningful. It also includes the phenomenon of "seekerism" in its narrower sense, in which people who currently are not involved in a religious tradition, and those who find their current religious tradition to be inadequate in some way, set out to find a better option, again often described as one that better suits their existing needs, beliefs, and preferences.

A short step from this rather focused definition of religious individualism is a second approach that I separate out here in order to examine it in its specificity. This is bricolage, the "found-object" approach to religion. Bricolage extends the narrow form of seekerism I described earlier in that its practitioners search not for an entire religious tradition that suits their beliefs, needs, and preferences but for specific beliefs and practices, often in separation from their broader traditions and divorced from their cultural and historical contexts. Pulling these together as an artist does a collection of found objects, altering them here and there to bring them into a more pleasing shape, reorienting them toward each other rather than toward their original source, these spiritual practitioners of found-object art create their spirituality in their own image and, importantly, in the image – even if at times in the negative – of the culture or cultures around them.[29]

Such approaches to religion have been invaluable for queer people in Western cultures, particularly those raised within the Abrahamic traditions where much of the homophobia and transphobia one might encounter is religiously rooted. I should hasten to note that this is not to claim that outside of the Abrahamic traditions there are no such sexual and gender biases; rather, same-sex-attracted and gender-variant people who practice other religions, or no religion at all, may encounter other sources of bias on the part of those around them. For many, the main source of that bias is a postcolonial resistance to the impositions of Western cultures, paired with a generally false claim that same sex eroticism and gender variance did not exist in their own culture prior to Western colonization and the attendant introduction of exotic Western vices. For those who follow Abrahamic traditions and also are part of cultures resisting Western colonization and neocolonialism, the claims against same-sex eroticism and gender variance often combine religious and anticolonial arguments.

While effective approaches to these various forms of bias against same-sex-attracted and gender-variant people are shaped to a great extent by cultural, national, historical, religious, local, familial, and personal contexts, in the case of religious biases and especially of internalized religious biases religious individualism has appeared repeatedly as an important and even lifesaving resource. Some practitioners of this individualism become seekers, joining queer-positive alternative traditions such as inclusive neopagan groups, inclusive houses of African diasporic traditions, or the seeker- and bricolage-oriented Unitarian Universalism; others embrace religious brico-lage and become full-fledged proponents of SBNR. Attending drum circles, Hindu-based meditation classes, Zen Buddhist retreats, and the occasional Episcopal church service for the "smells and bells," lighting candles and studying tantric sex, assembling altars made up of a mélange of Buddha stat-ues, Kali images, ancient Egyptian goddesses, and sage bundles – often all bought online or at pricey boutique stores catering to the more than century-old Western infatuation with so-called Asian mystical wisdom and the more recent attachment to a fantasy of the primitive, these queer bricole-urs are seasoned shoppers in the neoliberal spiritual marketplace. Like their straight and cisgender counterparts, they mine the "religions of the world" – that infelicitous invention of the Western intellectual tradition – for intellec-tual and cultural resources, and representatives of those religions are at times also eager to sell. Here the parallels to neoliberal economics become too glar-ing to ignore, and it is here that the circulation between religion, homona-tionalism, neoliberalism, and colonialism – whether settler colonialism places like the United States, Canada, Australia, and New Zealand or whether fran-chise colonialism in Europe – becomes particularly clear. Morgensen's analy-sis might fruitfully be expanded, then, from his focus on the Radical Faeries to queer spirituality and to the SBNR phenomenon as a whole.

Neoliberal capitalism relies on not only the alienation of the worker from the product but also the alienation of the consumer from the worker. It encourages consumption through individual fulfillment, marketing prod-ucts through promises of intangible goods such as happiness, beauty, fam-ily togetherness, national belonging, and even – perhaps especially – the attainment of an elusive cismasculine or cisfeminine, heteronormative ideal. Increasingly, therefore, neoliberal consumers are encouraged to evaluate our purchasing activity on the basis of personal fulfillment. And the heart of the issue when it comes to spirituality and neoliberalism is that this personal fulfillment is exactly the rationale most commonly offered in the face of concerns about appropriation. Religion, the argument goes, is for everyone. It can't be held, selfishly, by one culture and not shared with others. As long as one's consumption or usage of a religious commodity – belief, practice, person, nonhuman entity, or material object – is sincere and fulfilling, then it must be ethical. Yet the claim that religion, like air perhaps, though cer-tainly not like water or land in a colonial and neocolonial world, cannot be owned hides the reality that it already is owned: copyrighted by those who've figured out how to monetize it, marketed on eBay and Amazon, and packaged into podcasts, weekend retreats, and spiritual vacations. Imagine someone who supports a boycott against a politically oppressive regime or someone who believes in disinvestment from environmentally destructive corporations, claiming that certain purchases or investments are acceptable because they are personally fulfilling. Neoliberal spirituality often seems exempt from similarly critical analyses.

Concluding complexities: managing the neoliberal management of religion?

Broadening the application of Morgensen's analysis of white supremacist settler colonialism in queer communities must also involve broadening the application of his point that not all non-Native queer activists agree with settler colonialism, that some insightfully oppose all structural oppressions, and that nevertheless they still find themselves caught up within the very dynamics they oppose. In a Foucauldian understanding of power there is no outside on which to stand, no foothold from which to lay siege to the walls of the citadel; instead, the complex dynamics of Foucauldian power must be resisted – subverted, really – from within. From this perspective of an almost ontological complicity it seems that perhaps SBNR can be used in a resistant way, or at least that it may be impossible to tell a simple story of neoliberal cultural appropriation and consumption about the phenomenon of SBNR, and perhaps especially about spirituality in queer communities. Since telling a more complex story requires a close reading of specific cases, I return now to my tale of two Sisters.

In framing this chapter, I elected to focus on Sister Baba's and Sister Krissy's stories because they evince precisely the sort of complexity I see in queer spiritualities. Sister Baba moves nimbly between calling her novice project a hajj, a form of darshan, and a prayer; she dressed at one time in what could be termed primitivist ways; and despite not being or having ever been Hindu that mode of dress earned her a Sister name referencing Ganesh, which she now proudly bears as a reference to a queer god who exemplifies her work as a Sister. Sister Krissy is drawn to the religious aspect of the primitivism that Morgensen critiques, especially in her work with the Unnamed Path but also, in a more historical way, with her devotion to Antinous. Yet both Sisters are committed antiracist activists, one as a person of color and one as a white ally; both spoke passionately about inclusion and justice in my interviews with them, in casual conversations, and even in writing; neither could ever be described as a slave to consumer capitalism; both belong to fairly activist houses of the Sisters, especially Sister Baba in San Francisco; and both attempt to live out those commitments through their work with the Sisters as well as in their personal lives. If the work of the Sisters is an expression of spirituality for both of these queer nuns, and if they dedicate their own work as nuns to social justice, then the spirituality that they practice is in some way also a spirituality of justice. So how does this square with neoliberal complicities?

In attempting a response to this question, it may be worth asking more focused questions about the boundaries of neoliberal spiritual consumption; these questions may point in the right direction for sorting out the possibility of resistance from within neoliberal spiritualities. One such question has to do with the precise definition of appropriation. For instance, Sister Baba's use of the terms *hajj*, *darshan*, and *prayer* to describe the meditative procession seems to have been an attempt to triangulate between metaphors, to describe what she elsewhere termed the "spiritual blueprint" that she sees the Sisters as developing, rather than an attempt to lay claim to practicing a new form of Islam, Buddhism, or Catholicism or even an amalgamation of the three. In the absence of words for a new phenomenon, how does one describe it except by likening it to what one already knows, even if one only knows those things through a neoliberal process of fragmentation? The question of complicity is still not far off. Furthermore, this collection of metaphors may be drawing on the idea, produced and now problematized by religious studies, that there exist parallel human phenomena across cultures and periods that are called "religions" and that can be compared or used as parallel metaphors to describe a new phenomenon within this category. Scholars like Talal Asad and Tomoko Masuzawa have demonstrated the ways in which world religions and comparative religions discourses such as these have functioned to support European colonial and imperialist enterprises, so it's advisable to remain suspicious of such use of metaphors;[30] at the same time, though, it bears repeating that in Sister Baba's hands these appear to be attempts to describe a brand-new phenomenon and a practice that may hold different meanings or resonances for different people and therefore may need a variety of metaphors to clearly define it. *What counts as appropriation, then? And more specifically, are all uses of such metaphors and comparisons automatically colonialist and appropriative, simply because they're mobilized through neoliberal and colonialist processes?* This is my first concluding question.

Another example is Sister Krissy's involvement in a shamanic movement. On one hand, Western anthropology and religious studies have produced the very idea of a "primitive" or indigenous religious practice called "shamanism" that supposedly exists in comparable form among cultures across the world; on the other hand, some shamanic movements (which almost inevitably draw primarily whites, and certainly non-Natives, to their practice) actively appropriate contemporary Native practices or imagined or actual Native pasts. While the latter are clearly settler colonial and neoliberal appropriations and commodifications of culture, we might ask whether shamanic movements that rely only on the already-Western, already-invented concept of shamanism are indeed of the same ilk. Are there forms of non-Native "shamanic" practice that are not appropriative or settler colonial? To frame the question more broadly as my second concluding question: *What is the extent or the nature of neoliberal and colonial complicity in a practice that focuses solely on a Western invention and not on direct appropriation, even when that invention is based on Western colonial fantasies and neoliberal assumptions about the availability for consumption of personally fulfilling religious practices and beliefs?*

A third example is Sister Baba's use of Ganesh in her name and her claim to him as a queer god. On one hand, such usage of Ganesh by a non-Hindu in the United States, regardless of that person's national origin, can be fairly clearly described as appropriative, as a part of the neoliberal phenomenon of the fragmenting and mining of colonized religious traditions. On the other hand, there are also interesting questions to ask here about who can and cannot queer religious traditions. This is not to argue that appropriation becomes justifiable or leaves the bounds of neoliberalism when it is done for the sake of queer reclaiming; that would be to deny the validity of Morgensen's very strong claim to the contrary. It is instead to point out that some might find Sister Baba's nod to Ganesh problematic precisely because of her claim that he is a queer god and that such an analysis rests on the false assumption that same-sex eroticism and gender variance are limited to the West and to the human realm. In fact, both phenomena appear in Hindu sacred story, and as Devdutt Pattanaik pointed out some years ago, there is ample material for Hindu queer reclamation.[31] The question, then, is not whether it is appropriate to queer a tradition, but *who* can queer it, and this points beyond the role of neoliberalism to the complexity of a neocolonial, globalized world. So my third concluding question is, *How do we navigate analytically through the intertwining power dynamics of neoliberalism and colonialism in a globalized world when the lines of transmission and the dynamics of power are this deeply tangled?*

The connection between SBNR and neoliberalism is one of both complicity and complexity. Because of neoliberalism's thorough and mutual alliance with both settler and franchise colonialism, and the linkages between this alliance and contemporary conceptualizations and practices of religion, a circulation of power exists between these various socio-political-economic structures. Because of the centrality of sexuality and gender to biopolitics, the forces of homonationalism draw queer communities, explicitly homonational or not, into this circulation in particular ways. And yet because of the complexities and complicities of these circulations of power, and because of the all-pervasive nature of power itself, there are no simple answers, no simple critiques, by which queer activists caught up in these circulations can find their way out. Instead, those like Sister Krissy and Sister Baba continue to navigate within these circulations to address the intersections of power within their communities. And who knows, perhaps a prophet and a shamanic spiritual slut within an order of queer nuns are those best positioned to dance their way through this conundrum.

Notes

1 The full study can be found in Melissa M. Wilcox, *Queer Nuns: Religion, Activism, and Serious Parody* (New York: New York University Press, 2018).
2 The following narrative is drawn from Sister Baba Ganesh, Sisters of Perpetual Indulgence – San Francisco house, interview with the author, 11 July 2012.
3 The following narrative is drawn from Sister Krissy Fiction, Order of Benevolent Bliss (Portland, Oregon), interview with the author, 1 November 2009.
4 For a good overview of the literature on religion and spirituality in LGBTQ communities, see Andrew K. T. Yip, "Coming Home from the Wilderness: An Overview of Recent Scholarly Research on LGBTQI Religiosity/Spirituality in the

West," in *Queer Spiritual Spaces: Sexuality and Sacred Places*, ed. Kath Browne, Sally R. Munt and Andrew K.T. Yip (New York: Routledge), 35–50.

5 On bricolage see, for example, Danièle Hervieu-Léger, "Bricolage Vaut-Il Dissémination? Quelques Réflexions sur l'Operationnalité Sociologique d'une Metaphore Problématique," *Social Compass* 52, no. 3 (2005): 295–308.

6 See Jeremy Carrette and Richard King, *Selling Spirituality: The Silent Takeover of Religion* (New York: Routledge, 2005).

7 See especially Robert N. Bellah et al., *Habits of the Heart: Individualism and Commitment in American Life* (Berkeley: University of California Press, 1985).

8 Tuomas Martikainen and François Gauthier, eds., *Religion in the Neoliberal Age: Political Economy and Modes of Governance* (Burlington, VT: Ashgate, 2013).

9 François Gauthier et al., "Introduction: Religion in Market Society," in *Religion in the Neoliberal Age*, 13–14 (n. 45).

10 Breda Gray, "Catholic Church Civil Society Activism and the Neoliberal Governmental Project of Migrant Integration in Ireland," in *Religion in the Neoliberal Age*, 72. Gray is here quoting Thomas Lemke, "Foucault, Governmentality, and Critique: Rethinking Marxism," *Economy and Society* 14, no. 3 (2002): 49–64.

11 Subjectification, sometimes subjectivation, refers to the simultaneous and intertwined construction and subjection of the subject. See, for example, Judith Butler, *Gender Trouble: Feminism and the Subversion of Identity* (New York: Routledge, 1990) and *Bodies That Matter: On the Discursive Limits of "Sex"* (New York: Routledge, 1993).

12 Michel Foucault, *The Birth of Biopolitics: Lectures at the Collège de France, 1978–1979*, ed. Michel Senellart, trans. Graham Burchell (New York: Palgrave MacMillan, 2008), 131.

13 Ibid., 132.

14 Ibid., 226 (italics in original).

15 Ibid., 241.

16 See, for example, ibid., 243.

17 Ibid., 270–1.

18 On Foucault and religion, though, see Mark D. Jordan, *Convulsing Bodies: Religion and Resistance in Foucault* (Stanford, CA: Stanford University Press, 2015).

19 Foucault, *The Birth of Biopolitics*, 297.

20 For example, Tomoko Masuzawa, *The Invention of World Religions, or, How European Universalism Was Preserved in the Language of Pluralism* (Chicago: University of Chicago Press, 2005).

21 See especially chapter 1 of *Selling Spirituality*.

22 Michel Foucault, *The History of Sexuality, Volume 1: An Introduction* (New York: Vintage, [1978] 1990).

23 Lisa Duggan, "The New Homonormativity: The Sexual Politics of Neoliberalism," in *Materializing Democracy: Toward a Revitalized Cultural Politics*, ed. Russ Castronovo and Dana D. Nelson (Durham, NC: Duke University Press, 2002), 179. On the privatization of sexuality, see also the path-clearing essay by Lauren Berlant and Michael Warner, "Sex in Public," *Critical Inquiry* 24, no. 2 (1998): 547–66.

24 Jasbir K. Puar, *Terrorist Assemblages: Homonationalism in Queer Times* (Durham, NC: Duke University Press, 2007). On the privatization of sexuality, see the path-clearing essay by Lauren Berlant and Michael Warner, "Sex in Public," *Critical Inquiry* 24, no. 2 (1998): 547–66.

25 Melissa M. Wilcox, "The Separation of Church and Sex: Conservative Catholics and the Sisters of Perpetual Indulgence," *e-misférica* 12, no. 2 (2016): n.p.

26 Scott Lauria Morgensen, *Spaces Between Us: Queer Settler Colonialism and Indigenous Decolonization* (Minneapolis: University of Minnesota Press, 2011), 6.
27 Ibid., 27.
28 Ibid., 48.
29 A nuanced discussion of religious individualism, framed through the concept of "the subjective turn," can be found in Paul Heelas and Linda Woodhead, *The Spiritual Revolution: Why Religion is Giving Way to Spirituality* (Malden, MA: Blackwell, 2005).
30 See Talal Asad, *Genealogies of Religion: Discipline and Reasons of Power in Christianity and Islam* (Baltimore, MD: The Johns Hopkins University Press, 1993); Masuzawa, *The Invention of World Religions*.
31 Devdutt Pattanaik, *The Man Who Was a Woman and Other Queer Tales from Hindu Lore* (New York: Harrington Park Press, 2002).

References

Asad, Talal. *Genealogies of Religion: Discipline and Reasons of Power in Christianity and Islam*. Baltimore, MD: The Johns Hopkins University Press, 1993.
Bellah, Robert, Richard Madsen, Robert Neelly Bellah, Steven M. Tipton and William M Sullivan. *Habits of the Heart: Individualism and Commitment in American Life*. Berkeley, CA: University of California Press, 1985.
Berlant, Lauren and Michael Warner. "Sex in Public." *Critical Inquiry* 24, no. 2 (1998): 547–66.
Butler, Judith. *Gender Trouble: Feminism and the Subversion of Identity*. New York: Routledge, 1990.
———. *Bodies That Matter: On the Discursive Limits of "Sex."* New York: Routledge, 1993.
Carrette, Jeremy and Richard King. *Selling Spirituality: The Silent Takeover of Religion*. New York: Routledge, 2005.
Duggan, Lisa. "The New Homonormativity: The Sexual Politics of Neoliberalism." In *Materializing Democracy: Toward a Revitalized Cultural Politics*, 175–94. Edited by Russ Castronovo and Dana D. Nelson. Durham, NC: Duke University Press, 2002.
Foucault, Michel. *The Birth of Biopolitics: Lectures at the Collège de France, 1978–1979*. Edited by Michel Senellart, translated by Graham Burchell. New York: Palgrave MacMillan, 2008.
———. *The History of Sexuality, Volume 1: An Introduction*. New York: Vintage, [1978] 1990.
Gauthier, François, Tuomas Martikainen and Linda Woodhead. "Introduction: Religion in Market Society." In *Religion in the Neoliberal Age: Political Economy and Modes of Governance*, 1–20. Edited by T. Martikainen and F. Gauthier. Burlington, VT: Ashgate, 2013.
Gray, Breda. "Catholic Church Civil Society Activism and the Neoliberal Governmental Project of Migrant Integration in Ireland." In *Religion in the Neoliberal Age: Political Economy and Modes of Governance*, 69–91. Edited by Martikainen and Gauthier. Burlington, VT: Ashgate, 2013.
Heelas, Paul and Linda Woodhead. *The Spiritual Revolution: Why Religion Is Giving Way to Spirituality*. Malden, MA: Blackwell, 2005.

Hervieu-Léger, Danièle. "Bricolage Vaut-Il Dissémination? Quelques Réflexions sur l'Operationnalité Sociologique d'une Metaphore Problématique." *Social Compass* 52, no. 3 (2005): 295–308.

Jordan, Mark. *Convulsing Bodies: Religion and Resistance in Foucault*. Stanford, CA: Stanford University Press, 2015.

Martikainen, Tuomas and François Gauthier, eds. *Religion in the Neoliberal Age: Political Economy and Modes of Governance*. Burlington, VT: Ashgate, 2013.

Masuzawa, Tomoko. *The Invention of World Religions, or, How European Universalism was Preserved in the Language of Pluralism*. Chicago: University of Chicago Press, 2005.

Morgensen, Scott L. *Spaces Between Us: Queer Settler Colonialism and Indigenous Decolonization*. Minneapolis, MN: University of Minnesota Press, 2011.

Pattanaik, Devdutt. *The Man Who Was a Woman and Other Queer Tales from Hindu Lore*. New York: Harrington Park Press, 2002.

Puar, Jasbir. *Terrorist Assemblages: Homonationalism in Queer Times*. Durham, NC: Duke University Press, 2007.

Wilcox, Melissa M. "The Separation of Church and Sex: Conservative Catholics and the Sisters of Perpetual Indulgence." *e-misférica* 12, no. 2 (2016).

———. *Queer Nuns: Religion, Activism, and Serious Parody*. New York: New York University Press, 2018.

Yip, Andrew K.T. "Coming Home from the Wilderness: An Overview of Recent Scholarly Research on LGBTQI Religiosity/Spirituality in the West." In *Queer Spiritual Spaces: Sexuality and Sacred Places*, 35–50. Edited by Kath Browne, Sally R. Munt and Andrew K.T. Yip. New York: Routledge, 2010.

9 Yogi superman, master capitalist
Bikram Choudhury and the religion of commercial spirituality

Andrea R. Jain

Bikram Choudhury is a multimillionaire who has exploited the cultural cache and economic capital of yoga, claimed copyrights on yoga postural sequences, pursued litigation against rival yoga studio owners and teachers, and battled allegations of sexual harassment and rape all while serving as the self-proclaimed guru of Bikram Yoga and a teacher of spirituality.[1]

Bikram has been accused of serious abuses of power, especially sexual misconduct. For years, a general reputation as "yoga's bad boy" (as *Yoga Journal* dubbed him in 2000) was a part of, not damaging to, Bikram Yoga's brand image.[2] In 2013, however, a *Vanity Fair* article titled "Bikram Yoga's Embattled Founder: The Alleged Rapes and Sexual Harassment Claims Against Guru Bikram" represented the shift from Bikram's sex life being an enticing part of Bikram Yoga's mischievous brand image to it being a damaging public scandal. The success of Bikram Yoga's brand image steadily declined, and many of the yoga studios that promoted themselves as offering Bikram Yoga rebranded as "hot yoga" studios.[3]

Increasingly, women publicly accused Bikram of harassing them and, in some cases, raping them. Several filed lawsuits. In 2016, a Los Angeles jury ordered Bikram to pay more than $7 million to his former head of legal and international affairs Minakshi Jafa-Bodden who said the guru sexually harassed her and wrongfully fired her for investigating another woman's rape allegation. Shortly after the ruling, Bikram left the country and went into hiding. In 2017, a California judge issued an arrest warrant for Bikram stating that he had yet to pay any of the nearly $7 million awarded to Jafa-Bodden. Later that year, Bikram Choudhury Yoga Inc. filed for bankruptcy. At the time of writing, Bikram's whereabouts remain unknown.

This chapter analyzes the values, aims, ontology, rituals, aesthetics, mythology, and community-making activities promoted through Bikram Yoga in order to illustrate the ways commercial spiritualities often represent, in and through their commodities, bodies of religious practice. Bikram is the paragon of commercial spirituality. He is one among many entrepreneurs in the global spirituality market who have become frontline agents of commercial empires. He is also a yoga guru worshiped by adoring disciples and a purveyor of spiritual commodities that transform the bodies, lives, and relationships of those who consume them.

I use *body of religious practice* here to refer to a set of behaviors characterized by the following: they are treated as sacred, set apart from the ordinary or mundane;[4] they are grounded in a shared ontology or worldview (though that ontology may not be all-encompassing); they are grounded in a shared axiology or set of values or goals concerned with resolving weakness, suffering, or death; and the preceding qualities are reinforced through narrative and ritual.[5] Religion also concerns things that are shared. It is therefore *social*; religious behaviors demarcate social structures and organize social interactions. They are therefore also political insofar as they set the boundaries of authority and frequently organize people and other living beings into hierarchies.

In lamenting the reconfiguration of spirituality in the context of consumer culture, cultural and social analysts often overlook the religious behaviors in commercial spirituality.[6] Scholarship buttresses popular discussions of spirituality, which are often based on the assumption that you are either religious, spiritual, or neither but cannot be religious and spiritual. In other words, you are inside religion (and therefore outside spirituality), you are inside spirituality (and therefore outside religion), or you reject both.

We see the dichotomy between religion and spirituality in some high-profile quantitative research. Consider, for example, the high-profile study by the Pew Forum on Religion & Public Life, which suggests that the "nones" are "on the rise" and are "less religious than the public at large." According to the survey, about 18% of the U.S. population identifies as "spiritual, not religious," including 37% of the nones or unaffiliated and only 15% of the affiliated. The so-called rise of the nones reported in such surveys misses much of what is significant about spirituality and the direction of religion as it is *done*, as people *do* religion. Problems with the Pew report – for example, asking respondents to define their spirituality as a negation of their religiosity, "religious" or "spiritual, not religious," suggests that the increasingly frequent efforts to quantify religion and spirituality distract from more nuanced understandings. Respondents were asked, for example, not whether they do yoga and to what religious or spiritual effect, but rather whether they "believe" in yoga "not just as exercise, but as a spiritual practice."[7]

Yoga insiders frequently suggest yoga is secular or that it is "Spiritual but Not Religious." Bikram himself has proclaimed, "I teach spirituality. I use the body as a medium. I use the body to control your mind, to make your spirit happy."[8] Yoga insiders often avoid the category *religion* because for them, religion is narrowly defined primarily in terms of shared belief, implying that a person cannot rationally adopt two or more religions at the same time because that would entail commitment to different and incompatible belief systems. Many yoga practitioners, even when they self-describe themselves as "spiritual, not religious," would probably not describe themselves as "believers in yoga." Bikram himself rejects that Bikram Yoga is *religious*: "Religion is the biggest piece of shit created in all time!"[9]

Furthermore, scholarly inquiry on commercial spirituality tends to reduce it to the products of capitalism, that is, to mere consumer sellouts or commodities.[10] Such critiques are correct in pointing out that, since the Enlightenment and the birth of modern political liberalism, religion has become privatized, a process that preceded the rise of market capitalism, which facilitated the contemporary notion of consumer-oriented and individualized spiritualities. Those critiques are also correct that many spiritualities have been tailored to fit the needs of and to reflect the neoliberal values of corporate culture in its demand for an efficient, productive, and pacified workforce and for profit, which is concentrated in the hands of the super wealthy.[11]

The yoga industry, in particular, is known for a consumer idiom that attempts to sell evocative objects, images, or ideas appropriated from South Asian cultural complexes, resulting in countless commodities guaranteed to purify the spirit, mind, and body. Although the yoga industry is largely made up of forms of postural yoga, a 20th-century transnationally produced body of practices that focuses on the health benefits of certain postures, it thrives on widespread stereotypes of India as spiritually rich.[12] The industry is also known for its focus on self-care and personal improvement – more specifically, adopting a privatized and personalized notion of lifestyle and worldview; wedding a nostalgia for ancient symbols and traditions to modern ideals of beauty, fitness, health, and well-being; and valorizing and profiting off of the free market (even as cultural appropriation is in large part what makes profit possible).

Religious behaviors in commercial spirituality are not necessarily ethical ones.[13] There is no doubt that commercial yoga's spiritual discourses construct convenient masks for the neoliberal establishment and that its capitalist discourses equally mask the religious dimensions of spirituality; nevertheless, neoliberal and capitalist influences do not render it less religious than traditional religions. As I have said elsewhere, that there are ethical problems with market capitalism, given its dire consequences for individuals, communities, and the natural environment, is indisputable. That those ethical problems make the behaviors found therein nonreligious, however, is disputable.[14]

In contrast to dichotomous approaches to spirituality and religion in contemporary society, I suggest we should imagine commercial spirituality, not as a *takeover* or *replacement* of religion or as an *alternative* to religion, but as a modern *manifestation* of religion. What popular and scholarly assumptions about spirituality often miss are the ways commercial spiritualities share a lot with traditional religions. Social and cultural critiques that attend exclusively to commodity exchange remove narrated experiences from their embedded socioeconomic context and setting, therefore reducing the spirituality industry to socioeconomic dynamics in order to fit spiritualities into a theoretical discourse on capitalism and neoliberalism. In other words, they divest religious ways of organizing, approaching, and interacting with the social world from their view of consumer culture. However, the spirituality industry is not immune from the religiosity of consumer culture at large. As Kathryn Lofton argues, how we organize our consumer life and how consumer practices organize us are religious issues.[15] The religion of corporate culture "is in the consumer interests they protect, the social possibilities they promote, the hierarchies they reiterate, and the commodities they sell."[16] Religion is in everything spiritual consumers do.[17] The relationship between religious and consumer behaviors in commercial spirituality is a dynamic and mutually constitutive one. Bikram's efforts to become a yogi superman, for example, are concurrent with his efforts to become a master capitalist. In both ways, Bikram believes he has become more powerful than Superman. In his own words, "I'm beyond Superman . . . Because I have balls like atom bombs, two of them, 100 megatons each. Nobody fucks with me."[18]

Bikram Yoga, commodification, and religion

Bikram Choudhury (born in 1946 in Kolkata) is the CEO of Bikram Yoga Inc. and founder of Bikram's Yoga College of India, which provides certification in Bikram Yoga, a school of modern postural yoga performed as a series of twenty-six postures (each of which is performed twice) and two breathing exercises in a room heated to 105 degrees Fahrenheit.

Biographical details about Bikram depend heavily on his autohagiography.[19] Having practiced yoga since age three, at age five, Choudhury began studying with Indian physical culture advocate Bishnu Ghosh (younger brother of Paramahansa Yogananda, who in 1920 traveled to the United States where he founded the Self Realization Fellowship and authored the acclaimed book *Autobiography of a Yogi*). Bikram won the Indian National Yoga Competition at age thirteen. He tells the mythical narrative of how, as a teenager, he dropped an almost-four-hundred-pound weight on his knee, shattering his patella. Doctors said Bikram would never walk again, but he turned to Ghosh, who used yogic techniques to rebuild the young man. Bikram emerged completely cured after only six months. He moved to Bombay, where he became immersed in Bollywood culture, which remains a central part of Bikram Yoga teacher training programs to this day – trainees gather at night to watch Bollywood films until two or three in the morning – and a daily pastime of Bikram himself.

Soon after Bikram's guru's death in 1970, having been charged with the mission to finish Yoganananda's project of delivering yoga to the world, Bikram left for Japan, where he used heated rooms to replicate the conditions of Calcutta. He also claims to have aided Japanese scientists studying tissue regeneration and to have healed Richard Nixon of chronic phlebitis using nothing but Epsom salts.

In 1973, Bikram came to the United States and opened a small yoga school in the basement of a Beverly Hills bank building where he taught a twenty-six-posture yoga program, which he claimed would maintain and restore health even to those with grave injuries and illnesses. There, he very much represented the ascetic ideal of a traditional celibate yogi, sleeping on the studio floor and offering donation-only classes.

According to Bikram, all that changed when his student, the famous actress Shirley MacLaine, approached him and advised, "In America, if you don't charge money . . . people won't respect you."[20] Rather than allow capitalism to restrain him, Bikram became a master capitalist. He changed his approach, becoming one of the first entrepreneurs to build a commodified, franchised, and merchandized yoga brand.

The growth in demand was exponential. In 1994, Bikram hosted his first teacher-training program in Los Angeles. Training programs would eventually boast upwards of six hundred registrants. The cost for training steadily rose. A 2018 training costs $16,600. If, as Lofton suggests, "religion manifests in efforts to mass-produce relations of value," then Bikram Yoga teacher training programs represent consumer religion.[21] Teachers who have completed the training have opened more than five thousand yoga studios worldwide. In addition to charging for his yoga classes and teacher training programs, Bikram merchandise has included CDs, DVDs, apparel, towels, mats, books, and water bottles. In Bikram's rise-to-the-top story, we witness what Philip Goodchild described as a general consequence of neoliberalism: "The spheres of piety . . . have been increasingly appropriated by finance capital itself. Religions adapt to make themselves more appealing in a competitive market."[22]

The convocational meetings of Bikram Yoga teacher training programs occur in front of wreathed portraits of Bikram, Ghosh, and Yogananda, a devotional gesture that situates Bikram within an authoritative, Indian yogic lineage and narrative. Though it has been suggested that spiritualities are averse to history – Courtney Bender, for example, suggests that "[n]arrating spirituality in a way that gives it a past and affords it a tradition makes it unrecognizable to those who practice and produce it" – Bikram Yoga conveys the way narrative mythology can serve as the very nucleus of commercial spirituality.[23] Multiple intersecting narratives about free enterprise, the individual and his or her well-being, and long Indian lineages or ancient origins shoulder commercial spirituality.[24] Bikram is among the many charismatic capitalists responsible for producing the narratives that sustain capitalist empires today.[25] Branding and mythologizing go hand in hand.[26]

Though some might retort that "fitness," "stress-relief," and "health" are the "final objectives" of Bikram Yoga and serve utilitarian or hedonistic self-interest as opposed to salvation or other truly religious aims, a full understanding of Bikram Yoga qua religion requires reflection on the human tendency to seek resolutions to the problems of weakness and suffering. Wouter J. Hanegraaff suggests New Age healing systems, for example, are not concerned only with utilitarian aims of physical and psychological healing but also with the religious problem of human weakness and suffering:

> In a general sense, "personal growth" can be understood as the shape "religious salvation" takes in the New Age movement; it is affirmed that deliverance from human suffering and weakness will be reached by developing our human potential, which results in our increasingly getting in touch with our inner divinity. Considering the general affinity between salvation and healing, the close connection between personal growth and healing . . . is hardly surprising in itself. It is important to note however, that therapy and religious "salvation" tend to merge to an extent perhaps unprecedented in other traditions.[27]

In turn, "religious salvation in fact amounts to a radical form of 'healing.' "[28]

Bikram Yoga is a commodity as well as a radical form of healing. Representatives of Bikram's Yoga College takes seriously the charge to deliver universal healing through yoga, proclaiming on the Bikram Yoga website, "We are fully dedicated to the wellness of the millions of people around the world."[29]

Bikram's overt economics, rooted in the neoliberal emphasis on the individual, press for a lifestyle of physiotherapeutic consumption. On the one hand, at times, Bikram resorts to overtly religious terms to convey the purpose of yoga: "The spirit is nothing without the body. And the body is nothing without the spirit. Our body is God's temple. We must take care of it, keep it healthy, by coming to yoga class every day."[30] On the other hand, Bikram has denied that many practitioners of Bikram Yoga are capable of "spiritual growth," telling one white American journalist, for example,

> You Westerners are like spiritual babies. You were born in the wrong country, with the wrong skin color, in the wrong culture. You can never be spiritual! It is not your fault. I'm sorry about that. If you can even get the body right, that much is good enough for you![31]

But getting the body "right" is itself a form of radical healing, as Bikram adds:

> It is very simple. Go do good in the world, like me. Teach them their mind has a screw loose. It hates itself, it hates its body. But the lotus can grow in the garbage! Make them fall in love with themselves! That is the secret.[32]

The constant effort to situate Bikram Yoga within larger narratives testifies to their importance to identity construction for teachers and other practitioners. At teacher trainings, lectures deliver complex, intersecting narratives on Bikram Yoga's capacity to prolong youth and heal the body of disease as well as its rootedness in allopathic medicine, nutritional sciences, pathology, subtle energy, and the chakra system. Bikram and the most advanced teachers in Bikram Yoga lecture on the theory and practice of yoga and yoga therapy and on the setting up and marketing of a yoga studio.

If the mythological narratives underlying Bikram Yoga reconcile the contradictions – the pervasive yet impossible aims – between unquestioned devotion to youth and the inevitability of aging, then it is the Bikram Yoga rituals that unite individuals into a community of assent. Bikram Yoga's rituals are in large part concerned with activities through which yoga practitioners conceptualize and reinforce their value systems, goals, space, and relationships. Bikram's Yoga College of India provides teachers with "basic guidelines" for constructing and managing a predetermined ritual space and ritual process. All Bikram Yoga approved studios, for example, are required to meticulously follow a particular format. All teachers are required to memorize a forty-five-page script, which they call the "dialogue," to be recited verbatim so that classes across studios are identical to taking a class with Bikram himself. Every class is supposed to follow additional specific requirements and contain a series of postures instructed in the same way every time all of which serves to buttress the concentration of authority in Bikram and, as an extension of Bikram, Bikram Yoga-trained teachers. A sample of the guidelines includes the following:

> Carpet is the only approved flooring. No other flooring is allowed . . .
> Mirrors must be on the front wall . . .
> Temperature: 105 degree heat/40% humidity.
> Only Bikram certified teachers can instruct classes
> Bikram's Beginning Yoga Class of 26 postures and 2 breathing exercises is permitted. No other styles of yoga . . . can be conducted . . .
> No physical contact, hands on corrections or adjustments of students is permitted (with the exception of Bikram) . . .
> Do not turn yoga mats at any point during the class . . .[33]

One Bikram Yoga–trained teacher testified to the power of that space to transform the practitioner:

> Those who ignore the Bikram types of yoga may not understand what yoga is – there is something very real that happens in there once you overcome your self (lower case) and that real thing is yoga pure and simple. You connect to truth."[34]

Healing through Bikram Yoga requires hard work. In fact, Bikram calls approved Bikram Yoga studios "torture chambers." Although critics are quick to write off yoga practitioners as hedonistic or utilitarian consumers, ascetic behaviors are essential to advancement in Bikram Yoga.[35] One student describes a not-uncommon experience in a class led by Bikram himself:

> Before I can do the Head-to-Knee Pose . . . I have to wipe the sweat out of my eyes and dry my hands and foot to stop them from slipping. Even so, I topple over immediately. I look around. A few of the students can hold the poses until the bitter end, but most, like me, are tortured and teetering while Bikram urges us on, admonishing us to work harder, stretch harder. "Pain is good. You Americans taught me, no pain no gain. In India we say, No hell, no heaven.[36]

All that suffering is for the sake of miraculous healing, enhanced life expectancy, and self-perfection as embodied by Bikram himself. Bikram frequently enrobes his muscular body in little more than his signature speedo. He wears a diamond-encrusted watch, has an eight-thousand-square-foot Beverly Hills mansion, and dons a Rolls-Royce and Bentley collection. Bikram's skimpy Speedo bears some resemblance to the emblematic loincloth associated with the master yogi, and when he sits to rest at teacher-training programs, the guru reclines on a chair covered with an ochre-colored towel, resembling the ochre robes donned by many renunciates in South Asia. Yet Bikram's consumer behaviors are a far cry from the renunciatory behaviors we envision when we think of an Indian master yogi who is poor, celibate, free of superfluous possessions and, as a consequence of his ascetic behaviors, has developed endless sorts of powers to the point of being inhuman or superhuman, from being able to read minds to living for extraordinary lengths of time.

Although Bikram's biography is often interpreted as a tale of an ascetic yogi-turned-capitalist entrepreneur – Anya Foxen describes him, for example, as evoking the "ascetic-turned-capitalist Maharaja" – the guru does not represent a shift from the yogi to the entrepreneur; rather, he represents the juxtaposition of the two.[37] In other words, however much Bikram serves as an entrepreneurial guru, he is also a supernatural yogi. Bikram claims to eat only one meal a day (only chicken or beef), drink nothing but water and Coke, and sleep only two hours per night.[38] In a claim evoking images of yogis believed to have transmutated their semen into Soma by means of their extreme *tapas* or ascetic activities, Bikram once claimed he had no need to sexually harass or assault women because "[p]eople spend one million dollars for a drop of [his] sperm."[39] Based on calculations of the average time human beings spend sleeping, Bikram once determined that he was approximately 220 years old.[40]

These narratives serve to vindicate Bikram's authoritative excesses. The famously intensive Bikram Yoga teacher training has a schedule that starts daily at seven in the morning and ends at ten at night. The schedule includes classes in the postures, lectures, and demonstrations. During postural classes, Bikram alternates between standing and hollering corrections, oftentimes with expletives, into his headset and lounging on his throne set on a stage at the front of the class. Beautiful women comb his hair and massage his feet. There are other physical and verbal gestures of devotion. One of Bikram's employees told an interviewer, "I'm in love! I'm in love with Bikram! I'm in love with our life! I'm in love with what we are doing for people!"[41] Others declare that supernormal nature of Bikram Yoga and the superhuman nature of Bikram more publicly. When Bikram asked students to introduce themselves at a 2002 teacher training in Los Angeles, one student rose and exclaimed, "I'm from San Diego. I've been doing yoga for eleven months. I love Bikram. He is God."[42]

Scandal, the guru model, and corporate corruption

In 2002, there was a transnational public outcry in response to Bikram and Bikram's Yoga College when they attempted to enforce copyrights over Bikram Yoga's sequence of twenty-six postures on yoga studios claiming to teach Bikram Yoga but not conforming to Bikram's standards. Bikram's attorney, Jacob Reibolt, suggested that "[m]any people think yoga belongs to the world. That is wrong."[43] In February 2003, Reinbolt announced that Bikram secured federal copyright registration for his series of twenty-six postures and two breathing exercises.

Bikram threatened to pursue legal action against anyone who copied his sequence or created a derivative work that uses even a small number of consecutive postures; the addition of different postures or breathing exercises to the sequence (with or without the dialogue); or the introduction of elements, such as music, to the sequence. Bikram sent "cease and desist" letters, warning yoga studio owners and teachers not to teach his style or anything derivative unless they graduated from his teacher training program and paid a franchise fee. Through these activities, Bikram has maintained an iron grip on the hot yoga industry – teachers have to undergo a nine-week costly teacher training offered by Bikram Choudhury Yoga if they want to teach the same postural sequence or something derivative. Bikram and his Yoga College were involved in two U.S. federal court lawsuits, which were settled out of court under nondisclosure agreements, and they threatened many more around the world.[44]

Allison Fish suggests this case serves as an example of how the yoga industry, given the difficulty in locating and defining yoga, has consequences for how open-source and intellectual property rights are defined and how information management strategies emerge.[45] The case, indeed, forced those concerned about the question of who owns yoga to take a stand with regard to how to define and categorize new conceptualizations or applications of what are popularly considered preexisting materials, traditional knowledge, or spiritual practices.

In 2012, the U.S. Copyright Office slighted Bikram's claims of ownership when they concluded that the copyrights issued to him were issued in error.[46] Neither Bikram and the Yoga College nor any other individual or organization could copyright yoga postures or their sequences. In response to the question of whether "the selection and arrangement of preexisting exercises, such as yoga poses" are copyrightable, the office answered with a definitive "no."[47] The refusal to grant copyrights to yoga posture "compilations" or sequences is based on the idea that "exercise is not a category of authorship."[48] Therefore, it is based on the assumption that postural yoga, by definition, is "exercise."[49]

The government of the United States was not the only one to respond to Bikram and the Yoga College's efforts to establish and enforce copyrights on yoga postural sequences. In 2002, in part as an act of resistance to Bikram's attempts to claim yoga ownership, the Indian government-run Traditional Knowledge Digital Library created a database of 1,300 yoga postures believed to be documented in ancient Indian texts.[50] The Indian government's agenda, which has expanded to include many strategies on the part of Prime Minister Narendra Modi to "reclaim yoga for India," is akin to that of Bikram's in the sense that both betray a corporate logic in claiming some kind of ownership of yoga to prevent what they perceive as the inequitable profiteering off knowledge they perceive as belonging to them.[51]

From one perspective, Bikram joins rank orientalists, essentializing yoga and profiting off the exploitation of yoga's cultural cache for the purposes of power and profit. He sees yoga as a commodity that can be bought and sold and reflects the neoliberal emphasis on corporate rights over respect for community rights. From another perspective, as Foxen notes, his claim to ownership can also be read as an attempt to control a model of initiatory yogic transmission through modern structures of economic and legal power.[52]

Though they earned him many adversaries, tensions and debates over copyright issues did not lead to the demise of Bikram Yoga's brand image. His reputation as a womanizer did not either. In a 2011 interview, when asked if he has sex with students, Bikram exclaimed, "Only when they give me no choice! If they say to me, 'Boss, you must fuck me or I will kill myself,' then I do it! Think if I don't! The karma!"[53] Despite such explicit confessions to sexual exploitation, Bikram Yoga continued to grow and expand. It was not until there were legal proceedings that delegitimized Bikram's abuses of power that the brand image went into steady decline.

Popular media has since primarily envisioned Bikram as an abusive guru and his organization as a spiritual cult. This situates him within the broader context of guru sex scandals that have erupted since the 1960s and the larger narrative that envisions religion and especially non-Protestant forms of spirituality as inevitably despotic and abusive. It is true that, even as gurus have idealized celibacy and ethical integrity, many late 20th-century and 21st-century scandals have revealed sexual corruption. A number of yoga gurus have been outed as sexually active, usually with young, white, female students. These scandals have left the public thinking the "guru model" is problematic for its inherently undemocratic tendencies, suspecting the model is an extreme form of authoritarianism that inevitably leads to demise. In 1993, for example, Joel Kramer and Diana Alstad warned against the dangers of the guru–disciple relationship, suggesting it displays "the seductions, predictable patterns, and corruptions contained in any essentially authoritarian form" and "the epitome of surrender to a living person, and thus clearly exhibits what it means to trust another more than oneself."[54]

Though yoga gurus certainly can slip into authoritarianism, the assumption that corruption is somehow inherent to that model betrays an Orientalist stereotype of South Asians, their religions, and other cultural products as despotic in contrast to white, so-called democratic religions or cultures. I suggest we avoid falling into dichotomous, Orientalist traps by too simplistically subsuming Bikram and his financial and sex scandals into "guru scandals," as if this is simply a result of an essentialized "guru model" or, more generally, of religious authoritarianism. If one imagines Bikram Yoga as offering a profile of commercial spirituality, it becomes readily apparent that this type of corruption, which is found in all forms of authoritarianism, is as much a reflection of capitalist corporate culture as it is a reflection of patriarchal religious hierarchy.

Corporate control of the globe is at an all-time high, and the super wealthy (who are only sometimes also religious authorities) have little reason to fear the average global citizen. CEOs, after all, regularly get away with making over three hundred times the average wages of workers.[55]

Bikram's efforts to establish himself as the living embodiment of an authoritative lineage that offers a form of salvation through a healing kinesthetic ritual are mutually constitutive with, not mutually exclusive with, his efforts to establish himself as a member of the super wealthy, free from many of the limitations on ordinary citizens' behaviors. When Bikram Choudhury Yoga Inc. filed for chapter eleven bankruptcy protection on November 9, 2017, the corporation listed more than $16 million owed in legal judgments, many related to Bikram's sexual scandals, with the biggest creditors being former employees. The company epitomizes corporate corruption. And, as we have learned from Donald Trump, bankruptcy is not sufficient to destroy the super wealthy in the neoliberal age – in fact, such an entrepreneur can rise to one of the most powerful positions in the world. Considering that, in the United States, there are more arrests for marijuana charges than for violent crimes, and many of those arrested for marijuana, especially black youth, end up serving prison time, this cost to an entrepreneur of Bikram's magnitude is a mere slap on the wrist for charges of violent behavior.[56]

Conclusion

Bikram's religious efforts to achieve the status of a yogi superman are mutually constitutive with his capitalist activities as an entrepreneur. The values, ontology, rituals, aesthetics, mythology, and community-making activities underlying Bikram Yoga make up a religious operation that makes capitalism seem desirable and perhaps even necessary. In scenes from Bikram Yoga's corporate culture, underwritten by market capitalist discourse about individualist personhood, are beliefs about the world, a world in which God is present as a yogi superman. Bikram creates and profits off all these discourses.

Though it is a mistake to overlook the religious dimensions of commercial spirituality, it is also a mistake to overlook the real ethical problems with them, namely, the moments when they are complicit with neoliberalism and market capitalism and, more specifically, embody the abusive and exploitative activities of the super wealthy.

Neoliberal ideologies and the corporate model are infiltrating every aspect of contemporary culture and subordinating of social and ethical concerns associated with social justice to the realm of economics. Spiritualities, like traditional religions institutions, accommodate the neoliberal and capitalist social, economic, and political mores of the day. Also like traditional religions, they can bring about a significant change in one's lifestyle or fundamental behavior pattern while locating the spiritual firmly within a privatized space and multinational corporate model. In other words, as evidenced in Bikram, spiritual entrepreneurs can be both frontline agents of neoliberalism's commercial empires and gurus worshipped by adoring disciples.

The yoga industry provides an apt example of an individualized spirituality of the self, packaged over and over again as a commodity to be sold to the consumer for her or his own perfection according to capitalist-consumer standards and at the cost of social equality – one should also add environmental costs. Many yoga commodities, Bikram Yoga commodities included, are methods for pacifying and accommodating individuals to the neoliberal and capitalist world in which they find themselves. Bikram Yoga is a neoliberal religion. Neoliberalism, in Chomsky's words, values "profit over people," or, as Bikram might put it, measures the superman by his power to heal, though only those willing to pay the price.

Notes

1 This chapter first appeared as a conference paper titled "Being a Superman Who Can't be F*$#d With: Bikram Choudhury, the Yoga Industry, and Neoliberal Religion," which I delivered at the Being Spiritual but Not Religious: Past, Present, and Future(s) conference in 2016 at Rice University, and then in another incarnation as "The Case of Bikram Yoga: Can 'Pop Spiritualities' Be Truly Transformative," *Tricycle* (Spring 2017).

2 Loraine Despres, "Yoga's Bad Boy: Bikram Choudhury," *Yoga Journal* (March/April 2000).

3 For example, in 2017, the first Bikram Yoga studio in New York City (founded in 1999 as "Bikram Yoga NYC") dropped the Bikram name in its rebranding efforts. It was renamed "Bode NYC" (see Bode NYC, https://bodenyc.com).

4 This use of *sacred* comes from Émile Durkheim in his famous *The Elementary Forms of Religious Life* (Oxford: Oxford University Press, 2001 [1912]).

Durkheim used *sacred* to describe that which is set apart from the ordinary or mundane. Sacred things are antagonistic to profane things (*Elementary Forms of Religious Life*, 38).

5 I am drawing on my definition of *body of religious practice* first discussed in Andrea R. Jain, *Selling Yoga: From Counterculture to Pop Culture* (New York: Oxford University Press, 2014).

6 The study *Selling Spirituality* (2005) by Jeremy Carrette and Richard King serves as the paragon of the tendency to reduce spiritualities to mere consumer sell-outs (Jeremy Carrette and Richard King, *Selling Spirituality: The Silent Takeover of Religion* [New York: Routledge, 2005]). See also, for example, Wade Clark Roof, *Spiritual Marketplace: Baby Boomers and the Remaking of American Religion* (Princeton, NJ: Princeton University Press, 1999); Kimberly J. Lau, *New Age Capitalism: Making Money East of Eden* (Philadelphia: University of Pennsylvania Press, 2000). The authors target the "big business" of spirituality, including postural yoga. Though the authors claim that their concern is with the sociopolitical consequences of the spiritual marketplace and not with the truth, authenticity, or the question of "what counts as real spirituality," their analysis of the spiritual marketplace is framed as the capitalist "takeover," "commercialization," and "replacement" of religion. This opposition between capitalist commodification and religion amounts to an assessment of what counts as real religion. For example, the reduction of spiritual products to the mere commodification of what were traditional religious wares – "What is being sold to us as radical, trendy and transformative spirituality in fact produces little in the way of a significant change in one's lifestyle or fundamental behaviour patterns" (Carrette and King, *Selling Spirituality*, 5) – frames spiritualities as distinct from religion and presumes, therefore, that practices identified by insiders as *spiritual* are not religious. In short, there is no religious substance to self-proclaimed spiritualities. Some recent work on spirituality and religion in consumer culture avoids the dichotomy between spirituality and religion (see, for example, Kathryn Lofton, *Oprah: The Gospel of an Icon* [Los Angeles: University of California Press, 2011]; Jain, *Selling Yoga*; Nicole Aschoff, *The New Prophets of Capital* [New York: Verso Press, 2015]; Philip Goodchild, *Capitalism and Religion: The Price of Piety* [New York: Routledge, 2002]; and Lofton, *Consuming Religion*).

7 Pew Research Center, "Nones on the Rise," October 9, 2012, www.pewforum.org/2012/10/09/nones.

8 Ed Staskus, "The Torture Chamber," *Elephant Journal*, May 4, 2012, www.elephantjournal.com/2012/05/the-torture-chamber-ed-staskus/.

9 Clancy Martin, "The Overheated, Oversexed Cult of Bikram Choudhury," *GQ*, February 1, 2011.

10 Some critiques of spirituality point to postural yoga as an especially apt example of the capitalist replacement of religion, suggesting that postural yoga separates yoga from its religio-philosophical, ascetic, and ethical dimensions (Carrette and King, *Selling Spirituality*, 117–18) or suggesting that it relies on physical practice exclusively and at the loss of a "complete" lifestyle (Carrette and King, *Selling Spirituality*, 117; see also, Lau, *New Age Capitalism*, 104). Carrette and King lament, "Yoga essentially became a form of exercise and stress-relief to be classified alongside the other health and 'sports-related' practices and fads of the late twentieth century" (*Selling Spirituality*, 119).

11 "Neoliberalism is in the first instance a theory of political economic practices that proposes that human well-being can best be advanced by liberating individual entrepreneurial freedoms and skills within an institutional framework characterized by strong private property rights, free markets, and free trade" (David Harvey, *A Brief History of Neoliberalism* [New York: Oxford University Press, 2005], 2). Neoliberalism promotes privatization of public utilities, services, and

resources. Under neoliberalism, everything is a commodity that can be bought and sold, and corporate rights are privileged over community rights.

12 For a history of modern yoga and its transnational constructions and relationship to globalization, see Elizabeth de Michelis, *A History of Modern Yoga: Patañjali and Western Esotericism* (New York: Continuum, 2004); Mark Singleton, *Yoga Body: The Origins of Modern Posture Practice* (New York: Oxford University Press, 2010); and Jain, *Selling Yoga*.

13 The problem is not with the critiques of consumer culture – such critiques, in fact, speak to the undeniable ethical problems with capitalism and corporate culture. Rather, the problem is that the critiques miss much about consumer culture. Commercial engagement has frequently been dismissed as antithetical to true religious aims, but the dynamics of the market are integral to the whole practice of religion in the context of consumer culture. In reality, in consumer culture, there is no distinction between the market or commercial production and consumption and sacred space or religious or spiritual activity (see, e.g., Jain, *Selling Yoga* and Lofton, *Consuming Religion*).

14 Jain, *Selling Yoga*, 115, 121. To reiterate, market capitalism and neoliberalism are no doubt ethical problems. Critiques of neoliberalism are understandably concerned about its real negative social and ecological consequences, including the corporate takeover of society and the displacement of questions of social justice. The ethical implications of market capitalism in light of modern commitments to the individual (or human rights), the social world (or social justice), and the natural environment (or sustainability) are dire. In other words, if a person's ethical agenda includes maintaining a stable global community of equal persons and a sustainable natural environment, market capitalism and neoliberalism are rightfully perceived as obstacles.

15 Lofton, *Consuming Religion*.

16 Lofton, *Consuming Religion*, xii.

17 I made a related argument regarding the religious practices of yoga consumers in *Selling Yoga*, 95–129.

18 Quoted by Paul Keegan, "Yogis Behaving Badly," *Business 2.0*, September 2002.

19 See, for example, Bikram Choudhury, *Bikram Yoga: The Guru Behind Hot Yoga Shows the Way to Radiant Health and Personal Fulfillment* (New York: Harper Collins Publishers, 2007).

20 Choudhury, *Bikram Yoga*, 32.

21 Lofton, *Consuming Religion*, 2.

22 Goodchild, *Capitalism and Religion*, 248.

23 Courtney Bender, *The New Metaphysicals* (Chicago, IL: University of Chicago Press, 2010), 185.

24 For additional examples, see Jain, *Selling Yoga*; and Aschoff, *New Prophets of Capital*.

25 Ardent pro-capitalists in the spirituality industry, as Aschoff demonstrates, situate their products within narratives about self-improvement and actualization (*New Prophets of Capital*).

26 Mara Einstein suggests that mythologizing is at work in branding, which requires marketers to uniquely package their products (*Brands of Faith: Marketing Religion in a Commercial Age* [New York: Routledge Press, 2008]). On mythologizing practices in the yoga industry at large, see Jain, *Selling Yoga*, 95–129.

27 Wouter J. Hanegraaff, *New Age Religion and Western Culture: Esotericism in the Mirror of Secular Thought* (Albany: State University of New York Press, 1998), 46.

28 Hanegraaff, *New Age Religion*, 44.

29 Bikram Yoga, "What Is Bikram Yoga?" www.bikramyoga.com/about/bikram-yoga/.

30 Despres, "Yoga's Bad Boy."
31 Martin, "Overheated, Oversexed Cult."
32 Martin, "Overheated, Oversexed Cult."
33 Bikram Yoga, "Bikram Yoga Franchise," www.bikramyoga.com/franchise/.
34 Anonymous source, email correspondence, February 28, 2014.
35 Many of the ascetic dimensions of Bikram Yoga are present in other schools of modern yoga (see Jain, *Selling Yoga*, 95–129).
36 Despres, "Yoga's Bad Boy."
37 Anya P. Foxen, *Biography of a Yogi: Paramahansa Yogananda and the Origins of Modern Yoga* (New York: Oxford University Press, 2017), 180.
38 Martin, "Overheated, Oversexed Cult."
39 For Bikram's interview in which he makes this claim, see HBO Real Sports, "Bikram Choudhury Sexual Misconduct Allegations," October 21, 2016, www.youtube.com/watch?v=NZ4BF0WdY1s&feature=youtu.be. For examples of myths about the yogic transmutation of semen, see Wendy Doniger O'Flaherty, *Women, Androgynes, and Other Mythical Beasts* (Chicago: University of Chicago Press, 1980), 20, 43–7.
40 Benjamin Lorr, *Hell-Bent: Obsession, Pain, and the Search for Something Like Transcendence in Bikram Yoga* (London: Bloomsbury, 2012), 140.
41 Martin, "Overheated, Oversexed Cult."
42 Hilary E. MacGregor, "Had Your McYoga Today? A Stretch of Success," *Los Angeles Times*, July 7, 2002, http://articles.latimes.com/2002/jul/07/news/lv-bikram7.
43 MacGregor, "Had Your McYoga Today?
44 Allison Fish, "The Commodification and Exchange of Knowledge in the Case of Transnational Commercial Yoga," *International Journal of Cultural Property* 13 (2006): 192.
45 Ibid.
46 Office of the Federal Register, "Registration of Claims to Copyright," *Federal Register: The Daily Journal of the United States Government*, June 22, 2012, www.federalregister.gov/articles/2012/06/22/2012-15235/registration-of-claims-to-copyright.
47 Ibid., 37607.
48 Ibid.
49 In the view of the Copyright Office, a selection, coordination, or arrangement of exercise movements, such as a compilation of yoga poses, may be precluded from registration as a functional system or process in cases where the particular movements and the order in which they are to be performed are said to result in improvements in one's health or physical or mental condition. See, for example, *Open Source Yoga Unity v. Choudhury*, 2005 WL 756558, *4, 74 U.S.P.Q.2d 1434 (N.D. Cal. 2005; "Here, Choudhury claims that he arranged the asanas in a manner that was both aesthetically pleasing and in a way that he believes is best designed to improve the practitioner's health."). While such a functional system or process may be aesthetically appealing, it is nevertheless uncopyrightable subject matter. (Office of the Federal Register, "Registration of Claims to Copyright," 37607).
50 Kounteya Sinha, "India Pulls the Plug on Yoga as Business," *The Times of India*, February 6, 2011, http://articles.timesofindia.indiatimes.com/2011-02-06/india/2835560 2_1_hot-yoga-patanjali-tkdl.
51 See Andrea R. Jain and Michael Schulson, "The World's Most Influential Yoga Teacher Is a Homophobic Right-Wing Activist," *Religion Dispatches*, October 4, 2016; and Andrea R. Jain, *Peace, Love, Yoga: The Politics of Global Spirituality* (New York, NY: Oxford University Press, forthcoming).
52 Foxen, *Biography of a Yogi*, 182.

53 Martin, "Overheated, Oversexed Cult."
54 Joel Kramer and Diana Alstad, *The Guru Papers: Masks of Authoritarian Power* (Berkeley, CA: Frog Books, 1993).
55 AFL-CIO, https://aflcio.org/paywatch.
56 Timothy Williams, "Marijuana Arrests Outnumber Those for Violent Crimes, Study Finds," *The New York Times*, October 12, 2016, www.nytimes.com/2016/10/13/us/marijuana-arrests.html.

References

AFL-CIO. https://aflcio.org/paywatch.

Aschoff, Nicole. *The New Prophets of Capital*. New York, NY: Verso Books, 2015.

Bender, Courtney. *The New Metaphysicals*. Chicago, IL: University of Chicago Press, 2010.

Bikram Yoga. www.bikramyoga.com.

Bode NYC. https://bodenyc.com.

Carrette, Jeremy and Richard King. *Selling Spirituality: The Silent Takeover of Religion*. New York, NY: Routledge, 2005.

Choudhury, Bikram. *Bikram Yoga: The Guru Behind Hot Yoga Shows the Way to Radiant Health and Personal Fulfillment*. New York, NY: Harper Collins Publishers, 2007.

Corrigan, John. "Emotions Research and the Academic Study of Religion." In *Religion and Emotion: Approaches and Interpretations*, 3–32. Edited by John Corrigan. Oxford: Oxford University Press, 2004.

de Michelis, Elizabeth. *A History of Modern Yoga: Patañjali and Western Esotericism*. New York, NY: Continuum, 2004.

Despres, Loraine. "Yoga's Bad Boy: Bikram Choudhury." *Yoga Journal* (March/April 2000).

Durkheim, Émile. *The Elementary Forms of Religious Life*. Translated by Carol Cosman. Oxford: Oxford University Press, 2001 [1912].

Einstein, Mara. *Brands of Faith: Marketing Religion in a Commercial Age*. New York, NY: Routledge Press, 2008.

Fish, Allison. "The Commodification and Exchange of Knowledge in the Case of Transnational Commercial Yoga." *International Journal of Cultural Property* 13 (2006): 189–206.

Foxen, Anya P. *Biography of a Yogi: Paramahansa Yogananda and the Origins of Modern Yoga*. New York: Oxford University Press, 2017.

Goodchild, Philip. *Capitalism and Religion: The Price of Piety*. New York, NY: Routledge, 2002.

Hanegraaff, Wouter J. *New Age Religion and Western Culture: Esotericism in the Mirror of Secular Thought*. Albany: State University of New York Press, 1998.

Harvey, David. *A Brief History of Neoliberalism*. New York, NY: Oxford University Press, 2005.

HBO Real Sports. "Bikram Choudhury Sexual Misconduct Allegations." October 21, 2016. www.youtube.com/watch?v=NZ4BF0WdY1s&feature=youtu.be.

Jain, Andrea R. *Selling Yoga: From Counterculture to Pop Culture*. New York, NY: Oxford University Press, 2014.

———. "Being a Superman Who Can't Be F*$#d With: Bikram Choudhury, the Yoga Industry, and Neoliberal Religion." Being Spiritual But Not Religious: Past, Present, and Future(s). Conference presentation at Rice University, 2016.

———. "The Case of Bikram Yoga: Can 'Pop Spiritualities' Be Truly Transformative." *Tricycle* (Spring 2017).

———. *Peace, Love, Yoga: The Politics of Global Spirituality*. New York, NY: Oxford University Press, forthcoming.

Jain, Andrea R. and Michael Schulson. "The World's Most Influential Yoga Teacher Is a Homophobic Right-Wing Activist." *Religion Dispatches*, October 4, 2016. http://religiondispatches.org/baba-ramdev/.

Keegan, Paul. "Yogis Behaving Badly." *Business 2.0*, September 2002.

Kramer, Joel and Diana Alstad. *The Guru Papers: Masks of Authoritarian Power*. Berkeley, CA: Frog Books, 1993.

Lau, Kimberly J. *New Age Capitalism: Making Money East of Eden*. Philadelphia: The University of Pennsylvania Press, 2000.

Lofton, Kathryn. *Oprah: The Gospel of an Icon*. Los Angeles: University of California Press, 2011.

———. *Consuming Religion*. Chicago, IL: University of Chicago Press, 2017.

Lorr, Benjamin. *Hell-Bent: Obsession, Pain, and the Search for Something Like Transcendence in Bikram Yoga*. London: Bloomsbury, 2012.

MacGregor, Hilary E. "Had Your McYoga Today? A Stretch of Success." *Los Angeles Times*, July 7, 2002. http://articles.latimes.com/2002/jul/07/news/lv-bikram7.

Martin, Clancy. "The Overheated, Oversexed Cult of Bikram Choudhury." *GQ*, February 1, 2011.

Office of the Federal Register. "Registration of Claims to Copyright." *Federal Register: The Daily Journal of the United States Government*, June 22, 2012. www.federalregister.gov/articles/2012/06/22/2012-15235/registration-of-claims-to-copyright.

Open Source Yoga Unity v. Choudhury. 2005 WL 756558, *4, 74 U.S.P.Q.2d 1434 (N.D. Cal. 2005.

Pew Research Center. "Nones on the Rise." 2012. www.pewforum.org/2012/10/09/nones-on-the-rise/.

Roof, Wade Clark. *Spiritual Marketplace: Baby Boomers and the Remaking of American Religion*. Princeton, NJ: Princeton University Press, 1999.

Singleton, Mark. *Yoga Body: The Origins of Modern Posture Practice*. New York, NY: Oxford University Press, 2010.

Sinha, Kounteya. "India Pulls the Plug on Yoga as Business." *The Times of India*, February 6, 2011. http://articles.timesofindia.indiatimes.com/2011-02-06/india/2835560 2_1_hot-yoga-patanjali-tkdl.

Staskus, Ed. "The Torture Chamber." *Elephant Journal*, May 4, 2012. www.elephantjournal.com/2012/05/the-torture-chamber-ed-staskus/.

Wendy Doniger O'Flaherty. *Women, Androgynes, and Other Mythical Beasts*. Chicago, IL: University of Chicago Press, 1980.

Williams, Timothy. "Marijuana Arrests Outnumber Those for Violent Crimes, Study Finds." *The New York Times*, October 12, 2016. www.nytimes.com/2016/10/13/us/marijuana-arrests.html.

10 Global spirituality among scientists

Elaine Howard Ecklund and Di Di

Scholars see the rise of spirituality – a quest for transcendence without affiliation with a religious tradition – as a celebration of individualism.[1] Some argue that, after the baby-boomer generation (those born between 1946 and 1964), many people were not so willing to submit to an organized religious authority.[2] Instead, individuals began to value the freedom to choose and combine different cultural resources, either religious or secular, after self-reflection.[3] In particular, it is possible that spirituality is a unique phenomenon in the United States and the United Kingdom – two societies in which the culture of individualism is prevalent.[4]

Nevertheless, an emerging strand of literature suggests that spirituality is not necessarily a celebration of individualism but, rather, a product of the operation among multiple cultural authorities.[5] According to these and other scholars, people in modern societies are situated in distinctive social institutions and hence are subsumed under different cultural authorities. Rather than relying exclusively on one religious authority to construct their religiosity, many people turn to multiple cultural authorities to construct their spirituality.

If, as the literature suggests, modern spirituality is a product of social differentiation in modern societies, there should be an emergent group in societies outside the United Kingdom and the United States, which constructs its own spirituality. Recent empirical studies on spirituality, however, have focused on the United Kingdom and the United States almost exclusively, which makes it difficult to answer the general question of whether spirituality is dependent on the culture of individualism. And so, to identify whether and to what extent spirituality is a global phenomenon, this chapter looks at how scientists in different contexts construct spirituality.

But why study scientists in particular? Science was once considered the dominant social institution contributing to secularization at the societal, institutional, and individual levels.[6] Although scholars acknowledge that science is not the only factor that drives secularization,[7] scholars and members of different publics still often view science and religion as competing and parallel cultural authorities.[8] For instance, people who deeply embrace scientific views are particularly attracted to New Atheism – a social movement that strives to eliminate the influence of religion from multiple social institutions.[9] Since they are situated at the intersection of two competing, parallel social institutions, scientists should, in theory, experience the most salient tensions and navigations in their construction of spirituality, making them an important group to expand our understanding of spirituality.

The contribution of this chapter, then, is twofold. First, it provides a systematic comparison of scientists' spirituality in different countries. Second, it advances extant scholarship on spirituality by arguing that it is a product of the tension between nonreligious scientists and their religious "others" and, in order to reduce this tension, nonreligious scientists often reconstruct the concept of the sacred, retaining the cultural meanings bundled with religion but without affiliating with any faith tradition. We further argue that whether spirituality can serve an ambassadorial role between science and religion depends on the national contexts in which science and religion are situated. Given that the interface between science and religion is still, more or less, a Western-based, Christian-centric conversation,[10] science was not – and currently is not – bundled with religion in all national contexts, especially Eastern societies.

The rise of (Western) spirituality

Scholars of religion in the West are curious about the changing religious landscape,[11] not least because "non religion" is rising in many Western societies.[12] But close inspection reveals that the rise of religious nonaffiliation is not indicative of the decline or disappearance of religion. Rather, it suggests a change in how individuals construct transcendence;[13] that is, a growing number of people are less satisfied by the faith tradition into which they were born or by the constructions of transcendent worlds offered by "the formal context of organized religion."[14] Indeed, many find that they can meet their individualistic spiritual needs by joining a new religious movement[15] or by seeking various unconventional modes of spirituality.[16]

Even so, scholars raise different opinions regarding the level of "individualism" of such socio-syncretic constructions of spirituality. These scholars argue that spirituality is not a celebration of individualism but a cooperation of multiple cultural authorities.[17] For certain groups of people who are immersed in or more impacted by certain cultural authorities, their spirituality is more loosely institutionalized than truly individualistic. For instance, science is a highly influential cultural authority, more than others, in the construction of spirituality among elite scientists in the United States.[18]

Regardless of its specific forms, Western spirituality is viewed as a syncretism of different cultural resources that include – but are not limited to – philosophy, religion, science, and embodied practices. Spiritual but Not

Religious (SBNR) people are seen as potential ambassadors who facilitate conversations among different social institutions.[19] This role might be particularly intriguing to SBNR scientists, who may facilitate the conversation between science and religion, historically two social institutions that have on occasion had a competitive and troubled relationship.

Spirituality and science

Prominent social theorists have considered science to be one of if not *the* leading institutions responsible for secularization.[20] Although the evidence suggests that scientists in certain contexts tend to be less religious than the general public,[21] recent studies have shown that beliefs about the secularizing effect of science are often inaccurate, exaggerated, or oversimplified.[22] By expanding their interest in scientists' religiosity from the West to other countries, scholars have found that scientists in Asian societies, such as Taiwan and Hong Kong, for example, are slightly *more* religious than the public. Even in countries where scientists are less religious than the public, they do not always attribute their low level of religiosity to their exposure to science but, rather, to their self-selecting from less religious and even irreligious backgrounds.[23]

Cultural boundaries between science and religion still persist.[24] A majority of scientists around the world adopt an "independence" narrative, seeing science and religion as separate authorities – the former authority of the natural world and the latter of the world of values and meaning. Sharing Stephen Jay Gould's idea of science and religion as non-overlapping magisteria, only a minority of academic scientists around the globe think that the two magisteria can collaboratively construct knowledge.[25] Nevertheless, the prevalence of the independence narrative over the collaboration narrative indicates that scientists, as insiders of the scientific community, are both constrained by and actively reinforce the cultural boundaries between science and religion.[26]

For this reason, scholars are increasingly interested in understanding scientists' religiosity, arguing that they might be social carriers of secularization, in Weber's sense,[27] thereby changing the role and importance of religion in modern societies.[28] While scholars generally recognize that modernity does not refer to a decline of religion but to the transformation of its appearance,[29] still by focusing predominantly on the construction of *religiosity* among scientists, they implicitly situate scientists as either religious or non-religious. The nascent literature on scientists' spirituality suggests that being SBNR might be an innovative way for scientists to navigate the apparent tension between science and religion.[30] In fact, this chapter expands on this idea by discussing how SBNR scientists in different contexts construct spirituality and how this construction leads to a better understanding of religion's role in modern societies.

Cases and concepts

Scientists' narratives come from the larger Religion among Scientists in International Context (RASIC) study. RASIC examines physicists' and biologists' views on the relationship of religion and science, their understandings of religion and spirituality, and the role of religion and spirituality in their lives and work, among other things. We studied these topics in eight nations and regions comprising: France, Hong Kong, India, Italy, Taiwan, Turkey, the United States, and the United Kingdom.

We used both a survey and in-depth interviews (more information about the survey can be found here in the cited article).[31] Relying on our survey, we identified the four national/social contexts where spirituality is the most prevalent among scientists – Taiwan, France, the United Kingdom, and the United States – as our focus for this chapter. In addition to the survey, we conducted in-depth interviews with a selection of survey respondents in each region among those who indicated that they would be willing to do an interview. A total of 609 interviews were completed in the eight regions we studied. For this chapter, we identify SBNR interview respondents according to their responses on the survey, only analyzing the interviews of those who identified themselves as Spiritual but Not Religious. We analyzed interviews of a total of 53 scientists in these four national contexts: 22 in the United Kingdom, 11 in the United States, 8 in France, and 12 in Taiwan.

Specifically, we asked respondents about their current religious/spiritual identities and practices, their religious history, and how they answer the big questions, such as questions about the meaning of life. When analyzing the data, we did a two-cycle coding that is generally inductive.[32] Our in-depth interviews allowed us to address scientists' own understandings and perspectives of spirituality without requiring them to choose from researcher-created categories.

Constructing spirituality in Taiwan: practicing folk religions, preserving Taiwanese traditions

Taiwan has the highest proportion of scientists who identified themselves as "not following religion but being a spiritual person interested in the sacred and the supernatural." Surprisingly, in our interviews, the word *spirituality* and its Chinese translation, *Ling Xing*, was not immediately intuitive to Taiwanese scientists. Most scientists were confused by the word and offered various definitions: "spirituality is an intuition,"[33] "a level of mental adjustment,"[34] and that it "is related to supernatural beings."[35] None of their definitions could be mapped onto the largely U.S.-based scholarship, which views spirituality as a socio-syncretic religious concept.[36] *Spirituality* is simply not the best word to capture the categories Taiwanese scientists chose on our survey, namely, "not following a religion" but still being "interested in the sacred and the supernatural."

In our subsequent questions about whether Taiwanese scientists adopt religious or spiritual practices, we found that all spiritual scientists in Taiwan maintain some folk religious practices. Folk religion is a major religion in Taiwan with 44.2% of the general population affiliated.[37] Folk religion is also bundled with profound cultural meanings there[38] – the folk religious conceptualization of the universe being composed of five elements and a belief in the balance between *yin* and *yang* constitute the core of Chinese cultures.[39] Hence, although folk religion is synonymous with superstition for many educated Taiwanese, it is still widely practiced by the general population.[40]

Like many nonscientists in Taiwan, Taiwanese scientists often adopt certain folk religious practices, such as *bai bai* (worshipping), on traditional holidays – on *Qi Xi*, for example, Chinese Valentine's Day. Some simply "follow the tradition in Taiwan," worshipping in ghost festivals once or twice every year[41] and view such "worshipping of the *Guan Yin* Bodhisattva and ancestors" as part of their families' lives.[42] However, although many say that practicing folk religions does not entail a folk religion affiliation, most feel a tension between their beliefs and their practices. A physicist[43] said,

> It's just that my elders have such a practice and so I do it, but rationally, I don't [believe in it]. With the contours that we are given, it is unnecessary for us to pick a fight with what our ancestors believed. Lots of times, we do follow their [practices]. Unless you are totally unwilling to [do so], more or less you would pick up some [ancestral worshipping] practices.

This scientist, grounded in empiricism, does not believe in the supernatural connotations associated with folk religions, but he follows folk religious practices to accommodate family traditions. His claim of "not following religion but being a spiritual person interested in the sacred and the supernatural," is, by and large, a way for him to resolve the tension between not believing in supernatural connotations and taking part in his family's religious practices.

Almost all self-identified Taiwanese SBNR scientists adhere to some folk religious practices. However, instead of recognizing gods and deities as supernatural beings, they see folk religious practices pragmatically, as a way to connect with family or cultural traditions. As a male professor in physics said, "[t]hat's not a religion. It is more a family [thing] or connection to tradition."[44] As reflected in their narratives, the construction of spirituality is a way for SBNR scientists in Taiwan to re-create the sacred, disconnect it from the supernatural, and link it to Chinese culture.

Spirituality in France: detaching supernatural meanings, caring for the human world

Although all four societies – Taiwan, France, the United Kingdom, and the United States – are secular societies to some degree, secularization is most assertive in France.[45] The French government explicitly endorses secularity, excluding religion from many public domains. Having a governmental stance on assertive secularization, however, does not entail the eradication of religion. Instead, Catholicism, the country's major religion, serves as an important cultural resource that formulates French understanding of nationalism, ethics, and cultural values.[46] In this context, French SBNR scientists see their spirituality as a set of ethical values that include empathy and an implicit moral code.

This sort of spirituality is illustrated by the response of a male biology researcher[47] who identified himself as a spiritual atheist. Born into a Catholic family, he became an atheist because he disagreed with his perception of the Catholic Church's perspective on evolution (the Catholic Church *actually* accepts evolution). He said, "Very early I got interested in evolution, and the notion of evolution is blatantly in total opposition to a religious version of the world." Although an atheist, he is still spiritual, and spirituality for him does not have supernatural connotations. Instead, it involves "humanism, relationships, and the duties [he has] towards [his] peers and the whole living world." His atheism entails "a conception of the universe that is materialistic" but without "a creator." As a spiritual person, however, he is sensitive to his "relations and duties with respect to my human peers, to my human environment, and to the living world I am in." There is a noticeable tension in his description between his scientific interests and his Catholic upbringing. To construct his spirituality, this scientist denies the existence of a supernatural creator but finds a sense of transcendence in the human world.

To be sure, some SBNR scientists in France experience tension with their country's dominant religion. They resolve such tensions by describing their concern for and care of the human world as a sacred duty, but they reject any affiliation with Catholicism. As one of our respondents[48] said, "[s]pirituality doesn't necessarily involve God, it's more about life, what we think of our life values, which are not necessarily related to whether you believe in God or not."

Spirituality in the United Kingdom and the United States: disaffiliated with religion, retaining a value system

Not surprisingly, religious contexts in the United Kingdom and the United States share many similarities. Both countries are secular in the sense that state and church are separate,[49] and religion is seen as the foundation of morality, politics, civic participation, and even citizenship.[50] Still, the U.K. and U.S. religious contexts are not identical. In the latter, there is (generally) a positive perception of religion and (generally) a pejorative stance against atheism,[51] but in the former there is both a positive perception of religion and a nondiscriminatory stance against atheists.

Living in such contexts where religion is still socially important, nonreligious scientists wonder whether their religious peers will perceive them as having the cultural and ethical values that are made synonymous with being religious. To respond to this fear, SBNR scientists purposefully construct their spirituality to highlight that, even without a religious affiliation, they can have sound ethical values. A female biologist,[52] for instance, said that she was "raised atheist by an ex-Catholic," and therefore was "told there was no God." Asked about the afterlife she said,

> The desire to understand my own spirituality came from my internal knowledge that I was a good person, and the idea that other people would tell me that I was going to go to hell . . . But I wasn't going to buy all of that stuff because it just didn't work for me, so that was where a lot of thinking and trying to figure out, just what do I believe? How does it fit in, what does it mean?

Such conversations motivated her to establish her own values, and she refused to accept the value system of an organized religion. She continually engages in dialogues with people from different faith traditions, such as Greek Orthodoxy and Quakerism, which expose her to other cultural resources:

> I think I accept that we are here and that my point of being here is that I need to try to be a good contributor. That my job is to be a positive influence on it all . . . [It is like] the philosophy [that] when you visit somebody, leave things better than you found them. That's my philosophy of life. Leave the place better than you found it.

Although her exposure to and reinterpretation of different religious and philosophical traditions enables her to construct an alternative value system by having a positive influence on the world, the value system is not dependent on an affiliation with any religion.

In the United Kingdom one of our respondents, a biologist,[53] experienced tension with the "religious other." Born into a Muslim family, she began questioning her religion as a teenager. She did not think that being religious means being a good person or vice versa. For her the construction of spirituality contains two important parts. The first is to consciously seek alternative values in place of religion. As she said, "I consciously had to think because I rejected religion; I consciously had to think what are my values? What kind of person do I want to be?" A second part of her spirituality is the instinctive feeling she has that there is something bigger and deeper than her own life.

Like their colleagues in the United States, SBNR scientists in the United Kingdom experience similar tensions with the religious other. Many do not accept the values constructed by most organized religions and implicitly assert, through their construction of spirituality, that they are still moral without being affiliated with any religion. For some, the construction of an alternative value system may be influenced by a previous religion – or as one self-identified SBNR biologist,[54] born into a religious family with "very dedicated Christians," for parents, said, "Spiritually, I would say that [Christianity] is always a part." However, for others, this alternative value system is independent of their earlier religion. An SBNR scientist in the United Kingdom[55] said that he was previously a Sikh, but now, as a spiritual person, he holds "common values and common beliefs about the world and the universe and how people should treat each other." These values are "independent of the Sikh religion."

Similar to the construction of spirituality in France, for SBNR scientists in the United Kingdom and the United States the construction of spirituality is a claim on value systems and moralities. Yet in France, SBNR scientists connect their spirituality to an explicitly humanistic view that centers on this world. SBNR scientists in the United Kingdom and the United States also search for an alternative value system without affiliating with any religious tradition, but many scientists are still open to the possibility of having a god or a greater force that can be broadly understood as God. Spirituality in the United Kingdom and the United States, therefore, is more apt to serve as an individualistic bridge that connects the secular and the sacred, this-world values with other-world beliefs.

Perceptions of the science and religion interface

SBNR scientists are sometimes seen as ambassadors bridging the cultural and ideological divide between science and religion. Indeed, as reflected in our survey results, being spiritual cushions the "conflict narrative" between science and religion in most national/social contexts. Our interviews provide further understanding of how SBNR scientists see the science–religion interface. In fact, we found that, in most national/social contexts, SBNR scientists do not see science and religion in conflict at all as long as religious people do not accept their sacred texts literally. For example, a graduate student in physics[56] in the U.S. said,

> I can see where there would be a conflict if you follow, you know, a certain religious text, word-for-word, without any sort of interpretation. If you believe that the world was created in seven days, clearly that wasn't the case. But without taking that literally, I think you could still believe in your system of beliefs pretty well.

Although she did not think religion was capable of offering a plausible explanation for the origins of life, she readily accepts that it might have something important to add to the scientific narrative and that the two need not necessarily conflict.

The notion that only literal interpretations of religion lead to conflicts between science and religion appeared in our conversations with almost all SBNR scientists in France, the United Kingdom, the United States, and – in some cases – in Taiwan. Respondents told us that "the whole point of the Bible or the Qur'an is why we're here, not how it all happened" and that, therefore, from that perspective, "science and religion can sit reasonably comfortably together."[57] However, "if you're taking every religious aspect and accepting it as undeniable, literal, factual truth, then, sure, there's probably somewhere in the Bible or somewhere in the Qur'an"[58] that will conflict with an evidence-based explanation. As one Taiwanese physicist said,[59] "[i]f you define religion in a fundamental sense, then maybe there will be conflict."

It is worth noting that, for SBNR scientists in Taiwan, their perspectives on the science–religion interface are diverse. Some, such as the physics research fellow quoted earlier, share the perspective of colleagues in other countries. Others frame science and religion as two independent entities triggering different parts of the brain.[60] A small number of SBNR scientists in Taiwan implicitly hold a conflict perspective between science and religion. A religious scientist, in their opinion, is "not a purely scientific person."[61]

Our analysis of how SBNR scientists perceive the science–religion interface illustrates that they do not reject wholesale the argument that science and religion are destined to conflict. Instead, they qualify it by saying that, even if people hold religious beliefs but accept that religious discourse can coexist with science, there need be no conflict between them. Such narratives consistently appear in France, the United Kingdom, and the United States, but are less salient in Taiwan.

Discussion and conclusion

In this chapter we compared scientists' construction of spirituality in four countries – France, Taiwan, the United Kingdom, and the United States. Previous studies on spirituality, in general, and on scientists, in particular, have focused on the construction of spirituality in the West, particularly in the United Kingdom and the United States, and yielded two implicit biases concerning spirituality: first, that it is peculiarly applicable to the United Kingdom and the United States, the two national contexts where individualism is most highly valued, and, second, that to be spiritual means to meditate, practice yoga, pray, read religious or sacred texts, or connect with the natural world in a mystical way.

A close analysis of the scientists' narratives of spirituality confirmed that SBNR scientists across the four national/social contexts construct various types of spirituality. For SBNR scientists in Taiwan, spirituality refers to the continuation of Taiwanese traditions through their occasional practice of folk religions; in France, spirituality refers to the negation of supernatural meaning and support for humanism; in the United Kingdom and the United

States, spirituality means constructing an alternative value system without affiliating with a specific religious tradition.

Certainly, at face value, the scientists' construction of spirituality varies according to the four national/regional contexts. At the same time, a close analysis also reveals considerable similarities. For example, scientists have experienced tension with religion and identify themselves as nonreligious. As a result, they refuse to accept the religious package or situate themselves in a society according to their religious affiliation. In all countries, however, religion is bundled with other cultural meanings – so that, while rejecting religious affiliation, SBNR scientists do not want to distance themselves from cultural-religious meaning entirely. In doing so, they reconstruct the traditional notion of the "sacred" for themselves.

This reconstructed sacred is different from the orthodox religious idea of a supernatural and transcendent power. Instead, it *only* reflects other cultural meanings that are bundled with religion, such as ethnicity, ethical values, and nationality. In different national/regional contexts, and to varying degrees, religion is accessorized with distinctive cultural meanings, which explains the cross-national (cross-regional) differences in scientists' construction of spirituality.

Specifically, Taiwanese folk religion is often bundled with a broadly defined Chinese culture, and the Taiwanese reconstructed sacred is, therefore, a guardian of their ethnicity. Similarly, in France, Catholicism influenced – and continues to influence – people's understanding of ethics and nationality even if such influence is now only implicit because of a muscular secularization favored by the French government.[62] Thus, the reconstructed sacred in France reflects the nation's role as guardian of secularism.

For their part, in the United Kingdom and the United States, religion is bundled with a set of cultural meanings, such as citizenship, morality, and politics,[63] and for SBNR scientists there, reconstructing spirituality means establishing an alternative ethical value system. Such scientists implicitly claim that, even without affiliation with any faith tradition, by drawing resources from different religions and philosophies, they can construct their own positive and enduring value systems.

The schema of detaching other cultural meanings that religion bequests is applicable also to SBNR scientists' understanding of the science–religion interface. By saying that science and religion do not conflict if people interpret religious texts on their own rather than accept their narratives as literal truths, SBNR scientists imply that people should detach the scientific connotations from religion. According to them, religion answers broader questions about life and its meaning but does not provide scientific explanations about our world. This also explains why, in Taiwan, there exist more diverse perspectives on the science–religion interface. It seems that, in the context of Taiwan, science is not necessarily a cultural meaning attached to religion. As one of our respondents said,[64] "I know that in other, more religious countries, there is some conflict between science and religion, particularly in some old doctrines," but "for a country like Taiwan, although people will say we have Confucianism or Buddhism, these are more like a philosophical type of religion," and that scientists "don't necessarily reject the idea or see that [science and religion are in] conflict."

Scholars have argued that modern secularization is not necessarily mirrored in the decline of religion but in its changing appearance.[65] If, in modern societies, religion is not a "sacred canopy" bundled with different sets of cultural meanings, then our analysis is a snapshot of the continuing change of religion in the modern world. Meanwhile, through their construction of spirituality, scientists continue to decouple religion from the other cultural meanings that come with it.

As we have expanded the interrogation of scientists' construction of spirituality from the United Kingdom and the United States to other national/ social contexts, we suggest that future scholars analyze spirituality as a reconstruction of the sacred rather than as an identity label that people adopt. If we conceptualize spiritual scientists according to their identity label, spirituality seems to be particularly applicable to Western societies, especially the United Kingdom and the United States, but "spirituality" – even its Chinese equivalent – is not intuitive to scientists in Taiwan, despite the high proportion of spiritual scientists there. The focus on spiritual labels constructed according to identities that people choose narrows the relevance of spirituality. If we understand, however, that being SBNR might be for some a reconstruction of the sacred, detached of religious cultural meaning, we can see that spirituality is applicable not only to national contexts that value individualism but also to those contexts that are moving towards modernity and religious diversity while placing high importance on the communal.

Notes

1 Robert N. Bellah et al., *Habits of the Heart: Individualism and Commitment in American Life* (Berkeley: University of California Press, 1985); Robert Wuthnow, *After Heaven: Spirituality in America Since the 1950s* (Berkeley and Los Angeles: University of California Press, 1998).
2 Steve Bruce, *God Is Dead: Secularization in the West* (Malden, MA: Wiley-Blackwell, 2002); Paul Heelas, "Challenging Secularization Theory: The Growth of 'New Age' Spiritualties of Life," *Hedgehog Review* 8, no. 1/2 (2006): 46.
3 Stef Aupers and Dick Houtman, "Beyond the Spiritual Supermarket: The Social and Public Significance of New Age Spirituality," *Journal of Contemporary Religion* 21, no. 2 (2006): 201–22.
4 Harry Triandis, "Collectivism v. Individualism: A Reconceptualisation of a Basic Concept in Cross-Cultural Social Psychology," in *Cross-Cultural Studies of Personality, Attitudes and Cognition*, ed. Christopher Bagley and Gajendra K. Verma (London: Palgrave Macmillan, 1988), 60–95.
5 Matthew Wood and Christopher Bunn, "Strategy in a Religious Network: A Bourdieuian Critique of the Sociology of Spirituality," *Sociology* 43, no. 2 (2009): 286–303.

6 Olivier Tschannen, "The Secularization Paradigm: A Systematization," *Journal for the Scientific Study of Religion* 30, no. 4 (1991): 395–415; Mark Chaves, "Secularization as Declining Religious Authority," *Social Forces* 72, no. 3 (1994): 749–74.

7 John H. Evans and Michael S. Evans, "Religion and Science: Beyond the Epistemological Conflict Narrative," *Annual Review of Sociology* 34, no. 1 (2008): 87–105.

8 Ibid.

9 Ryan Cragun, "Who Are the 'New Atheists?,'" in *Atheist Identities: Spaces and Social Contexts*, ed. Lori G. Beaman and Steven Tomlins (New York: Springer, 2014), 195–211.

10 Robert C. Fuller, *Spiritual, But Not Religious: Understanding Unchurched America* (New York: Oxford University Press, 2001).

11 Peter L. Berger, *The Sacred Canopy: Elements of a Sociological Theory of Religion* (New York: Open Road Media, 1967); Peter L. Berger, "Secularization Falsified," *First Things*, 2008, www.firstthings.com/article/2008/02/002-secularization-falsified

12 Grace Davie, *Religion in Britain Since 1945: Believing Without Belonging* (London: Blackwell, 1994); Sarah Wilkins-Laflamme, "Toward Religious Polarization? Time Effects on Religious Commitment in U.S., UK, and Canadian Regions," *Sociology of Religion* 75, no. 2 (2014): 284–308.

13 Gerardo Martí, "Religious Reflexivity: The Effect of Continual Novelty and Diversity on Individual Religiosity," *Sociology of Religion* 76, no. 1 (2015): 1–13.

14 Fuller, *Spiritual, But Not Religious*, 4.

15 Heelas, "Challenging Secularization Theory," 46.

16 Nancy T. Ammerman, "Spiritual But Not Religious? Beyond Binary Choices in the Study of Religion," *Journal for the Scientific Study of Religion* 52, no. 2 (2013): 258–78.

17 Wood and Bunn, "Strategy in a Religious Network," 286–303.

18 Elaine Howard Ecklund and Elizabeth Long, "Scientists and Spirituality," *Sociology of Religion* 72, no. 3 (2011): 253–74.

19 Giuseppe Giordan, "Spirituality: From a Religious Concept to a Sociological Theory," in *A Sociology of Spirituality*, ed. Kieran Flanagan and Peter C. Jupp (New York: Ashgate Publishing, Ltd., 2007), 161–80.

20 Tschannen, "The Secularization Paradigm," 395–415.

21 Rodney Stark, "On the Incompatibility of Religion and Science: A Survey of American Graduate Students," *Journal for the Scientific Study of Religion* 3, no. 1 (1963): 3–20.

22 Elaine Howard Ecklund et al., "Religion Among Scientists in International Context a New Study of Scientists in Eight Regions," *Socius: Sociological Research for a Dynamic World* 2 (2016): 1–9.

23 Elaine Howard Ecklund and Christopher P. Scheitle, "Religion Among Academic Scientists: Distinctions, Disciplines, and Demographics," *Social Problems* 54, no. 2 (2007): 289–307.

24 Evans and Evans, "Religion and Science," 87–105.

25 Ibid.

26 Thomas F. Gieryn, *Cultural Boundaries of Science: Credibility on the Line* (Chicago: University of Chicago Press, 1999).

27 Stephen Kalberg, *Max Weber's Comparative-Historical Sociology Today: Major Themes, Mode of Causal Analysis, and Applications* (New York: Routledge, 2017).

28 Elaine Howard Ecklund and Jerry Z. Park, "Conflict Between Religion and Science Among Academic Scientists?" *Journal for the Scientific Study of Religion* 48, no. 2 (2009): 276–92; Neil Gross and Solon Simmons, "The Religiosity of

American College and University Professors," *Sociology of Religion* 70, no. 2 (2009): 101–29.

29 Ulrich Beck, *A God of One's Own: Religion's Capacity for Peace and Potential for Violence* (New York: Polity, 2010).

30 Ecklund and Long, "Scientists and Spirituality," 253–74.

31 Elaine Howard Ecklund et al., "Religion Among Scientists in International Context a New Study of Scientists in Eight Regions," *Socius: Sociological Research for a Dynamic World* 2 (2016): 1–9.

32 Johnny Saldana, *The Coding Manual for Qualitative Researchers* (New York: SAGE Publications, 2015).

33 TW_14, Male, Research Fellow, Physics, Interviewed November 7, 2014.

34 TW_35, Female, Assistant Research Fellow, Biology, Interviewed December 5, 2014.

35 TW_34, Male, Research Fellow, Physics, Interviewed December 4, 2014.

36 Paul Heelas and Linda Woodhead, *The Spiritual Revolution: Why Religion Is Giving Way to Spirituality* (New York: Wiley, 2005).

37 Pew Research Center, "The Global Religious Landscape: A Report on the Size and Distribution of the Worlds' Major Religious Groups as of 2010," 2012, www.pewforum.org/2012/12/18/global-religious-landscape-exec

38 Anning Hu and Reid J. Leamaster, "Longitudinal Trends of Religious Groups in Deregulated Taiwan: 1990 to 2009," *The Sociological Quarterly* 54, no. 2 (2013): 254–77.

39 Ibid.

40 Chengpang Lee and Myungsahm Suh, "State Building and Religion: Explaining the Diverged Path of Religious Change in Taiwan and South Korea, 1950–1980," *American Journal of Sociology* 123, no. 2 (2017): 465–509.

41 TW_04, Male, Research Fellow, Biology, Interviewed December 4, 2014.

42 TW_34, Male, Research Fellow, Physics, Interviewed December 4, 2014.

43 TW_34, Male, Research Fellow, Physics, Interviewed December 4, 2014.

44 TW_22, Male, Professor, Physics, Interviewed November 12, 2014.

45 Ahmet T. Kuru, *Secularism and State Policies Toward Religion: The United States, France, and Turkey* (Cambridge: Cambridge University Press, 2009).

46 Leora Auslander, "Bavarian Crucifixes and French Headscarves: Religious Signs and the Postmodern European State," *Cultural Dynamics* 12, no. 3 (2000): 283–309; Ivan Strenski, *Contesting Sacrifice: Religion, Nationalism, and Social Thought in France* (Chicago: University of Chicago Press, 2002).

47 FR_63, Male, Research Director, Biology, Interviewed July 31, 2015.

48 FR_52, Female, Researcher, Biology, Interviewed July 20, 2015.

49 Philip Hamburger, *Separation of Church and State* (Cambridge, MA: Harvard University Press, 2009).

50 Lori G. Beaman and Steven Tomlins, *Atheist Identities: Spaces and Social Contexts* (New York: Springer International Publishing, 2014); Penny Edgell et al., "Atheists as 'Other': Moral Boundaries and Cultural Membership in American Society," *American Sociological Review* 71, no. 2 (2006): 211–34.

51 Beaman and Tomlins, *Atheist Identities*.

52 US_29, Female, Professor, Biology, Interviewed April 1, 2015.

53 UK_35, Female, Graduate Student, Physics, Interviewed April 2, 2015.

54 US_58, Female, Graduate Student, Biology, Interviewed April 29, 2015.

55 UK_70, Female, Associate Professor, Biology, Interviewed May 08, 2014.

56 US_05, Female, Graduate Student, Physics, Interviewed Marcy 24, 2015.

57 UK_45, Male, Postdoctoral Fellow, Physics, Interviewed April 6, 2015.

58 US_50, Female, Graduate Student, Physics, Interviewed April 9, 2015.

59 TW_14, Male, Research Fellow, Physics, Interviewed November 7, 2014.

60 TW_35, Female, Assistant Research Fellow, Biology, Interviewed December 5, 2014.

61 TW_04, Male, Research Fellow, Physics, interviewed December 4, 2014.
62 Kuru, *Secularism and State Policies Toward Religion.*
63 Penny Edgell et al., "Atheists as 'Other,'" 211–34.
64 TW_14, Male, Research Fellows, Physics, Interviewed.
65 Beck, *A God of One's Own*; Berger, "Secularization Falsified."

References

Ammerman, Nancy T. "Spiritual But Not Religious? Beyond Binary Choices in the Study of Religion." *Journal for the Scientific Study of Religion* 52, no. 2 (2013): 258–78.

Aupers, Stef and Dick Houtman. "Beyond the Spiritual Supermarket: The Social and Public Significance of New Age Spirituality." *Journal of Contemporary Religion* 21, no. 2 (2006): 201–22.

Auslander, Leora. "Bavarian Crucifixes and French Headscarves: Religious Signs and the Postmodern European State." *Cultural Dynamics* 12, no. 3 (2000): 283–309.

Beaman, Lori G. and Steven Tomlins. *Atheist Identities: Spaces and Social Contexts.* New York: Springer International Publishing, 2014.

Beck, Ulrich. *A God of One's Own: Religion's Capacity for Peace and Potential for Violence.* New York: Polity, 2010.

Bellah, Robert N., Richard Madsen, William M. Sullivan, Ann Swidler and Steven M. Tipton. *Habits of the Heart: Individualism and Commitment in American Life.* Berkeley, CA: University of California Press, 1985.

Berger, Peter L. *The Sacred Canopy: Elements of a Sociological Theory of Religion.* New York: Open Road Media, 1967.

———. "Secularization Falsified." First Things, 2008. www.firstthings.com/article/2008/02/002-secularization-falsified

Bruce, Steve. *God Is Dead: Secularization in the West.* New York: Wiley-Blackwell, 2002.

Chaves, Mark. "Secularization as Declining Religious Authority." *Social Forces* 72, no. 3 (1994): 749–74.

Cragun, Ryan. "Who Are The 'New Atheists?'" In *Atheist Identities: Spaces and Social Contexts*, 195–211. Edited by Lori G. Beaman and Steven Tomlins. New York: Springer, 2014.

Davie, Grace. *Religion in Britain Since 1945: Believing Without Belonging.* Oxford, Cambridge, MA: Blackwell, 1994.

Ecklund, Elaine Howard, David R. Johnson, Christopher P. Scheitle, Kirstin R.W. Matthews and Steven W. Lewis. "Religion Among Scientists in International Context a New Study of Scientists in Eight Regions." *Socius: Sociological Research for a Dynamic World* 2 (2016): 1–9.

Ecklund, Elaine Howard and Elizabeth Long. "Scientists and Spirituality." *Sociology of Religion* 72, no. 3 (2011): 253–74.

Ecklund, Elaine Howard and Jerry Z. Park. "Conflict Between Religion and Science Among Academic Scientists?" *Journal for the Scientific Study of Religion* 48, no. 2 (2009): 276–92.

Ecklund, Elaine Howard and Christopher P. Scheitle. "Religion Among Academic Scientists: Distinctions, Disciplines, and Demographics." *Social Problems* 54, no. 2 (2007): 289–307.

Edgell, Penny, Joseph Gerteis and Douglas Hartmann. "Atheists as 'Other': Moral Boundaries and Cultural Membership in American Society." *American Sociological Review* 71, no. 2 (2006): 211–34.

Evans, John H. and Michael S. Evans. "Religion and Science: Beyond the Epistemological Conflict Narrative." *Annual Review of Sociology* 34, no. 1 (2008): 87–105.

Fuller, Robert C. *Spiritual, But Not Religious: Understanding Unchurched America*. New York: Oxford University Press, 2001.

Gieryn, Thomas F. *Cultural Boundaries of Science: Credibility on the Line*. Chicago: University of Chicago Press, 1999.

Giordan, Giuseppe. "Spirituality: From a Religious Concept to a Sociological Theory." In *A Sociology of Spirituality*, 161–80. Edited by Kieran Flanagan and Peter C. Jupp. New York: Ashgate Publishing, Ltd., 2007.

Gross, Neil and Solon Simmons. "The Religiosity of American College and University Professors." *Sociology of Religion* 70, no. 2 (2009): 101–29.

Hamburger, Philip. *Separation of Church and State*. Cambridge, MA: Harvard University Press, 2009.

Heelas, Paul. "Challenging Secularization Theory: The Growth of 'New Age' Spiritualties of Life." *Hedgehog Review* 8, no. 1/2 (2006): 46–58.

Heelas, Paul and Linda Woodhead. *The Spiritual Revolution: Why Religion Is Giving Way to Spirituality*. New York: Wiley, 2005.

Hu, Anning and Reid J. Leamaster. "Longitudinal Trends of Religious Groups in Deregulated Taiwan: 1990 to 2009." *The Sociological Quarterly* 54, no. 2 (2013): 254–77.

Kalberg, Stephen. *Max Weber's Comparative-Historical Sociology Today: Major Themes, Mode of Causal Analysis, and Applications*. New York: Routledge, 2017.

Kuru, Ahmet T. *Secularism and State Policies Toward Religion: The United States, France, and Turkey*. Cambridge: Cambridge University Press, 2009.

Lee, Chengpang and Myungsahm Suh. "State Building and Religion: Explaining the Diverged Path of Religious Change in Taiwan and South Korea, 1950–1980." *American Journal of Sociology* 123, no. 2 (2017): 465–509.

Martí, Gerardo. "Religious Reflexivity: The Effect of Continual Novelty and Diversity on Individual Religiosity." *Sociology of Religion* 76, no. 1 (2015): 1–13.

Pew Research Center. "The Global Religious Landscape: A Report on the Size and Distribution of the Worlds' Major Religious Groups as of 2010." 2012. www.pewforum.org/2012/12/18/global-religious-landscape-exec

Saldana, Johnny. *The Coding Manual for Qualitative Researchers*. New York: SAGE Publications, 2015.

Stark, Rodney. "On the Incompatibility of Religion and Science: A Survey of American Graduate Students." *Journal for the Scientific Study of Religion* 3, no. 1 (1963): 3–20.

Strenski, Ivan. *Contesting Sacrifice: Religion, Nationalism, and Social Thought in France*. Chicago: University of Chicago Press, 2002.

Triandis, Harry. "Collectivism v. Individualism: A Reconceptualisation of a Basic Concept in Cross-Cultural Social Psychology." In *Cross-Cultural Studies of Personality, Attitudes and Cognition*, 60–95. Edited by Christopher Bagley and Gajendra K. Verma. London: Palgrave Macmillan, 1988.

Tschannen, Olivier. "The Secularization Paradigm: A Systematization." *Journal for the Scientific Study of Religion* 30, no. 4 (1991): 395–415.

Wilkins-Laflamme, Sarah. "Toward Religious Polarization? Time Effects on Religious Commitment in U.S., UK, and Canadian Regions." *Sociology of Religion* 75, no. 2 (2014): 284–308.

Wood, Matthew and Christopher Bunn. "Strategy in a Religious Network: A Bourdieuian Critique of the Sociology of Spirituality." *Sociology* 43, no. 2 (2009): 286–303.

Wuthnow, Robert. *After Heaven: Spirituality in America Since the 1950s.* Berkeley and Los Angeles, CA: University of California Press, 1998.

Part III

Future(s)

11 Rogue mystics

The ecology of cosmic consciousness

Jason James Kelly

Have you reckoned the earth much?

– Walt Whitman

In light of the alarming evidence on climate change provided by the scientific community it is difficult to question the fact that we are living amid an ecological crisis that threatens the very existence of all life on our planet. Yet, despite this knowledge powerful nations throughout the world continue to support neoliberal social and economic policies that fail to address the urgency of the situation. The question is, what steps can we take as a global community to stave off disaster? In her compelling work *This Changes Everything* (2014) the Canadian philosopher and social critic Naomi Klein argues that the hopes of turning to science for answers to the ecological crisis is shortsighted because such a move fails to address the heart of the issue, which is that we have been encultured by religious and secular ideologies that have normalized the central conceit of modernity – namely, our mastery over nature. Klein and other progressive environmentalists are convinced that what is required is a fundamental change in how human beings relate to the environment. In other words, we need new ways of *being-in-the-world*. Is it possible that spirituality might play a role in helping us create a more ecological way of *being-in-the-world*, one that privileges the intrinsic value of nature?

The history of the early environmental movement in America seems to suggest as much. Consider, for example, Ralph Waldo Emerson's classic essay *Nature* (1836), in which he identifies an "occult relation between man and the vegetable,"[1] or Henry David Thoreau's observation that "the earth I tread on is not dead, inert mass; it is a body, has a spirit, is organic, and fluid to the influence of spirit, and to whatever particle of that spirit is in me."[2] In the early to mid-19th century these two transcendentalist philosopher's presented the American public with a new way of thinking about nature that suggested our capacity to spiritually identify with nature was key to unlocking the full potential of our moral lives. And they were not alone. Emerson's and Thoreau's influence on other intellectuals and activists, such as John

Burroughs (1837–1921), John Muir (1838–1914), and, a little later, Aldo Leopold (1887–1948), would help spark a public debate about the merits of conservationism, which, in turn, would serve as a rallying point for the rise of the early environmental movement. The emergence of transcendentalism, then, signals an important milestone in the history of environmentalism in America in that its spiritual philosophy provided a moral justification to protect nature by suggesting that, in the words of Thoreau, "heaven is below our feet as well as over our heads."[3] In other words, nature is divine and ought to be treated as such.

The influential role transcendentalism has played in shaping our understanding of spirituality in America has been well documented by a range of scholars, including Leigh E. Schmidt (2005) and Arthur Versluis (2014). Both Schmidt and Versluis, for example, suggest that many of our contemporary views about spirituality and what is now commonly called "Spiritual but Not Religious" (SBNR)[4] can be traced to the teachings of various figures associated with transcendentalism.[5] By encouraging self-reliance, liberalism, social reform, and a deep love of nature, the teachings of the transcendentalist's presented an unorthodox, if not radical, response to the social and political challenges of their times, leading many of the movements most prominent figures to question the authority of traditional religion. Ultimately, the transcendentalists called for a new way of *being-in-the-world*, one that valued spiritual experience over religious belief. This move to privilege spiritual experience over religious belief continues to inform the way we conceptualize the meaning of being "Spiritual but Not Religious" and underscores the importance of Robert C. Fuller and William B. Parsons's characterization of the SBNR as "unchurched, nontraditional, and noninstitutional."[6] I suggest that the teachings of the transcendentalists still have a lot to offer our contemporary understanding of the SBNR, particularly when it comes to the question of how human beings view and value nature. Most significantly, I argue that the future relevance of the SBNR is tied to the field's capacity to engage in a more robust dialogue with ecological issues. Perhaps a broader engagement with ecology could help the SBNR address some its social and political defects and possibly even demonstrate another dimension to the field – a countercultural dimension, which contests the commodification of nature and our social and political realities?

This chapter aims to address some of these issues by tracing the intellectual history of a particular concept that emerged in the West during the late 19th and early 20th centuries called "cosmic consciousness." I suggest that a deeper understanding of cosmic consciousness, which I characterize as the experiential awareness of one's connection to or unity with the cosmos, can provide a solid historical context to ground ecological theorizing about the future direction of the SBNR and perhaps even unsettle some common misconceptions about the social and political significance of spirituality. In basic terms, I want to revisit the history of cosmic consciousness to demonstrate how the concept can be utilized by contemporary theorists interested in learning more about the connection between spirituality and ecology and what this connection could mean for our understanding of environmental ethics and the future direction of the SBNR.

In more specific terms, I argue that the move to characterize cosmic consciousness as an ecological concept has a distinct, yet largely unacknowledged, history that can be traced to the teachings of three *rogue mystics* who were deeply influenced by the philosophy of transcendentalism: the American poet Walt Whitman, the Canadian psychiatrist R. M. Bucke, and the English author and activist Edward Carpenter. It was Carpenter who first coined the term *cosmic consciousness* and Bucke who popularized it, but their shared understanding of its significance was shaped by the teachings of their mentor, Walt Whitman. In this chapter I propose a new study of cosmic consciousness that can perhaps enhance our understanding of the SBNR and, by extension, help broaden the scope of the field to include a more critical engagement with ecology. My discussion consists of two parts that will unfold as follows: first, I examine how the concept of cosmic consciousness evolved in the work of Whitman, Bucke, and Carpenter, and, second, I address the ecological significance of cosmic consciousness in relation to the SBNR movement as a whole.

The good gray poet

The American literary critic and author Harold Bloom describes Walt Whitman (1819–1892) as "the greatest artist this nation has brought forth."[7] Over the past century and a half, Whitman's book of free-verse poetry, *Leaves of Grass* (1855), has spawned an enormous amount of commentary and the scholarly material detailing the literary genius of the Brooklyn-born poet is in no short supply. Hence, I have no interest in discussing the literary merit of his work. Rather, I want to call attention to the underlining philosophy that shaped Whitman's genius, particularly, as it relates to his ideas about our spiritual connection to the "kosmos." The first thing we must consider is how to make sense of Whitman's mysticism. Scholars working in the field of religious studies often characterize Whitman as a "nature mystic." Nature mysticism has been defined in various ways in the west, but perhaps "the key characteristic of natural mystical experience is a sense of union or identity with the natural world."[8] In a certain sense this is an accurate characterization of Whitman's mysticism. But in other ways it is slightly misleading to define Whitman as simply a nature mystic. For example, this characterization completely misses the social and political element of his mysticism, let alone its fundamental eroticism. Nor does it address his abiding interest in modern science, which he held in the highest esteem as the harbinger of human progress.[9] From this perspective, I believe nature mysticism is too restrictive of a category to accurately capture Whitman's position.

Why then do religious scholars insist on defining Whitman as a nature mystic? Perhaps because it is easier to dismiss the more radical dimensions of his mysticism if it is defined as "nature mysticism." Historically, certain scholars of religion, such as W. T. Stace and R. C. Zaehner, for example, have characterized nature mysticism as a less developed or "lower" form of mysticism compared to the more traditional "religious" forms of mysticism.[10] Such a rhetorical move, I argue, is a means for conservative scholars to pacify and mute any alternative conceptions of the mystical that contest the legitimacy of the status quo. At issue here is a question of power and authority: who possesses the power to dictate what constitutes an authentic form of mysticism? Who has the authority to exercise such power? Traditionally, the study of mysticism in the west has largely been defined in relation to a specific religious standard that privileges the ideological interests of certain religious institutions, particularly the monotheistic traditions of Judaism, Christianity, and Islam. Religious scholars who have an interest in preserving the dominance of this monotheistic ideology tend to address mysticism in terms that advocate this religious standard as normative, universal, and even "natural." The problem with this approach is that it not only conceals the socially constructed nature of "the mystical," but it is methodologically flawed because its scope is too narrow to accommodate the views of mystics, such as Whitman, Bucke, and Carpenter, who do not conform to this religious standard. Hence, I characterize Whitman as a "rogue mystic," by which I mean a mystic who does not identify with any particular religious tradition and is often quite hostile towards the exclusive claims of organized religion. Consider, for example, the following lines from the original preface of *Leaves*, which underscore Whitman's "rogue" position:

> There will soon be no more priests. Their work is done. A new order shall arise, and they shall be priests of man, and every man shall be his own priest. They shall find their inspiration in real objects to-day, symptoms of the past and future. They shall not deign or defend immortality or God, or the perfection of things, or liberty, or the exquisite beauty and reality of the soul.[11]

"It is as if the beasts spoke." That is how Thoreau described his first impression of reading *Leaves of Grass*. Although Thoreau would eventually champion the brilliance of this little book of free-verse poetry, critics and most of the public were unimpressed with the work on its first publication in 1855. Whitman envisioned his book as a "new bible" that would unify a fractured country under the erotic banner of democratic comradeship. With such high hopes it is understandable that Whitman was devastated when his "new bible" flopped. However, he would receive help from an unlikely savior, which came in the form of a letter from the most well-respected philosopher in America at the time, Ralph Waldo Emerson, who described *Leaves of Grass* as "the most extraordinary piece of wit and wisdom that America has yet contributed."[12] Emerson's endorsement changed Whitman's fortunes for the better, and in time, *Leaves* would come to be considered one of the greatest works of poetry in the world – and Whitman, America's greatest poet.

"I contain multitudes," writes Whitman. Indeed, he does. He is at once a shameless self-promoter, egotist, *and* the charitable "good gray poet" who worked tirelessly to ease the suffering of thousands of wounded Civil War soldiers. He stands as a fierce advocate for sexual freedom but internally struggled with his own homoerotic desires. He is widely recognized not only as the quintessential nature mystic but also celebrated as a poetic advocate for scientific innovation and intellectual progress. What are we to make of these multitudes? Whitman was first and foremost an artist, and his creative genius was complex and encompassing. Interestingly, his artistic focus was largely spiritual in nature; that is, with the Civil War looming, Whitman was convinced that America was in the midst of a profound crisis, one that could only be averted by constructing a new spiritual vision for the country based on the democratic principles of equality and comradeship.

Ever the Romantic, Whitman's spiritual vision transcended the dogmatic constraints of traditional religion. In fact, it's safe to say that Whitman was no friend of organized religion and was convinced that spiritual illumination was ultimately a matter of self-realization: "This head more than churches, bibles, and all the creeds."[13] Religious beliefs, Whitman suggests, are secondary to the existential "fact" of our *being-in-the-world*, which is infused with mystical significance. Realizing the mystical dimensions of our Being, Whitman believed, is not a matter of belonging to the right religious institution; it is a matter of individual effort: "Bibles may convey, and priest expound, but it is exclusively for the noiseless operation of one's isolated Self, to enter the pure ether of veneration, reach the divine levels, and commune with the unutterable."[14]

Whitman presents a radical vision of the mystical in *Leaves of Grass* that celebrates the body as a sacred site of spiritual and social liberation. All human beings are embodied, sexualized beings. Regardless of circumstance, we all share this erotic bond we each other and with the natural world. The attainment of spiritual and social liberation, according to Whitman, rests with our capacity to realize the existential significance of this erotic bond between "I" and "Other." This move to erotically fuse the subject and object lies at the heart of Whitman's mysticism and even shaped the way he valued such notions as equality and democracy – two key concepts that define his social philosophy. Whitman believed that it is not possible to divorce the mystical from the social; every aspect of our daily lives, that which we consider routine and commonplace is invested with mystical significance. And therein lies the secret to understanding Whitman's spirituality: to see the average as divine.

Perhaps no human desire was more divine to Whitman than erotic desire. He was convinced that "there was a close connection – a very close connection – between the state we call religious ecstasy and the desire to copulate."[15] In contrast to the puritanical nature of classical (male) mysticism,

Whitman tends to describe the mystical in highly erotic terms. Consider, for example, one of most oft-cited passages from "Song of Myself," which dramatizes Whitman's erotic encounter with his own soul:

> I mind how we lay in June, such a transparent summer morning;
>   You settled your head athwart my hips and gently turned over upon me,
>   And parted the shirt from my bosom-bone, and plunged your tongue to my barestript heart,
>   And reached till you felt my beard, and reached till you held my feet.[16]

As this erotic encounter with his soul reaches its climax, Whitman describes the onset of a unitive state of illumination, framed in terms that are familiar to most mystical literature in the West:

> Swiftly arose and spread around me the peace and joy and knowledge that pass all the art and argument of the earth;
>   And I know that the hand of God is the elderhand of my own,
>   And I know that the spirit of God is the eldest brother of my own,
>   And that all men ever born are also my brother . . . and the Women my sisters and lovers,
>   And that a keelson of the creation is love;[17]

As the preceding passage indicates, Whitman's ideas about the mystical are grounded in an expansive sense of self-identity with God, which includes the whole of creation. Notably, Whitman is explicit that the driving force of creation is love.[18] The subtextual significance of the above two passages is that the spiritual (soul) and material (body) domains are coextensive expressions of a single, overarching energy, that is, love, which he often characterized as "the procreant urge of the world."[19] Love is the vital force that unifies the disparate elements of creation, and such a nondualistic perspective permits Whitman to proclaim himself as poet of both body and soul. He refused to separate the body from the soul because he believed that materiality *is* mystical: "The scent of these arm-pits, aroma finer than prayer."[20] Ultimately, it was this world, the impermanent world of body, blood, and bone where Whitman believed the divine truly resides: "I believe in flesh and the appetites. Seeing hearing and feeling are miracles, and each part and tag of me is a miracle."[21] I suggest that it was precisely Whitman's willingness to invest the natural world with spiritual value that encouraged him to frame his call for social reform as a moral obligation. If we are all intimately connected by the erotic energies of the "kosmos," which Whitman firmly believed, then the recognition of this knowledge compels us to treat each other – and all of nature – with the dignity and respect that comes by virtue of our shared interdependence with the "kosmos."

Eroticism, embodiment, immanence – these were all essential elements of Whitman's mystical philosophy. They are all united by his abiding passion for nature. Following his mentor Emerson, Whitman viewed and valued nature as humanity's greatest teacher. He writes,

> After you have exhausted what there is in business, politics, conviviality, love, and so on – have found that none of these finally satisfy, or permanently wear – what remains? Nature remains; to bring out from their torpid recesses, the affinities of a man or woman with the open air, the trees, fields, the changes of seasons – the sun by day and the stars of heaven by night.[22]

In this passage we can discern Whitman's attempt to imbue nature with intrinsic value; the power of nature is framed as source of fulfillment that transcends the triviality of common human desires. Moreover, similar to his views on sexual liberation and social reform, his overall take on nature was both critical of convention and cosmic in scope:

> Nature, true Nature, and the true idea of Nature, long absent, must, above all, become fully restored, enlarged . . . I do not mean the smooth walks, trimm'd hedges, poesy's and nightingales of the English poets, but the whole orb, with it geologic history, the kosmos, carrying fire and snow, that rolls through the illimitable areas, light as a feather, though weighing billions of tons.[23]

In this passage we see Whitman expanding the conventional aesthetic of the Romantics to include a much broader interpretation of nature, which exchanges the obvious beauty of the "trimm'd hedges, poesy's and nightingales," for a more nuanced appreciation of the cosmic processes that gave rise to such beauty. Perhaps most significantly, at the heart of Whitman's interpretation of nature is an overarching sense of mystical identification: "I see my soul reflected in nature."[24] Here then, is a poet of both nature and God, body and soul, science and spirituality, who wrote his poems for a future audience that could appreciate the ethical implications that comes with placing oneself in creative harmony with what he believed to be the ultimate driving force of the cosmos: love.

The moral mystic

The Canadian psychiatrist R.M. Bucke (1837–1902) was one of the first biographers of Whitman to underscore the mystical element of his poetry. As their friendship blossomed, Bucke would eventually take on the role of Whitman's personal physician and staunchest advocate for reading *Leaves of Grass* as a "new bible."[25] If *Leaves* is a new bible, then it followed for

Bucke that Whitman was indeed a kind of prophet, set upon the world to usher in the dawn of a new "kosmic" religion based on the democratic principles of equality and comradeship. Bucke's affection for Whitman was immense, going so far as to compare the importance of the poet's teachings to that of Socrates, Jesus, and the Buddha. There is no question that Bucke was enchanted by Whitman, but he also possessed a critical mind and independent spirit. In fact, Bucke was a highly respected medical professional and superintendent of the London asylum in Ontario, considered by many to be one of the most progressive psychiatric institutes in North America at the time.

Bucke's interest in Whitman began when he first read *Leaves of Grass* in 1867. Five years later he would finally experience his own encounter with the mystical. Bucke was at a gathering with a few friends, reading and discussing poetry – particularly, the work of Whitman, late into the evening. While traveling home in his carriage, an intense feeling came upon him, and he felt as though he was being immersed in a "flame-colored cloud" that overwhelmed him with "a sense of exultation, of immense joyousness accompanied or immediately followed by an intellectual illumination quite impossible to describe."[26] He does, however, go to identify two essential insights he gleaned from this state of illumination – namely, "that the Cosmos is not dead matter but a living Presence" and that "the foundation principle of the world is what we call love." This extraordinary experience would provide the theoretical foundation for Bucke's most influential work, *Cosmic Consciousness* (1901). With the possible exception of William James's *The Varieties of Religious Experience* (1902), no other work played a more influential role in shaping the direction of the modern study of mysticism than Bucke's *Cosmic Consciousness*. Similar to James, Bucke was no longer content to rely on theology to explain mystical states of consciousness. Rather, he sought to naturalize mystical states of consciousness by constructing a psychological study of its characteristics. However, Bucke took his scientific speculations a step further than James by framing cosmic consciousness as a product of evolution. Bucke not only believed that cosmic consciousness was a natural phenomenon but that it also foreshadowed the moral and spiritual potential of our species.

Bucke borrowed the term *cosmic consciousness* from his English colleague Edward Carpenter, who was also a "hot little prophet" of the Whitman gospel. Bucke and Carpenter engaged in a friendly correspondence and shared many ideas about their interpretation of cosmic consciousness and Whitman's teachings in general.[27] But whereas Carpenter emphasized the social and political import of cosmic consciousness, Bucke was content to focus on its scientific relevance. Drawing on his background in psychiatry, Bucke understood consciousness as a spectrum consisting of three primary stages of awareness. The first stage, *simple consciousness*, he associated with the brute instinctual awareness of animal life. The second stage, *self-consciousness*, he identified with the advanced state of self-awareness found in human beings who are capable of high-order abstraction and symbolization. The third and final stage in Bucke's model is *cosmic consciousness*, which he associated with the emergence of the moral and spiritual heights of our species as exemplified in the lives and teaching of such historical figures as Socrates, Jesus, Buddha, and especially Whitman.

What exactly are the characteristics of cosmic consciousness? According to Bucke, there are basically three main characteristics: illumination, moral elevation, and a sense of ineffable connection or unity with the cosmos that finds its closest corollary in the human conception of love. According to Bucke, cosmic consciousness

> shows the cosmos to consist not of dead matter governed by unconscious, rigid, and unintending law; it shows it on the contrary as entirely immaterial, entirely spiritual and entirely alive . . . it shows that the universe is God and that God is the universe.[28]

From this perspective it is clear that following Whitman, Bucke was advocating a form of mysticism that invested the natural world with spiritual value. Most significantly, by investing the natural world with spiritual value vis-à-vis his conception of cosmic consciousness, Bucke affirms a nondualistic conception of the relationship between mind (consciousness) and body (matter).

Certainly, there are numerous limitations to Bucke's study of cosmic consciousness. First, by today's standards his scientific method was questionable to say the least, akin more to a form of pseudoscience. Second, Bucke's study was misogynistic and racist and lacked any kind of nuanced discussion about social and historical context. Third and finally, Bucke's interpretation of cosmic consciousness largely omitted any kind of critical engagement with eroticism, which is quite surprising given how central erotic ideas are to his most exemplary figure of cosmic consciousness, Whitman. However, his study was the first of its kind to undertake a systematic interpretation of mystical states of consciousness from an evolutionary perspective. In today's climate of New Age spiritualities it is difficult to really appreciate how revolutionary of an idea this truly was at the time. Consider for a moment that Bucke outlined a model of spiritual expression that essentially privileges *experience over belief* more than a century before the SBNR was even acknowledged as a legitimate category of academic study. In other words, Bucke's evolutionary model of cosmic consciousness sought to liberate spirituality from the exclusive confines of traditional religion by placing his analysis within a scientific register. To this end, Bucke was indeed a pioneer in the early field of the SBNR who deserves to be acknowledged for his effort to separate the study of mystical experience from the domain of organized religion.

The revolutionary mystic

Unlike Whitman and Bucke, the name of Edward Carpenter (1844–1929) is rarely recognized today. This is a shame really, given that his views on the relationship between spirituality and nature and his stinging critique of capitalism are so relevant to the contemporary conditions of society in the 21st century. Similar to Bucke, Carpenter's initial interest in studying cosmic consciousness was prompted by his own mystical experience, and he also shared Bucke's schematic of consciousness that consists of three overlapping stages of awareness: simple, self, and cosmic. In such works as *Civilization: Its Cause and Cure* (1891) and *The Art of Creation* (1904), Carpenter presents a comprehensive model of mystical consciousness that he believed would someday play a pivotal role in catalyzing a radical transformation of the social and political order. Often characterized as the "English Whitman," Carpenter took the label as a badge of honor because like Bucke, he viewed Whitman as a kind of prophet declaring the creation of a new era of erotic liberation and harmony with nature.

Carpenter's most famous work, *Towards Democracy* (1883) is a free-verse book of poetry reminiscent of Whitman's first edition of *Leaves*. However, unlike Whitman, whose ideas about social reform remained safely ensconced in the written word, Carpenter made every effort to put his theories into practice and remained politically engaged for the entirety of his adult life. Carpenter was a vocal critic of British imperialism and a well-respected advocate of such progressive causes as socialism, prison reform, free love, women's liberation, gay rights, animal rights, and environmentalism – long before any of these issues were a serious concern of the public.[29] Despite the wide range of his interests, Carpenter was no fly-by-night dilettante; he earned a degree in mathematics from Cambridge University, and for an early part of his career he lectured on astronomy, music, and science.

It was while working as a lecturer in the countryside of northern England where Carpenter's eyes were first opened to the miserable conditions of the working class. Inspired by the simplicity of country living, Carpenter invested his inheritance in the purchase of a small-hold farm and retired from teaching to focus on writing, while making a modest living as a market gardener. Drawing on both Whitman and various Eastern philosophies,[30] Carpenter began writing his most famous book of poetry, *Towards Democracy*, which details the evolution of cosmic consciousness as a movement of the soul's awakening to and eventual identity with nature:

> I arise out of the dewy night and shake my wings. Tears and lamentations are no more. Life and death lie stretched below me. I breathe the sweet aether blowing of the breath of God.
>
> Deep as the universe is my life – and I know it; nothing can dislodge the knowledge of it; nothing can destroy, nothing can harm me.

Joy, joy arises – I arise. The sun darts overpowering piercing rays of joy through me, the night radiates it from me.[31]

Alongside his spiritual identification with nature, like Whitman before him, Carpenter presents a highly erotized and fully embodied vision of cosmic consciousness: "Sex still goes first, and hands eyes mouth brain follow; from the midst of belly and thighs radiate the knowledge of self, religion, and immortality."[32] And again, following Whitman, Carpenter affirms a nondualistic interpretation of the relationship between body and soul:

The body is a root of the soul. As the body in air, so the soul sustains itself in Love. The medium in which the Knowledge of Yourself subsists in Equality. When you have penetrated into that medium (as the young shoot penetrates into the sunlight) you shall know that it is so – you shall realize Yourself – but not till then.[33]

Carpenter viewed this erotic relationship between body and soul as an evolutionary process that was driven by a fundamental element: desire. According to Carpenter, "there is a force at work throughout creation, ever urging each type onward into new and newer forms. This force appears first in consciousness in the form of desire."[34] This begs the question, what is desire? Carpenter framed his understanding of desire in relation to love: "Love is the sum and the solution of all desires of man – that in which they converge; the interpretation of them; for which they all exist, and without which they would be considered useless."[35] Again, similar to Whitman, Carpenter valued love as an expansive, all-encompassing principle that runs through all creation, unifying its diverse forms. This is a love, then, cosmic at its core, which lures creation into being and blurs the boundary between subject and object.

Carpenter believed that our misplaced identification with Cartesian dualism was the chief culprit behind all our psychological and social woes. More specifically, argues Carpenter, our incapacity to transcend this dualism is a symptom of our overidentification with self-consciousness:

The perception of matter and mind as distinct things belongs only to our ordinary (self) consciousness. This distinction is not known in the earlier stage of simple consciousness, and it passes away again in the higher and more perfect stage of the cosmic consciousness.[36]

An experience of cosmic consciousness expands one's perspective so radically that he or she no longer identities solely with the ego-as-entity, but rather the idea of "self" is enlarged to include the entire cosmos so that,

[S]ubject and the object are felt, are *known*, to be united and one – in which the Self is felt to *be* the object perceived, or at least in which the subject and the object are felt to be parts of the same being, of the same including Self of All.[37]

It is precisely this sense of self-realization and identification with the "All" that defines Carpenter's conception of cosmic consciousness.

In a remarkable move that clearly sets Carpenter's model apart from Bucke's, he asks if we are all cosmically connected, then why should we not try to realize this connection – with all the ethical and existential implications it entails – in our social and political lives? And that is exactly what Carpenter set about to do. In numerous books, pamphlets, lectures and organized protests, Carpenter sought to mobilize the masses by appealing to the spiritual and social liberation that comes with shrugging off the shackles of "Commercial Civilization." Thus, at the heart of Carpenter's vision of cosmic consciousness is an emancipatory discourse dedicated to restoring our lost kinship with nature. But how do we begin such a massive endeavor? Quite simply argues Carpenter, we can begin at the individual level by reconfiguring our relationship with nature and seek out "the life of the open air, familiarity with the winds and waves, clean and pure food, the companionship of animals,"[38] and such a move will ideally lead to a new sense of *being-in-the-world* that prohibits the normalization of social injustice. Carpenter identified a close link between our alienation from nature and our alienation from each other; by renewing our connection to nature we empower ourselves with a larger perspective of *being-in-the-world*, which, in turn, will help foster our interest in cultivating a more authentic love for one another in the social domain. Carpenter writes,

> To become united and in line with the beauty and vitality of Nature (but, Lord help us! We are far enough off from that at present), and to become united with those we love – what other ultimate object in life is there? Surely all these other things – these games and examinations, these churches and chapels, these distinct councils and money markets, these top-hats and telephones and even the general necessity of earning one's living – if they are not ultimately for that, what are they for?[39]

Throughout his life Carpenter held a deep and abiding reverence for nature. Writing about his childhood, he notes, "Nature was more to me, I believe, than any human attachment."[40] But it was not until he encountered cosmic consciousness when he finally realized how precious of an objective it was to protect nature (and thus humanity) from the vile exploitations of mass industrialization. Carpenter was one of the earliest advocates of land conservation in England and campaigned heavily against air pollution, or as he called it, "the smoke nuisance." His views on the matter were perhaps articulated most eloquently in a newspaper article he wrote for the *Sheffield*

Independent in 1889. Carpenter describes the unsettling impression he had while looking down on Sheffield from atop a hill. He writes:

> [O]nly a vast dense cloud, so thick that I wondered how any human being could support life in it, went up to heaven like the smoke from a great alter. An alter, indeed, it seemed to me, whereon thousands of lives were being yearly sacrificed. Beside me on the hills the sun was shining, the larks were singing; but down there a hundred thousand grown people, let alone children, were struggling for a little sun and air, toiling, moiling, living a life of suffocation, dying of diseases caused by foul air and want of light – all for what? To make a few people rich! And this was not a lunatic asylum! I descended into the smoke. The sun went out; the chimneys towered round me, belching forth thick volumes.[41]

This passage is key to appreciating the foresight of Carpenter's ecological sensibilities. He makes an explicit link between pollution and the suffering of the working class, which in my estimate prefigures in many ways, socially, politically, and economically, the claims that have come to characterize the environmental justice movement, which, like Carpenter, identify a systemic link among class, capitalism, and environmental degradation.[42] And like the advocates of the environmental justice movement, Carpenter was adamant that the cause of environmentalism is tied to the call for social justice. To borrow a slogan from the American civil rights movement, Carpenter ultimately believed that "nobody is free, until everybody is free," and "everybody" in this context includes nature.

Overall, Carpenter's vision of cosmic consciousness can be characterized as revolutionary in the sense that if his most essential insight – namely, the fusion of subject (self) and object (nature) – were to be actualized on a practical level of our lived existence, it would entail a radical contestation of our conventional understanding of reality. And Carpenter would settle for nothing less. His calls for social and political reform, sexual justice, and gender equality and a renewed rapport with nature are all tied to his fundamental teaching on cosmic consciousness, which stipulated that "the whole of Creation is *alive*."[43] Like Whitman and Bucke, Carpenter lost faith in organized religion and sought to construct a "rational mysticism" that could accommodate the finding of both modern science and mystical experience. But unlike Bucke, Carpenter was keenly aware of the limitations of science; that is, he recognized that science alone ultimately fails to address the essential nature of our humanity, which consists of not merely a desire to know the facts of the world but also to appreciate the value of *being a part* of the world.

Cosmic consciousness and the SBNR

Earlier in this volume Robert C. Fuller and William B. Parsons characterize the type of spirituality often associated with those who profess to being

SBNR as "unchurched, nontraditional, and noninstitutional."[44] Likewise, Whitman, Bucke and Carpenter's conceptualization of cosmic consciousness share these same characteristics. For instance, Whitman, Bucke, and Carpenter were convinced that cosmic consciousness is essentially incompatible with the dogmatic claims of organized religion; that is, cosmic consciousness refers to a spiritual/mystical state of awareness that is essentially "unchurched" or even hostile to the exclusive claims of organized religion. Moreover, Whitman, Bucke, and Carpenter also characterize cosmic consciousness in nontraditional terms that place emphasis on science, evolution, and eroticism, which are all fields of study that tend to be marginalized in traditional religious discourse. Furthermore, Whitman, Bucke, and Carpenter claim that cosmic consciousness is at the root of all religion but essentially transcends the authoritative reach of any particular religious, social, or political institution. In fact, it could be argued that the spiritual knowledge engendered by cosmic consciousness empowers subjects to call into question all forms of institutional authority that fail to acknowledge the emancipatory quality of unitive experience. Thus, given these levels of similarity, I think it is safe to suggest that Whitman, Bucke, and Carpenter would identify their teachings as "Spiritual but Not Religious" and, moreover, that their concept of cosmic consciousness has played a formative – yet often underappreciated – role in popularizing spirituality to the American public and beyond.

Perhaps one of the most stinging criticisms often leveled at the SBNR movement is that it promotes and perpetuates an insidious form of hyperindividualism that tends to collaborate with rather than contest the exploitative agenda of neoliberal philosophy and the consumerist ethos it entails.[45] But the writings of Whitman and Carpenter, for example, suggest that an experience of cosmic consciousness *can* enhance a subject's sense of agency and empower him or her to develop alternative strategies of social and political engagement. By investing the natural world with spiritual value both Whitman and Carpenter essentially favor an existential interpretation of cosmic consciousness in that the locus of spiritual meaning remains *in this world* and not in the hereafter. And it is precisely the immanent dimension of their spiritual vision that informs the ethical contours of their social/political critique. Such a perspective I believe can serve as a response to critics of the SBNR movement who fail to fully address the substantive quality of spiritual experience as a source of both ethical reflection and political engagement.

But perhaps the most valuable contribution that a deeper study of cosmic consciousness can make to broaden our understanding of the SBNR movement lies with its ecological significance. Drawing on the teachings of Whitman, Bucke, and Carpenter, I argue that cosmic consciousness can be interpreted as an ecological principle in the sense that it presents a nondualistic or "holistic" understanding of the relationship between spirituality and materiality, which, in turn, fosters an attitude of reverence for nature based on the idea that nature is an extension of God. Or, to put the matter another way, cosmic consciousness affirms both our spiritual *and* material bond with nature and the moral realization of this bond presents us with an opportunity to cultivate an environmental ethic that can accommodate the findings of both science *and* spirituality.

Why is this knowledge important to the future of the SBNR? Because if the study of the SBNR is to remain relevant into the future then it must make more of an effort to critically engage with ecological issues. A significant portion of our population identifies as being SBNR. In fact, it is the youngest generation, the millennials, who will likely decide the future fate of this planet and it is the millennial generation that most identify with being SBNR.[46] Aside from the threat of nuclear war, there is no question that the biggest issue confronting millennials will be how to address the ecological crisis. Thus, it only makes sense that we try to cultivate a more sophisticated understanding of the connection between spirituality and ecology because the fate of future generations might literally depend on it.

Conclusion

Following the work of such scholar's as Leigh Schmidt (2005) and Arthur Versluis (2014), I believe a convincing argument can be made that links the earliest rise of the SBNR movement in America to the influential teachings of various 19th-century intellectuals associated with the philosophy of transcendentalism. The emphasis on self-reliance, liberalism, and social reform that has come to characterize transcendentalist philosophy are ideas that still play a formative role in shaping how we comprehend the meaning of being SBNR. But my brief study suggests that our contemporary understanding of the SBNR still has a lot to learn from the history of transcendentalism, particularly, as it relates to the question of nature and ecology. To this end, I've tried to call attention to a specific dimension of this history by demonstrating the ecological significance of cosmic consciousness. This type of research is important because it provides us with an opportunity to carve new paths of theorizing about the future direction of the SBNR – ones that hopefully lead in a more ecological direction!

Bucke's contributions to popularizing the idea of cosmic consciousness cannot be underestimated. But as a whole, his perspective is only marginally valuable to our effort to reconfigure cosmic consciousness as an ecological principle. The work of Whitman and Carpenter, in contrast, present a spiritual viewpoint that clearly aligns with the ideals that define our contemporary understanding of ecology.[47] Whitman and Carpenter were also profoundly concerned about the social and political conditions of their time and believed that the erotic realization of this cosmic bond between "I" and "Other," could inspire the creation of a new social order based on the democratic ideals of equality and comradeship. I would even go so far as to suggest that even though Carpenter's conception of cosmic consciousness was developed well over a century ago, the environmental perspective it presents, it is still ahead of its time in the sense that it can accommodate the multidimensionality of the ecocrisis we are facing; that what we think about as environmentalism is not only tied to how we view and value nature, but it also entails an overhaul how we view and value the body, sexuality, and social justice. In other words, Carpenter's social and environmental critique is at the core ontological; only by cultivating a new way of being, particularly, a new way of *being-in-the-world* that embraces the existential implications of the erotic body, will we be able to restore some semblance of balance in our relationship with nature that can hopefully bring us back from the brink of ecological disaster.

As the rise of popular interest in spirituality continues to grow and our culture becomes more attuned to the consequences of the ecological crisis, the need to historically contextualize cosmic consciousness and its relationship to the SBNR becomes ever more pressing. In this chapter I've tried to demonstrate how the concept of cosmic consciousness can be reconfigured as an ecological principle and provide a solid historical context to ground ecological theorizing about the future direction of the SBNR. At the very least, my study suggests that there are new spiritual narratives waiting to be written in terms of how we think and feel about nature and a deeper exploration of the ethical and ontological significance of cosmic consciousness could play an important role in this endeavor. Ultimately, as we consider the fate of our ecological future we must keep our hearts and minds open to the possibility that the flourishing of our planet rests on our collective capacity to appreciate the spiritual significance of knowing that "a leaf of grass is no less than the journeywork of the stars."[48]

Notes

1 Ralph Waldo Emerson, *Nature* (Boston, MA: James Munroe and Company, 1979), 13.
2 Henry David Thoreau as quoted by Robert L. Dorman in *A Word for Nature: Four Pioneering Environmental Advocates, 1845–1913* (Durham, NC: Duke University Press, 1998), 63.
3 Henry David Thoreau, *Walden* (New York: AMS Press, 1982), 211.
4 For a detailed discussion of the SBNR movement see Robert C. Fuller's *Spiritual, But Not Religious: Understanding Unchurched America* (New York: Oxford, 2001) and Linda A. Mercadante's *Belief Without Borders: Inside the Minds of the Spiritual But Not Religious* (New York: Oxford, 2014).
5 For a more comprehensive account on the history of transcendentalism see Philip F. Gura's *American Transcendentalism: A History* (New York: Hill and Wang, 2008).
6 See Robert C. Fuller and William B. Parsons chapter, "Spiritual But Not Religious: A Brief Introduction" in this volume.
7 Harold Bloom, "Whitman's America," *The Wall Street Journal*, July 29, 2005.
8 Paul Marshall, *Mystical Encounters with the Natural World* (New York: Oxford University Press, 2008), 57.
9 For a detailed discussion of Whitman and science see Joseph Beaver's *Walt Whitman: Poet of Science* (New York: King's Crown Press, 1951).

10 See Walter T. Stace's *Mysticism and Philosophy* (London: Macmillan, 1961) and R.C. Zaehner's *Mysticism: Sacred and Profane* (Oxford: Clarendon Press, 1957).

11 Walt Whitman, *Prose Works* (Philadelphia: David McKay, 1892), 274. According to David S. Reynold's, Whitman "accepted all religions but believed in no single church. It was difficult for him to have faith in the churches at a time when he felt they had become poisoned by association with economic injustice and chattel slavery" (David S. Reynolds, *Walt Whitman* [New York: Oxford University Press], 77).

12 James E. Miller Jr., *Walt Whitman* (Boston, MA: Twayne Publishers, 1990), 119.

13 Walt Whitman, *Leaves of Grass* (New York: Bantam Books, 2004), 45.

14 Walt Whitman, *Prose Works* (Philadelphia, PA: David McKay, 1892), 234.

15 Walt Whitman as quoted by David S. Reynolds, in *Walt Whitman*, 96.

16 Whitman, *Leaves of Grass*, 29.

17 Ibid.

18 According to James E. Miller Jr., "Through sexual imagery Whitman identifies the person with the fundamental generative forces of nature. In sexual identity and experience the person may discover harmony and unity with nature, the life-force that subterraneously unites all into one creative whole" (James E. Miller, *Walt Whitman* (Boston: Twayne Publishers, 1990), 131).

19 Whitman, *Leaves of Grass*, 26.

20 Ibid., 49.

21 Ibid.

22 Whitman, *Prose Works*, 82.

23 Ibid., 249.

24 Whitman, *Leaves of Grass*, 120.

25 Reynolds, *Walt Whitman*, 90.

26 Richard Maurice Bucke, *Cosmic Consciousness* (Secaucus, NJ: The Citadel Press, 1973), 8.

27 For a detailed account of their relationship see Lorna Weir's, "Cosmic Consciousness and the Love of Comrades: Contacts Between R. M. Bucke and Edward Carpenter," *Journal of Canadian Studies* 30, no. 2 (1995).

28 Bucke, *Cosmic Consciousness*, 14.

29 For a more detailed study of Carpenter's views on these issues see Sheila Rowbotham's biography, *Edward Carpenter: A Life of Liberty and Love* (New York: Verso, 2009).

30 See Carpenter's *From Adam's Peak to Elephanta* (London: Swan Sonnenschein, 1892) for a detailed examination of how Eastern philosophy influenced his understanding of cosmic consciousness.

31 Edward Carpenter, *Towards Democracy* (Charleston: Nabu Press, 2011), 3.

32 Ibid., 21.

33 Ibid., 41.

34 Edward Carpenter, *Civilization: Its Cause and Cure* (London: Humboldt Publishing, 1891), 52.

35 Ibid.

36 Edward Carpenter, *My Days and Dreams* (London: George Allen & Unwin, 1921), 5.

37 Ibid., 60.

38 Edward Carpenter, *Civilization: Its Cause and Cure* (London: Humboldt Publishing, 1891), 32.

39 Carpenter, *My Days and Dreams*, 302.

40 Ibid: 26.

41 Edward Carpenter, "The Smoke Nuisance," *Sheffield Independent*, May 25, 1889.

42 See Ronald Sandler and Phaedra C. Pezzullo, eds., *Environmental Justice and Environmentalism* (Cambridge, MA: The MIT Press, 2007).
43 Carpenter, *My Days and Dreams*, 110.
44 See Robert C. Fuller and William B. Parsons's chapter "Spiritual But Not Religious: A Brief Introduction" in this volume.
45 I am thinking in particular of the critiques presented by Jeremy Carrette and Richard King, in their influential work *Selling Spirituality*. Briefly put, Carrette and King claim that the growing popularity of the SBNR movement can be interpreted as a symptom of Western culture's overidentification with the (neoliberal) ideology of consumerism; that is, the social and political conditions of late capitalism have transformed "spirituality" into just another product of the market, designed to be consumed like any other commodity.
46 See the Pew Research Center's Religious Landscape Study: www.pewforum.org/religious-landscape-study/religious-denomination/spiritual-but-not-religious/.
47 See Leslie Sponsel, *Spiritual Ecology: A Quiet Revolution* (Santa Barbara, CA: Praeger, 2012).
48 Whitman, *Leaves of Grass*, 55.

References

Beaver, Joseph. *Walt Whitman: Poet of Science*. New York: King's Crown Press, 1951.
Bloom, Harold. "Whitman's America." *The Wall Street Journal*, July 29, 2005.
Bucke, Maurice Richard. *Cosmic Consciousness*. Secaucus, NJ: The Citadel Press, 1973 (1901).
Carpenter, Edward. "The Smoke Nuisance." *Sheffield Independent*, May 25, 1889.
———. *Civilization: Its Cause and Cure*. London: Humboldt Publishing, 1891.
———. *From Adam's Peak to Elephanta*. London: Swan Sonnenschein, 1892.
———. *The Art of Creation*. London: George Allen & Unwin, 1904.
———. *My Days and Dreams*. London: George Allen & Unwin, 1921.
———. *Towards Democracy*. Charleston: Nabu Press, 2011 (1883).
Carrette, Jeremym and Richard King. *Selling Spirituality: The Silent Takeover of Religion*. New York: Routledge, 2005.
Dorman, Robert, L. *A Word for Nature: Four Pioneering Environmental Advocates, 1845–1913*. Durham, NC: Duke University Press: 1998.
Emerson, Waldo Ralph. *Nature*. Boston, MA: James Munroe and Company, 1979 (1836).
Fuller, Robert, C. *Spiritual, But Not Religious: Unchurched America*. New York: Oxford University Press, 2001.
Gura, Philip, F. *American Transcendentalism: A History*. New York: Hill and Wang, 2008.
James, William. *The Varieties of Religious Experience*. New York: Penguin Books, 1958 (1901).
Klein, Naomi. *This Changes Everything: Capitalism vs. The Climate*. New York: Simon & Schuster, 2014.
Marshall, Paul. *Mystical Encounters with the Natural World: Experiences and Explanations*. New York: Oxford University Press, 2005.
Mercadante, Linda A. *Belief Without Borders: Inside the Minds of the Spiritual But Not Religious*. New York: Oxford University Press, 2014.
Miller, James E. *Walt Whitman*. Boston, MA: Twayne Publishers, 1990.

Reynolds, David S. *Walt Whitman*. New York: Oxford University Press, 2005.

Rowbotham, Sheila. *Edward Carpenter: A Life of Liberty and Love*. New York: Verso, 2009.

Sandler, Ronald and Phaedra C. Pezzullo, eds. *Environmental Justice and Environmentalism*. Cambridge, MA: The MIT Press, 2007.

Schmidt, Eric Leigh. *Restless Souls: The Making of American Spirituality*. New York: HarperCollins, 2005.

Sponsel, Leslie. *Spiritual Ecology: A Quiet Revolution*. Santa Barbara: Praeger, 2012.

Stace, Walter T. *Mysticism and Philosophy*. London: Macmillan, 1961.

Thoreau, David Henry. *Walden*. New York: AMS Press, 1982 (1854).

Versluis, Arthur. *American Gurus: From Transcendentalism to New Age Religion*. New York: Oxford University Press, 2014.

Weir, Lorna. "Cosmic Consciousness and the Love of Comrades: Contacts Between R.M. Bucke and Edward Carpenter." *Journal of Canadian Studies* 30, no. 2 (1995).

Whitman, Walt. *Prose Works*. Philadelphia, PA: David McKay, 1892.

———. *Leaves of Grass*. New York: Bantam Books, 2004 (1855).

Zaehner, R.C. *Mysticism: Sacred and Profane*. Oxford: Clarendon Press, 1957.

12 Toward a metamodern reading of Spiritual but Not Religious mysticisms

Linda C. Ceriello

The Spiritual but Not Religious (SBNR), the Nones, and the Unaffiliateds are contemporary alternative spiritualities whose apophatic appellations signal a new kind of secular spirituality. The interest they indicate in choosing ontological ambiguity – emphasizing what one is *not* as equal to or more important than what one *is* – accompanies an upsurge in popular treatments of mysticisms, often in contexts that are not particularly religious or spiritual. Understanding the current epistemic locus in which these expressions of individual spirituality are situated reveals a unique way in which mystical material "performs" for those who embrace these affiliations. Furthermore, it shows a way being paved for a consideration of universalist (modern) and constructivist (postmodern) cultural readings within a new narrative, one that offers a kind of reconciliation of the two while also reflecting the depth of influence of such contemporary secular spiritualities.

This chapter frames the SBNR as constitutive of a post-postmodern epistemic turn, one referred to by some under the rubric of *metamodernism*. The potential utility of the new theoretical category of metamodernism as successor to postmodernism lies in helping account for several factors that have contributed to the growth of the SBNR phenomenon. The first is the increased normalization of presentations of mystical experience in contemporary Western secular culture (for the present purpose, I use an intentionally wide, emic definition of a *mystical experience/encounter*: a vision or realization occurring as radically de-centering and life-altering in the perception of the experiencer). I work from the idea that mystical encounters – including fictionalized ones, as in film and television depictions that I refer to as "secondhand mysticism" – mirror and engage contemporary individuals' felt experience of being in-between, of being both secular and spiritual. Specifically, I employ metamodern theory to ask how the choice to identify as SBNR engages this *both/and* ontology via the reflexive construction of *liminalities* that, I propose here, act as analogs to the mystical encounter itself. While this sort of boundary-blurring ontology has been well articulated by a handful of scholars, what has room to be more fully explored are its epistemic basis and expressions in contemporary culture.[1]

Second, deploying *metamodernism* as a distinction will serve to help update the cumulative effect of 19th- and 20th-century alternative spirituality's emphasis on individual experience. There should be little doubt of that particular "baton" having now passed to SBNRs, evinced by their move toward a further reclamation of personal and felt experience, as I will explain. My analysis begins where existing historiographies, with their important genealogies of Western metaphysical religious movements that detail the epistemologies of experience, leave off and focuses on charting shifts that occur between the decline of the New Age and the present in the public sharing of mystical accounts and truth claims.

Third, the theorization of metamodernism will afford proper emphasis to be placed on specific forms of "participatory" popular culture and media practices as contemporary social forces that exert undeniable influence upon new spiritualities. Since *millennials*, along with the emerging generation referred to as the *plurals*, are the cultural dominants with respect to engagement with media influences, I shall to some extent emphasize these younger generations' manifestations of secular spiritualities while attempting to track their concomitant influence on the metamodern epistemic shift.[2]

The epistemic usage of metamodernism that I employ here was first proposed early in the first decade of the 2000s and comes into more active scholarly use primarily in cultural studies, literary critical, and art historical capacities later in the decade. Only in the last few years have a small handful of scholars of religion made forays into exploring its theoretical use for the field.[3] In Timotheus Vermeulen and Robin van den Akker's influential conception of it, the term *metamodernism* names

> a continuous oscillation, a constant repositioning between attitudes and mindsets that are evocative of the modern and of the postmodern but are ultimately suggestive of another sensibility that is neither of them. A discourse that negotiates between a yearning for universal truths but also an (a)political relativism, between a desire for sense and a doubt about the sense of it all, between . . . sincerity and irony, knowingness and naivety, construction and deconstruction.[4]

The relevance of these negotiations of *betweens* to the SBNR, which will be elaborated on shortly, should be readily recognizable: the SBNR is already acknowledged as a contemporary spirituality that "challenges the division created in the modern era between religious and secular realms of life and enables the formation of new lifestyles, social practices, and cultural artifacts that cannot be defined as either religious or secular."[5] Put simply, the bifurcative stance of *you are or you aren't* (i.e., either you are or are not a mystic, a religious person, a spiritual seeker, an atheist, etc.) seems to reflect less than ever the felt reality of SBNRs. Millennials and plurals especially are seen engaging their spiritualities with an increasingly egalitarian stance toward beliefs, worldviews, and practices different from their own. Relatedly, they evince what I am calling *fluid identity narratives* – identities freely constructed and reconstructed in an increasingly more public fashion and with an increased sense of personal agency. They do so partly through engagement with mystical and spiritual phenomena. Courtney Bender's 2010 ethnographic study suggested that the worlds of SBNRs are shaped by numinous encounters and mystical experiences of *flow*, synchronicity, or oneness.[6] I expand this observation about everyday spiritual encounters to highlight their occurrences in certain secular environments, such as those available secondhand through TV/film, and through lifestyle technologies such as internet-based fandoms and social media.

Last, I ask what these intersections portend about the future of being SBNR: its sustainability as an affiliation and its potential growth and social influence as a movement. I introduce the idea of a metamodern soteriology to address whether the SBNR will exhibit a (continued) promotion of pluralist, inclusivist community engagement, or perhaps something else altogether.

The New Age rebranded? The work of the "SBNR" moniker

Wouter Hanegraaff ended his *New Age Religion and Western Culture* by giving the last word to Gershom Scholem in a pronouncement that has significance four decades later. Scholem wrote, "If humanity should ever lose the feeling that there is mystery – a secret – in the world, then it's all over with us."[7] Hanegraaff and Scholem each asked whether the secularization trend, with its emphasis on individualism, might threaten the bedrock of shared symbolism that foregrounds *mystery* as central to the human quest for meaning.[8] Viewed from the perspective of 21st-century popular mysticisms, however, I contend that mystery and the mystical have reestablished themselves as central in the cultural conversation and are, in fact, reframed by the concerns of SBNRs. Hanegraaff also commented that he doubted if the term *New Age* would survive the 20th century, given that it had "acquired negative connotations, and many people no longer want to be associated with it."[9] His remark turns out to have been prescient – partly. While the term *New Age* is indeed embraced less and less frequently as an identity in much of the West after the turn of the millennium, it appears to continue to do some important signifying work as a pejorative – a point whose significance for understanding the SBNR has, I believe, gone undernoticed.[10]

What specific cultural shifts might account for the New Age's falling out of favor, while its beliefs and practices seem to persist to the present day? To answer that, let us examine an instance of the derisive use of the term *New Age* found in the web magazine *Elephant Journal*. This magazine describes its demographic, those interested in "the mindful life" as being "about yoga, organics, sustainability, conscious consumerism, enlightened education, the contemplative arts, adventure, bicycling, family . . . everything. But mostly it's about this present moment, right here, right now, and how we can best be of benefit, and have a good time doing so."[11] On *Elephant Journal's* home page, alongside topic tabs such as *WELLNESS, GREEN,* and *ENLIGHT-ENED SOCIETY,* one finds *NON NEW-AGEY SPIRITUALITY.* Articles under that tab include some that frankly epitomize the stereotypes of the New Age and some that seem aimed at differentiating a newer kind of eclectic spirituality. Author David Zenon Starlyte's article titled "Darkness Can't Exist in the Light" exemplifies a meeting of the New Age and SBNR ideologies. Arguing against traditional religions, both West and East, he argues that a *multiplicity* is a more apt, and even socially responsive, rewrite: "Complexity and multiplicity, which is the nature of existence, has been maligned and even suppressed" by these "old perspectives." . . . "An inseparable duality runs through the matrix of our thinking . . . encouraged by institutions . . . Perhaps our traditions have misled us or simply polarized our view into black and white thinking?"[12]

This argument runs a circuit familiar for anyone acquainted with New Age tenets: railing against the hegemonies of organized religions by proposing a universalist philosophy that is inclusive of scientific perspectives, friendly to relativism, and still arrives at the monist position that all is God. Epistemically, this presents a kind of clash among traditional (or premodern), modern, and postmodern epistemes. The simultaneous borrowing from and critiquing of religious ideas reflect both a suspicious stance toward them and a disinclination to discard them. The tone of this and other articles in *Elephant Journal* suggests that anyone can offer their take on *the mindful life* and that the project of engaging with and rewriting the ancient wisdoms to incorporate contemporary values is ongoing and open to all comers.

Elephant Journal's telling tab appealing to the "non-New-Agey" underscore the relevance of my question about what exactly happened to sully the designation *New Age.* Part of the sullying surely had to do with a backlash against the simultaneous popularization, and commodification of contemporary expressions of New Age spiritualities.[13] Still, one suspects that the surfacing of the SBNR reflects more than a simple rebranding attempt.

To address this more closely, let us consider the work performed by the ambiguity inherent in the phrase "Spiritual but Not Religious." With its apophatic quality, the name *SBNR* subverts the expectation of specificity, in that it signals both an opening ("spiritual" with that intentionally wide set of meanings) and, in the same breath, a vehement closing (*not* "religious"). So *SBNR* as a moniker may be deployed as a creative, ontological strategy to uphold the right to one's eclecticism and to avoid being pigeonholed with any single affiliation that could be commodified and/or derided away. To call oneself SBNR is to produce a subtext highlighting one's individual choice-making agency and thus declaring oneself the arbiter of what is to be deemed "spiritual." This produces an interesting relational aspect of SBNR as simultaneously denying that any stamp of approval from extrinsic religious authorities should be needed and, at the same time, inviting participation with the individual as her own spiritual authority. That is, unlike most religious affiliations, since the SBNR encompasses a large array of traditions, teachers, beliefs, and practices, if one wants to know which of these a given SBNR individual follows, one has to ask.

And finally, we should notice one rather unambiguous aspect of this name designation, which is that no telos or soteriology is subtly suggested in the phrase "Spiritual but Not Religious." No definitive creed is announced, no call for anything "new," or a connotation of SBNR as somehow an improved version of what came before. SBNR can be thought of, then, as a horizontal move of sorts, one that reflects a position *between*: between the New Age's modernist grand narratives and notions of progress, on one hand, and the overtly constructed, postmodernist stance, on the other.

Being between epistemes

Where my analysis differs from other scholars working to unpack metamodern theory who do not attend to religious historiographies is in regarding the SBNR's emergence as a specific response to the New Age as an important factor in this epistemic turn. To plug this observation into the epistemic schema depends first on typifying the New Age as essentially modern. On this point, I follow Paul Heelas, who wrote that the New Age is a spirituality *of and for modernity* in the sense that it "provides a *sacralized rendering* of widely held values (equality, dignity, tranquility, harmony, love, peace, creative expressivity, being positive and, above all, *the self* as a value in and of itself)"[14] and, in its conception of a *Higher Self*, regarded as the *real you*. The dualistic split that occurs when sacralizing these values in effect means that New Age narratives pit the light, the good, the positive, the transcendent, and the idea of a universal Real against "darker," more ethically ambiguous, more immanent, local, felt realities. The postmodern turn, which comes along, in part, in reaction to these sorts of universalisms and bifurcations, enacts its own kind of split with the deconstruction of unmediated meanings, and of the notion of any *stable subject* to derive such meanings, as invoked in shorthand by the expression, "no *there* there." This stance produces an affective constriction in the academy – one that had a particular impact on scholars of mysticism who broached the affective domain of *experience*, and who still to some extent face an implicit accusation of failing to recognize the Derridean gospel of "nothing outside the text." As Raoul Eshelman quipped, "[n]o one wants to get caught practicing metaphysics."[15]

Calling out the affective limitations of this postmodern *removal* as well as alluding to its social consequences, David Foster Wallace's 1993 essay "E Unibus Pluram" is thought to have articulated what would become one of metamodernism's anchoring sentiments. In it, he wrote against irony culture and the passivity and cynicism portended by being always "behind the scenes" rather than *in* the scene.[16] Wallace wrote,

> The next real literary 'rebels' in this country might well emerge as some weird bunch of 'anti-rebels,' born oglers who dare to back away from ironic watching, who have the childish gall actually to endorse single-entendre values. Who treat old untrendy human troubles and emotions in U.S. life with reverence and conviction. Who eschew self-consciousness and fatigue.[17]

Indeed, as Wallace foresaw, the postmodern ironic culture with its employment of aesthetic and discursive techniques aimed at the decentering and scrambling of meanings – has in some respects been running its course since around the turn of the millennium. Echoing the pronouncements about the death of postmodernism of numerous literary scholars from Wallace onward, Eshelman writes,

> We are now leaving the postmodern era, with its essentially dualist notions of textuality, virtuality, belatedness, endless irony, and metaphysical skepticism and entering an era in which specifically monist virtues are again coming to the fore. For the most part, this process has been taking place directly in living culture, around and outside the purview of academic theory.[18]

This latter observation of Eshelman's squares with my own and, I might add, makes post-postmodernisms extra fascinating and at the same time extra tricky to track. My own working theory – hardly provable – is that millennials have felt something amiss with the always-ironic postmodern disaffection into which they came of age, and have begun constructing a new sensibility around an attitude something like *OK, there may be no 'there' there, but yet . . . I'm here! That has got to count for something . . . !* Indeed, it has amounted to a calling-out of the paradox of negating oneself as subject. This becomes one place we might look to locate the ground of the metamodern turn. Today's SBNRs might then be considered the rebel *antirebels* in the sense Wallace conveys.

Metamodern millennial spiritualities, then, are marked by a desire to *reclaim* that which had somehow gone underground under postmodernism: affect, emotional sincerity, felt experience and agency or authority in meaning making. This reclamation will be taken here as a key characteristic of the metamodern cultural sensibility and its newly configured soteriological perspective. For one thing, such reclamation has made it possible for secular individuals to also be spiritual – publicly – without shame or embarrassment at somehow getting caught having missed the joke. As I have written elsewhere, metamodernism performs the existential move out from under the thumb of postmodern irony, producing artifacts that show individuals (re)claiming ownership of a breadth of human vicissitudes experientially felt to be real – and more so when they stand messily entangled together rather than tidily sorted out into either modern universalisms or postmodern deconstructions.[19] Important for the study of religion, the cultural manifestation of this reclamation is a general gravitation toward – even a kind of *sacralizing* of – individual felt experience, though inclusive now of the rougher, flawed, more shadowy, and even the weirder and quirkier human qualities, emotions, and experiences.[20] So, SBNRs project an insistence that the spiritual can be found anywhere and in everything. But this time, they seem to really mean *everything*.[21] This is one aspect of a soteriological shift in the script that, I submit, should be central to an attempt to define SBNR spirituality.

In sum, the cultural position out of which the SBNR arises speaks to a disenchantment with the New Age's lopsidedly light, power-of-positive-thinking-fueled soteriology, as well as a disenchantment with postmodern disenchantment, as it were.[22] (A double negative becomes, in effect, a positive.) Starlyte pushed back against a duality that would banish "the dark" and overemphasize "the light" when he wrote, "When we fear the dark, we give it power over us. We tend to view darkness as bad and light as good, and place them on opposite ends of the spectrum."[23] His argument for a place for the full spectrum of human experience is the sort of *both/and* likely to be endorsed by metamodern SBNRs.

A metamodern narrative analysis of a mystical account

A brief close reading of a narrative account of mystical awareness may help illustrate the secular-informed spiritual immanence I've identified here as part of a metamodern soteriological shift. The following account was submitted anonymously to the Alister Hardy Archive of Religious Experience in the early 2000s.[24] I have excerpted three short passages. The subject begins by describing her own process of painting as a portal to mystical states of awareness. She reports "*an extreme continuity between you and the material world around you . . . an extremely heightened awareness of . . . the interaction of earth, air, ground, sky and water . . . an experience of unity with the forces of both the material world and the spiritual world within that.*"

She then characterizes the spiritual state as "within" the material realm, rather than outside, above, or in some way superseding it, by qualifying with apophatic remarks on what the experience is *not*:

> *You could not say from this experience that life had a special meaning and purpose. You could only say: 'Life has a meaning, and it is this: We are continuously a part of this material and spiritual world.' It is not that, 'There is a transcendent world.' I don't think we need to go so far as*

to say this is a vision of a new world, nor of a new heaven and earth. . . .
What is important is the enhancement of creativity and awareness in
the moment. The reason we don't have to do that 'transcendent-for-
evermore' bit is because, by this means, we can have great, great eternity
in one great, great moment.

"Awareness in the moment" by means of ordinary activities like painting,
the subject feels, can bring access to a kind of transformational awareness
that, finally, anchors one in the world. The subject then details her means
of "returning" from this state of awareness back to the "everyday world"
before concluding,

> *Whilst such moments are great ones, we have to absorb what has hap-*
> *pened, and go on from there in the everyday world. I would argue that to*
> *look for universal insights from this experience of unity is not the right*
> *way to go about it. I do not think this means we will be joining a con-*
> *tinuously unified world . . . I feel that this does not matter too much. . . .*
> *we can personally have a great life in this life and from this kind of*
> *experience. . . . As ever, we return to everyday life, problems, conflicts,*
> *perceptions, and failures of communication. That is life.*

In my brief comments on the subject's rich account, I want to especially
underscore the fact that it is largely *not* centered on transcendence. The
salient element of the mystical realization, for her, is not one of feeling trans-
ported or of spiritual attaining from another source, but more of informing
and augmenting ordinary existence. As such, it stands in contrast to mystical narratives which commonly use a type of developmental progression
that Mark Freeman has called the *process narrative*.[25] Freeman has found
that subjects often interpret their experiences through a kind of ranking of
their own previous mystical/spiritual experiences as less powerful, concluding that prior experiences have led them toward, and finally culminated in,
the new "higher" realization/state of consciousness. Our present subject's
tone, by contrast, does not imply that she feels she has reached any such
pinnacle, nor does she lead her presumptive interlocutor to a suggestion that
her mystical awareness provides her any real resolution for everyday problems. On the contrary, what is conveyed is a feeling that she has glimpsed a
part of the transformative capacities inherent in human experience, perhaps
one mode of awareness among many. Her manner of validating her experience via ordinary lived reality rather than in the context of a transcendent
reality marks her account as an example of a metamodern mysticism.[26]

Media culture and participatory rescripting of spiritualities

Spirituality in the millennial era and beyond simply cannot be addressed
without accounting for its embeddedness in media culture. As observed

already in 2006, "[m]edia technologies are a core aspect of spiritual access and religious community in contemporary [Western] societies."[27] What I specifically wish to add to the mix here is the significance of new norms and practices influenced by social media and by portrayals of the religious, spiritual, and mystical/nonordinary in the media. For brevity's sake, my treatment must bypass critical issues such as uneven access to technology by different socioeconomic groups and other social factors of import. My comments will necessarily be general signposts rather than pointed dissections of any specific group's usages of specific media.

As anyone who lives in the contemporary West and owns even one "device" is aware, a world in which individuals are composites is now upon us. Social media's ubiquity, its popularity, and its structural egalitarianism have now made normative each person's ability to in a certain sense operate as an array of differing personal identities.[28] Younger generations especially have grown accustomed to forming, framing, and displaying their identities through momentary snapshots on their numerous social media platforms. In the current *sharing economy*, liking, posting, and sharing as forms of endorsement amount now to literal engines of economics, overtly tying this manner of identity construction to social as well as market capital.

Furthermore, this processing and viewing moments in one's life as snapshots or scenes for consumption by one's network of followers – framing reality *through the lens* – is a recent reflexive propensity that one can speculate may perform several significant ontological functions. For instance, blurring the lines between lived and constructed realities, may encourage this sense of fluid identity narratives I mentioned. The transient, snapshotted realities and identities, when read as any number of available storylines, may also foster future forms of community that do not insist on adherence to a single, totalizing truth but, in fact, tolerate or even thrive on multiple perspectives. Indeed, as metamodern viewers feel their sensibilities and experiences reflected in mystical pop culture, the epistemological undercurrent for millennial SBNRs may be one that leads them to feel as if a metaphysics of shared agency exists. That is, when there is a multivalent reality, manipulable right here, on one's own screen, not in a transcendent elsewhere, it may be apprehended as a co-creation, no less meaning-filled for its accessibility in ordinary, secular terms. I will return to this discussion shortly.

Here I might add that it is common to negatively construe and pin this situation on millennials, lamenting how they seem content to morph and shape-shift per the collective cultural allegiance to the economy of *likes* and *followers* on their various social media platforms. Be that as it may, I suggest it fruitful to also explore their fluid identity constructions and polyvalent, public ontologies as a sophisticated, pluralistic, metamodern move of both integrating and recovering from dead-ended aspects of the postmodern ironic they inherited, their creative means, perhaps, of finding their "place at the table." At a minimum, and more germane to the current topic, these newer generations have found ways of engaging their media and technologies in a manner that does not necessarily pit them *against* an interest in spiritual, as evidenced by what they watch and how they engage as viewers.

Current television and film are not only reflecting the apparent appetite of contemporary viewers for spiritual and religious themes. They also have engendered ancillary forms of participatory community. Consider that each of the top five "most watched TV shows" among millennials in 2014 – *The Walking Dead, American Horror Story, The Big Bang Theory, Game of Thrones,* and *NCIS*[29] – situate their numerous spiritual or supernatural themes and plot arcs in secular settings. They also work in messages of religious pluralism and humanism – something a nonviewer might be especially surprised to see playing a significant part in the formulaic crime drama, *NCIS,* or in the sitcom *The Big Bang Theory.* On *The Big Bang Theory,* for example, strident adherence to religious beliefs or to scientific epistemologies are mocked in equal measure. With respect to their efficacy as tools for negotiating social realities, both are lampooned as laughably ineffectual. That they are placed on equal ground – tacitly critiqued as for their insensitivity to human vulnerabilities, I suggest is a metamodern aspect of the show. Attending to feelings and relationships rights the situation better than ideologies can, is the message. On *NCIS,* where religious metaphors direct some of the storylines and episode names include "Saviors," "Resurrection," "Shiva," "Devil's Triad," "Shabbat Shalom," "Better Angels," "Judgment Day," "Witch Hunt," and "See No Evil," the collision of secular and spiritual values and themes is overt and seems to create moral arcs meant to span both.

Viewer "participation" takes virtual engagement with these themes even further. Fans can "add" numinosity, in a manner of speaking, to their show-watching experience. *NCIS*'s *fanfic* writers posting their stories in online fan groups liberally interweave supernatural and mystical elements, for example, taking the show's crime-solving storylines into alternate realities, where the cop characters are turned into shape-shifters and telepaths, among other alternate-reality plot twists.[30] *The Big Bang Theory*'s lively online chat boards show participants of various persuasions from atheist to fundamentalist discussing theological topics. One thread asks, "Can theist's enjoy the show The Big Bang Theory?"[31] (And, incidentally, the answer would appear to be yes, because, according to the aforementioned poll, the show ranked second among "practicing Christians.")[32] This demonstrates viewers' interest in seeing the intersections of the religious and secular interrogated more fully and their desire to ask deep questions, even of a comedic program.

There are numerous other examples of television shows drawing big ratings that point to an apparent interest by both secularly and spiritually minded audiences in the intersection of the two. Subsequent fan and audience studies may confirm what we here surmise is the case: popular culture acts as an engine of an ongoing *intertextual rescripting of the sacred,* to borrow a phrase from Richard Santana and Gregory Erickson.[33] And increasingly technologically enabled viewers can become quasi-spiritual practitioners – actively participating in this rescripting in ever more inventive ways. It can be expected that technology and media will only continue to augment the means by which people engage their spiritual proclivities. Subsequent studies may draw more data relevant to understanding the effects on consumers by looking even more closely at what meanings are performed by them for an increasingly participation-oriented, media-mediated audience.

Liminalizing: drawing and erasing boundaries

I now pull the above observations together to address the question that is in some ways at the heart of understanding secular-spiritual mysticisms: What meanings can we make of the popularity of the sorts of media representations of spirituality and mystical encounters under discussion here? More specifically, just how does the move across the borders of ordinary and nonordinary realities entice a contemporary consumer of mystical material? While a complex inquiry to be sure, I offer a theory here – one that attempts to connect my epistemic, narrative, and phenomenological points for purposes of inquiring more deeply into the mechanics, if you will, of the secondhand mystical encounter. What may be occurring is that mystical and supernatural narratives, as they blur, bend, and reconfigure boundaries, perform the liminal states that mirror metamodern SBNRs' felt reality.[34] Put more radically, mystics and mystical activity may be construed by SBNRs on some level as "sacred sites." This idea I extrapolate from Carmel Bendan Davis's application of the Foucauldian concept of *heterotopic liminality*.[35] Heterotopias are "places which are '. . . a sort of simultaneously mythic and real contestation of space in which we live' . . . representing something that is *beyond* that society."[36] Could the *media-mystic* be acting as a heterotopia, enacting or even triggering a felt negotiation of ordinary and nonordinary states?

Narratives of mystical encounters, though diverse and heterogeneous, very often focus on this powerful period of negotiation, sometimes referred to as the "descent" period, in which the mystic is straddling several perceptual realities: cognizant of her liminality, experiencing a multiplicity of identities, and also in some sense aware of the requirements of the "ordinary" state, as in our earlier account. Mystical narratives, to a great extent, are about this negotiation, about a "process of drawing and erasing lines and boundaries."[37] Furthermore, they very naturally problematize the boundaries between good and evil, between believers and nonbelievers or ordinary and nonordinary realities, boundaries that, as Santana and Erickson rightly insist, are "kept alive by both faith *and* doubt, located *between* existence and non-existence."[38] The suggestion here then is that a secondhand encounter with mystical material as on the television screen may also set up a similarly inflected sense of ontological negotiation for the viewer – a kind of performance of this drawing and erasing. I am emphasizing the action of *liminalizing* as a verbal construction, a performative process – one that reflects the metamodern oscillation between identities by means of this stepping back and forth between domains. Put more directly, the notion here is that the active riding of tensions between the secular and spiritual is an important aspect of how SBNRs forge their identities – how their public ontologies are performatively generated – both inside and outside their secular and their spiritual identities and in constant negotiation between these realities – not unlike the mystic.

The metamodernization of spiritual figures

In this final section, I describe what I am calling the "metamodernization" of spiritual figures – which can apply to both living teachers and to repackagings of historical saints and others. I use the term as a way of pointing to the current trend of emphasizing the human, often quirky, aspects of spiritual figures, endeavoring to make them seem more ordinary and their lives relatable, rather than emphasizing their specialness, extraordinariness, or otherworldliness. One figure in contemporary spirituality illustrative of such metamodernization is popular British spiritual teacher Jeff Foster. Foster's teaching, in my estimation, could be described as Neo-Advaita Vedanta, though he takes pains to avoid any such labels. His website, *Life Without a Centre*, appears to be designed to reflect millennial sensibilities.[39] For instance, the headshot on his homepage avoids stereotypes of a "spiritual look," instead presenting a visage that seems to signal an ordinary moment for a not-*too*-radiantly-blissed-out person, someone who, with his incomplete scruff of beard, might, like you, be "in progress." The *Life Without a Centre* homepage links to Foster's writings on very human and ordinary topics such as depression, heartbreak, addiction, activism, passion, and grief. Foster seems to aim to offer a relational, feeling-centered approach that addresses average people's this-worldly emotions and concerns. He intones that the real work lies in "BLESSING THE MESS OF YOUR LIFE!" writing, "Thoughts and feelings are not mistakes, and they are not asking to be HEALED. They are asking to be HELD, here, now, lightly, in the loving arms of present awareness. . . ."[40]

The content of his writings avoids reflecting any ascetic form of spirituality and, moreover, references no originating tradition. The subtitle of the site reads, *My guru is this moment. My lineage is this moment. My spiritual path is this moment. And my home is this moment.* In his writing and public talks, negation is also employed heavily. A bio for Foster included in an interview echoes this negation:

> Jeff belongs to no tradition or lineage but has a deep respect for traditions and lineages. Jeff is not an 'authority' on life. His words are equal to the sound of a bird singing, or a cat miaowing. All are expressions

of the One Life. And when all words have disappeared, as they do, all that's left is laughter.[41]

This verbiage would feel familiar to millennial SBNRs such as those we would expect to find at the *Elephant Journal*, where language about spirituality often conveys a kind of negotiation or oscillation between epistemic positions; a performance of their complex and sometimes contradictory relationships around authority, meaning and truth.

Another way Foster metamodernizes his teachings, making them "broachable" by Western audiences, is to lightly poke fun at ideas like spiritual perfection and seekership, disarming any esoteric connections that could be an affront to secular audiences. For example, his site includes a short video of "bloopers" of himself screwing up on camera, self-effacingly titled "I'm a Useless Spiritual Teacher."[42] Also, in a short video called "The Advaita Trap," he stages what I would call a metamodern spiritual intervention, a scene in which one spiritual seeker finds she must confront her companion about his annoyingly didactic preachiness:

> Can I be honest with you? Since you've, well, in your own words, recognized your true nature, all the joy seems to have gone out of you. I'm sure you've found some clarity in one way or another, but it's almost like you've lost the ability to relate as a human being to me. . . . You're playing the guru and it's getting tiresome. . . . I'm trying to talk to you in a down to earth, ordinary, human way; not asking for help but sharing. . . . You're no fun anymore.[43]

The content and the construction of these videos invoke simplicity and innocence and the desire to connect. Each video reflects the metamodern course correction after postmodernism – that is, to become more attentive to relationality, that which simply makes one human. These artifacts, moreover, exemplify the negotiation between universalism and constructivism *through* felt experience, which, again, appeals to contemporary secular concerns about spirituality by intoning that one needn't discard everyday feelings and emotions in the pursuit of spiritual fulfillment.

Futures

To summarize what I have tried to convey here, *metamodernism* has been employed as replacement for the ill-defined and vaguely ouroboric *post-postmodernism*, specifically to reflect the millennial-era desire to recover one's right to personal, earnest pursuit of *Truth*, while acknowledging *truth* as constantly on the move. I have asked whether the performing of this negotiation may have a more-than-coincidental relationship to the current preponderance of public portrayals of mystical encounters and if this confluence helps us understand anything about the rise of secular spiritualities like the SBNR. My answer has been to propose that metamodernism's calling attention to the full reflexive awareness of the human penchant to seek a grand theory, and the simultaneous contemporary understanding that history will continually belie that effort, initiates ontological oscillations that can bring contemporary subjects into relationship with some aspect of the mechanics of mystical realization, whether strictly cognitive or more experiential.

Some will wish to ascertain whether a metamodern-informed SBNR avails itself of any particular social mission. If it does, it will be partly in spite of itself, as a metamodern-inflected idea of "mission" would tend to be written not as grand but as personal. The locus of meaning and agency becoming centered more around the individual, one surmises that as individuals' self-reflexive awareness increases and the language and practices of cultivating it become even more culturally normative (e.g., through the popularity of *mindfulness* as a simple means of being present to the individual moment) then modern narratives of progress with prescripted outcomes, those that redirect back to a static *either/or*, may naturally start to feel less relevant. To put it another way, the metamodern perspective, itself reliant on self-reflexivity tacitly refutes the assumption that meaningful moments must necessarily add up to any single soteriological outcome. For some metamodern SBNRs, the fact that "the search is off" for the immaculate moment in which one might hope to find an *answer* means that no idea, moment or point of view is thought of as necessarily salvific. I am not suggesting so much that specific social agendas would be deemphasized but that they would not be approached as grand fixes to all social ills. If one's felt experience is of fluidity, in terms of the sense that some multivalent identity narratives/storylines will be wrapping up, while other narratives take their place, the rewritten soteriology would surely reflect this sense of no single storyline, no grand salvific end.

From another perspective, the metamodern swapping out of soteriologies for storylines that emphasize personal, felt experience might indicate the potential for an *increased* emphasis on a social mission by SBNR millennials. Pundits who call out millennials' selfishness and their entitled behaviors or their lack of community-mindedness perhaps miss the way in which individuals of these newer generations are more likely to take the state of the world, and their roles in it, much more personally. Again, the personal is paramount for metamodern spiritualities. Furthermore, assuming the SBNR movement to be the spawn of unchurched seeker spiritualities that began appropriating tenets of influential Eastern philosophies over a century ago, affiliants would be influenced by appropriated versions of traditions (such as the Vedanta and Buddhism) that tend to present global issues as directly reflective of individual's inner, spiritual issues *and* vice versa. Perhaps we can therefore presume that metamodern millennial SBNRs have inherited a sense of their responsibility and place within a social schema. To put it plainly, the metamodern savior is not likely to be a removed, perfected, immaculate, unified, transcendent force.[44] It is not necessarily "someone else" at all. If there is to be world-saving, it will be ordinary, warts and all, human-led, and evaluated from here on the ground.

As for the future of being SBNR, whether their beliefs, philosophies, and practices (and, not irrelevantly, their consumer habits) will be sustainable or will be supplanted by the next spiritual fad will in my view be connected to the staying power of metamodernism. Just as postmodern sensibilities began to undo the attraction of the New Age as an identity and each began to give way as their operative narratives stopped fitting with the current-day constituents, there is every reason to expect the same of metamodernism and the SBNR. That said, the fact of metamodernism being by nature oscillative, absorptive, and pluralistic – allowing for contradictions of other epistemes to be creative fodder, rather than seeking to supplant them – may be expected to contribute to the SBNR movement's longevity.

Notes

1 Jeffrey J. Kripal's *The Serpent's Gift* (Chicago: University of Chicago Press, 2007) develops the both/and concept I refer to here. In his "Introduction," Kripal also proposes something that has similarities to metamodernism, which he refers to as "(post)modernity."

2 Here I should clarify that the epistemes I speak of are not meant to be regarded as wholly determined by a given generation, even if coeval. That is, in the same way that not all generation Xers, or the cultural artifacts generated by them, are postmodern, similarly, not everything millennials say and do is metamodern. Having come of age together, however, millennials have done the most to develop the metamodern sensibility.

3 Metamodernism's genealogy and its earliest ideological underpinnings are contested. It is located by some as stemming from Frederic Jameson and his criticism of postmodern fragmentation and late capitalism (1984) and by others with Mus'ad Zavarzadeh, who, as early as 1975, examined an emerging aesthetic in fiction in which there exists no sharp division between life and art. While I read Zavarzadeh's essay, "The Apocalyptic Fact and the Eclipse of Fiction in Recent American Prose Narratives," *Journal of American Studies*, April 1975, as outlining a postmodern literary move, I do feel that ground is nonetheless laid there for a later shift more closely resembling literary metamodernism. In 2001 Alexandra Dumitrescu began proposing an idea of metamodernism and began publishing on it starting in 2002. She theorized it both as a literary modality and a cultural "paradigm," with its ethical implications foregrounded. Also in 2002, Andre Furlani published an essay delineating metamodernism as a literary movement. These two early versions of metamodernism have resemblances as well as important differences from each other, as well as from the later work of Timotheus Vermeulen and Robin van den Akker, who brought their version of the term to the fore in 2010. The present author began theorizing metamodernism for the field of religious studies in conference papers and unpublished essays in 2012 and has maintained a popular-audience website and blog on metamodernism with co-creator Greg Dember since 2013. Our version also differs somewhat from each of the aforementioned theorists.

4 World Heritage Encyclopedia, "Post-Postmodern." Timotheus Vermeulen and Robin van den Akker are the founders of the webzine, *Notes on Metamodernism*, the first online presence dedicated to theoretical and general-culture exploration of metamodernism.

5 Boaz Huss, "Spirituality: The Emergence of a New Cultural Category and Its Challenge to the Religious and the Secular," *Journal of Contemporary Religion* (January 2014): 47.

6 Courtney Bender, *The New Metaphysicals: Spirituality and the American Religious Imagination* (Chicago: University of Chicago Press, 2010), 2.

7 Gershom Scholem qtd. in Wouter Hanegraaff, *New Age Religion and Western Culture* (Albany, NY: State University of New York Press, 1998), 524.

8 Hanegraaff, *New Age Religion*, 524.

9 Ibid., 17n49.

10 Robert Fuller, one of the first to offer a characterization of the SBNR, suggested in *Spiritual, But Not Religious: Understanding Unchurched America* (New York: Oxford University Press, 2001) that the SBNR shares much with the New Age. Fuller's intention in focusing on their common ancestry was to show that both have roots as part of an "unchurched movement," which he conceives of as a tradition in its own right. With respect to their shared roots in the early Western metaphysical traditions of the 19th century and forward, I find this reading quite on point. However, with the benefit of hindsight, I believe we can now see that the SBNR "culture" diverges from the New Age in significant ways that I deal with here.

11 *The Elephant Journal*, www.elephantjournal.com/.

12 David Starlyte, "Darkness Can't Exist in the Light," www.elephantjournal.com/2017/05/darkness-cant-exist-in-the-light.

13 Paul Heelas reviews the literature that addresses how what he calls "New Age spiritualities of life," which would include the SBNR, have become an integral tool of capitalism in *Spiritualities of Life: New Age Romanticism and Consumptive Capitalism* (Malden, MA: Blackwell, 2008). Boaz Huss also addresses this topic in "Spirituality: The Emergence," 58. Jeremy Carette and Richard King focus on this in their 2005 volume, *Selling Spirituality: The Silent Takeover of Religion* (London: Routledge, 2005).

14 Paul Heelas, *The New Age Movement: The Celebration of the Self and the Sacralization of Modernity* (Cambridge, MA: Blackwell, 1996), 169.

15 Raoul Eshelman, *Performatism, or the End of Postmodernism* (Aurora, CO: The Davies Group Publishers, 2008), xi.

16 It would be incorrect to paint irony as an always-negative cultural influence, even within metamodernism, my compacted portrayal notwithstanding. Metamodernism is necessarily replete with irony, having been born of postmodern irony culture, but utilizes it differently. For a fascinating tracking of the scope and history of the ironic as both a literary device and a social standard, see Lee Konstantinou's *Cool Characters: Irony and American Fiction* (Cambridge, MA: Harvard University Press, 2016).

17 David Foster Wallace, "E Unibus Plurum: Television and U.S. Fiction," *Review of Contemporary Fiction*, June 22, 1993, www.thefreelibrary.com/E+unibus+pluram%3A+television+and+U.S.+fiction.-a013952319.

18 Eshelman, *Performatism*, xi.

19 Paraphrased from Linda Ceriello and Greg Dember, "What Is 'What Is Metamodern?'" on website *What Is Metamodern?*, http://whatismetamodern.com/post/47887761163/hello-world-what-is-what-is-metamodern.

20 Lynne Hume and Kathleen McPhillips also mention new forms of spirituality that embrace the "dark aspects to enchantment." *Popular Spiritualities: The Politics of Contemporary Enchantment* (Burlington, VT: Ashgate, 2006), xvi.

21 Raoul Eshelman's "new monism" is relevant here. He describes a move beyond an "ironic regress" or beyond any one frame at all and wherein "metaphysical skepticism and irony aren't eliminated but are held in check by the frame (*Performatism*, 2–5).

22 The manifold historical outcomes of epistemic modernism and postmodernism are certainly more complicated than can be conveyed in brief here. For one thing,

the secularization argument generally locates the rise of disenchantment in the modern period. That said, Jason A. Josephson-Storm's recent *The Myth of Disenchantment: Magic, Modernity, and the Birth of the Human Sciences* (Chicago, University of Chicago Press, 2017) argues against that too-ready conclusion. His treatment of the shortcomings of unilinear portrayals of enchantment and disenchantment is an important contribution to the discussion with which I find sympathy, and one that I finally feel does not undercut my reading of the New Age as a bastion of modernist master-narrativizing.

23 David Starlyte, "Darkness Can't Exist in the Light," www.elephantjournal.com/2017/05/darkness-cant-exist-in-the-light.

24 Anonymous account# 200025, Archive of the Alister Hardy Religious Experience Research Centre, University of Wales Trinity Saint David, Lampeter, UK. This archive houses more than six thousand anonymously submitted accounts of ordinary individuals' self-described "religious experiences." The term "mystical" here is my own application.

25 The New Age trope of "old self" and "new self," Freeman writes in *Rewriting the Self: History, Memory, Narrative* (New York: Routledge, 1993), creates a kind of developmental narrative, made coherent when such identity conflicts are reconciled, one into the other. The new self gains ascendency after having articulated the falsity of the previous version (see especially chapter 2). This is suggestive of the kind of either/or narrativization that the metamodern SBNR troubles and rewrites with a both/and of secular and spiritual identity narratives.

26 This brief analysis admittedly bypasses important issues of gender and social location in examining personal experience and agency. Also, my synchronic approach does not address whether mystics writing their narratives in other periods might have also made similar discursive choices. Subsequent analyses of narratives of mystical experience from the millennial era will reveal whether there is a pattern of decreased emphasis on the spiritual goal of transcendence, with mystical realizations portrayed as ordinary, accessible, frameable in terms of everyday life, as this one seems to.

27 Hume and McPhillips, *Popular Spiritualities*, xix.

28 This is a qualified egalitarianism – Obviously, one must have a computing device and access to the internet. Beyond that, users anywhere, of any race and socio-economic background, are able to participate largely equally in a way incomparable to any other period.

29 Barna Group, "What Americans Are Watching," www.barna.org/barna-update/media-watch/670-what-americans-are-watching-in-2014. For another example of how pluralist, humanist and religious values are commuted in secular TV, see my article on AMC's *The Walking Dead*, "What Popular TV Shows Reveal About Contemporary Views of Religion in Society: Pt 1 – the Walking Dead," *Huffington Post*, June 7, 2016, www.huffingtonpost.com/linda-ceriello/what-popular-tv-shows-rev_b_10229348.html.

30 See, for example, fanfic stories in the genre "alternate universe" such as "Dino Undercover" by "anny385" published March 13, 2013 on NCIS FanFiction Archive https://www.ncisfiction.com/browse.php?type=class&type_id=3&classid=8.

31 Quora, n.d., accessed January 11, 2018, www.quora.com/Can-theists-enjoy-the-show-The-Big-Bang-Theory.

32 Barna Group, "What Americans Are Watching."

33 Borrowed from the title of Richard W. Santana and Timothy Erickson's *Religion and Popular Culture: Rescripting the Sacred* (Jefferson, NC: McFarland, 2008).

34 This idea also draws on the Kripalean thesis of how consciousness and culture "make each other up" – see Jeffrey J. Kripal, *Mutants and Mystics: Science Fiction, Superhero Comics, and the Paranormal* (Chicago: University of Chicago Press, 2011).

35 See Bendan Davis, *Mysticism and Space: Space and Spatiality in the Works of Richard Rolle, the Cloud of Unknowing Author* (Washington, DC: Catholic University of America Press, 2008), and Julian of Norwich. Davis credits the idea to Caroline Walker Bynum, who presented the notion of monks as vicarious worshippers for all of society. Lynn Hume employs liminality in a somewhat similar manner to mine in her essay "Liminal Beings and the Undead" in *Popular Spiritualities*, 3–16.
36 Davis, *Mysticism and Space*, 93.
37 Santana and Erickson, *Religion and Popular Culture*, 151.
38 Santana and Erickson, Religion and Popular Culture, 151 (emphasis mine).
39 Jeff Foster, www.lifewithoutacentre.com.
40 Jeff Foster, www.lifewithoutacentre.com.
41 Interview of Foster on Buddha at the Gas Pump, November 3, 2011, https://batgap.com/jeff-foster/.
42 Jeff Foster, "Useless Spiritual Teacher," www.lifewithoutacentre.com/watch-listen/video-clips/.
43 Foster, "The Advaita Trap."
44 For more on metamodern saviors and soteriologies, see my chapter, "The Big Bad and the Big 'Aha!': Metamodern Monsters as Transformational Figures of Instability," in *Holy Monsters, Sacred Grotesques: Monstrosity and Religion in Europe and the U.S.* (Lanham, MD: Lexington Books, forthcoming).

References

Anonymous, Account# 200025, Electronic Archive, Alister Hardy Religious Experience Research Centre, University of Wales Trinity Saint David, Lampeter, UK.
Barna Group. "What Americans Are Watching in 2014." www.barna.org/barna-update/media watch/670-what-americans-are-watching-in-2014.
Bender, Courtney. *The New Metaphysicals: Spirituality and the American Religious Imagination*. Chicago: University of Chicago Press, 2010.
Ceriello, Linda and Greg Dember. "What Is '*What Is Metamodern?*'" Accessed February 1, 2017. *What Is Metamodern?* (website). http://whatismetamodern.com/about.
Davis, Carmel Bendon. *Mysticism and Space: Space and Spatiality in the Works of Richard Rolle, the Cloud of Unknowing Author, and Julian of Norwich*. Washington, DC: Catholic University of America Press, 2008.
Eshelman, Raoul. *Performatism, or the End of Postmodernism*. Aurora, CO: Davies Group Publishers, 2009.
Foster, Jeff. *Life Without a Centre* (website). www.lifewithoutacentre.com.
———."The Advaita Trap." *Life Without a Centre* (website). www.lifewithouta centre.com/writings/the-advaita-trap-a-one-act-play/.
———. Interview of Foster on *Buddha at the Gas Pump*. November 3, 2011. https://batgap.com/jeff-foster.
Freeman, Mark. *Rewriting the Self: History, Memory, Narrative*. New York: Routledge, 1993.
Hanegraaff, Wouter. *New Age Religion and Western Culture: Esotericism in the Mirror of Secular Thought*. Albany, NY: State University of New York Press, 1998.
Heelas, Paul. *The New Age Movement: The Celebration of the Self and the Sacralization of Modernity*. Cambridge, MA: Blackwell, 1996.
———. *Spiritualities of Life: New Age Romanticism and Consumptive Capitalism*. Malden, MA: Blackwell, 2008.

Hume, Lynne and Kathleen McPhillips, eds. *Popular Spiritualities: The Politics of Contemporary Enchantment*. Burlington, VT: Ashgate, 2006.

Huss, Boaz. "Spirituality: The Emergence of a New Cultural Category and Its Challenge to the Religious and the Secular." *Journal of Contemporary Religion* 29, no. 1 (2014): 47–60.

Kripal, Jeffrey J. *The Serpent's Gift: Gnostic Reflections on the Study of Religion*. Chicago: University of Chicago Press, 2007.

Santana, Richard W. and Timothy Erickson. *Religion and Popular Culture: Rescripting the Sacred*. 2nd ed. Jefferson, NC: McFarland, 2016.

Starlyte, David Zenon. "Darkness Cannot Exist in the Light" (website). www.elephantjournal.com/2017/05/darkness-cant-exist-in-the-light/.

Wallace, David Foster. "E Unibus Plurum: Television and U.S. Fiction." *Review of Contemporary Fiction*, June 22, 1993. www.thefreelibrary.com/E+unibus+pluram%3A+television+and+U.S.+fiction.- a013952319

World Heritage Encyclopedia. "Post-Postmodern." Accessed April 11, 2017. http://self.gutenberg.org/articles/post-postmodern.

13 Transpersonal psychology and the Spiritual but Not Religious movement

Beyond spiritual narcissism in a postsecular age

Jorge N. Ferrer and William Z. Vickery

It was once believed that the rise of modernity would predictably lead to secularization and the decline of religion in North America.[1] However, although recent surveys show some signs of decline in organized religion, an increasing number of people consider themselves Spiritual but Not Religious.[2] The Spiritual but Not Religious (SBNR) movement is now a large and influential phenomenon that is altering the spiritual and religious landscape of not only North America but also many European countries.[3]

In a way, the SBNR movement is a predictable outcome of the confluence of two different sociocultural processes in the (post)modern West: the *secularization* of traditional religious authority, on one hand, and the *resacralization* of self, nature, and the cosmos, on the other.[4] In this postsecular context, an SBNR "affiliation" becomes an essential – conscious, semiconscious, or unconscious – self-identification strategy to minimize the cognitive dissonance stemming from reenchanting subjective life and world while simultaneously feeling that one may be regressing to problematically perceived, past religious attitudes (e.g., dogmatism, exclusivism, authoritarianism). Thus, SBNR might well become – or be seen as – the postsecular spiritual identity *par excellence*.

The SBNR movement has many arguably positive attributes (e.g., holism, openness to hybridity, anti-authoritarianism), but also some problematic features; in this chapter, we explore one major problem. What we call *spiritual narcissism* can be understood in two different but often interrelated ways: (a) the appropriation of spirituality to bolster egoic ways of life (i.e., spiritual materialism) and (b) the belief in the universal superiority of one's favored spiritual choice, path, or account of ultimate reality (i.e., sectarianism).

Two major conceptual frameworks fueling spiritual narcissism in the SBNR movement are *experientialism* and *perennialism*. Experientialism refers to the assumption that spiritual phenomena are fundamentally individual inner experiences, as seen in the SBNR movement's prioritizing of individualism and personal experience.[5] Perennialism refers to the assumption that there is one single spiritual ultimate (and associated liberated state) underlying all religions, as suggested in the SBNR movement's anti-exclusivism and belief that all religions teach the same thing.[6] As Schneider points out, both orientations tend to come together in the SBNR movement: "The repudiation of institutional religion in favor of personal spirituality is . . . actually the repudiation of denominational belonging rather than of religion as such."[7] Whereas experientialism tends to foster spiritual narcissism of the egoic appropriation type (i.e., by framing spirituality as inner experiences the ego can possess) and perennialism usually results in spiritual narcissism of the universalist type (discussed in the following), in this chapter we argue that both assumptions reinforce sectarianism.

Since the egoic type has been already discussed in detail elsewhere,[8] this chapter focuses on the universalist version of spiritual narcissism. Spiritual narcissism can be found throughout the world's religious literature, as well as in the field of transpersonal psychology and transpersonal theory more generally. To address spiritual narcissism in transpersonal studies there is a contemporary movement, often framed under the banner of *participatory*, concerned with reformulating underlying philosophical assumptions of classical transpersonal psychology (e.g., experientialism and perennialism) in order to minimize or eradicate its limitations and inadequacies. Realigning the SBNR movement with the participatory approach in transpersonal psychology may thus help to undermine the SBNR movement's spiritual narcissism. After a brief review of experientialism and perennialism in the SBNR movement, in this chapter we discuss two waves of transpersonalism (perennialist and participatory), suggesting that the SBNR movement can learn important lessons from the evolution of the transpersonal field to minimize sectarianism and better embody its anti-exclusivist ethos. The chapter concludes with some general reflections on the (im)possibility of fully avoiding sectarian spiritual narcissism in intellectual discourse.

The SBNR movement's experientialism and perennialism

This section documents the SBNR movement's allegiance to experientialism and perennialism. *Experientialism* arises in the SBNR movement when discussing the differences between spirituality and religion, as much of the literature emphasizes the movement's centrality of the personal interior life over external religious institutions. For example, in his study of the ongoing shift from religion to spirituality, Heelas states that while religion is concerned with a god and external structures, spirituality has to do with the personal, interior, and immanent.[9] Dogma and traditional religion are rejected for a customized spiritual path that specifically works for the particular individual. Mercadante makes the same distinction between spirituality and religion by stating that the former refers to the inner life of faith while the latter refers to organizational communal components.[10] For Schneiders, whereas spirituality is "the experience of conscious involvement in the project of life-integration through self-transcendence toward the ultimate value one perceives,"[11] religion entails belief in a transcendent reality in the context of a cultural system or institution external to the individual. However, all the preceding thinkers acknowledge a significant overlap between spirituality and religion.[12]

Empirical research corroborates the prevalence of experientialism in the SBNR movement. For example, Roof interviewed about 1,599 members of the baby-boomer generation over eight to nine years and identified a great number of what he calls "seekers"[13] – those who have generally rejected organized religion to adopt a highly individualized spirituality that emphasizes direct spiritual experience. Zinnbauer et al. found similar results for the SBNR group in their survey of 346 individuals.[14] In Mercadante's study of the SBNR movement, one of the defining characteristics of the "nones" (i.e., the religiously unaffiliated) is the affirmation of individual rights, self-determination, and personal responsibility. Nones value individual choice and personal preference in matters of spirituality. They are moral individualists who make decisions on ethical matters based on individual perceptions rather than religious dogma.[15]

In this context, *perennialism* enters SBNR discourse through the often-made distinction between *exclusive* religions (to be rejected) and an *inclusive* spirituality (to be embraced).[16] On one hand, institutional forms of religion are rejected for claiming to have the correct answers concerning spiritual matters – a claim that renders alternate religious systems incorrect or partial. As Mercadante discovered, one main position rejected by SBNRs (i.e., those who consider themselves SBNR) is "an exclusivism that rejects all religions but one's own."[17] On the other hand, SBNRs generally believe that all traditions have something valuable to offer and can be taken on more or less equal footing. A common belief in the SBNR movement, Mercadante writes, is that "[a]ll religions, at base, are seeking the same thing or teach the same basic principles."[18]

But, what is the essential spiritual belief of the SBNR movement? As Houtman and Aupers conclude in their multicountry study of post-Christian spirituality, the contemporary "spiritual turn" is characterized by "the idea that the self is divine and by the immanent conception of the sacred."[19] This immanent monism, they add, not only is the often-neglected "main tenet of post-Christian spirituality" but also "contradicts SBNRs' alleged individualism."[20]

Despite the asserted emancipatory and reconciliatory nature of SBNR experientialism and perennialism, a pernicious individualistic relativism and hidden exclusivism lurk behind them. Since the spiritual path is taken to be highly unique to each individual, SBNRs often believe that the various spiritual paths are all equally good but for different people – that is, no path can be said to be superior or inferior. This account can easily lead to a banalization of differences, lack of critical discernment, and even moral perniciousness. On what grounds can one then denounce patriarchal, oppressive, repressive, or eco-destructive spiritualities? Furthermore, the SBNR movement's emphasis on inner experience as the privileged location for the sacred inadvertently fuels sectarian tendencies. As we have seen, the divine is understood as an all-pervasive force residing in the world and within people's deepest selves.[21] This immanent-monistic sectarianism is further cemented by the SBNR movement's commitment to perennialism. Like the perennial philosophy (discussed in the following), SBNRs believe that a nondual, monistic account of spirituality accurately reflects the mystical or esoteric core of all traditions. Privileging such a particular version of the sacred, however, ends up devaluing other views of what the ultimate spiritual goal entails (e.g., transcendentalist, personal, and dual accounts of the divine are demoted). Thus, when considering the primary aim of the spiritual path, SBNR experientialist perennialism is actually exclusive of many alternate spiritual perspectives.

As a way to assist with these issues in the SBNR movement, we find it helpful to examine the field of transpersonal psychology. Classical transpersonal psychology prefigured many of the themes found in the SBNR movement, and they have much in common with each other. For example, both are heavily influenced by Eastern traditions, tend to psychologize spirituality, seek to integrate science and spirituality, emphasize self-growth and spiritual transformation, hold an anti-exclusivist stance that is open to all spiritual traditions, and generally assume a perennialist outlook of spirituality. In addition, both transpersonal psychology and the SBNR movement were, in part, born out of reactionary movements against social and religious conventions that were seen as downplaying or suppressing authentic spirituality. The next section introduces transpersonal psychology and maps the evolution of the field from a perennialist to a participatory orientation.

Transpersonal psychology: from perennialism to participation

Transpersonal psychology originated in the mid-1960s out of the interest of a group of psychologists and psychiatrists (Anthony Sutich, Abraham Maslow, Stanislav Grof, Miles Vich) in expanding the field of humanistic psychology beyond its focus on the individual self. Etymologically, the prefix *trans* – means "beyond" or "through." *Transpersonal* was originally coined in the field of transpersonal psychology to refer to experiences, motivations, developmental stages (e.g., cognitive, moral, emotional, interpersonal), modes of being and other phenomena that include but transcend the sphere of the individual personality, self, or ego.[22] Historically, the transpersonal orientation emerged out of the encounter among Western psychology (psychoanalytic, Jungian, humanistic, and Existentialist schools in particular), Eastern contemplative traditions (especially Zen, Advaita Vedanta, and Taoism), and the psychedelic counterculture of 1960s' California. The transpersonal perspective also finds precedents in a plethora of spiritual traditions that are of great interest to many in the SBNR movement, such as Neoplatonism, Gnosticism, Hermeticism, Christian mysticism, Kabbalah, and the various schools usually amalgamated under the name of Western esotericism.[23]

The transpersonal anthropologist Lahood describes two turns or waves in transpersonal scholarship. The first began with the birth of transpersonal psychology in the late 1960s and can be defined as "an attempt to integrate psychologies East and West; an attempt to map the farthest shores of consciousness; and the merging of pragmatic science and spiritual concerns."[24] Lahood characterizes this turn with a commitment to religious universalism (or perennialism) and included the work of Maslow, Grof, and Wilber as representative. The perennialist era in transpersonal scholarship prevailed from 1977 to the mid-1990s and was dominated by the work of Ken Wilber, who sought to integrate Western and Eastern philosophy, psychology, and religion into an evolutionary framework structured according to a supposedly universal teleological process whose ultimate aim is a Zen-like nondual realization. The second turn is the participatory one (as exemplified by Lahood in the works of Tarnas, Heron, and Ferrer), which represents a departure from transpersonal psychology's allegiance to perennialism and emphasizes the embodied, relational, creative, and pluralistic dimensions of transpersonal events.[25] According to Dale, the participatory paradigm correlates with the nonlinear paradigm in contemporary science (i.e., moving beyond mainstream psychology's linear statistical averaging) and provides the best explanation of transpersonal inquiry and development.[26]

The second wave of transpersonal psychology emerged, in part, as a response to problems and shortcomings increasingly perceived in the first wave. In particular, as discussed in the following, the first wave operated under particular philosophical assumptions that were fueling spiritual narcissism in various ways. Two of these premises are experientialism and perennialism, which also heavily influence the SBNR movement. The next two sections offer a closer examination of the problems of perennialism and our suggested participatory solution.

The fundamental problems of perennialism

Both first-wave transpersonalism and the SBNR movement generally adopt a perennialist outlook of spirituality. Before examining the problems of perennialism, it is useful to review the origins of its popular understanding.

Although perennialist ideas had already been reintroduced in the West, it was not until the publication of Aldous Huxley that they reached the masses and became popular beyond esoteric and academic elites.[27] Huxley famously described the perennial philosophy as

> the metaphysics that recognizes a divine Reality substantial to the world of things and lives and minds; the psychology that finds in the soul something similar to, or even identical with, divine Reality; the ethic

that places man's final end in the knowledge of the immanent and transcendent Ground of all being.[28]

What characterizes Huxley's perennialism, as well as the one of the so-called traditionalists such as René Guénon, Ananda K. Coomaraswamy, or Frithjof Schuon, is the conviction that this single perennial truth can be found at the heart of the mystical teachings of all the world religious traditions.[29]

Although with different emphases, these authors claim that whereas the exoteric beliefs of religious traditions are assorted and at times even incompatible, their esoteric or mystical dimension reveals an essential unity that transcends this doctrinal pluralism. According to this view, for example, the same mystical experience of the nondual Ground of Being would be interpreted as emptiness (*sunyata*) by a Mahayana Buddhist, as Brahman by an Advaita Vedantin, as the union with God by a Christian, or as an objectless absorption (*asamprajñata samadhi*) by a practitioner of Patañjali's yoga. In all cases, the experience is the same, the interpretation different. In sum, perennialists maintain not only the existence of an experiential contemplative consensus about the ultimate nature of reality but also the objective truth of such a vision (i.e., it depicts "things as they really are").

Perennialism is burdened with three fundamental difficulties. The first is that it privileges a nondual monistic metaphysics. Perennialist models typically assume the existence of a universal spiritual reality that is the Ground of all that is, and of which the contemplative insights are an expression. Despite their insistence on the ineffable and unqualifiable nature of this Ground, perennialists consistently characterize it as nondual, the One, or the Absolute. The perennialist Ground of Being, that is, strikingly resembles the Neoplatonic Godhead or the Advaitin Brahman. As Schuon states, "the perspective of Sankara is one of the most adequate expressions possible of the philosophia perennis or sapiential esoterism."[30] The Absolute of the perennial philosophy, far from being a neutral and truly unqualifiable ground, is represented as supporting a nondual or monistic metaphysics. Both first-wave transpersonal psychology and the SBNR movement elevate monistic and nondual states to the zenith of spiritual development.[31]

A second problematic issue is that perennialism is geared toward an objectivist epistemology. The perennialist vision falls back into objectivism with its insistence on a pregiven ultimate reality that can be objectively known by the human Intellect (intuitive knowing). As Schuon states, "[t]he prerogative of the human state is objectivity, the essential content of which is the Absolute."[32] Although objectivity should not be understood as limited to the empirical and external, Schuon writes that "knowledge is 'objective' when it is capable of grasping the object as it is and not as it may be deformed by the subject."[33] These assumptions make the perennial philosophy subject to all the anxieties of Cartesian consciousness, such as the false dichotomy between objectivism and relativism.[34]

Third, these universalist and objectivist assumptions generally lead perennial philosophers to recede into dogmatism and intolerance toward different spiritual worldviews. In spite of the different metaphysical universes espoused by the contemplative traditions, perennialists insist "there is only one metaphysic but many traditional languages through which it is expressed."[35] But what about spiritual traditions that do not posit a metaphysical Absolute or transcendent ultimate reality? What about spiritual traditions that refuse to fit into the perennialist scheme? The perennialist solution to conflicting spiritual traditions is to regard religious traditions and doctrines that do not accept the perennial vision as inauthentic, merely exoteric, or representing lower levels of insight in a hierarchy of revelations whose culmination is the perennial truth.[36] In this scheme, the different spiritual Ultimates, although absolute within their own specific religious universe, are merely relative in relation to the single Absolute that perennialism champions. With this move, perennialism relativizes the goals of the various traditions by positing a pregiven supra-ultimate referent beyond them, out of which all spiritual ultimates are merely partial aspects, dimensions, or perspectives. Furthermore, while ecumenically claiming to honor all spiritual truths, perennialists consistently grades spiritual insights and traditions according to how closely they approach or represent the supposed attributes of this pregiven Absolute reality (e.g., nondual traditions over dual ones, monistic over theistic, impersonal over personal).[37]

Perennialists justify these rankings on the basis of metaphysical intuitions about the ultimate nature of the Absolute. The problem with this claim is that mystics from the most diverse times and places have reported metaphysical intuitions that not only did not conform to the perennialist cosmology but also were fundamentally at odds with each other. Generations of mystics from different traditions, and often from a single tradition, have debated metaphysical issues for centuries without substantial signs of agreement – the everlasting quarrels between Buddhist and Hindu contemplatives about the ultimate nature of the self and reality come quickly to mind in this regard.[38] These differences did not arise only among the exoteric representatives of the traditions (as perennialists accept) but also among the mystical or esoteric contemplatives themselves.

The perennialist certainty about the nondual or monistic nature of ultimate reality too easily results in spiritual narcissism. By adopting a perennialist framework, one might view oneself as having the higher-ranking perspective that subsumes all other spiritual perspectives. Believing each tradition is essentially talking about the same goal devalues their differences and promotes the egocentric belief that oneself truly knows what every spiritual seeker's ultimate goal is – or should be. Despite their strong anti-exclusivist character, transpersonal psychology's and the SBNR movement's allegiance to perennialism catapults them back to a sectarianism that privileges particular spiritual traditions over all others.

The participatory turn as a solution to perennialist sectarianism

Can sectarianism be avoided without resorting to either (a) an ideological perennialism that hides exclusivist claims or (b) an individualistic or cultural relativism that banalizes differences and offers no grounds for critical discernment? We believe that this aspiration is (largely) achievable, and together with a number of scholars in the field of religious studies, we have called this third possible way the "participatory turn" in the study of religion and spirituality.[39] Originally articulated in the field of transpersonal psychology, the participatory turn proposed a shift from perennialism to participatory pluralism in the understanding of religious diversity. Since the participatory approach in transpersonal psychology was partly aimed at undercutting the spiritual narcissism rampant in perennialist transpersonalism, it may also provide assistance in deflating spiritual narcissism in the SBNR movement.

The *participatory approach* holds that human spirituality essentially emerges from human co-creative participation in an undetermined mystery or generative power of life, the cosmos, or reality.[40] It also reframes spiritual experiences as multilocal participatory *events* that can occur not only in the locus of an individual but also in a relationship, a community, or a place (countering thereby experientialism and egoic appropriation). Spiritual participatory events can engage the entire range of human epistemic faculties (e.g., rational, imaginal, somatic, vital, aesthetic) with both the creative unfolding of the mystery in the enactment – or "bringing forth" – of ontologically rich religious worlds. Extending Varela, Rosch, and Thompson's enactive paradigm to spiritual cognition,[41] the participatory approach presents an understanding of the sacred that conceives spiritual phenomena, experiences, and insights as *co-created events*. Spiritual knowing, thus, is not a representation of pregiven, independent spiritual objects, but an enaction of a world or domain of distinctions co-created by the different elements involved in the participatory event. In the same way that Rorty debunked the myth of the human "mind as mirror of nature,"[42] we suggest it is important to put to rest the equally problematic image of contemplative or visionary "consciousness as mirror of spirit" implicit in much classical and contemporary spiritual discourse. By locating the emergence of spiritual knowing at the interface of human multidimensional cognition, cultural context, subtle worlds, and the deep generativity of life or the cosmos, this account avoids both the secular post/modernist reduction of religion to cultural-linguistic artifact and the religionist and perennialist privileging of a single tradition as superior or paradigmatic.

Participatory pluralism conceives a multiplicity of not only spiritual paths but also spiritual liberations and spiritual ultimates. On one hand, besides affirming the historical existence of multiple spiritual goals or "salvations," the increased embodied openness to the generative power of the mystery fostered by the participatory approach can naturally engender a number of novel holistic spiritual realizations that cannot be reduced to traditional states of enlightenment or liberation. On the other hand, participatory pluralism proposes that different spiritual ultimates can be enacted through participation in an undetermined mystery or generative force of life or reality. The participatory perspective does not contend that there are two, three, or any limited quantity of pregiven spiritual ultimates but, rather, that the radical openness, interrelatedness, and creativity of the mystery or the cosmos allows for the participatory cocreation of an indefinite number of ultimate self-disclosures of reality and corresponding religious worlds. Whether there is an ultimate end point to overall spiritual evolution is an open question, but given the rich variety of spiritual cosmologies it can be reasonably conjectured that the mystery co-creatively unfolds in multiple ontological directions.

A participatory understanding of spiritual knowing should not then be confused with the view that mystics of the various kinds and traditions simply access different dimensions or perspectives of a readymade single ultimate reality – a view which merely admits that this pregiven spiritual referent can be approached from different vantage points. In contrast, the view advanced here is that no pregiven ultimate reality exists and that different spiritual worlds and ultimates can be enacted through human co-creative participation.

Participatory approaches seek to enact with body, mind, heart, and consciousness a creative spirituality that lets a thousand spiritual flowers bloom. To be sure, once enacted, spiritual phenomena become more easily accessible and, in a way, "given" to some extent for individual consciousness to participate in. In other words, spiritual forms that have been enacted so far are more readily available and tend more naturally to emerge (from mudras to visionary landscapes, from liberating insights to ecstatic types of consciousness, and so on). But the fact that enacted phenomena become more available does not mean that they are predetermined, limited in number, organized in a transcultural hierarchical fashion, or universally sequential in their unfolding, or that no new spiritual manifestations can be enacted through co-creative participation.

Although this may at first sound like a rather "anything goes" approach to religious claims, we hold to the contrary that recognizing a diversity of co-created religious worlds, in fact, asks both scholars and practitioners to be more perspicuous in discerning the differences and merits of those worlds. Specifically, we suggest three basic guidelines: the *egocentrism test*, which assesses the extent to which spiritual traditions, teachings, and practices free practitioners from gross and subtle forms of narcissism and self-centeredness; the *dissociation test*, which evaluates the extent to which spiritual traditions foster the integrated blossoming of all dimensions of the person; and the *eco-socio-political test*, which assesses the extent to which spiritual systems foster ecological balance, social and economic justice, religious and political freedom, class and gender equality, and other funda-mental human rights.

Since it is likely that most religious traditions would not rank too highly in these tests, it should be obvious that the participatory approach leads to a strong ranking of spiritual orientations. Thus, although this approach does not privilege any tradition or type of spirituality over others on *doctrinal, objectivist*, or *ontological grounds* (i.e., saying that theism, monism, or non-dualism corresponds to the nature of ultimate reality or is soteriologically superior), it does offer criteria for making qualitative distinctions among spiritual systems on *pragmatic* and *transformational grounds*. The crucial difference in relation to perennialist gradations, thus, is that participatory rankings are not ideologically based on a priori ontological doctrines or putative correspondence to a single pregiven ultimate reality, but instead ground critical discernment in the practical values of integrated selflessness and eco-socio-political justice. We stand by these values – not because we think they are universal, objective, or ahistorical (they are not), but because we firmly believe that their cultivation can effectively reduce today's per-sonal, relational, social, and planetary suffering.

To further minimize the problem of sectarianism, participatory pluralism rejects the *dualism of mystery and enactions*, thus considering these enac-tions to be ultimate in their respective spiritual universes.[43] In other words, a participatory enactive epistemology affirms the radical identity of the mani-fold spiritual ultimates and the mystery, even if the former does not exhaust the ontological possibilities of the latter. The mystery–enactions dualism is pernicious: it not only binds scholars and practitioners alike to objectiv-ist and hierarchical frameworks but also paves the way for interreligious exclusivism and spiritual narcissism (i.e., once a supra-ultimate Absolute is posited, practitioners can – and often do – claim their own religion's Abso-lute to be the closer, better, or more accurate account of the supra-ultimate Absolute). Building on the enactive paradigm's rejection of representational theories of knowledge,[44] we maintain that in the same way an individual is her actions (whether perceptual, cognitive, emotional, or subtle), the mys-tery is its enactions. In this understanding, emptiness (*sunyata*), the Tao, and the Christian God (in their many inflections) can be seen as creative gestures of the mystery enacted through participating human (and perhaps nonhu-man) individuals and collectives.

Not positing a supra-ultimate spiritual referent beyond its specific enac-tions has two very important consequences. First, it preserves the ontologi-cal ultimacy of those enactions (e.g., God, emptiness, Tao, Brahman) in their respective spiritual universes, avoiding the traditionalist and neo-Kantian demotion of those ultimates to penultimate stations.[45] Second, it short-cir-cuits the feasibility of promoting one tradition as objectively superior (i.e., holding the most accurate picture of the mystery), excising ontological com-petitiveness at its root and arguably settling one of the main challenges of religious pluralism.

To return to the SBNR movement, we argue that this participatory plural- ist perspective can effectively erode the hidden exclusivism and sectarianism of the SBNR movement while avoiding cultural and individualist relativ- isms. Once the very idea of a pregiven ultimate is rejected, ranking particular spiritual states and associated traditions according to how they accurately represent or mirror such an ultimate becomes meaningless. Furthermore, the radical undeterminacy of the mystery undermines the objectivism of the perennial philosophy, preventing the mystery from being reified. Whether these moves are enough to entirely eradicate spiritual narcissism is a ques- tion for this chapter's conclusion.

Conclusion: beyond spiritual narcissism?

Legions of spiritual practitioners are rummaging through the spiritual marketplace in an attempt to optimize their well-being and attain one or another particular spiritual state they have come to believe is universal or most liberating. According to the participatory approach, however, a spir- itual practitioner is expanding consciousness not just to access pregiven spiritual contents but also to enact or bring forth a rich variety of spiritual phenomena. In this light, spiritual identity becomes an ongoing participa- tory process arising from the confluence of human knowing, cultural con- text, spiritual aims and expectations, and the creative power of the mystery. Hyphenated spiritual identities, common in the SBNR movement, can then be seen as the fruit of participatory events enacted in interaction with such factors, including possible interactions with a diversity of subtle worlds.[46] The highly syncretic nature of the SBNR movement typically entails both a firm rejection of any kind of religious exclusivism and an openness to the wisdom of all spiritual traditions. Nevertheless, by adhering to the per- ennialist belief that all traditions ultimately deliver the same message or lead to the same place, SBNRs unknowingly fall back to sectarianism. Such a sectarianism becomes evident both whenever such a perennial truth is described (e.g., as nondual, monistic, immanent), and in the inclusivist claim that the perennial truth (with its favored spiritual ultimate) encompasses all other spiritual truths but not vice versa.[47]

A chief way in which the participatory approach minimizes sectarianism is by holding the undetermined nature of the mystery, leaving open the pos- sibility of both determinacy and indeterminacy within – as well as the para- doxical confluence or even identity of – these two apparently polar accounts. As Duckworth observes regarding this proposal, metaphysical biases are thus neutralized for the most part: such an "undetermined ultimate pre- cludes emptiness from being the final word on reality because, being unde- termined, ultimate reality can also be disclosed as theistic in a personal God. And importantly, this 'God' is not a lower reality than emptiness."[48]

That said, it is important to note that participatory approaches do not completely eradicate sectarianism. No conceptual framework can successfully avoid privileging one or another perspective. As Derrida underlines, hierarchy is intrinsic to Western thinking and language.[49] To affirm or deny one thing implicitly denies or affirms, respectively, its opposite, polar, or alternate reality. In the present case, the idea of an undetermined mystery does not entirely settle the issue because it questions the legitimacy of exclusively positive or negative metaphysical accounts of the mystery.

Mindful of this predicament, we stress that the use of the term *undetermined mystery* should be understood to be mostly *performative* – that is, seeking to evoke the sense of not knowing and intellectual humility that might be most fruitful in approaching that creative power of life and reality that is the source of our being. In this regard, Duckworth argues that whereas to claim the determinacy–indeterminacy of the mystery bounds one to a closed model of truth, the undetermined fosters a humble and open-ended approach to such a mystery.[50] Doctrinal rankings are further minimized by the participatory grounding of qualitative distinctions on pragmatic values (e.g., integrated selflessness, embodiment, eco-socio-political justice). In addition, the participatory turn holds that there can potentially be different spiritual enactions that are nonetheless equally holistic, emancipatory, and ethically just, which further minimizes rankings; for example, fully embodied liberated states could be arguably achieved through Christian incarnation or Yogic integration of *purusa* (consciousness) and *prakriti* (nature) in the context of radically different ontologies.

Summing up, the participatory approach provides a framework that minimizes problematic hierarchies based on doctrinal ontological beliefs about the mystery, while conserving grounds for the criticism of dissociated, narcissistic, and oppressive visions and practices. While the participatory proposal might not entirely resolve the question of ontological ranking, we maintain that the question is significantly relaxed through the qualification of the mystery as undetermined, the overcoming of the dualism of mystery and enactions, the affirmation of a potential plurality of equally holistic visions, and the focus on transformational outcomes to make spiritual qualitative distinctions. Sectarianism and spiritual narcissism cannot be fully overcome conceptually (i.e., through any theoretical framework, whether participatory or not), but we propose that it can be transcended in the realm of human experience. This transcendence comes through an attitude of intellectual humility and genuine openness to the other, as well as to the world's mysteries – particularly those mysteries that surpass the conceptual mind and can paradoxically (for the human mind) house incompatible spiritual enactions, orientations, and values.

In closing, we propose that the understanding of SBNR as a plural, hybrid, and participatory spiritual identity holds the promise to overcome its hidden sectarianism and achieve greater fidelity to the SBNR movement's anti-exclusivist ideals. Will postsecular spiritualities eventually free themselves from the spiritual narcissism that has plagued most of the world's religious history? Only time will tell.

Notes

1 José Casanova, *Public Religions in the Modern World* (Chicago, IL: University of Chicago Press, 1994); Steve Bruce, *God Is Dead: Secularization in the West* (Malden, MA: Blackwell, 2002).

2 Robert C. Fuller, *Spiritual, But Not Religious: Understanding Unchurched America* (New York: Oxford University Press, 2001); Paul Heelas and Linda Woodhead, *The Spiritual Revolution: Why Religion Is Giving Way to Spirituality* (Maiden, MA: Blackwell, 2005); Linda Mercadante, *Belief Without Borders: Inside the Minds of the Spiritual But Not Religious* (Oxford, UK: Oxford University Press, 2014).

3 Joantine Berghuijs et al., "Being 'Spiritual' and Being 'Religious' in Europe: Diverging Life Orientations," *Journal of Contemporary Religion* 28, no. 1 (2013): 15–32.

4 Charles Taylor, *A Secular Age* (Cambridge, MA: Harvard University Press, 2007); Jürgen Habermas, "Secularism's Crisis of Faith: Notes on Post-Secular Society," *New Perspectives Quarterly* 25 (2008): 17–29.

5 Mercadante, *Belief Without Borders*.

6 Ibid.

7 Sandra M. Schneiders, "Religion vs. Spirituality: A Contemporary Conundrum," *Spiritus: A Journal of Christian Spirituality* 3, no. 2 (2003): 175.

8 Jorge N. Ferrer, *Revisioning Transpersonal Theory: A Participatory Vision of Human Spirituality* (Albany: State University of New York Press, 2002)

9 Paul Heelas, "The Spiritual Revolution: From 'Religion' to 'Spirituality,'" in *Religions in the Modern World: Traditions and Transformations*, ed. Paul Fletcher, Hiroko Kawanami, and David Smith (London, UK: Routledge, 2002), 358–9.

10 Mercadante, *Belief Without Borders*.

11 Schneiders, "Religion vs. Spirituality: A Contemporary Conundrum," 166.

12 See Tom Boyd, "Is Spirituality Possible Without Religion? A Query for the Postmodern Era," in *Divine Representations: Postmodernism and Spirituality*, ed. Ann W. Astell (New York: Paulist Press, 1994), 83–101; Nancy T. Ammerman, "Spiritual But Not Religious: Beyond Binary Choices in the Study of Religion," *Journal for the Scientific Study of Religion* 52, no. 2 (2013): 258–78.

13 Wade C. Roof, *A Generation of Seekers: The Spiritual Journeys of the Baby Boom Generation* (San Francisco, CA: Harper, 1993); Wade C. Roof, *Spiritual Marketplace: Baby Boomers and the Remaking of American Religion* (Princeton, NJ: Princeton University Press, 1999).

14 Brian J. Zinnbauer et al., "Religion and Spirituality: Unfuzzing the Fuzzy," *Journal for the Scientific Study of Religion* 36, no. 4 (1997): 549–64.

15 Mercadante, *Belief Without Borders*.

16 Roof, *Spiritual Marketplace*; Mercadante, *Belief Without Borders*.

17 Ibid., 230.

18 Ibid., 8.

19 Dick Houtman and Stef Aupers, "The Spiritual Turn and the Decline of Tradition: The Spread of Post-Christian Spirituality in 14 Western Countries, 1981–2000," *Journal for the Scientific Study of Religion* 46, no. 3(2007): 305–20.

20 Ibid., 306, 307.

21 Ibid.

22 Miles A. Vich, "The Origins and Growth of Transpersonal Psychology," *Journal of Humanistic Psychology* 30, no. 2 (1990): 47–50; Roger N. Walsh, "The Transpersonal Movement: A History and State of the Art," *The Journal of Transpersonal Psychology* 25, no. 3 (1993): 123–39.

23 Harris L. Friedman and Glenn Hartelius, eds., *The Wiley-Blackwell Handbook of Transpersonal Psychology* (Malden, MA: John Wiley & Sons, 2013). Ferrer, *Revisioning Transpersonal Theory*.

24 Gregg Lahood, "The Participatory Turn and the Transpersonal Movement: A Brief Introduction," *ReVision: A Journal of Consciousness and Transformation* 29 (2007): 2.

25 Ibid., 2–6. See also Richard Tarnas, "A New Birth in Freedom: A (P)review of Jorge Ferrer's Revisioning Transpersonal Theory: A Participatory Vision of Human Spirituality," *The Journal of Transpersonal Psychology* 33, no. 1 (2001): 64–71; Glenn Hartelius and Jorge N. Ferrer, "Transpersonal Philosophy: The Participatory Turn," in *The Wiley-Blackwell Handbook of Transpersonal Psychology*, ed. Friedman and Hartelius (Malden, MA: John Wiley & Sons, 2013), 187–202.

26 Edward J. Dale, *Completing Piaget's Project: Transpersonal Philosophy and the Future of Psychology* (St. Paul, MN: Paragon House, 2014).

27 J. J. Clarke, *Oriental Enlightenment: The Encounter Between Asian and Western Thought* (New York: Routledge, 1997); Antoine Faivre, *Access to Western Esoterism* (Albany, NY: State University of New York Press, 1994).

28 Aldous Huxley, *The Perennial Philosophy* (New York: Harper & Row, 1945), vii.

29 William W. Quinn, *The Only Tradition* (Albany, NY: State University of New York Press, 1997).

30 Frithjof Schuon, *Esoterism as Principle and as Way* (Bedfont, Middlesex, UK: Perennial Books, 1981), 21.

31 Stanislav Grof, *The Cosmic Game: Explorations of the Frontiers of Human Consciousness* (Albany, NY: State University of New York Press, 1998); Ken Wilber, *One Taste: Daily Reflections on Integral Spirituality* (Boston, MA: Shambhala, 1999); Mercadante, *Belief Without Borders*; Houtman and Aupers, "The Spiritual Turn and the Decline of Tradition."

32 Schuon, *Esoterism as Principle and as Way*, 15.

33 Ibid.

34 Richard J. Bernstein, *Beyond Objectivism and Relativism: Science, Hermeneutics, and Praxis* (Philadelphia: University of Pennsylvania Press, 1985)

35 Seyyed H. Nasr, "Response to Thomas Dean's Review of Knowledge and the Sacred," *Philosophy East and West* 35, no. 1 (1985): 89.

36 cf. Wouter J. Hanegraaff, *New Age Religion and Western Culture: Esotericism in the Mirror of Secular Thought* (Albany: State University of New York Press, 1998).

37 Schuon, *Esoterism as Principle and as Way*; Ken Wilber, *Sex, Ecology, and Spirituality: The Spirit of Evolution* (Boston, MA: Shambhala, 1995).

38 Mangala R. Chinchore, *Anatta/Anatmata: An Analysis of the Buddhist Anti-Substantialist Crusade* (New Delhi, India: Sri Satguru Publications, 1995).

39 Jorge N. Ferrer and Jacob H. Sherman, eds., *The Participatory Turn: Spirituality, Mysticism, Religious Studies* (Albany: State University of New York Press, 2008).

40 Ferrer, *Revisioning Transpersonal Theory*; Jorge N. Ferrer, *Participation and the Mystery: Transpersonal Essays in Psychology, Education, and Religion* (Albany: State University of New York Press, 2017).

41 Francisco J. Varela, Evan Thompson, and Eleanor Rosch, *The Embodied Mind: Cognitive Science and Human Experience* (Cambridge, MA: The MIT Press, 1991).

42 Richard Rorty, *Philosophy and the Mirror of Nature* (Princeton, NJ: Princeton University Press, 1979).

43 Ferrer, *Participation and the Mystery*.

44 Anthony Chemero, *Radical Embodied Cognitive Science* (Cambridge, MA: The MIT Press, 2009); Warren G. Frisina, *The Unity of Knowledge and Action: Toward a Nonrepresentational Theory of Knowledge* (Albany: State University of New York Press, 2002).
45 Sally B. King, "The Philosophia Perennis and the Religions of the World," in *The Philosophy of Seyyed Hassein Nasr: The Library of Living Philosophers*, Vol. 28, ed. Lewis Edwin Hahn, Randall E. Auxier and Lucian W. Stone (Chicago, IL: Open Court, 2001), 203–20; David S. Nah, *Religious Pluralism and Christian Theology: A Critical Evaluation of John Hick* (Cambridge, UK: James Clarke, 2013).
46 Duane R. Bidwell, "Enacting the Spiritual Self: Buddhist-Christian Identity as Participatory Action," *Spiritus: A Journal of Christian Spirituality* 15, no. 1 (2015): 105–12.
47 Wilhelm Halbfass, *Tradition and Reflection: Explorations in Indian Thought* (Albany: State University of New York Press, 1991).
48 Douglas Duckworth, "How Nonsectarian Is 'Nonsectarian?': Jorge Ferrer's Pluralist Alternative to Tibetan Buddhist Inclusivism," *Sophia* 53, no. 3 (2014): 346–7.
49 Jacques Derrida, *Positions*, trans. Alan Bass (Chicago, IL: University of Chicago Press, 1981).
50 Douglas Duckworth, "Buddhism and Beyond: The Question of Pluralism," in *Buddhist and Christian Responses to Religious Diversity*, ed. Abraham Vélez de Cea (Leiden, The Netherlands: Brill, forthcoming).

References

Ammerman, Nancy, T. "Spiritual But Not Religious: Beyond Binary Choices in the Study of Religion." *Journal for the Scientific Study of Religion* 52, no. 2 (2013): 258–78.

Berghuijs, Joantine, Jos Pieper and Cok Bakker. "Being 'Spiritual' and Being 'Religious' in Europe: Diverging Life Orientations." *Journal of Contemporary Religion* 28, no. 1 (2013): 15–32.

Bernstein, Richard J. *Beyond Objectivism and Relativism: Science, Hermeneutics, and Praxis*. Philadelphia, PA: University of Pennsylvania Press, 1985.

Bidwell, Duane R. "Enacting the Spiritual Self: Buddhist-Christian Identity as Participatory Action." *Spiritus: A Journal of Christian Spirituality* 15, no. 1 (2015): 105–12.

Boyd, Tom. "Is Spirituality Possible Without Religion? A Query for the Postmodern Era." In *Divine Representations: Postmodernism and Spirituality*. Edited by Ann W. Astell. New York: Paulist Press, 1994.

Bruce, Steve. *God Is Dead: Secularization in the West*. Malden, MA: Blackwell, 2002.

Casanova, José. *Public Religions in the Modern World*. Chicago, IL: University of Chicago Press, 1994.

Chemero, Anthony. *Radical Embodied Cognitive Science*. Cambridge, MA: The MIT Press, 2009.

Chinchore, Mangala R. *Anatta/Anatmata: An Analysis of the Buddhist Anti-Substantialist Crusade*. New Delhi, India: Sri Satguru Publications, 1995.

Clarke, J.J. *Oriental Enlightenment: The Encounter Between Asian and Western Though*. New York: Routledge, 1997.

Dale, Edward J. *Completing Piaget's Project: Transpersonal Philosophy and the Future of Psychology*. St. Paul, MN: Paragon House, 2014.

Derrida, Jacques. *Positions*. Translated by Alan Bass. Chicago, IL: University of Chicago Press, 1981.

Duckworth, Douglas. "How Nonsectarian Is "Nonsectarian?": Jorge Ferrer's Religious Pluralist Alternative to Tibetan Buddhist Inclusivism." *Sophia* 53, no. 3 (2014): 346–47.

———. "Buddhism and Beyond: The Question of Pluralism." In *Buddhist and Christian Responses to Religious Diversity*. Edited by Abraham Vélez de Cea. Leiden, The Netherlands: Brill, forthcoming.

Faivre, Antoine. *Access to Western Esoterism*. Albany, NY: State University of New York Press, 1994.

Ferrer, Jorge N. *Revisioning Transpersonal Theory: A Participatory Vision of Human Spirituality*. Albany, NY: State University of New York Press, 2002.

———. *Participation and the Mystery: Essays in Psychology, Education, and Religion*. Albany, NY: State University of New York Press, 2017.

Ferrer, Jorge N. and Jacob H. Sherman, eds. *The Participatory Turn: Spirituality, Mysticism, Religious Studies*. Albany, NY: State University of New York Press, 2008.

Friedman, Harris L. and Glenn Hartelius, eds. *The Wiley-Blackwell Handbook of Transpersonal Psychology*. Malden, MA: John Wiley & Sons, 2013.

Frisina, Warren G. *The Unity of Knowledge and Action: Toward a Nonrepresentational Theory of Knowledge*. Albany, NY: State University of New York Press, 2002.

Fuller, Robert C. *Spiritual, But Not Religious: Understanding Unchurched America*. New York: Oxford University Press, 2001.

Grof, Stanislav. *The Cosmic Game: Explorations of the Frontiers of Human Consciousness*. Albany, NY: State University of New York Press, 1998.

Habermas, Jürgen. "Secularism's Crisis of Faith: Notes on Post-Secular Society." *New Perspectives Quarterly* 25 (2008): 17–29.

Halbfass, Wilhelm. *Tradition and Reflection: Explorations in Indian Thought*. Albany, NY: State University of New York Press, 1991.

Hanegraaff, Wouter J. *New Age Religion and Western Culture: Esotericism in the Mirror of Secular Thought*. Albany, NY: State University of New York Press, 1998.

Heelas, Paul. "The Spiritual Revolution: From 'Religion' to 'Spirituality.' " In *Religions in the Modern World: Traditions and Transformations*, 357–77. Edited by Paul Fletcher, Hiroko Kawanami and David Smith. London, UK: Routledge, 2002.

Heelas, Paul and Linda Woodhead. *The Spiritual Revolution: Why Religion Is Giving Way to Spirituality*. Malden, MA: Blackwell, 2005.

Houtman, Dick and Stef Aupers. "The Spread of Post-Christian Spirituality in 14 Western Countries, 1981–2000." *Journal for the Scientific Study of Religion* 46, no. 3 (2007): 305–20.

Huxley, Aldous. *The Perennial Philosophy*. New York: Harper & Row, 1945.

King, Sally B. "The Philosophia Perennis and the Religions of the World." In *The Philosophy of Seyyed Hassein Nasr: The Library of Living Philosophers*, Vol. 28, 203–20. Edited by Lewis Edwin Hahn, Randall E. Auxier and Lucian W. Stone. Chicago, IL: Open Court, 2001.

Lahood, Greg. "The Participatory Turn and the Transpersonal Movement: A Brief Introduction." *ReVision: A Journal of Consciousness and Transformation* 29 (2007): 2–6.

Mercadante, Linda A. *Belief Without Borders: Inside the Minds of the Spiritual But Not Religious*. Oxford, UK: Oxford University Press, 2014.

Nah, David S. *Religious Pluralism and Christian Theology: A Critical Evaluation of John Hick*. Cambridge, UK: James Clarke, 2013.

Nasr, Seyyed H. "Response to Thomas Dean's Review of Knowledge and the Sacred." *Philosophy East and West* 35, no. 1 (1985): 87–90.

Quinn, William W. *The Only Tradition*. Albany, NY: State University of New York Press, 1997.

Roof, Wade Clark. *A Generation of Seekers: The Spiritual Journeys of the Baby Boom Generation*. San Francisco, CA: Harper, 1993.

———. *Spiritual Marketplace: Baby Boomers and the Remaking of American Religion*. Princeton, NJ: Princeton University Press, 1999.

Rorty, Richard. *Philosophy and the Mirror of Nature*. Princeton, NJ: Princeton University Press, 1979.

Schneiders, Sandra M. "Religion vs. Spirituality: A Contemporary Conundrum." *Spiritus: A Journal of Christian Spirituality* 3, no. 2 (2003): 163–85.

Schuon, Frithjof. *Esoterism as Principle and as Way*. Pates Manor, Bedfont, Middlesex, UK: Perennial Books, 1981.

Tarnas, Richard. "A New Birth in Freedom: A (P)review of Jorge Ferrer's *Revisioning Transpersonal Theory: A Participatory Vision of Human Spirituality*." *The Journal of Transpersonal Psychology* 33, no. 1 (2001): 64–71.

Taylor, Charles. *A Secular Age*. Cambridge, MA: Harvard University Press, 2007.

Varela, Francisco J., Evan Thompson and Eleanor Rosch. *The Embodied Mind: Cognitive Science and Human Experience*. Cambridge, MA: The MIT Press, 1991.

Vich, Miles A. "The Origins and Growth of Transpersonal Psychology." *Journal of Humanistic Psychology* 30, no. 2 (1990): 47–50.

Walsh, Roger N. "The Transpersonal Movement: A History and State of the Art." *Journal of Transpersonal Psychology* 25, no. 3 (1993): 123–39.

Wilber, Ken. *Sex, Ecology, Spirituality: The Spirit of Evolution*. Boston, MA: Shambhala, 1995.

———. *One Taste: Daily Reflections on Integral Spirituality*. Boston, MA: Shambhala, 1999.

Zinnbauer, Brian J., Kenneth I. Pargament, Brenda Cole, Mark S. Rye, Eric M. Butter, Timothy G. Belavich, Kathleen M. Hipp, Allie B. Scott and Jill L. Kader. "Religion and Spirituality: Unfuzzing the Fuzzy." *Journal for the Scientific Study of Religion* 36, no. 4 (1997): 549–56.

14 Being spiritual but not hierarchical

Chad J. Pevateaux

In her essay "Spiritual But Not Religious: The Vital Interplay between Submission and Freedom," Amy Hollywood argues that those seeking spiritual experience but not religious adherence do so in large part because they want to relate to a higher power through the freedom of their interior individuality rather than through submission to the external community. What they miss that medieval monks knew, she argues, is that we are constituted communally whether we want to be or not. Being human means being ever already with others. "Isn't the desire to constitute oneself as a spiritual person outside of the framework of larger communities illusory," Hollywood asks, "in that we are always constituted in and through our interactions with others and their texts, practices, and traditions?"[1] While I agree about communal constitution, I doubt that so many spiritual seekers desire such detached autonomy. "Let's face it," Judith Butler writes, "[w]e're undone by each other. And if we're not, we're missing something."[2] Far from missing it, many who desire to be "spiritual but not religious" (SBNR), I argue, well know that we are constituted as persons through our interrelations, and precisely because of that gnosis they reject the patriarchal and hierarchical historical structures of restrictive religion in favor of more inclusive and egalitarian cosmic communities of expansive spirituality.

Of all systems of human cultures, those we deem religious perhaps fare among the worst with respect to hierarchical oppression – of women and people of color, of nonhuman animals, and of the natural world. Yet, they also offer some of the greatest resources for countering such horrors and hate. Thus, powerful recent movements of people reject traditional hierarchical systems deemed religious but seek to retain resources deemed spiritual. Among the fastest-growing segments of American society today, those who proclaim, "none of the above," in regard to the historical traditions on offer testify to the desire for new modes of living. Given our current state of social injustice and environmental crisis, we need resources for thinking and doing otherwise than our past histories of domination if we are to live to see a future at all.

This rising tide of "nones," those who disavow explicit affiliation with religions, especially the cresting wave of those who embrace spirituality yet reject religiosity, flows in part from the history of mystics, or those who speak of an interconnection with a "More" yet disavow that any words or concepts can capture that reality. Historically, the uses and meanings of spiritual and mystical have been inextricably entwined.[3] They also have been entangled with hierarchy. The very word *hierarchy* appears to have been coined by the 5th- or 6th-century figure Dionysius the Areopagite, in whose Greek corpus we also find the first mention of *mystical theology*, which later would morph first in French from *la théologie mystique* to the elliptical *la mystique*, then turn in English into *mysticism*.[4] Thus, if we can envision mysticism and spirituality without hierarchy, then perhaps we also may find resources to transform historical oppressions, which I argue is a central desire at the heart of many SBNR movements of today that are working to form a better tomorrow.

Mystical human nature

The person perhaps foremost responsible for the modern promotion of mysticism is William James (1842–1910). In his *Varieties of Religious Experience: A Study in Human Nature* (1902), James famously separates religion from institutional religious traditions by defining it as "the feelings, acts, and experiences of individual men in their solitude, so far as they apprehend themselves to stand in relation to whatever they may consider the divine."[5] Later in *Varieties*, James further reduces religion to the mystical, and the mystical to an interrelation with whatever may be "More" at work with us in the universe. Actually, he reduces the mystical to mere potentiality – the hope in what may come to help or save that currently eludes our powers to perceive or conceive.

Though often accused of individualism at the expense of communalism, James does include *acts* in his definition of religion, which would encompass liturgical participation and hymn singing. Moreover, he also includes the cultivated mysticisms of the world's religious traditions in the final rung of his mystical ladder, but he definitely demonstrates a marked preference for individual expression apart from communal submission, at least to traditional religions. Surrendering to the hope of possible cosmic consciousnesses at work in, around, and beyond us, though, is James's core affirmation. After witnessing the horrors of the Civil War, James hopes that uniting with such a mystical More might help us form more perfect political and spiritual unions. Unfortunately, James remains fairly hierarchical, racist, and sexist. The subtitle of *Varieties* may say it's a study in human nature, but the emphasis falls on *man* and one who looks suspiciously like James himself.

More than half a century before James's *Varieties*, though, Margaret Fuller (1810–1850), in *Woman in the Nineteenth Century*, turns to mystical experiencing as a resource to help uplift women in society. "Mysticism, which may be defined as the brooding soul of the world," she writes, "cannot fail of its oracular promise as to woman."[6] For Fuller, that mystical promise whispers that if humanity suffers because sin entered the world through a woman, then mothers will be the ones to birth a new earth. Conjoining the spiritual with the mystical, Fuller contends that its "tendency is towards the elevation of woman."[7] According to Fuller, women need uplifting because they are so often put down. All too often, the direction down itself has been associated with women, whereas up, and all associated with it, has been mapped as masculine. Following ancient patterns, Fuller links the spiritual more with emotion, nature, and the feminine and the intellectual with the masculine as defined in opposition to supposedly lower modes of embodiment and animality. Contrary to ancient valuations, though, she argues for their transvaluation:

> Plato, the man of intellect, treats woman in the Republic as property, and, in the Timaeus, says that man, if he misuse the privileges of one life, shall be degraded into the form of woman, and then, if he do not redeem himself, into that of a bird. . . . But the intellect, cold, is ever more masculine than feminine; warmed by emotion, it rushes towards mother earth, and puts on the forms of beauty."[8]

The love of wisdom as intellectual represented here by Plato shows a love of the Greek male as the normative human. Detached and cold, he needs a connection to warmth and emotion. Fuller argues that man needs woman.

Above the normative Greek Man in this ancient cosmology are the realms of the forms, the gods, and the Good, which later Christian thinkers will populate with truth, angels, and God. Down from Man are the realms of women, animals, and materiality, all overwhelmingly deemed negative. The way of salvation, according to this ancient hierarchy, goes away from the material, animal, and maternal toward the immaterial, angelic, and paternal, to "our Father, who art in Heaven." Traditionally, the spiritual path runs up and out of messy materiality through intellectual mastery. The spiritual leads to the intellectual. Fuller, however, argues the reverse. The intellectual needs to be brought into balance by the spiritual, down through emotion, femininity, and the natural world. If we follow Fuller's lead, we need to rethink the mystical, the human, and nature. Such rethinking requires more understanding of how we got here.

From renaissance humanism to rationalism and fundamentalism

We could perhaps credit Martin Luther (1483–1546) with making the first move of the SBNR movements when five hundred years ago he rejected the trappings of the church hierarchy in favor of faith alone. Some even credit (or blame) him with the invention of what would become modern individualism, though he would have been aghast at the secular consumer subjects so many have become.[9] Or, we could trace the currents back to the earliest

Renaissance Humanists because of their elevation of broad human capacity over and above narrow church Scholasticism. For example, Pico della Mirandola (1463–1494) in his *Oration on the Dignity of Man*, composed about the time that Luther was born, placed the human at the center of the cosmos, marking us as unique in God's creation because of our capacity to determine our own natures. Although, like other humanists, Pico returned to ancient wisdom, and thus the hierarchy of angels above animals, he also affirmed a hopeful resource that the human is in the image of God because of our indeterminate image, able to climb or descend the chain of being according to our desires. Shape-shifting humans can degrade, through sensitivity, into animals and further down into plants or be reborn into the higher orders through the capacity of our intellect. We might even become divine by dwelling in the inmost reaches of our mind.

René Descartes (1596–1650), the French philosopher whom many consider to be among the most influential on creating modern scientific notions of rationality, and on creating modernity itself, dramatically increased the ancient emphasis of mind over body, with all the hierarchical currents that flow from it, famously proclaiming humans preeminently to be thinking things, *res cogitans*. Seeking to avoid the horrors of the religious wars resulting from the divisions in the wake of the Reformation, Descartes sought certainty as a common ground apart from disputed sacred ground. As Stephen Toulmin convincingly argues, Descartes turned to rational certainty because religious toleration in France under King Henry of Navarre (1553–1610) had been tried and failed.[10] Born just before Henry's Edict of Nantes, which established religious toleration and rights for Huguenots (French Calvinist Protestants), Descartes was a young teen when Henry IV was stabbed to death by an assassin on the streets of Paris. The young René even saw the king's heart ceremonially displayed in a silver chalice before being enshrined in the chapel of the Jesuit school at La Flèche where he was a student.[11] Clearly, one may see the appeal of ascending to mind and being rational but not religious for Descartes after witnessing this literal broken heart.

Near the time in France, then, that *la théologie mystique* becomes *la mystique*, or mystical theology becomes the mystical, Descartes turns to the rational. After deciding to doubt all of which he is not certain, Descartes's doubt ends when he concedes that he cannot doubt his own existence. From the fact of doubting, he infers there must be something there to do the doubting. To doubt, a doubter has to exist. Hence, when the question of existence appears, already the answer is certain because the question itself entails the existence of a questioner. In a sense, doubting is beyond doubt. Thus, in *Meditations on First Philosophy*, Descartes declares, "[T]his proposition, *I am, I exist*, is necessarily true whenever it is put forward by me or conceived by my mind" (II, 17). In *Discourse on the Method*, he puts the point more poetically: "*cogito ergo sum*" in Latin, "*je pense, donc je suis*" in French, or in English – "I think, therefore I am." In other words, the sound of his own voice soothes his anxiety about doubt. Descartes trusts the promise that he is actually talking to himself. Cartesian certainty involves a certain circularity: I (as hearing-myself-think) guarantee me (my existence as thinking thing). Faith, albeit the minimal amount required by the context of truth telling, even if just to oneself as another, seems foundational even for Descartes.

Similarly, we might see the emphasis on faith alone to which Luther gave rise as ultimately giving way to later biblical literalist fundamentalist fideism that likewise shares the circular: God guarantees God and textual clarity. More accurately perhaps, faith alone depends on scripture alone: "Jesus loves me, this I know *for the Bible tells me so*." As the word of God, the Bible plays largely the same role for Christian fundamentalists as the voice does for Descartes, and perhaps, *mutatis mutandis*, so, too, the diverse sacred texts for religionists of other faiths. If both reason and religion, however, rest on the not-so-firm foundation of circular paradox, testimonial trust, or, essentially, faith, how different are they?

Hierarchies after Enlightenment

Against both a dogmatic Enlightenment rationalism that identifies man as immaterial mind measured by the ideals of logic and a dogmatic biblical fideism that asserts man as disembodied soul judged by submission to divine authority (and for both it is indeed overwhelmingly *man* and not woman), the Romantics reacted by affirming the divinity of the human spirit arising from feelings within the heart and flowing around through and from nature. Rather than solely up and out, the Romantic path leads in and around. Hence Friedrich Schleiermacher (1768–1834) famously and influentially argues in his *On Religion: Speeches to Its Cultured Despisers* (1799) that "[i]f you have only given attention to these dogmas and opinions, therefore, you do not yet know religion itself, and what you despise is not it."[12] Instead, religion, according to Schleiermacher, is piety or "the immediate feeling of the Infinite and Eternal." This feeling, Schleiermacher affirms, is the "mystic tendency," involving "consciousness of the salvation of man to a higher world." His higher world, however, arises from a felt dependency on the universe itself and the feeling of finite life entwined with the Infinite. Though Schleiermacher undoubtedly furthers the modern subjective turn, he nevertheless thinks this feeling of connection to the universe is best con-textualized and channeled by the Christian church. It takes until William James to really free this mystic tendency.

Crossing the pond, European Romanticism becomes American Tran-scendentalism, with currents furtively flowing through Fuller and others to James, eventually giving rise to the recent SBNR movements. We might argue that none of these reactions actually escape the dualisms they reject, unfortunately, but, rather, favor the opposite side of every dichotomy. Try as they might, these European and American thinkers seem still caught in the wake of Plato and ancient hierarchies. Rejecting the total history of western thought, or "footnotes to Plato," as the philosopher Alfred North Whitehead famously quipped, many seekers turned east for resources to think otherwise about the hierarchical dualisms that place mind over body, reason over emotion, and male over female in order to propel the soul up and out of messy materiality.

Embraced by many who aspire to be SBNR, though often in bowdlerized forms, Asian traditions also all too often show similar divisions between transcendence and immanence. In *A New Buddhist Path: Enlightenment, Evolution, and Ethics in the Modern World*, David R. Loy argues that early Buddhism, like the traditions of Judaism, Christianity, and Islam, entails a cosmological dualism. "Instead of God and his creation," Loy says, "samsara is contrasted with nirvana, with a similar depreciation of this world as a place of suffering, craving, and delusion."[13] Loy argues that, like the Abrahamic traditions, the goal of Buddhist practice often is to go up and out, or ultimately transcend this world. Moreover, this cosmological dualism becomes embodied dualism, with the higher parts of the human more identified with salvific ascension while the lower gets denigrated as dirty. Anthropology mirrors cosmology.

"The dualism between the transcendent and this world," Loy argues, "became reproduced within us, between the 'higher part of ourselves (the soul, rationality) that yearns for escape from this vale of sorrow and the 'lower' part that is of the earth (our physical bodies with their emotions and desires)."[14] Loy notes as well that Descartes turns the pressure up on these cosmological and anthropological dualisms, giving rise today to fantasies of transhumanism that envision escape from the vulnerability of embodiment and unavoidable exposure to ultimate death by becoming pure consciousness. Whether through spiritual means like meditation or technological modes like uploading minds onto a mainframe, such desires to attain the transcendent tend to denigrate the immanent, making it more difficult for us to confront the all-too-physical problems of social justice, animal suffering, and environmental cataclysm. Yearning for the hereafter may hurt the here and now.

If, however, our basic problems arise primarily because of unhealthy views of ourselves and our world, especially indulgence in the fantasy of being individual egos autonomously able to detach from embodiment and avoid death, then perhaps our path forward might be further embracing, albeit otherwise than hierarchy, our communal constitution with others amidst a context that precedes and exceeds us. "If our fundamental *dukkha* is due to the delusion of a self that feels separate from the rest of the world," Loy argues, "then enlightenment should not be understood as that self attaining some other reality."[15] Rather than up and out, maybe our desires should flow down and around. Down, however, reminds us of death since we all know that our bodily destiny is to go down to the grave – ashes to ashes, dust to dust. "Dread of death," Loy argues, "also explains our fear and degradation of nature, animal, physical bodies, sex, and women (who bleed and remind us that we are conceived and born like other mammals)."[16] Anything and everything that reminds us of this frightening fate we also associate with the lower, more earthly realms of reality and ourselves, which we then reject. "We don't want to be of the earth," writes Loy, "because we don't want to perish like other animals: we want to be immortal souls that can qualify for heaven. Or nonselves that might attain nirvana!"[17] Rethinking our lives and how we live, thus, also will mean rethinking embodiment, earthiness, and death. The processes of reimagining ourselves, the up and down, and the more or less human, may mean reimagining who and what "we" are.

Spirituality, sexuality, and fear of death

Perhaps to overturn dualities and hierarchies, then, we should think of ourselves radically otherwise than as autonomous rational egos, and instead contemplatively accept our communal constitution and unavoidable vulnerability. Traditional ritualized religions, however, are both helps and hindrances for such a path. We need more healthy ways to engage our vulnerability without indulging the fantasy of escaping it.

In his essay "The Compatibility of Reason and Orgasm in Tibetan Buddhism: Reflections on Sexual Violence and Homophobia," Jeffrey Hopkins shows how the fear of death arises in spiritual and sexual experiencing when the borders of the ego become porous, exposing our unavoidable vulnerability to our usually repressed constitutive outside.[18] From the feeling of this fragility, he argues, self-loathing and sexual violence may come. Hopkins maintains that a potential psychological defense mechanism against death and the onslaught of everything that might remind us of death, especially the loss of control in orgasm, is to project onto the object of desire all that we loathe in ourselves because of our mortality and vulnerability. Whatever draws us toward a loss of control, draws us deeper down into the body, and away from the sublimated mental ascent away from materiality, we must shun because that reminds us of mortality. Of course, the "we" and "us" of those preceding sentences would be overmuch the "masculine" – those aspects of our psyches that identify with control, activity, and autonomy. Thus, all too poignantly, women and "passive" men mirror back to "active" and heterosexual men all the weakness and fragility in themselves that they want to deny and destroy. In grasping after control and autonomy, men historically have denigrated women and homosexual men, subjugating them to all sorts of abuse and hatred because, Hopkins argues, the controlling men hate themselves, their vulnerable bodies, and their own fear of death.

Since reason is identified with mind, then anything having to do with its opposite of body must be repressed, disparaged, and destroyed. Opposing disconnection, Hopkins argues that reason and embodied states like orgasm are continuous, much like some Jewish and Christian mystics and many Romantic thinkers argue as well. "It is my contention," Hopkins argues,

> that this Indo-Tibetan perspective of continuity could help to alleviate the sense of loathing that some males experience with respect to the power that sexual pleasure has over them, when the surface personality is collapsed in orgasm and the panic of annihilation sets in.

This strikes me as a powerful analysis and a very plausible psychological diagnosis of one of the continuing roots of patriarchy and indeed all forms of hierarchical domination.

The desire to dominate and control others arises in part from the desire to avoid the loss of control and autonomy experienced in sexual desire and (male) orgasm, as well as mystical experiencing and spiritual desire for a Wholly Other. Hopkins argues that men seek domination of others because they fear the dissolution of the ego that comes with such experiencing that reminds them of death. "At once attracted to and repelled by their own inner nature," says Hopkins, "they lash out in distorted disgust, attempting to claim a privileged position over a process that does indeed undermine their identification with superficial states."[19] The patriarchal and hierarchical structures and rituals of those systems of human cultures that we call religions, then, could serve to harness these spiritual and sexual powers or powerlessnesses, bringing them under a measure of control. This analysis provides another way of understanding why women and gay men have been and still oftentimes are prevented from participating in the performance of these rituals – because their presence could disrupt the heterosexual male control of the very energies the rituals are designed to sublimate.

Hence, a ritual like Christian baptism through which believers are "born again" can be seen as childbirth done better, cleaner, and clearer, with the role of the man visible to all, unlike natural, bloody human birth in which the role of the father remains largely unseen. Through baptism and the attendant naming, men assuage the anxiety of uncertain paternity coming from their relatively tiny role in natural procreation. Effacing women's labor in all its senses, men value the fruits of invisible mind over embodied birthing because they want to live forever in disembodied form. As Grace Jantzen argues in her *Power, Gender, and Christian Mysticism*, ancient hierarchical thought holds that

> a lover of wisdom must overcome the desires of the flesh, and in so doing can actually appropriate at the level of spirit the reproductive function which in physical terms is uniquely women's. . . . As Plato says in the Symposium, 'who would not prefer such [spiritual] fatherhood to merely human propagation?' This appropriation of reasoning to the male sex only, and the valorisation of the offspring of male intellect

above the reproductive capacity of the female, was to have a very long run in western thought, very much at the expense of women.[20]

What we could be seeing with many of the rituals in the history of religions, then, would be the desire to control the loss of control experienced through desire. Or more specifically, we see rituals and hierarchical structures designed to repress and sublimate the ways orgasm and death upset subjectivity and open it onto its other – the unconscious realm of the body, emotions, and everything deemed negative by the gender hierarchy.

Moreover, practitioners of such rituals and enforcers of such hierarchies perhaps fear the way the power of procreation, and thus potential immortality by living on through offspring, seems ceded to women in the paradoxical moment of orgasm, when men perhaps feel most powerful yet spasmatically lose control only to then feel their power pathetically wane through detumescence. Even Aristotle, as April D. DeConick writes, shared such a fear of losing control of the power of procreation to women when,

> in his argument against pangenesis, he said that the denial of female seed was intellectually satisfying because it put to rest any fear one might have that a woman, since she had a uterus and could produce menses for the nourishment of the embryo, might put forth her own seed and produce a child without the contribution of a father.[21]

We also find hints of such fear in the Hermetic text *Asclepius*:

> For if you take note of that final moment to which we come after constant rubbing when each of the two natures pours its issue into the other and one hungrily snatches <love> from the other and buries it deeper, finally at that moment from the common coupling females gain the potency of males and males are exhausted with the lethargy of females.[22]

If to be "male" means avoiding vulnerability and maintaining a controlling and rational grasp on one's self, then the loss of control in orgasm would involve a fear of the loss of one's very "maleness" or self into the unknown, destabilizing "feminine."

"Once reason is separated out as an autonomous entity and once persons identify mainly with this disembodied faculty," Hopkins argues, "it is all too easy to view states and impulses that are actually part and parcel of one's own mind as threateningly impinging from the outside."[23] We then deem this outside as the demonic other. "Fear and rejection of sexuality," Hopkins continues, "lead to projection of sexuality onto women and homosexuals."[24] Thus, some heterosexual men project their self-loathing of their own sexuality – which reminds them of their exposure to their constitutive outside – onto those others whom they deem associated with the loss of control that comes in orgasm, thereby giving rise to all manner of social ill in the erection of hierarchies that seek domination of all below transcendent, immaterial mind – namely, everything from women to nonhuman animals to materiality itself.

To transform such hierarchies, then, requires embracing embodiment with a clear mind and feeling our passivity in balance with how we think our agency. "Such a revolution in perspective," writes Hopkins, "requires recognition of vulnerability and thus is not easy."[25] Fearing our own deaths, and feeling the deaths of friends and family, or perhaps seeing the horrors on the news of those even far away, we realize our exposure to loss, grief, and pain. We can try avoiding, denying, or repressing this realization of vulnerability to death, as we have seen attempted perhaps through all the hierarchies in the history of the world, or we can engage with it differently.

Embracing vulnerability otherwise

Several recent attempts by academic philosophers and theorists to reject religions yet retain their resources have been understudied in connection to "Spiritual but Not Religious" movements of more popular culture, though they may be mutually reinforcing. If, moving toward a conclusion, we compare some ways that recent writers theorize how the human is haunted by its marginalized others with the ways mystical practitioners theologize how the self is daunted by an incomprehensible Other, then perhaps we may find more ways to move otherwise than oppressive hierarchies.

For example, Luce Irigaray argues that, rather than simply a valorization of the formerly marginalized feminine, we need to maintain woman as a conceptual elsewhere to man in much the same way that mystical theologies maintain a God beyond all perceptions and conceptions.[26] She is his unattainable elsewhere, always eluding controlling masculinist reason. "But what," Judith Butler asks, "is the 'elsewhere' of Irigaray's 'elsewhere'?"[27] Butler argues that the human is constituted not only through community but also through exclusion, always producing an outside that can never be delimited, whether to women, animals, nature, or any recognizable other (or Other). Whatever we recognize as constituting the here and now, whether our egos, sexualities, societies, religions or Gods, something else remains elsewhere, outside, and hidden. "The task," she says, "is to refigure this necessary 'outside' as a future horizon, one in which the violence of exclusion is perpetually in the process of being overcome."[28] With the future horizon of Butler's outside, we return to a similar affirmation to James's mystical More, but one with more resources for countering sexism, racism, and xenophobia.

Moreover, Butler increasingly sounds mystical as she invokes a constitutive opacity at the heart of the human. As in the image of an incomprehensible Trinity, mystics from Gregory of Nyssa through Dionysius to Teresa of Avila speak of approaching the love of God by "knowing through unknowing," whereas Butler says "that we are compelled in love means that we are, in part, unknowing about why we love as we do."[29] Hers is no mystical or negative theology of dazzling darkness, however, but simply the mundane realization that we do not know everything and that a dizzying doubt seems ever already to haunt all of our apparent certainties and engagements in the world. For Butler, no union, whether an individual ego or a democracy, can or should be conclusively closed and secure. "It may be that what is right and what is good," she argues, "consist in staying open to the tensions that beset the most fundamental categories we require. . . ." And Butler continues in language that sounds not dissimilar from mystics: "in knowing unknowingness at the core of what we know, and what we need, and in recognizing the sign of life in what we undergo without certainty about what will come."[30]

If, however, whatever or whoever haunts the human remains unrecognizable within the parameters of the presently possible, then it may be indistinguishable from death (Heidegger), face or call (Levinas), excess (Marion), the messianic to come (Derrida), more (James), or less (Beast or Abyss).[31] "In order to be authentic," Jacques Derrida argues, "the belief in God must be exposed to absolute doubt. I know that the great mystics experience this."[32] Such experiencing of exposure Derrida discusses in terms of a "religion without religion," which is a phrasing "permitting a discourse to be developed without reference to a religion as institutional dogma, and proposing a genealogy of thinking concerning the possibility and essence of the religious that doesn't amount to an article of faith."[33] Though rejecting organized religions as traditionally inherited, Derrida nevertheless wants to retain a relation with faith, which he argues is absolutely universal.

"We have to find in our experience, each as a living being," he argues, "the experience of faith far beyond any received religious tradition, any teaching."[34] "That is why," he therefore continues, "I constantly refer to the experience of faith as simply a speech act, as simply the social experience; and this is true even for animals."[35] Already before the first speech act, the conditions that make it possible to say "I" already entail trust. One has to promise to oneself that one is really talking to oneself. In forming a world or in coming to consciousness, we have to trust that this is indeed happening. "When I speak to you," Derrida says, "I am telling you that I promise to tell you something, to tell you the truth."[36] Derrida thus displaces Cartesian subjectivity that knows itself in talking to itself by pointing to the prior context of trust. This testimonial promise of truth-telling, with the faith it entails, Derrida argues, precedes and makes possible both reason and religion.

"Religion and reason," Derrida writes, "develop in tandem, drawing from this common resource: the testimonial pledge of every performative."[37] For either religion or reason to get going, one already will have had to communicate to some other, even if only to oneself as if one were another. Even if I'm only talking to myself or attesting to myself in my inner intimacy that this is indeed what is taking place, this act involves the basic division of an "I" and a "me": I am talking to me. We thus find ourselves amid a relation with something more or other than ourselves. In a sense, we are ever already two. Such is our relation with a world.

Faith, as testimonial speech act from before the start is a social experience, involves nonhuman animals and the material world and is absolutely universal. Such faith, then, is intimately interconnected with whatever comes, including all those aspects of ourselves and the cosmos that we historically deem "lower" on the hierarchies. Hence, Derrida declares that his constant project is the thinking of "interconnectedness," though he adds, "albeit otherwise."[38]

As extreme examples of those who might profess "none of the above," some recent thinkers use Derrida's analyses, though, to think the end of being spiritual or religious. Adding to the new atheisms, Martin Hägglund, in his book *Radical Atheism: Derrida and the Time of Life*, for example, counters theological interpretations of deconstruction to argue for the death of God. Moreover, Catherine Malabou and other new materialists argue that Derrida's deconstruction of the duality between speech and writing entails a radical plasticity to reality that discounts supernatural, nonmaterial possibilities. What they miss, I fear, are the ways deconstruction opens us and all radically to whatever other(s) may come, and thus possibilities in excess of any and all of our abilities to currently or ever confidently circumscribe. True, Derrida does think a radical mortality: "My death," argues Derrida, "is structurally necessary to the pronouncing of the *I*."[39] For speech to work, like when Descartes declares, "I think, therefore I am," that language has to be able to function even if the speaker is dead. For speech to make sense it also would have to be sensible in your absence. Entailing intelligibility at other places and times, even if the speaker is absent or dead, the conditions of possibility for speech share the instability of writing.

All language, then, even if spoken, bears the capacity of writing to be communicated at some other place and some other time. This unavoidable possibility of altered and altering repetition, and thus vulnerability to death, Derrida famously dubs "*différance*." His analysis applies not simply to writing, or, more specifically, this analysis of writing applies to everything, or at least to anything that comes into presence as a "thing." According to Derrida, the quasi-mystical traits of possible disappearance and reappearance across space and time are valid "beyond semio-linguistic communication, for the entire field of what philosophy would call experience, even the experience of being: the above-mentioned 'presence.'"[40] Moreover, any presence, even the presence of God, would be unavoidably exposed to the possibility of disappearance and thus death:

> The appearing of the *I* to itself in the *I am* is thus originally a relation with its own possible disappearance. Therefore, *I am* originally means *I am mortal*. *I am immortal* is an impossible proposition. We can go further: as a linguistic statement "I am he who am" is the admission of a mortal.[41]

If with the power to say "I am" also comes the powerlessness of vulner-ability to mortality, then even the God of Abraham, Isaac, and Jacob, who declares "I Am Who I Am" (Exodus 3:14) suffers exposure to the possibility of death. Such is why Derrida refers to a religion *without* religion, because according to his analysis any specific affirmation like a creed, any institu-tional edifice like a church hierarchy, or even the simplest rudiment of say-ing, "I am," is ever already exposed to a context that precedes and exceeds it, making it open and vulnerable to being recontextualized at some other place and time, interconnected to whatever may come.

Derrida takes his use of *without* from Augustine, who also had his own quest for certainty. Before Descartes, Augustine addressed the question of existence, saying, "if I am deceived, I am. For he who does not exist can-not be deceived. And if I am deceived, by this same token I am" (City of God, 11:26). Descartes's logic thus followed a Christian tradition. Must we, though, try to protect ourselves from the vulnerability to uncertainty and death with the ascent out of questioning to rational or religious certainty? "I have become a question to myself," Augustine famously writes in *Confes-sions* just after describing his temptation to love the rhythm of chants and hymns more than the words themselves – the embodied feeling more than the mental meaning. Augustine views this ability to be moved by music as a threat because it tempts him into his lower being, causing him to lose his sense of who he is. The Christian theologian Jean-Luc Marion in his "The Privilege of Unknowing" has sought to return to rhythmic embodied ques-tioning or embodiment of the question in order to interpret it anew as a resource rather than a threat. "Such avoidance of definition and concept," argues Thomas A. Carlson of Marion's effort to valorize unknowing at the heart of the human, "seems to depend nonetheless on a fundamental gesture of exclusion, directed first at the animal, and then . . . at all other nonhuman and nondivine beings – which are termed the 'world.'"[42] What then, would it mean to attend otherwise to the dichotomies of body and mind? Self and other? The more or less human – God and animal?

If we acknowledged their intimate interconnections, what might such an integrated consciousness feel like? "Embarrassing, probably," says Allen Ginsberg, the Beat poet from the counterculture movements quintessentially caught up in "Spiritual but Not Religious" circles, in response to a question about why the full embodied effects of chant have been so resisted in Chris-tianity from Augustine to today. In an interview titled "Gnostic Conscious-ness," he says people resist such vibratory embodiment beyond intellection

> because it's a whole area of feeling of communal family ritual feeling, which is feared. And the reason it's feared is because it's a breakthrough onto a new consciousness which is not like the social consciousness inculcated by television or radio or newspapers or politics, it's another animal mammal consciousness that we share, the compassionate consciousness of the mind and the heart that we share with the bald

eagles and the blue whales. And since we keep killing all the whales and the bald eagles it wouldn't be appropriate to voice that conscious-ness – I mean it would be revolutionary to voice that consciousness, to articulate that consciousness and welcome it to surface front-brain awareness.[43]

Welcoming awareness of our deep ecological interrelations would be revo-lutionary. Voicing consciousness of our communal constitution, however, also reveals our exposure to we know not what. Able to reverberate across time and clime, the call of consciousness bears the differential power or powerlessness of writing and arouses us to respond to unavoidable openness to whatever may come (back), perhaps even cosmic consciousnesses. Thus, the possibility appears that mind, body, and wor(l)d are interconnected, as if mystically, whether we like it or not. The material, it seems, is spiritual, and vice versa.

Lastly, let me close with a further both academic and popular expression of thinking and feeling such communal interconnection. If the "let there be light" of the God of Genesis gave rise to a light supremacy that supports and reinforces white supremacy, then the astrophysicist Neil deGrasse Tyson offers us a way of reconceiving our creation story that helps us embrace rather than reject our dark earthiness. Our lives, he explains, are not simply ashes to ashes, dust to dust, but more expansively stardust to stardust. In his book, *Astrophysics for People in a Hurry*, Tyson calls the sense of connect-edness with the stars and all that is that comes through knowledge of phys-ics the "cosmic perspective," sounding not dissimilar from Schleiermacher, Fuller, or James. "The cosmic perspective," he writes, "is spiritual – even redemptive – but not religious."[44] Science has not meant the end of religions but, rather, new modes of religiosity and spirituality. Always opening to new data to come that may revise all previous paradigms, science itself partakes of a sort of mystical hope. Spiritual traditions and scientific ones align in the perpetual practice of contemplative awareness of awe at the past, wonder at the present, and hope in what may come.

Notes

1 Amy Hollywood, "Spiritual But Not Religious: The Vital Interplay of Submis-sion and Freedom," *Harvard Divinity Bulletin* (Winter / Spring 2010): 26.
2 Judith Butler, Undoing Gender (New York: Routledge, 2004), 19.
3 See Robert C. Fuller and William B. Parsons, "Spiritual But Not Religious: A Brief Introduction," in this volume.
4 See Certeau's Fable. See also Leigh Eric Schmidt, "The Making of Modern 'Mys-ticism,'" *Journal of the American Academy of Religion* 71, no. 2 (2003). Also Chad J. Pevateaux, "Mysticism Emergent: The Beginning of the Study of Mysti-cism in the Academy," in *Religion: Secret Religion, Macmillan Interdisciplinary Handbooks* (Farmington Hills, MI: Macmillan Reference USA, 2016).
5 William James, *William James: Writings 1902–1910* (New York: Library of America, 1988), 36.

6 Margaret Fuller, *Woman in the Nineteenth Century* (New York: Greeley & McElrath, 1845), 90.
7 Ibid, 90.
8 Ibid., 90–1.
9 See Mark C. Taylor, *After God* (Chicago: University of Chicago Press, 2009).
10 Stephen Toulmin, *Cosmopolis: The Hidden Agenda of Modernity* (Chicago: University of Chicago Press, 1990).
11 Ibid., 56–7.
12 James C. Livingston, *Modern Christian Thought, Volume I: The Enlightenment and the Nineteenth Century*, 2nd ed. (Upper Saddle River, NJ: Prentice Hall, 1996), 93–105.
13 David R. Loy, *A New Buddhist Path: Enlightenment, Evolution, and Ethics in the Modern World*, 1st ed. (Boston, MA: Wisdom Publications, 2015), 20.
14 Ibid., 23.
15 Ibid., 20.
16 Ibid., 24.
17 Ibid., 24.
18 Jeffrey Hopkins, "The Compatibility of Reason and Orgasm in Tibetan Buddhism: Reflections on Sexual Violence and Homophobia," in *Que(e)Rying Religion: A Critical Anthology*, ed. Gary Comstock and Susan E. Henking (New York: Continuum, 1997), 382–3.
19 Ibid., 382–3.
20 Grace Jantzen, *Power, Gender, and Christian Mysticism* (Cambridge: Cambridge University Press, 1996).
21 April D. DeConick, "The Great Mystery of Marriage: Sex and Conception in Ancient Valentinian Traditions," *Vigiliae Christianae* 57, no. 3 (2003): 322.
22 Brian P. Copenhaver, ed., *Hermetica: The Greek Corpus Hermeticum and the Latin Asclepius in a New English Translation, with Notes and Introduction*, Reprint ed. (Cambridge: Cambridge University Press, 1995), 79.
23 Hopkins, "Compatibility of Reason and Orgasm," 383.
24 Ibid., 383.
25 Ibid.
26 Luce Irigaray, *This Sex Which Is Not One* (Ithaca, NY: Cornell University Press, 1985), 76. See also, Anne-Marie Priest, "Woman as God, God as Woman: Mysticism, Negative Theology, and Luce Irigaray," *The Journal of Religion* 83, no. 1 (January 2003): 1–23.
27 Judith Butler, *Bodies That Matter: On the Discursive Limits of Sex* (New York: Routledge, 1993), 49.
28 Ibid., 53.
29 Judith Butler, *Giving an Account of Oneself* (New York: Fordham University Press, 2005), 103.
30 Butler, *Undoing Gender*, 39.
31 For an intriguing study on the expansion of the possible, see Jeffrey J. Kripal, *Authors of the Impossible: The Paranormal and the Sacred*, Reprint ed. (Chicago: University of Chicago Press, 2011). On the undecidability between the analogies of death and an incomprehensible God, see Thomas A. Carlson, *Indiscretion: Finitude and the Naming of God*, 1st ed. (Chicago: University of Chicago Press, 1999). On the passivity of the affected subject and an undecidability between death and the call of the other, see Jeffrey L. Kosky, *Levinas and the Philosophy of Religion* (Bloomington: Indiana University Press, 2001). On the undecidability between saturated phenomena and aporias, see Robyn Horner, "Aporia or Excess? Two Strategies for Thinking r/Revelation," in *Derrida and Religion: Other Testaments*, ed. Yvonne Sherwood and Kevin Hart (New York:

Routledge, 2004). On the messianic, see especially Jacques Derrida, *Specters of Marx* (New York: Routledge, 1994).

32 Jacques Derrida, "Epoché and Faith: An Interview with Jacques Derrida," in *Derrida and Religion: Other Testaments*, ed. Yvonne Sherwood and Kevin Hart (New York: Routledge, 2004), 46.

33 Jacques Derrida, *The Gift of Death* (Chicago: University of Chicago Press, 1996), 49.

34 Derrida, "Epoché and Faith: An Interview with Jacques Derrida," 45.

35 Ibid., 45.

36 Jacques Derrida and John D. Caputo, *Deconstruction in a Nutshell* (New York: Fordham University Press, 1997), 23.

37 Jacques Derrida, "Faith and Knowledge: The Two Sources of 'Religion' at the Limits of Reason Alone," in *Acts of Religion*, ed. Gil Anidjar (New York: Routledge, 2002), 66.

38 Ibid., 90.

39 Jacques Derrida, *Speech and Phenomena: And Other Essays on Husserl's Theory of Signs* (Evanston, IL: Northwestern University Press, 1973), 96.

40 Jacques Derrida, *Of Grammatology*, trans. Gayatri Chakravorty Spivak, Corrected ed. (Baltimore, MD: Johns Hopkins University Press, 1974).

41 Derrida, *Speech and Phenomena* (Evanston, IL: Northwestern University Press, 1973), 54–5.

42 Thomas A. Carlson, *The Indiscrete Image: Infinitude and Creation of the Human* (Chicago: University of Chicago Press, 2008), 123.

43 Allen Ginsberg, *Allen Verbatim: Lectures on Poetry, Politics, Consciousness* (New York: McGraw-Hill, 1974), 34.

44 Neil deGrasse Tyson, *Astrophysics for People in a Hurry*, 1st ed. (New York: W. W. Norton & Company, 2017), 206.

References

Butler, Judith. *Bodies That Matter: On the Discursive Limits of Sex*. New York: Routledge, 1993.

———. *Undoing Gender*. New York: Routledge, 2004.

———. *Giving an Account of Oneself*. New York: Fordham University Press, 2005.

Carlson, Thomas A. *Indiscretion: Finitude and the Naming of God*. 1st ed. Chicago: University of Chicago Press, 1999.

———. *The Indiscrete Image: Infinitude and Creation of the Human*. Chicago: University Of Chicago Press, 2008.

Copenhaver, Brian P., ed. *Hermetica: The Greek Corpus Hermeticum and the Latin Asclepius in a New English Translation, with Notes and Introduction*. Reprint ed. Cambridge: Cambridge University Press, 1995.

DeConick, April D. "The Great Mystery of Marriage: Sex and Conception in Ancient Valentinian Traditions." *Vigiliae Christianae* 57, no. 3 (2003).

Derrida, Jacques. *Speech and Phenomena: And Other Essays on Husserl's Theory of Signs*. Evanston: Northwestern University Press, 1973.

———. *Of Grammatology*. Translated by Gayatri Chakravorty Spivak. Corrected ed. Baltimore, MD: Johns Hopkins University Press, 1974.

———. *Specters of Marx*. New York: Routledge, 1994.

———. *The Gift of Death*. Chicago: University Of Chicago Press, 1996.

———. "Faith and Knowledge: The Two Sources of 'Religion' at the Limits of Reason Alone." In *Acts of Religion*, 40–101. Edited by Gil Anidjar. New York: Routledge, 2002.

———. "Epoché and Faith: An Interview with Jacques Derrida." In *Derrida and Religion: Other Testaments*. Edited by Yvonne Sherwood and Kevin Hart. New York: Routledge, 2004.

Derrida, Jacques and John D. Caputo. *Deconstruction in a Nutshell*. New York: Fordham University Press, 1997.

Fuller, Margaret. *Woman in the Nineteenth Century*. New York: Greeley & McElrath, 1845.

Ginsberg, Allen. *Allen Verbatim: Lectures on Poetry, Politics, Consciousness*. New York: McGraw-Hill, 1974.

Hollywood, Amy. "Spiritual But Not Religious: The Vital Interplay of Submission and Freedom." *Harvard Divinity Bulletin* (Winter/Spring 2010).

Hopkins, Jeffrey. "The Compatibility of Reason and Orgasm in Tibetan Buddhism: Reflections on Sexual Violence and Homophobia." In *Que(e)Rying Religion: A Critical Anthology*, 372–83. Edited by Gary Comstock and Susan E. Henking. New York: Continuum, 1997.

Horner, Robyn. "Aporia or Excess? Two Strategies for Thinking r/Revelation." In *Derrida and Religion: Other Testaments*, edited by Yvonne Sherwood and Kevin Hart. New York: Routledge, 2004.

Irigaray, Luce. *This Sex Which Is Not One*. Ithaca, NY: Cornell University Press, 1985.

James, William. *William James: Writings 1902–1910*. New York: Library of America, 1988.

Jantzen, Grace. *Power, Gender, and Christian Mysticism*. Cambridge: Cambridge University Press, 1996.

Kosky, Jeffrey L. *Levinas and the Philosophy of Religion*. Bloomington, IN: Indiana University Press, 2001.

Kripal, Jeffrey J. *Authors of the Impossible: The Paranormal and the Sacred*. Reprint ed. Chicago: University of Chicago Press, 2011.

Livingston, James C. *Modern Christian Thought, Volume I: The Enlightenment and the Nineteenth Century*. 2nd ed. Upper Saddle River, NJ: Prentice Hall, 1996.

Loy, David R. *A New Buddhist Path: Enlightenment, Evolution, and Ethics in the Modern World*. 1st ed. Boston, MA: Wisdom Publications, 2015.

Pevateaux, Chad J. "Mysticism Emergent: The Beginning of the Study of Mysticism in the Academy." In *Religion: Secret Religion. Macmillan Interdisciplinary Handbooks*. Farmington Hills, MI: Macmillan Reference USA, 2016.

Priest, Anne-Marie. "Woman as God, God as Woman: Mysticism, Negative Theology, and Luce Irigaray." *The Journal of Religion* 83, no. 1 (January 2003): 1–23.

Schmidt, Leigh Eric. "The Making of Modern 'Mysticism.'" *Journal of the American Academy of Religion* 71, no. 2 (2003).

Taylor, Mark C. *After God*. Chicago: University of Chicago Press, 2009.

Toulmin, Stephen. *Cosmopolis: The Hidden Agenda of Modernity*. Chicago: University of Chicago Press, 1990.

Tyson, Neil deGrasse. *Astrophysics for People in a Hurry*. 1st ed. New York: W. W. Norton & Company, 2017.

15 "Comparison gets you nowhere!"

The comparative study of religion and the Spiritual but Not Religious

Jeffrey J. Kripal

The comparative study of religion has been on the defensive for almost four decades now. Its alleged crimes and supposed failures are well known. I cannot count the times that I have read or heard someone reacting to it with a remarkably easy certainty about how comparison is always somehow colonizing, appropriating, hegemonic; how it denies social and political context; how it must be antihistorical; how it relies on the unreliable intuitions or simple whims of the comparativist; and how it is old-fashioned, out of date, and must now be left behind.

Behind all of these common complaints, I hear the presence of a series of unquestioned dogmas or unexamined philosophical assumptions: that the human being is only historical; that we somehow know what "matter" and "mind" are and even how they are related; that the experience of transcendence, however universally reported, is nothing more than a ruse; and that time is a straight, linear arrow and nothing more.

Behind both the complaints and the dogmas, moreover, I hear the distant echoes of a deep and abiding existential fear: the fear of comparison as deconstructive of *all* local truth claims (including the secular and materialist ones); the fear of having to admit to ourselves that we are all enacting and performing our worlds, not finding or discovering them as some kind of absolute eternal things. The basic anxiety here boils down to a conviction that, if we took comparison *really* seriously, that is, if we really followed it through and applied it fairly and equally to every religious or cultural world, including and especially our own, we would lose all stable ground. We would, in effect, be lost at sea. The basic fear here is that comparison gets us literally nowhere.

I think such fears are reasonable and well-founded ones. It is just that I am not at all certain that some of us should not get lost at sea anyway, should not venture into this Nowhere of Comparison. Perhaps many of us already are. Perhaps it is only a matter of looking around, admitting as much, and moving on – into what, I freely admit, it is not at all clear.

I think we do have a fairly good sense, though, of where we have been on the supposed dry land of "religion. And it is not good. It has been a long history of certainties and subsequent conflicts and exclusions about and around those certainties, and at times it has been a literal bloodbath. As we can see all too clearly now, hatred, ignorance, and bigotry sit perfectly well with faith, established religion, and firm belief. I think many of us do not want to return to that land. I think many of us would much prefer to be lost at sea. I know I would.

* * * *

It is always telling what one remembers. I remember many things about my graduate training in the History of Religions at the University of Chicago in the late 1980s and early 1990s. But one memory stands out in particularly bright colors. It was a stray comment that I heard, I forget from whom, which went something like this: "The shadow of the History of Religions is the New Age."

Whoever said it and whatever was actually said, it did not mean a great deal to me when I first heard it. I was working in medieval Christianity with Latin texts and in 19th-century Calcutta with Bengali texts. I was a *real* scholar and would not deign to stoop to dedicate my days to lowbrow interests like the counterculture or, God forbid, the New Age movement.

Nor had I had any real involvement with either movement. I came into adolescence and early adulthood too late (in the 1970s) and in the wrong place (in a small farming community in Nebraska). I was a psychedelic virgin. The only memories I have of the counterculture are, in effect, stray flashes. I remember, for example, being scared as a young boy by a Volkswagen Bug spattered with peace signs and flowers and filled with loud music and some rambunctious teenagers whom my mom and dad called "hippies." Those hippies scared me. I also recall being quite puzzled by a red wax fat Buddha that my uncle Lonnie had in his room on my grandparents' Nebraska farm – the red thing seemed vaguely inappropriate and certainly out of place, somehow just "wrong."

These things did not carry any clear meanings for me as a boy. How could they? My childish psyche lacked any sufficient context to understand them, to place them. Accordingly, these experiences registered only as fears, gaps, or fissures in my otherwise stable familial and cultural worlds.

Still, at middle age, I ended up in northern California writing, among other things, about the mystical and paranormal currents of the human potential movement, the counterculture of the 1960s and 1970s, and the New Age movement of the 1980s and 1990s, movements which in turn, of course, morphed into the contemporary "Spiritual but Not Religious" (SBNR) scene – our present concern.

In full disclosure, I am also a happy participant in much of this now. I finished writing a history of the human potential movement via the prism of the Esalen Institute in Big Sur, California, in 2006.[1] About eight years later, I joined the board of trustees of the same institute. In the fall of 2015, I was elected chair of the board. Obviously, I can no longer claim any plausible objectivity. Nor would I want to do so. Of course, there are real limitations here, but this same situation gives me a certain double lens through which to see and analyze something like the SBNR movement. As Michael Murphy, the co-founder of Esalen, often humorously puts it to me: it is one thing to eat sausage; it is quite another to see how it is made in the back kitchen. I have eaten the sausage. I have also been in the back kitchen. I can tell you a lot about both processes, probably more than you want to know.

The point of the present chapter is to return to that stray comment in Swift Hall about the History of Religions and the New Age and explore for a moment to what extent such a comment was accurate. I will do this through the logic of comparativism, which I think is what holds these two broad cultural movements – one intellectual and academic, the other social and experiential – together, what makes them echo back and forth in some-times resonant, sometimes dissonant ways. In the end, I observe that the History of Religions and the New Age are not the same, but neither are they entirely different. They share the same deep comparative logic. This deep comparative logic, moreover, can also function as a kind of inarticu-late comparative spirituality or underdeveloped mystical practice. I suggest that this is precisely what we see in the New Age movement and our present SBNR demographic.

That is what I see in such a demographic, anyway. I see a lot of people at sea. I see a lot of people who have refused the firm ground of an established religious tradition, often for very good moral and intellectual reasons, but who have really no idea what to do at sea and how to take advantage of the winds and currents. I think professional scholars of religion could help, if they wanted to help. I also think there are real resources in both the profes-sional study of religion and in the history of comparative mystical literature, which, it turns out, often bear an uncanny likeness. If there is a sustainable future in all of this, I think it lies somewhere here, out to sea but with some reliable navigation techniques, which, I would argue, we already possess in the academy and in the classroom.

The classroom of comparison

Although I briefly venture outside the academic context, my comments apply mostly to this professional world of the university and the college, that is, to the social spaces that professors and their students routinely inhabit. These social spaces, after all, are the main places where comparative acts with respect to religion are best modeled, taught, protected, encouraged, and promulgated through ritualized events and texts like courses and academic works of scholarship.

It is all too easy to forget, or simply not to see: professors create, con-trol, and enact ritual spaces whenever they teach their courses, and these rituals affect young people, sometimes quite profoundly. One of the central claims of the present chapter is that one of the fundamental effects of the comparative religion classroom over the last fifty years, that is, since the counterculture of the 1960s and 1970s (the most immediate and influential origin point of contemporary comparison),[2] has been a profound weakening of religious identity, an equally profound opening to other ways of being religious, and the subsequent social production of the SBNR orientation. In short, academics bear a real responsibility for the production or appearance of this modern phenomenon.

Academics are not the sole influencers or catalysts, of course, and they themselves have been shaped and influenced by the same social forces (like the liberalization of the counterculture and the subsequent right-wing religious and political backlash of the 1980s and 1990s) that have produced the SBNR phenomenon. But they have nevertheless played an outsized role and have thought and written about the implications of all this in ways that no other social group has. In some ways, the SBNR orientation is indeed the "other side," the popular and public side, of the professional study of comparative religion. They are two sides of the same cultural and historical coin.

I observe this with some trepidation and more than a little pride.

The trepidation is a function of my awareness of the largely unacknowledged but awesome political, social, and spiritual power of comparison. Honestly, I am of the opinion that just about all of our present political and social problems come down to this: our inability to compare one another fairly and accurately, that is, to honor both our sameness and our differences and to keep these in a constant tensive balance.

It is truly astonishing how bad we are at this balance, at holding this healthy tension. We are always either trying to subsume one another within some historically relative sameness and its subsequent violence (for contemporary examples, consider "America," "Merry Christmas," "the Christian nation," or "family values"), or we are overprivileging some religious, gendered, ethnic, or racial identity as the defining mark of being human and so making any larger community nearly impossible to imagine, much less actualize (well-meaning academics are particularly guilty of this). We do not see that difference only makes sense in a context of sameness. We do not see that social justice is itself always and everywhere a comparative act, a balancing of sameness and difference. We do not see that justice is always a search for recognizing difference in sameness and sameness in difference. We do not see that comparison *is* justice.

Comparison done well, anyway.

A few years ago, I was approached by an editor to write a textbook on how to compare religions. I initially declined the idea on the grounds that there are already many fine world religions textbooks out there. But this was not what she was asking. She was asking me to propose a different kind of approach.

That was attractive to me, as I had long grown frustrated with the stand-ard "world religions" model, mostly because of the way that it left the stu-dents with an easy certainty that everyone was a this or a that, and wasn't it all just great? In my own experience teaching these textbooks, religious identity itself is never really seriously questioned in this particular pedagogi-cal approach. Everyone is left in her or his religious silo or cultural box. As a consequence of this safe siloing, most, or all, of the tough questions are left unasked, much less answered. I saw the world religions approach as a perfectly legitimate remedial task, as something that needed to be done, for sure, but I was not at all sure that I wanted to spend an entire course doing it, particularly since I knew that, for most of these young adults, this would be their one and only course on religion that they would ever take.

We have them once. We can only have one four-month conversation with them. What did I *most* want them to learn? What did I *most* want them to know? Certainly not the details they could easily access on Wikipedia in about two minutes. I decided that I most wanted them to learn the intima-cies and nuances of comparison, and I wanted them to be able to process and integrate what this might mean for them, personally, socially, and mor-ally. This, in my mind, was the conversation that could change everything.

So I proposed to the editor an approach that backgrounded the religions themselves and foregrounded the comparative act. Moreover, I proposed that the textbook deal explicitly and consistently with the existential costs of fair and accurate comparison. It was my experience, borne out of over a decade of teaching thousands of students at that point, that comparison done well leaves the typical student in a kind of existential crisis, in that aforementioned "nowhere" in which every culture is enacting its own world but in which no such single world can function as a stable, permanent, or absolute place.

Comparison is always a dance or a high-wire act. It works with some model of sameness (myth and ritual, the natural world, the body, society, the brain, and so on), but it also works with a profound sensibility around difference (especially our present trio of race, class, and gender). As a result, comparison done well grounds, but it also destabilizes and deconstructs. One of our undergraduates here at Rice once captured this particular punch of the practice by suggesting we create a T-shirt to attract new majors. It would read: "Have your mid-life crisis now. Become a Religion Major."

After dozens, if not hundreds, of these moments, I decided to create not a T-shirt with the undergraduate but a textbook with the inquiring edi-tor. I wrote it with three of my PhD students from three entirely different religious backgrounds. We wanted to work openly and explicitly with this destabilization and deconstruction, but we also wanted to help the student arrive, at the end of the course, at some sort of tentative resolution.[3] For all of my admiration of radical criticism and the denial of universal or abso-lute truths, I had grown weary, and suspicious, of pure deconstruction. It seemed irresponsible and just a bit cruel. How to put the pieces together again before the course ended and they went on with their lives, never again to enter another social space dedicated solely to the study of religion? Again, generally speaking, we have them *once*.

Inspired by a conversation I had with my colleague Bryan Rennie, I conceived the textbook in three parts, after Arnold van Gennep and Victor Turner's model of an initiation ritual: pre-initiation identity, liminal deconstruction, and reconstitution. In the first part, we define our "place" in the present and its relationship to the past. We discuss the history of comparison and the study of religion, from the polytheisms and monotheisms of the ancient Mediterranean world (all comparative strategies, in this model) through the Renaissance, Reformation, and Enlightenment to European colonialism, modernity, counterculture, and contemporary anxieties over fundamentalism and religious violence. In the second part, we work through six chapters on various comparative acts with different "comparative grounds": myth and ritual, the natural world, the gendered sexual body, social institutions, the religious imagination, and, finally, death and the nature of the soul. The third part is the key. Here, we emerge from all of these prehistories and comparative acts in order to "put the pieces back together again." We give the student-readers both religious and secular ways of doing this. We give them the standard tools of comparative theology (exclusivism, inclusivism, and pluralism). We give them liberation theology and feminist, race, and queer theory. But we also give them the standard tools of the social sciences, particularly psychology, sociology, and cognitive science. We encourage them to deconstruct, but we also encourage them to reconstruct. We openly acknowledge the destabilizing force of comparison, and then we work with it.

I can tell you from consistent personal experience over the years that this approach works, and often in a quite profound way. I teach the textbook to a large survey course of hundreds of students each fall. The course enrollment ranges from about 130 to up to 275. I could tell you dozens, if not hundreds, of stories at this point. Allow me just one.

The suffering public

First, though, allow me some Texas context. Teaching the comparative study of religion in Texas is a uniquely rewarding vocation. I have taught comparison in Chicago, in Boston, in western Pennsylvania, in Boulder, in northern California, and in Houston now. I can tell you that teaching comparativism in Texas is more rewarding than teaching it in any of these other contexts, and for a fairly simple reason: *because it truly matters.*

One could just as well say: because it is so culturally dissonant. There are so many thoughtful and progressive people in Texas who feel at deep odds with the public ultra-conservative political culture of the state. Because of this conflict and the repressions it has necessitated, when they hear me speak about comparative religion, they often react in very emotional and openly cathartic ways. They tear up. They laugh aloud. "Did he really say that? Oh my God, he *really* said that! He said exactly what I have always thought but could not quite say!" They come up to me and tell me horrific stories about being emotionally traumatized or intellectually beaten down by their family religious cultures, mostly of a Christian fundamentalist or Evangelical sort (or should I not be honest here, not name names?).

These individuals, these souls, just assumed that no one understood them, that no one cared, and, certainly, that no one had a language to speak their pain or their most secret convictions. It turns out someone did. Actually, it turns out that there is an entire academic field that has been honing this language and these convictions for two hundred years now. They are just so happy about that. They no longer feel alone. They feel human once again.

Here is a single example. A few years ago, I was teaching a course, I forget on what, to a group of adults at the Houston Jung Center. After the course, one of the women approached me after class. She wanted to share something with me. She told me that her son had been in my comparative religion course the fall before and that it had changed his life. Actually, what she said was that the textbook had changed his life. She then told me that she read the textbook along with him, chapter by chapter, and that it also changed her life. She was getting teary-eyed at this point. I thanked her for sharing that with me. I did not know what else to say.

I was pretty certain, though, what she meant and what she did not mean. She was not saying that both of their lives were changed because they now knew the Four Noble Truths of Buddhism, the Five Pillars of Islam, and a very general history of the Bible. She was not referring to historical data. She meant that *the comparative method itself* had fundamentally changed their lives, that, through it, they now understood much better their own deepest intuitions and convictions about "religion" and could articulate these in more clear and concise ways. They could now explain to themselves, and to others, why *they* thought there were so many religions, and what this might mean. She was saying that "religion" just made better sense now and that the comparative method allowed her to feel at peace with her own comparative instincts and secret thoughts.

Afterward, I thought to myself, "But the student never told me this and probably never will. Just how many like him are in every course? Clearly, we should also be teaching the parents, and then the lawyers, the teachers, the politicians, and the public policy makers."

The chapel of dilemmas

And the doctors and nurses.

The college classroom is not the only social space of comparison in contemporary American culture. Certainly, there are few, if any, social spaces in our culture in which comparative questions and comparative problems are more obvious and acute than in the modern hospital. At least in the class-room, no one is dying or is seriously ill. That is not the case in the modern hospital. I can only imagine.

Consider the doctor or nurse working in a modern urban hospital. Such a medical professional will walk through and perhaps even talk with a dozen different religious worldviews in a single day, usually without even knowing it, much less understanding the nuances and differences of these competing worldviews and what these nuances and differences might mean for the poignant practicalities of medical care, moral decisions, and the inevitable endurance of suffering and, in some cases, death. How *does* the medical professional make sense of the base fact of religious pluralism, that is, how to understand and relate different religious faiths and traditions, while at the same time providing health care, spiritual comfort, and guidance to indi-viduals suffering (even dying) within only one of these worldviews.

The challenge here is not simply to reach a particular level of religious literacy, as if some kind of basic "world religions" summary would be suffi-cient: this religion teaches this; this religion teaches that. The more basic and more pressing question is this: How do we take up these different religious systems, which do not agree on the most basic questions of human life and death, and relate them to one another in a modern pluralistic society, urban hospital, or therapeutic setting in which the creation and sustainability of well-being, meaning and purpose are paramount? For example, do more nuanced comparative strategies make for better healthcare and more effec-tive clinical practices? Or do more nuanced comparative strategies frustrate the same?

And what are the spiritual effects of this constant floating through worlds on the medical or mental health professionals? How do they process it? How do they think about it? And does it exile them in any way from their birth cultures? How do they speak to and relate to their family members, who are generally not exposed to this kind of radical religious plurality and suffering?

A few years ago Rice University hosted a postdoc, an anthropologist who works on the cultural phenomenon of hospital chaplains. He pointed out that such a role is quite unique in modern history. In what other time and culture do we know of religious specialists who are required to minister to people of different faiths and even religions? In what other religious role is one required to become a kind of spiritual chameleon? It is really quite remarkable, and admirable, and no doubt difficult. Is there a special psy-chology of becoming a hospital chaplain? And does it look anything like the special psychology of the professor of comparative religion? They look similar and different.

But perhaps the most public and dramatic sign of the hospital's compara-tive dilemma is not the hospital chaplain but the hospital chapel. Such a social space, at least in a secular or religiously liberal hospital, must some-how function as a sacred space for the grieving and anxious but must not contain any specific religious symbols or icons, since any particular symbol will privilege a particular story or religion and so implicitly deny all the others. Here we have a telling sign of the "comparative crisis" of modernity, that is, the way the modern world's civil acceptance of religious pluralism necessarily relativizes, even erases, the specificities of each and every specific religion in a public space. The comparative dilemma of the modern medical world could not be on better display than in such an empty chapel.

But here is the interesting thing. "Emptiness" is also a classical mystical trope and, as such, can also be a sign of some of the further reaches of religious experience. We are floating back to sea. Is there any connection between the empty chapel and the emptiness of the mystical traditions, any legitimate comparison to be made here? Can being adrift at sea serve a further spiritual purpose? Is there a silver lining or hidden gift in the fuzziness and nondirection of the SBNR?

The religion of no religion

I suppose it all depends on what we do with that, on how an individual or a community responds. Certainly one can just remain lost at sea. Or drown. Or roast under the sun. Or starve. Or get eaten by sharks. But one might also learn to wave with the waves and wind with the winds until other lands and truths appear on the horizon. Perhaps one can even learn to navigate with the stars, whose sameness and whose differences in the sky are precisely the key to navigating the otherwise dangerous waters.

And I am not simply speaking metaphorically here. I cannot pursue the topic, but I think modern astronomy, cosmology, physics, and evolutionary biology will play an outsized role in any future shared mythology or worldview, including and especially the SBNR ones. A new cosmology has been forming among the sciences for about two centuries now (think "the Big Bang," "evolution," and all of modern science fiction). This new cosmology will likely eventually become the new consensus story, not because it is perfect or complete (it is not) but because it is literally universal (as in "the universe"), its truth claims are replicable and demonstrable, its knowledge claims can often be translated into pragmatic technologies, and, at its very best, its vision is both sublime and transcendent vis-à-vis our little Earth tribes and worn-out stories.

Such an attempted fusion of science and spirit was central to the founding inspirations of the community that I know best, the Esalen community. As I have explained at some length in my earlier work, the intellectual and spiritual origins of Esalen lie with a Stanford professor of comparative religion: Frederic Spiegelberg (1897–1994). Spiegelberg's comparative theology of "the religion of no religion" was a later intellectual framing of a profound mystical experience that he had known as a young man, in 1917, while he was studying medieval Latin theology at the University of Halle. The story goes like this.

One bright spring day during this time, he took a walk through a wheat field laced with blue cornflowers and red poppies. As he walked through the field, his "usual, every-day consciousness" vanished, and he felt instead "something deep, something holy." He calls this other being "his higher Self." Within this altered state, he now "sees the bright glance of some super-cosmic sun shining from the centre of every creature around him." All of reality "has become perfect and holy." What he calls "secular life" has faded away. Then something stops him in his tracks, something both traditionally religious and deeply disturbing:

> [H]e suddenly approaches around the corner of the road – a church. And the sight of the church gives him a shock. For what on earth is a church doing in his glorified world? . . . All the world around has been holy, has been God's eternal nature, has been His face and His expression. Therefore – and this is what shocks him – if there is really anything else, anything peculiar behind those walls, it could only be a matter outside God, in contrast with, or even in opposition to this eternal bliss of the all-penetrating holiness.

"Now such a feeling and such an experience," Spiegelberg tells his readers, has always meant the birth of "the religion of no religion."[4] Such a religion of no religion must deny the gods and the churches but not for the sake of denial or some antireligious platform. Rather, this denial of the gods, of the church and of every accepted notion of God "leads always to the conception of new names for God." The religion of no religion, in other words, is not the end of religion. Rather, it is the beginning of *new types of religion*, even and especially if that word "religion" eventually falls away as no longer useful.

It is surely no accident that the man who inspired the founders of Esalen with his notion of the religion of no religion was also a political refugee from Nazi Germany. Frederic was no fuzzy thinker or dilettante. He was a friend of Martin Heidegger and Paul Tillich. He was a radical theologian whose public speeches and writings were tracked by the Nazi thought police and who had to flee his own home country.

It was this religion of no religion that Michael Murphy and Dick Price learned from Prof. Spiegelberg at Stanford University in the early 1950s. Indeed, Murphy experienced a kind of conversion in a college classroom, in Spiegelberg's comparative religion course, no less. In some real sense, what would become "Esalen" and the human potential movement were born then and there, in a traditional academic space. It was there again that Murphy and Price learned about the Upanishads and Hinduism; about Tibetan Buddhism, Sufism, Neoplatonism; and about the basic methods of comparativism as they stood mid-century. Not surprisingly, both men dedicated themselves to a contemplative practice – Murphy's Hindu and Advaita Vedantic in accent, Price's Buddhist and Daoist, neither quite traditional.

Murphy would spend sixteen months in the ashram of Sri Aurobindo, a former Indian freedom fighter who spent his last decades in retreat in the French enclave of Pondicherry. There, watched by British spies, Aurobindo revisioned evolution as both a biological and an occult process that was leading to what he called, alternately, the descent of the Supermind or the coming of the Gnostic Superman. This, by the way, was well before the Superman of the World War II comic books, but it was well after Nietzsche and his *daimon* Zarathustra, whose "Superman" Aurobindo was obviously evoking but also changing in radical ways.

The point of the story is this: "comparative religion" did not function in the Esalen story as a colonial logic, a fuzzy dilettantism, or an anything-goes free association. It functioned as an elite intellectual practice at an elite American research university. Moreover, it resulted in conversion and contemplation that looked back to an Indian political and spiritual figure who lived his entire adult life in a French enclave in order to escape a British colonial prison and a German professor who had known a cosmic presence in a wheat field and had escaped with his and his family's lives to American universities from Nazi Germany. Comparison was not some abstract cognitive exercise. It was prison. It was mysticism. It was exile. And it was justice.

Efflorescence, eclipse, and return

These kinds of political radicalism and mystical deconstruction, of course, did not last. Many departments of religion may have been founded in the wake and presence of such acts, that is, during the countercultural period and all its civil rights, feminist, gay, psychedelic, and antiwar movements. Still, the mystical, literary, and intellectual foundations that were mostly set up in the 1950s and then blossomed in the 1960s and 1970s were eventually forgotten as the decades ticked by. I am thinking of moments like Spiegelberg's potent "religion of no religion," Aldous Huxley's psychedelically revealed "Mind at Large" and his sly, wicked rage against all "inspirational twaddle"; Jiddu Krishnamurti's "pathless path" and "choiceless awareness" that refuses all belief; and Alan Watts's call for us to take up our own "godhood."[5] *All* were made possible by radical acts of comparison, and all were subsequently tamed, domesticated, or deconstructed by academics and other methods, as we shall soon see.

This kind of radicalism slipped away, then, but it never quite disappeared. What became the New Age movement became "the New Age" through a kind of commercialization and popularization but also, please note, through new revelations, often of a channeled and quite serious nature. Even when the New Age appears "too nice" or "too saccharine," it often comes with a real bite. It is often a kind of smiling takedown of religion, as we know it. If the New Age had begun to sever its ties to the intellectual and literary roots of the earlier human potential movement, however, what eventually became the SBNR demographic appears to be almost completely ignorant of these deeper political, literary, and mystical roots.

What happened?

A number of things. For one thing, the countercultural enthusiasms, which were often destabilizing and openly transgressive vis-à-vis the mainline church and synagogues, became the object of a kind of backlash in the 1970s and 1980s, particularly with the rise of the Moral Majority and the Religious Right and its alliance with the Republican Party under Ronald Reagan.[6]

Ironically, a disturbingly resonant – I will not say similar – backlash occurred in the academy and the study of religion at the same time, with the rise of constructivism, localism, and postmodern relativism, all of which sought to deny any and all sameness for the absolute regime of difference. Everything and everyone was constructed now. Everything was nothing more than a social fact, a dubious ideology or a linguistic effect inappropriately posing as a revelatory experience or religious claim. Any hint of transcendence disappeared. There was no "outside" now, no place from which to compare. There was only the text. Or the body. Or the social politic. There was only immanence. Absence reigned the day. Presence became a bad word, a category to be exiled from all polite academic conversation.

These elite intellectual movements were in turn echoed by various populist and fundamentalist attempts to censor scholarship that the conservative religious communities found particularly offensive. Here again, the logic was driven by an intolerant ontology of pure difference that had been forged and perfected in the academy. These backlashes, of course, are very different and cannot be equated, but they shared a very similar anticomparative logic. They rejected robust comparison across cultural and religious boundaries. They wanted to deny sameness. They wanted to absolutize difference. They wanted to deny any kind of transcendence from which it might make perfect sense to treat all religious forms as relative, as forms to combine and recombine, as religious prodigies and communities have long done out of their own revelations.

There are other reasons for the eclipse of sophisticated comparison, of course. Here is one possible reason. I cannot help but think that a big part of the explosion of robust comparative thinking in the counterculture had something to do with what Alan Watts called the "joyous cosmology" and the "chemistry of consciousness" as revealed in psychedelic states. When those chemicals were readily available and consumed by intellectuals like Aldous Huxley, Huston Smith, and Alan Watts, comparativism flourished, often, interestingly enough, in perennialist forms. When those plants and substances were criminalized and abandoned by intellectuals, comparativism waned and disappeared. Perhaps it is relevant that one of the most sophisticated books on the new renaissance in psychedelic research today arrives at a very sophisticated perennialism once again and what the author calls a "mystic materialism."[7] This, of course, is a reboot of Watt's "chemistry of consciousness," an affirmation of sameness rooted in the universalism of matter, chemistry, and neurobiology now.

I am not proposing a new perennialism. Nor am I advocating a denial of difference, much less an abandonment of constructivist, postmodern, and postcolonial methods. That is not my point. I am trying to understand how and why comparativism waned when it did and why we might want to be suspicious of the suspicions around comparison – very suspicious.

I do not think this is the end of the story. Actually, I am hopeful about the return of comparison in the academy, and for one reason: the rise of the SBNR and the Nones. I believe that this new demographic will provide a new social base and logic for its return. It is not that the one will cause the other. It is rather the case that the two social movements will feed off one another in a synergistic way. That is my best guess anyway about where we are going, about what the near future might yet look like.

Lift off

I want to return to my opening memory. If the counterculture and the New Age are the cultural doubles of the comparative study of religion (and I think they are), and if the comparative study of religion bears deep historical connections to apophatic mystical literature (and I think it does), then does it not follow that the counterculture and the New Age, and by extension the SBNR, are distant echoes of these same mystical forms of experience and thought, now reframed in largely secular terms?

I think this is, in fact, the case. I am not suggesting, of course, that the man or woman who checks "SBNR" on a Match.com account or on a Pew Forum questionnaire is doing so for the same reasons that a Plotinus, an Ibn al-Arabi, or a Frederic Spiegelberg developed a mystical theology. But I am suggesting that their cognitive habits with respect to "comparing religions" display a most obvious resonance. If we want to frame this intellectually, we might say that the SBNR works almost entirely within an immanent frame but out of a pluralist logic that resonates well with some classical mystical literature. They are enacting a kind of unconscious mystical theology, even when they do not know it.

I once gave a lecture at the University of Texas, Austin, on the contemporary UFO phenomenon and its abduction literatures. Historian of American religion Bob Abzug made a most insightful point there, which I want to follow up on here. He observed, quite correctly, that the contemporary UFO esotericisms bear a very distinct similarity or relationship to the much older kabbalistic mystical literatures, particularly in their focus on Ezekiel's apparent "abduction" by the fiery spinning wheels of the spiritual vehicle he encountered in the first chapters of the biblical book. This, in fact, is a point that has been made by others, including the literary critic Michael Lieb with respect to the Nation of Islam, the Nation's ufology, and what Lieb calls the "new riders of the chariot," that is, the UFO mystics of today.

But here is Bob's point. He noted that, whereas the older kabbalistic streams were and still are embedded in extremely complex scriptural, ritual, and community structures, the new UFO mysticisms are no longer so embedded. Indeed, as I tried to show in my lecture at the University of Texas, abductees are often extremely confused by their experiences, since they lack the mythological and mystical systems that would have previously made sense of them. We might say that the new riders of the chariot have "lifted off" from their traditional and older mythical, scriptural, and ritual foundations and are now "floating in space," as it were. Another form of being lost at sea.

As I have tried to too briefly show here, we can observe a very similar pattern with respect to the SBNR and the much older mystical apophatic literatures. In effect, the SBNR has also "lifted off" from its traditional philosophical and religious landing pads, not through experiences of transcendence necessarily (although those are no doubt present, too – have we really bothered to look?), but through the inevitable pressure of a new social pluralism and the disembedding powers of new communication technologies, like the Internet. What will become of these new space travelers we cannot say. Perhaps they will perish in the void. Perhaps they will discover new planets of spirit and eventually create new religions, even new civilizations.

I do not know. I would only caution us to not prematurely judge these experiments. Human beings are both settlers and explorers. We did not inhabit the planet, from Africa to the tip of South America, by remaining in one place or by respecting any single culture. To be human is to move and to leave culture behind. It is also, as Walt Whitman had it, to both create and shed scriptures and beliefs, like a plant grows and sheds its leaves. That is the comparative logic of the SBNR. It is also the comparative logic of the study of religion. I see no way around these simple cognitions or any reason to deny them.

Notes

1 Jeffrey J. Kripal, *Esalen: America and the Religion of No Religion* (Chicago: University of Chicago Press, 2007).
2 For this historical argument about the countercultural origins of the field, see my *Secret Body: Erotic and Esoteric Currents in the History of Religions* (Chicago: University of Chicago Press, 2017), particularly the material on gnomon 9, "It's about Counterculture, not Colonialism."
3 Jeffrey J. Kripal et al., *Comparing Religions: Coming to Terms* (Oxford: Wiley-Blackwell, 2014).
4 Frederic Spiegelberg, *The Religion of No-Religion* (Stanford, CA: James Ladd Delkin, 1953), 18–19.
5 I am thinking of countercultural classics like Huxley's *The Doors of Perception* (1954) and *Island* (1962); Krishnamurti's *The First and Last Freedom* (1954), for which Huxley wrote a foreword; and Alan Watts's *The Way of Zen* (1957) and *Beyond Theology* (1973). The "inspirational twaddle" line appears in Huxley's foreword.

6 For another discussion of the backlash, see Jeffrey J. Kripal, "The Mythologies of Scholarship: The Deep Narratives of the Study of Religion and Some Possible Futures," for Sarah Johnston, ed., *Narrating Religion* (New York: Macmillan, 2016), 353–72.
7 Nicolas Langlitz, *Neuropsychedelia: The Revival of Hallucinogen Research since the Decade of the Brain* (Berkeley: University of California Press, 2012).

References

Kripal, Jeffrey J. *Esalen: America and the Religion of No Religion.* Chicago: University of Chicago Press, 2007.

———. "The Mythologies of Scholarship: The Deep Narratives of the Study of Religion and Some Possible Futures. In *Narrating Religion*, 353–72. Edited by Sarah Johnston. New York: Macmillan, 2016.

———. *Secret Body: Erotic and Esoteric Currents in the History of Religions.* Chicago: University of Chicago Press, 2017.

Kripal, Jeffrey J., Ata Anzali, Andrea R. Jain and Erin Prophet. *Comparing Religions: Coming to Terms.* Oxford: Wiley-Blackwell, 2014.

Langlitz, Nicolas. *Neuropsychedelia: The Revival of Hallucinogen Research Since the Decade of the Brain.* Berkeley, CA: University of California Press, 2012.

Spiegelberg, Frederic. *The Religion of No-Religion.* Stanford, CA: James Ladd Delkin, 1953.

Index